RIVER PUBLISHERS SERIES IN SOCIAL, URBAN, ECONOMIC AND ENVIRONMENTAL SUSTAINABILITY

Series Editors:

Medani P. Bhandari
Akamai University, USA; Summy State University, Ukraine and Atlantic State Legal Foundation, NY, USA

Jacek Binda
Rector of the International Affairs, Bielsko-Biala School of Finance and Law, Poland

Durga D. Poudel
University of Louisiana at Lafayette, Louisiana, USA

Hanna Shvindina
Sumy State University, Ukraine

Scott Garner
Asia Environmental Holdings Group (Asia ENV Group), Asia Environmental Daily, Beijing / Hong Kong, People's Republic of China

The River Series on Social, Urban, Economic and Environmental Sustainability is a series of comprehensive academic and professional books which focus on the societal side of sustainability. The series focuses on topics ranging from theory to policy and real-life case studies and applications.

Books published in the series include research monographs, edited volumes, handbooks and textbooks. The books provide professionals, researchers, educators, and advanced students in the field with an invaluable insight into the latest research and developments.

Topics covered in the series include, but are by no means restricted to the following:

- Climate Change Mitigation
- Renewable Energy Policy
- Urban sustainability
- Strategic environmental planning
- Environmental Systems Monitoring and Analysis
- Greening the World Economy
- Sustainable Development

For a list of other books in this series, visit www.riverpublishers.com

Perspectives on Sociological Theories, Methodological Debates, and Organizational Sociology

Medani P. Bhandari
Akamai University, Hawaii, USA;
Sumy State University, Ukraine;
Gandaki University, Nepal

LONDON AND NEW YORK

Published 2023 by River Publishers
River Publishers
Alsbjergvej 10, 9260 Gistrup, Denmark
www.riverpublishers.com

Distributed exclusively by Routledge
4 Park Square, Milton Park, Abingdon, Oxon OX14 4RN
605 Third Avenue, New York, NY 10017, USA

Perspectives on Sociological Theories, Methodological Debates, and Organizational Sociology / by Medani P. Bhandari.

© 2023 River Publishers. All rights reserved. No part of this publication may be reproduced, stored in a retrieval systems, or transmitted in any form or by any means, mechanical, photocopying, recording or otherwise, without prior written permission of the publishers.

Routledge is an imprint of the Taylor & Francis Group, an informa business

ISBN 978-87-7022-780-3 (print)
ISBN 978-10-0087-951-3 (online)
ISBN 978-1-003-39288-0 (ebook master)

While every effort is made to provide dependable information, the publisher, authors, and editors cannot be held responsible for any errors or omissions.

Dedication

TO MY FRIEND, WIFE, AND COAUTHOR IN CREATING WRITINGS, MRS. PRAJITA BHANDARI. WITHOUT YOUR HELP AND SUPPORT, THIS BOOK WOULD NOT HAVE BEEN POSSIBLE.

TOGETHER, WE HAVE MILES TO GO

Content

Dedication	**v**
Preface	**xi**
Forewords	**xxi**
Acknowledgment	**lix**
List of Figures	**lxiii**
List of Tables	**lxv**
List of Abbreviations	**lxvii**

1 The Major Theories of Sociology, and Contemporary Development of Organizational Perspectives in Social Sciences   **1**

Outline 1

Introduction 2

     Founders of Sociology – Theory and Perspectives 2

First Section 3

     The Founding Writers of Western Sociology 3

     Karl Marx 3

     Emile Durkheim 7

     Max Weber 9

Second Section 11

     The Development of Organizational Theory and the Emergence of Challenges to the Traditional Rational Approaches to Understanding the Organization. 11

     Classical Theorists. 12

Third Section 15

     Contemporary Theories and Perspectives 15

viii   *Content*

Fourth Section 21

    The Feminist Approach to Organizational Analysis. 21

Conclusion. 26

Endnotes 29

References 37

2   The Debates Between the Quantitative and Qualitative Methods: An Ontology and Epistemology of the Qualitative Method   61

Outline 61

Introduction 61

Section 1 62

    Debates on Quantitative Versus Qualitative
Historical Perspective 62

    The Distinction Between Qualitative and Quantitative 63

    Durkheimian Notion. 65

    Ontological Assumptions 65

        Max Weber. 65

    The Chicago School 67

    The Positivist Research Paradigms 68

        Bronislaw Malinowski. 68

        Robert E. Park 69

    The Qualitative Inquiry Accepts the Notion
of Social Variation. 73

    Qualitative Ontology and Epistemology 73

    Qualitative and Quantitative Debate is Still There 76

    The Paradigms of Qualitative Methods 76

    Theories and Approaches of Qualitative Method 78

    Phenomenology 79

    Hermeneutical Phenomenology 82

    Symbolic Interaction 82

    Bridging the Gap Between the Two Methods 84

Content ix

Section 2 86
    Features of Successful Qualitative-based Work by Discussing
    Three Exemplary Texts 86
    Three Successful Examples of Qualitative Research 86
    1. William Foote Whyte 86
    2. Erving Goffman 88
    3. Robert J. Thomas 91
Section 3 93
    Application of the Qualitative Method 93
Conclusion 94
    Why Qualitative Method? 94
References 96

**3 International Organization and Organizational Sociology
Theories and Perspectives**   **111**

Outline 111
Introduction 112
    How Were International Organizations Formed? 112
    The Origin of the Term International Organization 116
    Historical Roots of International Organization Studies 118
    Definition of International Organizations 119
    Types of International Organizations 122
    International Organizations in the Contemporary World 123
    International Relation (IR) Theory and International
    Organizations 126
    Regime Theory and International Organizations 130
    Globalization, Organizations, and International
    Organizations 132
    Organizational Sociology 138
    Organizations as Complex Phenomena 142
    Application Network Theory in the Study of International
    Organizations 144

x *Content*

Social Networks 147

Application of Sociological Institution Theory in the
Study of International Organizations 150

The Green Economic Initiatives (As Theory) and
International Organization. 159

The Stakeholder Theory and International Organization 160

The Governance Theory and International Organization 161

Conclusion. 162

References 165

4 Sustainability Theory   **195**

Outline. 195

Introduction – Questions – Coverage 197

The following questions are complicated and complex as
the notion of sustainability: 200

1. How Theoretically and Practically Sustainability
   Discourse is Developed? 200

2. What Are the Boundaries of Sustainability? 212

3. What Are the Linkages Between Creativeness and
   Sustainability? 221

4. What Is the Institutional Architecture to Attain the
   SDGs?. 226

Conclusion. 233

References 236

Index   **257**

About the Author   **261**

Preface

Informally, this book has a relatively long educational trajectory from the date my memory begins, and I remember the social events from my primary schooling days to date. As usual, as part of my socialization, at home, my parents, grandparents, relatives, siblings, neighbors, my playmates, and my surroundings tried to teach me how to live in a stratified, classified, caste, race, and ethnically divided unequal society. They also tried to impart ways to maintain social harmony with each other, where societal norms and values were primarily imposed by the elite high caste males and reinforced by females. I always wondered, why all my friend's parents did not equally participate in various social and cultural events and why even an elderly senior of low caste origin used to salute me or used to say JADAU to me, though I was below the age of his youngest grandchildren. Now I know this is primarily due to the prevalent social structuring of our society based on caste, where some individuals are privileged simply because they were born to a so-called high caste family and others were born to a so-called low caste family. Not only that, but I have also seen familial or social boycotting/ outcasting of my maternal aunt (as for all woman) once every month for about four days for the reason of her physiological menstrual cycle. First, she was considered impure and thus was treated as an untouchable and could not touch water and water sources during this period. There was the problem of water collection. Second, she could not enter the house and she could not cook food in the kitchen and perform other household chores. During this period, she was not supposed to touch anything that is in liquid form despite her being a major labor force to conduct household chores and maintain the house. Another indirect issue associated with this periodic menstrual cycle for a newly married woman was family distress. The underlining fact was the fear of physical and mental preparedness to have a baby. My uncle and aunt had no children for a long time for which my aunt was blamed. I think my grandparents might be held the hope of conceiving a baby with their daughter-in-law, and when there was a regular period cycle in her, I think they felt hopelessness, and my aunt was blamed. Even having a baby on time was not an issue. The sex of a newly born baby mattered and boys were expected over girls. That conflict remained in the family until my uncle and aunt had a baby boy after decades of their marriage.

xii *Preface*

Primarily, my young brain was disturbed due to the unseemly divided society due to the haves and have not situations of the society, and the divisions created in the name of tradition, culture, religion, and other social systems – norms, values, regulations, and rules. On the one hand, my surroundings were enforcing me to mingle or merge within the existing social systems; on the other hand, my inner self was questioning "why we all are not equal, why we all do not have the same access to social events, education, labor, food, and even in shelters" and "also why society is giving more priority and love to me and why not to girls of my age (like Indira, Yogi, Kali, and Bhunti). Why did even the elderly or senior people of the low caste family in our community treat me as the son of a so-called privileged high caste family? Why my aunt was not equally treated at home and my parents repeatedly called her PARAYA DHAN (the property of someone else – since my uncle and she had the same parents (my grandparents)). I was deeply shocked all the time without any clear answer – why was there unequal treatment between brothers and sisters? Why were sisters not the priority of education? As soon as I was able to have some courage to ask questions, first, I asked my grandfather, why they blamed my aunt (his daughter-in-law) who had not committed any mistake? Why does my uncle have an education option and why not for my aunt (though both were his children)? My grandfather never responded to my questions, and he always just praised me without any reason. I was not happy with such praise at all. However, nobody answered my questions.

My uncle was a school teacher. I thought he would answer, but he also simply replied that I was too young to discuss those matters. I asked those questions to my primary and secondary school teachers, as I grew up. However, no one gave me a clear answer to why there was inequality? What is a society and why the social system is not equal for everybody? Time never stops; it was the time to join high school. However, the closest high school was within three hours of walking – one way. I wanted to continue my studies and decided to join the school. My family members did not oppose my decision. However, I was the only student from my village who chose the six-hour-long walk. Although there were several children of my age, no one preferred to take the risk of six hours' every day walk to school. I still wonder why none of the children of my age joined that educational journey to school.

During the three years of walking to school from the home village, I saw such inequality in every step of my social, economic, political, and religious life. Even I saw such inequality in school because there were no female teachers in middle and high schools. I was surprised, and I raised that question in the school too. No one answered. There was a hostel in the

Preface xiii

school but only for boys. I wanted to know the cause of this problem. Once I reached grade ten, I asked the headmaster about this situation of inequality in the society. I also asked him – is there any subject that addresses these issues? He told me "**Yes**" and said that at college-level, there is a subject called SOCIOLOGY. So, that was the first time, I heard about this term. After 3–4 attempts, I passed high school, and I joined college. There was no sociology subject; however, I went to India for undergraduate college and took sociology as one of the subjects of my preference. I discontinued and continued with so many trajectories; however, after several years, I completed my doctorate in sociology. This book is the product of my qualifying exams – sociological theory, method, and a subject of my choice – organizational sociology. I must state that, still, the question of how and why the society has been biased, unequal, and uneven in economic, social, political, and religious systems is the subject matter of my research.

We learn from culture, traditions, education, and particularly through societal practices. Even if we do not agree with the situation, our mental and behavioral patterns become the same as we see and practice through our surroundings. I must acknowledge that I also built with the same male-centric, patriarchal mentality and behavior. Therefore, my behaviors were and are still unknowingly biased. Now, I feel that I might not have given the same importance to my grandmother, mother, aunts, sisters, and female friends' circle as I valued my grandfather, father, uncles, brothers, and male friends. Also, I must confess that I might not give the equal rights to my wife in family decision making, and I might have imposed my male-centric decisions in all social (son's or daughter's marriage), economic (purchasing of land, house building, loan, donation, saving, bank account holding, etc.), and educational matters (the choice of schooling for my son and daughter). I must confess that through my behavior, I might have been hurting many of my heartily closed ones including my mother, sisters, daughters, daughters-in-law, and my wife. I feel that I might have expressed my biased behaviors and hurt them directly or indirectly. Therefore, foremost, I beg for forgiveness from all of you for my every biased action, reaction, and behavior throughout my life. I am indebted to you all, especially who have to face my erratic behavior in day-to-day life because of my narrow and extended family members. As a by-product of the patriarchal, stratified, classified, caste, race, and ethnically divided unequal society, I cannot say that all my misbehaves were unintentional; however, now I accept all of my mistakes and I hereby plead for my guilt and beg for removal of all debts on me and pardon and forgive. Here, with this acknowledgment, I firmly accept that whatever I produce, write, and publish in the form of books, journal papers, poems,

xiv *Preface*

essays, philosophy, opinion pieces, or in any form, it is due to your support and due to the support of motherland's environment. Thanks to all whom I was, am, and will be connected until my last ride and beyond.

Here, I would also like to note that the role of social scientists is crucial and important because we belong to the varieties of complicated social, cultural, religious, economic, political, and traditional systems and our role is to reveal the positive and negative reality of this system and contribute for the betterment of the society directly or indirectly. Therefore, we must accept and acknowledge that many heads have worked extremely hard to bring us as sensible and responsible human beings. We should not feel ashamed to tell the truth and should not be scared to find the truth and produce the truth. Social scientists are those who understand the societal trajectory and thrive for social justice, well-being, inclusive and equitable society, and rational social change. Therefore, social scientists need to understand the social theories, applicable methods, and actual systems of the society as the body of knowledge – the mind (theories), methods (the pathways of research), and the heart part (the knowledge itself of the society). Until or unless we do not find our niche and the grounded reality of our surroundings, the sociological knowledge we possess cannot contribute to a meaningful social change and cannot reveal the underlined facts of the social system. Here, I would like to acknowledge the contributions of social scientists who provided the pathways to understand society through theories, methods, and their uses.

This book is my understanding of western theories of social sciences, a shallow answer to my thirst for knowledge of society. I must accept that my thirst has increased; I am not satisfied. Instead of satisfaction, I am thirstier now. I feel that we have not been able to explore our social theories, which are grounded more in ethical, traditional, spiritual, and harmonious structures. We have to reveal the reality of our path of knowledge, which holds thousands and thousands of years of history of epistemology. However, I think this book could provide the pathways to begin to search for theorists who build our society and we never recognized them.

The book stands as the full body of scholarly work on western theories of social sciences. The book contains four chapters. The first part gives the overall scenario of theories, the second part provides the pathway to the research destination, the research method, the third chapter is the destination of the substantive field of study and the roles of international organizations on social, political, economic, and environmental regime creation as well as to other social and development functions of international organizations, the forth chapter explains sustainability theories.

Sociology examines the social actors' activities in society and social problems. Western scholars have developed many social theories, which address the underlying causes such as social conflicts and inequalities, and the many formal and informal social organizations involved to minimize the challenges of inequalities. The study of social organizations is a new phenomenon in sociology. Broadly, its historical root can be traced to Greek civilization (Plato and Aristotle), and it mostly flourished since the Enlightenment Era. However, the empirical studies show that the scientific study of organizations began only in the 19th and 20th centuries. Among the scholars of these centuries, the contributions of Karl Marx, Ferdinand Tönnies, Émile Durkheim, Ludwig Gumplovicz, Vilfredo Pareto, Max Weber, and Talcott Parsons are considered pillars of sociology.

This book intends to answer the broad and major questions of theories, methods, and international organization studies in social sciences, particularly in sociology. Whereas *"Theory is always for someone and some purpose. All theories have a perspective. Perspectives derive from a position in time and space, especially social and political time, and space. The world is seen from a standpoint definable in terms of nation or social class, dominance, or subordination, of ring or declining power, of sense of immobility or the present crisis, of experience, and hopes and expectations for the future"* (Cox 1981, page 11).

This book is divided into four chapters. The first chapter, "The Major Theorists of Sociology, Theories, and Contemporary Development of Organizational Perspectives in Social Sciences," is designed to answer several questions. What are the major sociological theories? Who are the theorists? What are the contributions of the theorists? And how a theory can be applied to understand society? In addition, this chapter also answers the following questions: what is the development trend of sociological theory development? What is the current situation? And where does organizational sociology stand in the sociological study? This chapter primarily enlists the contribution of the founding writers of western sociology, with a focus on how they addressed (or did not address) organizations. Then, it discusses, in brief, the development of organizational theory and how organizational theorists are responding to the emergence of challenges to the traditional rational approaches to understanding organizations in the historical context. Furthermore, this chapter elaborates on the role of the western sociological theorist – in other words, the founding writers of western sociology such as Karl Marx, Emile Durkheim, and Max Weber.

The chapter elaborates on the development of organizational theory and the emergence of challenges to the traditional rational approaches to

xvi *Preface*

understanding the organization, where the roles of the classical theorists, for example, Talcott Parsons, Henri Fayol, Frederick Taylor, Luther Halsey Gulick, Herbert A. Simon, Berton H. Kaplan, Michel Foucault, Jurgen Habermas, Jacques Derrida, Jurgen Habermas, etc., are highlighted. The *third section* elaborates on contemporary theories and perspectives with the exemplary works of Philip Selznick, Peter Blau, James David Thompson, Charles Perrow, Paul DiMaggio, and Walter W. Powell. The *fourth section* presents the emerging feminist approach in social sciences as well as an understanding of the roles and responsibility of sociological organizational analysis. This covers the feminist approach in theory building with a focus on organizational analysis such as Arlene Daniels, Dorothy Smith, Marjorie DeVault, Gisela Bock, Susan James, Martha Calas, and Linda Smircich.

Likewise, chapter 2, "The Debates Between Quantitative and Qualitative Method: An Ontology and Epistemology of Qualitative Method," answers the following questions: why is there a debate on qualitative and quantitative research methods? What is the basis of the debate? How, when, and why do debates continue? And finally, how do we choose the current research method? This chapter discusses how to see the divide in sociology between researchers employing qualitative versus quantitative methods.

First, the chapters highlight the issues from a historical perspective by highlighting the philosophical commitments and political and/or ethical considerations that have shaped how social scientists approach or think about the problem of "qualitative versus quantitative." To understand the root cause of the debate, it is essential to understand its historical root, its ontological and epistemological position, as well as its paradigms and methodological approaches. What most consistently divides these schools are not their substantive claims but the meta-theoretical *cognitive structures* within which such claims are formulated. These structures shape what phenomena are considered important and explainable, how research questions about such phenomena are posed, what concepts and methods are most suited for investigating these questions, whether the objectives of the investigation are to confirm axiomatic laws or engender an interpretive understanding of contexts, and what standards are reasonable for evaluating specific research products. These questions elicit reflect enduring ontological and epistemological, that is meta-theoretical, assumptions shared by members of research communities but not others. Social scientific disciplines and subfields are often characterized by the emergence of, competition between, and evolution or degeneration of discrete traditions of scholarly research.

These traditions distinguish themselves based on programmatic understandings that provide the foundation for the construction,

Preface   xvii

communication, and evaluation of various forms of models or narratives. The chapter highlights these notions and highlights the features of successful qualitative-based work by discussing three exemplary texts. The chapter further reveals major indications of a core commitment to qualitative methodological principles in the exemplary works of major scholars of social sciences who utilized the qualitative method. And, finally, the chapter discusses how researchers can utilize the qualitative tradition of scholarship. The chapter begins by addressing why there are debates in research methods, i.e., quantitative versus qualitative, provides a brief outline of debate from a historical perspective, and further provides the major distinction between qualitative and quantitative. The chapter provides the theoretical ground of research methods with the example of the Durkheimian notion and presents the ontological assumptions of methodological principles. The chapter provides the role of Max Weber in using rational perspectives in the research method and the role of the Chicago School in fostering the qualitative method and elaborates on how the positivist research paradigms emerged and applied including the contribution of Bronislaw Malinowski and Robert E. Park. The chapter further explains the applicability of qualitative reasoning and the importance of the qualitative inquiry, which accepts the notion of social variation. This chapter tries to reveal the root of qualitative ontology and epistemology and presents why the debates are unsolved "qualitative and quantitative debate is still there."

The chapter further provides a brief outline of the paradigms of qualitative methods, their theories, and approaches. In brief, the chapter also explains the importance of the qualitative method to understand the phenomenology and hermeneutical phenomenology and linkages of the principles of the "symbolic interaction." Methods associated with positivism are grounded in the work of Comte, Mill, and Durkheim in social sciences, who believed that the social world can be viewed in the same way as natural sciences. In contrast, philosophers like Dilthey, Rickert, and Weber who followed the Kantian tradition challenged the positivist philosophy and developed the interpretive approach. The positivist tradition of social inquiry has been followed by the quantitative scholars and the interpretive path by the qualitative scholars

The chapter broadly tries to bridge the gap between the two methods and provides the pathways to choose the right research method based on the research topic. Further, it provides the features of successful qualitative-based work by discussing three exemplary works of William Foote Whyte, Erving Goffman, and Robert J. Thomas. Finally, the chapter shows the ways of the applicability of the qualitative method and concludes with the answer to

xviii *Preface*

"why qualitative method"? However, there are no debates on the objectives of research because both methods have been trying to capture the social reality and investigate the causes of social problems. To explore this situation, the chapters discuss the ontological, epistemological, and theoretical grounds and paradigms of the qualitative method. Quantitative scholars follow the positivist approach and qualitative scholars follow the constructivist and interpretive approaches. At the epistemological level, debates are about the application of knowledge. Quantitative scholars follow the established notion (deductive) to explore the social reality and qualitative scholars construct the knowledge by doing inductive research.

Similarly, chapter 3, "International Organization and Organizational Sociology Theories and Perspectives," broadly answers the following questions: what is the foundation, formation basis of an international organization, history, perspectives, definitions, and growth and what is the applicability of theories of social sciences to understand the international organization? When did international organizations become the topic of social sciences (political science, economics, and sociology)? The chapter summarizes the current literature (key theories and readings) that focus on the study of international organizations. How might the theories and perspectives of organizational sociology better inform the study of international organizations? There is not much historical literature available on how international organizations were formed and how their expansion occurred beyond state borders before 1900. The term international organizations was first used by a Professor of Law James, Lorimer, in 1867 and became a major field of study in political science by 1900. In the contemporary world, the role of international organizations is universal. International organizations represent a form of institution that refers to a formal system of rules and objectives, a rationalized administrative instrument. It is a known notion that the internationalization or formalization of organizations beyond state borders was aimed primarily at securing the political and legal security of the state. Another aim of formalizing organizations was to build cooperation between the nations' citizens for their welfare and the exchange of business commodities.

Social scientists believe that all forms of organizations follow certain norms, values, social order, legal and social rules, and regulations; they are established with a vision and mission and try to attain certain goals. The ultimate goal of any national or international organization is to help maintain and fulfill societal demands (which could be political, economic, or social). In this context, as sociologists, we know basic grounds of international organizations, their foundations, their bureaucratic functions, and their roles in the society. There is a large body of sociological knowledge which sits as a background to international organizational research, but little in the way of specific contributions. For the international organizations of the future, however, particularly those that will attempt to address global environmental concerns as they affect communities, there is a body of sociological knowledge poised to inform international organizations.

There is also a close relationship between international relations, regime formation and development, globalization, global transformation and internationalization of social movements, and organization and international organization theories. Historically, sociological epistemologies have been developed to tackle social problems and formal and informal organizations have been formed to address social issues as they appeared. When socioeconomic and political problems crossed the borders, international organizations were formed to tackle those issues on an international scale.

This chapter provides a general overview of how international organizations were formed, for what purposes, and how their structure has been changed. The distinction between formal organizational studies and studies of international organizations is minimal because both help to widen the idea of creating an original position for better combinations of favorable circumstances or situations in human affairs. The chapter will explain the origin of the term international organization (OR); the historical roots of studies; and define or analyze the types of ORs in the contemporary world; reveals the relationship between the international relation (IR) and regime theories application in the OR's studies; and the impact of the globalization. The chapter also unveils the relationships between organizational sociology and OR and finally it gives a general outline of the application of institutional theory in the study of OR following a summary. Organizations can inspire and bring people in concert to achieve combined goals. They are accountable for determining the intelligence needed to meet their goals. This chapter provides a glimmer of international organizations theory, origin, historical account, definitions, and utilization of the contemporary academic world intertwined with the international relations, regime, and globalization as well as the organizational sociological theories and perspectives that can be utilized to study of international organizations. This chapter will help understand the historical account of an international organization, pedagogical development, and contemporary theories and practices of international organizations and organizational sociology.

Chapter 4, "Sustainability Theories," is the notion of sustainable development and tries to answer whether sustainability paradigm is the remedy to all challenges? Does its goals capture the essence of real development

xx *Preface*

and sustainability? Concerning discourses, creativeness, boundaries, and institutional architecture.

There are overlaps of theories and paradigms among international relations theory, sociological theory, organizational theory, and international organization theory. This book broadly tries to bridge knowledge gaps of social science theories application to understand the organizations, particularly, the international organizations.

The purpose of the book is to provide the basic concepts of social theories and the application of research methods (qualitative) and elaborate on the factual reality of "why the study of an international organization is also the subject of sociological study." The book presents the perspectives of organizational sociology, in a way that scholarly readers can see the linkages between political sciences, sociology, and slightly economics in addressing the roles and issues of the international organizations; so far, those have been the subject matter of political sciences within the domain of international relation theory and sustainability theory.

Prof. Medani P. Bhandari, Ph.D.

Forewords

Prof. Medani P. Bhandari has written the "go-to" book on the topic of perspectives on sociological theories, methodological debates, and organizational sociology for the academic community in their search for pedagogical perspectives on these topics. This new resource book addresses the topics from a scholarly, comprehensive, humanistic, and honest perspective, capturing the essence of the topics to be covered. His preface lays out the foundation of what is to be addressed and how he was "driven" to choose a career path in sociology and its role in society.

As I delved into the book, I found that his opening story of growing up in Nepal and the influence of family on who he is today matched my experience as a psychiatric mental health family therapist needing to understand the influence today on both the strengths and weaknesses of our cultural heritage on who we are and who we become affecting health, well-being, and choices in life.

Today, as I walk that path with one of my doctoral students, I hear her firsthand experience of breathing past the cultural norms she was raised in even today in 2021 to uplift the role of women in her country, India. Hearing firsthand her story, I realize the importance of today's women in her country which also matches women in the USA, my home country, and in the other countries, I visited, worked in, and explored health and healing history since that is my topic of interest in the educational paradigm of society.

From this base, I take the points Prof. Bhandari makes in his newest book to heart and encourage others to take to heart and then uplift their souls to the perspective of facing the challenges of bringing equality throughout the world in *all* countries. We need to uplift the downtrodden, forgotten, and suffering and challenge the affluent, well-educated with privileges to use their gifts to stand alongside not above others to bring out each person's gift and contribution to the world as we *all* possess gifts to give. Gifts such as the strength of spirit or achievement even in the face of adversity. Gifts of the song of artistic creation that uplift spirits to continue and aspire to higher ground or these same that point to what is needed for social solutions of local, national, and international problems.

xxii *Forewords*

And, of course, we need solid research that shows solutions to the world's many problems not trusting only quantitative research but qualitative research and, yes, of course, the blending of the two: qualitative and quantitative.

Let us not forget the intuitive experts who have communicated from a higher source showing pathways to solutions not relying on the human ego capacity only but joining with multi-dimensional perspectives like what I have experienced my entire life.

Look where your feet have walked throughout your life, and you will see the footprints left behind for others to walk in your shoes to unfamiliar territory and discoveries that capture their soul. So, I invite you as you read Prof. Bhandari's message, to stop at times for the inward stimulus that touches you and explore the sociological perspectives that shaped who you are today and where you want to go tomorrow. Talk to the elders, to the unforgotten, to the downtrodden, to the rich and famous, the high and mighty, and those given a title of less than that is not deserving. From that platform, you too can "write your new text" of your soul's journey on the earth at this time with the challenges facing the human, animal, and planetary kind.

As I write this forward, we are experiencing the aftereffects and current effects of the worldwide COVID-19 pandemic that reshaped the world. At this moment, storms are racing throughout Southeast America wreaking havoc on people's lives. On the American–Mexican border, in this country and other countries, there are individuals, and children unaccompanied by parents and loved ones coming to seek education, knowledge, and support to uplift their lives to then, in turn, uplift the lives left behind. How can we help? Which problem or problems do we, do I, as an individual focus on. I asked myself this question last night as I returned home late from helping family and a senior friend I am caring for as well as meeting the challenges of the new role as the president of Akamai University.

I have in front of me my role of president and co-leader with faculty and students to uplift society while personally co-facing with my sister and her husband the hard life challenges as she moves to the end stage of life. I am torn between my presidential duties and my family heart space to assist my sister's life transition to what we believe in there is another side besides planet earth. How does she transition? How do we help all those affected by end of life in her and my family? Then, how do I present what I learned and experienced personally and take it to my professional arena to help others do the same?

Reading Dr. Bhandari's work did help me and will help you to get to a "different place" in this journey called "life." Enjoy that time spent opening your eyes and heart to innovations of the soul.

Dr. MJ Bulbrook
President

mj.bulbrook@akamai.university
1 (919) 724-9657

3211 Gibson Road
Durham, NC
27703-4622 USA

akamai.university

It is an immense pleasure to write a forward for the book "Perspectives on Sociological Theories, Methodological Debates, and Organizational Sociology" by Prof. Medani P. Bhandari Akamai University, Hawaii, USA, and Sumy State University, Ukraine.

With pleasure and pride, I would like to state that Medani was our master's student at the Central Department of Sociology/Anthropology, Tribhuvan University, Kirtipur, Kathmandu, Nepal from 1989 to 1990. Medani was a very normal student, a full-time jobholder at the Rastriya Banijya Bank as a head assistant, and an environment conservation activist. His noticeable character was his simplicity, honesty, and his respect for us as professors, and respect for all his friend circles. Even, I still remember that, sometimes, he used to come to the class with a two-year baby boy (his son). Back in 2001, I heard that Medani quit his then officer job at the bank and began to pursue advanced study abroad. And now, when I see his profile, his publications, his humanitarian approaches, his name, and fame in the world, I feel so good and proud that our educational approach has the power to help students to choose the right path. I am proud of you, Medani, and to be one of the teachers in your education journey.

Prof. Bhandari is a well-known humanitarian, author, editor, and co-editor of several books and the author of hundreds of scholarly papers on social and environmental sciences: a poet, essayist, environment, social

xxiv *Forewords*

activist, etc. Most importantly, I value him as a true educator, who advocates that education should not be only for education sake and for employment (get the position, earn money, etc.) but should bring meaningful change in students' lives, which could provide the inner peace in life and be able to face any kind of challenges. Prof. Bhandari is also a motivational speaker – life skill coach (how to remain in peace and calm when the situation is not in our control, with the application of Bashudaiva Kutumbakkam principles) – and in writings and teaching, he exemplifies how studies of scientific theories can be enjoyable and applicable in day-to-day life. As such the epistemology of knowledge, which is the basis of theory, the building is considered not a fun subject for everybody; however, Prof. Bhandari's works show that there is always a lucid and attractive side to a difficult subject. This book on social theories and methods is an example.

This book first summarizes the contribution of western social science theorists beginning from Karl Marx to contemporary theorists and, second, provides the root of research methods the ontology and epistemology of qualitative and quantitative methods, and gives an overview of debates on research methods. Third, the book provides the theoretical root of international organization formation, and its functions.

The book captures the core message of each theorist. Here is a paragraph from the book itself about Karl Marx:

> It is hard to summarize what major theoretical contributions Marx made in sociological theory building. He pointed out that whatever he is doing is in the society and for the society *"Even when I conduct scientific work... ....I perform a social because human act. It is only the material of my activity------like the language itself which the thinker uses-----which is given to me as a social product. My existence is a social product"* (as cited by Tucker 1969, page 89). His presence can be found in most of the subject matter of sociological epistemology. His notion of dialecticism provides new ways to examine society (According to the materialist conception of history, the ultimate determinant element in history is the production and reproduction of real life. . . . Hence if somebody twists this into saying that the economic element is the only determining one, he transforms that proposition into a meaningless, abstract, and senseless phrase. The economic situation is the basis, but the various elements of the superstructure . . . also exercise their influence upon the course of

the historical struggle and in many cases preponderate in determining their form" (1962, II, p. 488). Marx first examines the sociological reality through critical perspectives and proposes the optimal solution to resolve the underlying social problems. His critical reasoning on social development gave others the ground to oppose the positivist basis of social inquiry. In terms of his contribution to the sub-fields of sociology, such as political sociology, historical sociology, organizational sociology, feminist sociology, etc., he gave the insights to examine society on logical grounds. *"Marx's work has been the inspiration and constant touchstone for radical critiques of management under conditions of capitalist industrial development as exemplified in debates concerning the nature of the labor process under capitalism* (Braverman 1974 as cited by Starkey 1992:1). His writings on class struggle and conflict provide the basis to explore how important is power dynamism, the relationships between the social elite and the working class, and how capital formation occurs in feudalistic and capitalist societies. In general terms, Marxist notions can be applied to examine critically how organizations are formed, for whom, and with what purpose. Further his notions allow us to explore organizational conflict and how capital is formatted to run the organization. Marx introduced the concept of greed in the possession or consumption of goods and services.

Prof. Bhandari has provided the actual massages of the most important theorists of the western world, in a way that the general readers also can easily follow the contributions of Karl Marx, Ferdinand Tönnies, Émile Durkheim, Ludwig Gumplovicz, Vilfredo Pareto, Max Weber, and Talcott Parsons, Henri Fayol, Frederick Taylor, Luther Halsey Gulick, Herbert A. Simon, Berton H. Kaplan, Michel Foucault, Jurgen Habermas, Jacques Derrida, Jurgen Habermas, Philip Selznick, Peter Blau, James David Thompson, Charles Perrow, Paul J. DiMaggio, Walter W. Powell, Arlene Daniels, Dorothy Smith, etc.

In the method chapter, Prof. Bhandari follows the same tract. First, he presents the contributions of founding theorists on research methods – Comte, Mill, Kant, Durkheim, Dilthey, Rickert, Weber, Malinowski, Park, etc., to contemporary scholars, provides the nutshell of debates of qualitative and quantitative methods, and gives the arguments that both methods are equal including mix method; however, researchers need to know what is appropriate for her or his research. Prof. Bhandari states that the research method is the roadmap of the researcher's journey, and the method is like

xxvi   *Forewords*

GPS (global positioning system); however, sometimes, the driver may need to prepare their pathway, because research may not follow the linear path. Here is how Prof. Bhandari conceptualizes the debates in research methods:

> The debates between quantitative and qualitative methods are essential for and against positivism and interpretive perspectives of social inquiry. Methods associated with positivism are grounded in the work of Comte, Mill, and Durkheim in social sciences, who believed that the social world can be viewed in the same way as natural sciences. In contrast, philosophers like Dilthey, Rickert, and Weber who followed the Kantian tradition challenged the positivist philosophy and developed the interpretive approach (Smith 1983). The positivist tradition of social inquiry has been followed by the quantitative scholars and the interpretive path by the qualitative scholars (from Chapter 2).

There is a fundamental distinction between qualitative and quantitative studies. Both have different epistemological positions. Quantitative methodology is associated with positivist epistemology and qualitative method with interpretive epistemology. The quantitative method refers to the collection of numerical data and analysis through using statistical tools, with an emphasis on facts. On the other hand, qualitative methodologies refer to the forms of field data collection with an emphasis on meanings and rely on understanding (Marshall 1998). Quantitative and qualitative methods have different assumptions, purposes and approaches, and researchers' roles. For example, quantitative researchers assume that social facts have objective reality and can be separated into variables (Chapter 2).

This chapter provides the theorists' contribution to research design and provides the pathway to choosing the right method and producing reliable, valid, and useful knowledge.

The last chapter is the theoretical root of organizational sociology. The role of sociologists has been considered fundamental to understanding society; as a result, there has been always a high demand for sociological knowledge. There is no limit to knowledge and there is an interconnected relationship between sociology to all knowledge systems. There are varieties in society and the scope of sociological knowledge is divided by demand. As a result, there are many branches of sociology, i.e., organizational sociology, political sociology, medical sociology, criminal sociology, occupational sociology, economic sociology, religious sociology, environmental sociology, rural sociology, urban sociology, knowledge sociology, historical sociology, theoretical sociology, demography, industrial, family, education, and so on. However, Prof. Bhandari's focus in this book is mostly on theoretical sociology, organizational sociology, and partly environmental sociology. The nutshell of theoretical sociology, which is the fundamental knowledge, is illustrated in Chapter 1, and Chapter 3 shows the exemplary work in organizational sociology. Chapter 3 summarizes the current literature (key theories and readings) that focus on the study of international organizations and answers on how the theories and perspectives of organizational sociology might better inform the study of international organizations.

"The study of organizations provides a theoretical framework for knowledge about human behavior in organizations and reviews the empirical evidence for the propositions that make up the theory. The theory emphasizes the motivations for organizational participation and the processes of decision making within organizations" (Simon 1979).

Chapter 3 first provides the answer to how international organizations were formed, what they are, what their role is, and why sociologist should study and explain organizational sociology theories and perspectives. This chapter unveils how political science and sociology follow the same path to understanding the socio-political systems and where they differ. To elaborate on the knowledge paths of social sciences, Prof. Bhandari presents the epistemology of international relations (IR) theory, regime theory, globalization, network theory, governance theory, social networks, institution theory, the green economic initiatives, the stakeholder theory, etc., and shows the importance of organizational sociology in the contemporary world as well as for near future.

International organizations (IO) are not new phenomena. Broadly, international organizations' historical roots can be traced to Greek civilization (Plato and Aristotle), although they have mostly flourished since the Enlightenment era. However, empirical studies show that the scientific study of IOs begins only in the 19th century. Political scientists examine international organizations in terms of international relations, governance, and power dynamics. To examine society, they use various historical perspectives (developed by ancient and classical social thinkers) such as power and authority (rewards and punishment) and the political community (including nationalism).

Theoretically, organizational research broadly examines (1) producing units and what factors determine organizational effectiveness or productivity and (2) sets of individuals whose well-being is affected by the terms of

xxviii *Forewords*

organizational membership and whose motivation to continue that membership depends on their assessment of its comparative contribution to their well-being (Kahn 1990, page 3). This notion can be applied to investigating the role of international organizations because they follow more complex formalities than domestic formal organizations. The roles of organizations depend on the motives behind why, how, and for what purpose organizations were formed.

> Sociologists "who study organizations have been and are rendering more valuable services to organizational theory and practice by maintaining the sociology of organization as a more or less distinct specialty than by simply joining hands with others in an interdisciplinary approach to the field" (Lammers 1981). Differing from the political scientists, sociologists examine organizations through three major perspectives such as rational, natural, and open and developed, and various approaches from functionalism, neo-functionalism, structuralism, and neo-structuralism to postmodernism along with the other theories such as contingency, network, institution, resource dependency, transaction cost, ecology, demographic, and so on (Chapter 3).

To sum up, the book covers three fundamental aspects of social sciences, theory, method, application, and the chosen field of studies organizational sociology. Prof. Bhandari has summarized the major social sciences theorists' contributions from beginning to date, provided the epistemology of research methods (quantitative and qualitative) with examples of applicability, and showed the importance of interdisciplinary research practices. I am really surprised to see how a scholar can reproduce the most difficult knowledge in a very general language. Each chapter is worth hundreds of pages of books within the social science domain. This book can be useful not only for the scholars of social science, sociology, political sciences, and economics but also to all scholars who need to understand the importance of theory, method, and application.

As such, this book can be useful to all scholars and general readers who thrive on the knowledge. For the universities, this book can be a major sourcebook mostly for sociology, anthropology, political sciences, and economics (bachelor level to Ph.D. level) where understanding of theory and method is a major pillar of knowledge.

And, finally, I thank Prof. Medani for your knowledge of production and distribution. I am proud to be your professor, and on behalf of all colleagues,

I express my best wishes and expect more valuable knowledge in the coming days as well.

Thank you,
Prof. Ganesh Man Gurung, Ph.D.
Chancellor
Gandaki University, Pokhara, Nepal

Prof. Medani P. Bhandari is a leading academic in the fields of sociology, environment, and climate change research methodology to reap this academic excellence from a developing country Nepal with the untiring struggle in life to gain this summit of the academia renowned among the eminent academicians and researchers in the world. His attempt to bring this book on social theories, methodologies, and organizational sociology is a monumental creation and to share with us making a publication from Nepal is praiseworthy. This book is a creation from his years of experiences, practices, and research in the fields that he worked as a professor, researcher, an advocate of climate change, and environmental conservation, and an expert in the field of organizational management. He has made several seminal publications in the form of books, journal articles, research reports, and advocacy documents for saving the nature earth for the common use of all the creatures on the earth.

This book is a complete whole, though it has not covered all the major social theories, for a reader who wants to do research in the fields of social sciences and education, making an understanding of social theories and their use in seeing the problems, putting theories in designing research methodologies, and selecting appropriate methods and tools. As a professor and a researcher active in the network of academia of the global North and South, his book brings up-to-date knowledge on theory, research methodology, and practices that could contribute to conducting research both in the developing and developed world. As he says in the preface of the book "…social scientists need to understand the social theories, applicable methods, and actual system of the society as the body of knowledge – the mind(theories), methods (the pathways of research) and the heart part(the knowledge itself of the society)…." Having said this, he has cleared his position in the book that from a practitioner's perspective, he wants to provide

xxx *Forewords*

ample knowledge of the theories and their use in the research. He intends to help the readers to understand the contributions of the great social scientists and to understand society through theories, methods, and their use. As an author from the eastern world, he has tried to speak his understanding of the western theories of social sciences that can provide ideas to contrast with the eastern social theories that build the society and continued till date.

As the book is organized into three chapters, interrelating each other gives an understanding of theory, methods, and its appropriate application in understanding and interpreting the social reality inherent in the particular context of time and space; and the growing field of organizational sociology different from the rationalist perspectives of creation and working of national and international organizational sociological theories and perspectives. The first chapter gives a brief version but a critical perspective of major social theories with an introduction of the theorists, their contributions, and the use of the theory in understanding society including the development trend of social theories and the position of organizational sociology in the social theories from the western theoretical perspectives. In discussing the theories, the author is using the exemplary works of scholars that can help understand the use of theories in understanding society and doing research on social problems under research in social sciences. In the second chapter, the origin and debate in the research methods from the historical, ontological, and epistemological perspectives can help to understand the different research paradigms meaningfully. Furthermore, it has shade light on why the debates remain ongoing and contribute to developing new perspectives in research paradigms. This explanation makes readers clear for not being slavish in one research paradigm tradition rather than using them as required to understand and answer the social and cultural issues as research problems in the academia and client research. The third chapter is related to international organization and organizational sociology theories and perspectives and broadly explains how an organization is born and exists in the society and becomes a topic of study in social sciences, and how it should be studied. A critical reflection from the history to the present scene of the organization is captured in this chapter, giving ideas on analyzing the national and international organizations from the perspectives of the social sciences, particularly from the sociological perspectives. This chapter can give an analytical tool to the researchers interested to make a study of the international organization from the perspectives of social theories and pragmatics, a critical perspective connected to values and power of the socio-political structure of the time for the formation of the organization. This book has made an interesting amalgamation of social theories, research methods, and methodological debates and their appropriate use in the study of society and social issues as research problems and tools for research and study of international organizations from the perspectives of the social theories and research methodologies focusing on qualitative research.

As I was trained in mathematics and taught many years of mathematics and mathematics education courses in university, favored quantitative methods in the early days. In the later part of my life, I developed a course of qualitative research for the students of mathematics education through my study. My experiences as teaching quantitative and qualitative research and supervising research students say that early scholars have much confusion in understanding the relation between theories, methodologies, and treating theories appropriately in research, and it is a problem even for the supervisors to bring them on board in this matter. As I went through this book, I am fully convinced that it will fill this gap of understanding and competencies of the early beginner researchers in the field of social science and education. Prof. Bhandari has worked among the Nepali scholars and the students too and knows the background of the students and the epistemology in them doing research. This book, I expect, will meet the needs of the students from the eastern academic culture, but, no less, it will be equally valuable for students and scholars of other parts of the world.

Thank you!!!
Prof. Lekhnath Sharma, Ph.D.
Former Vice-Chancellor

Manbhawan, Lalitpur, Nepal
TEL: +977-01-5008047, 5008048
e-mail: info@nou.edu.np

Prof. Medani P. Bhandari has brought his childhood, boyhood, and mature human-hood experiences in particular to questions of inequality in society in this book. They are in many ways the products of evolving human

xxxii *Forewords*

society, the hierarchal system that those contemporary society thoughts were appropriate, be it culturally or religiously the arena of men-hood and women-hood. The human thought process requires time to evolve and adopt new ways of doing things and change the societal norms and value systems. Even despite changes, there are mental biases in the so-called developed liberal democratic countries. We can see and feel the discrimination among European descent people against men and women, man and man, women and women, supremacy over black, yellow races, and other fellow *homo sapiens*. This is ongoing and they and we consider it still normal. In the name of such supremacy, much has happened, and many wars have undergone in human history and are continued today. Thus, the question of global inequality in all spheres of human society is one of the most important challenges to address in the 21st century by homo sapie*n*s. Prof. Bhandari talks about patriarchal society; inequality is even more prevalent in matrilineal society between women folks and men.

Social science is not a new subject. There were societies and social norms when *homo sapiens* lived along with other hominies about 250 thousand years ago and beyond. Modern social scientists like Auguste Comte, Max Weber, Karl Marx, William du Bois, James Festiringer, and many other philosophers have tried to postulate social theory and its evolution and talked about moral values. Eminent among those which still vibrantly exists and continues to exist in the future is the social theory of **Karl Marx** which has been applied in different parts of the world with varying degrees of success. The principle and theory on inequality in the social life of society have applied in the form of improving governance, judiciary, and legal aspects in the current world. But future generation problems of inequality are cropping up. The challenge of our time is how to address those in the contemporary world. For example, Prof. Bhandari's childhood, boyhood, and even manhood experiences are now becoming absolute. In many countries, to address such issues, a legal framework is in place. But the challenge is in their effective implementation. Revealing social theories and digging into the past will not help, except to learn lessons if we can adapt and move ahead. Part of the problem of the contemporary world is to try to adopt a carbon copy of western theory which is developed in different situations and circumstances. Good and practical ideas can be brought and applied, while new ways of governing society must evolve from the respective land.

Prof. Bhandari has tried to review and revisit the social theory and how they can be incorporated, and the roles modern institutions could play in the existing unequal human society. This book will be a reference material for students of social science and social works. I wish for his continuous and prolific writing a complete success.

Dr. Krishna Prasad Oli, Ph.D.
Former Member
National Planning Commission
Government of Nepal

I am thrilled to write a foreword for the book by Prof. Medani P. Bhandari, Akamai University, Hawaii, USA, and Sumy State University, Ukraine, titled "Perspectives on Sociological Theories, Methodological Debates, and Organizational Sociology."

Prof. Bhandari holds multidisciplinary academic background – Doctor of Philosophy (Ph.D.) in Sociology (USA), Master of Sociology (USA), Anthropology (Nepal), Sustainable International Development (USA), Master of Science (The Netherlands), Advance Diploma in Wildlife Management (UK), Ecology and Environment (India), Environmental Education (India), and so on. As multidisciplinary academic background, his area of expertise covers both core sciences and social sciences. This book is an example of his dedicated knowledge base on social sciences.

Prof. Bhandari is a globally known humanitarian, author, editor, editor-in-chief, and co-editor of several books and has authored hundreds of scholarly papers on environmental and social sciences. Most of his works are related to innovation and technology, entrepreneurship and development, climate change, biodiversity conservation, sustainable development, and humanism to create an inclusive society. Prof. Bhandari is also a well-known poet, essayist, and environmental and social activist. In our conversation, Prof. Bhandari repeatedly mentions that education should not be only for education but should be for EDUCARE which gives the pathway to living in peace in a worse situation. Prof. Bhandari advocates the principle of Bashudaiva Kutumbakkam – all living beings are relatives to humans; therefore, one should treat equally to each other as well as another living being to maintain harmony with nature. Prof. Bhandari states that nothing is impossible to the resolute, disciplined person and none of the subjects are difficult for those who enjoy challenging work.

xxxiv *Forewords*

This book is an example of how studies of scientific theories can be enjoyable and applicable in day-to-day life. As such, the epistemology of knowledge which is the basis of theory building is considered not a fun topic. However, Prof. Bhandari's works show that there is always a lucid and attractive side to a difficult subject. This book on social theories and methods is written in a way that readers will enjoy and understand social sciences theory development.

The book covers all aspects of theory building and utilization. The book is a kind of histography. "Social science, any branch of academic study or science that deals with human behavior in its social and cultural aspects." Usually included within the social sciences are cultural (or social) anthropology, sociology, psychology, political science, and economics.

"The discipline of historiography is regarded by many as social science, and certain areas of historical study are almost indistinguishable from work done in the social sciences" (https://www.britannica.com/topic/social-science). The book first presents the contributions of western social science theorists in chronological order, elaborates on their contributions, and provides the rationality of those epistemologies. Second, it talks about the fundamentals of research methods, the debates on methods application, and practical examples of how methods should be chosen for good scientific research. Third, the book provides the essence of theories building with the details of international organization formation and with the exemplary works of major theorists in disciple formation. It presents how all scientific theories are interconnected and how they can be utilized.

This book is a superb example of academic artisanship, where theories speak layperson languages, and researchers mingle with the method and create and produce new knowledge and perform in daily life. Prof. Bhandari presents this book as a knowledge tree, where roots are theories, and fruits are knowledge "beneficial to all knowledge seekers."

Prof. Bhandari presents his lifelong acquired knowledge of science. This example of arduous work, perseverance, dedication, and willingness to give to society. This book is useful to all scholars and general readers who thrive on knowledge. For universities, this book can be a major sourcebook for core sciences and social (high school to Ph.D. level) where understanding of theory and method is a major pillar of knowledge.

Finally, I thank Prof. Bhandari for your willingness to give back knowledge to society in the form of books, scientific papers, poems, essays, and other forms like talks, chats, knowledge production, and distribution. I am proud to know you, and on behalf of all my colleagues, I express my best wishes and we expect more valuable knowledge in near future.

Thank you,

Dr. Subash Shree Pokhrel, Ph.D.
Vice-Chancellor
Manmohan Technical University,
Budhiganga-4, Morang, Province 1, Nepal

The book "**Perspectives on Sociological Theories, Methodological Debate, and Organizational Sociology**" by Prof. Dr. Medani P. Bhandari is the finest example of the artistic presentation of social science principles and practices. The book jointly answers what the social theorist's contributions to mobilizing the current scholarship of social science are, why they are important, and why we should understand them. The book adds a new understanding of the debates of social science research methods and answers why scholars should not engage in debates but utilize the beauty of qualitative, quantitative, and mix-methods. In the current world, the role of an international organization is almost unchallengeable. However, there is little scholarly work, to give an overview of the historical account of multidisciplinary utilization of organizational knowledge. This book helps to understand the organization as architecture which helps the society to attain the desired goals.

I am particularly pleased with Dr. Bhandari's high standards and adeptness at directing and counseling adult students. He has demonstrated a sincere commitment to the teaching profession and has been effective at structuring the curriculum and assuring an important level of quality assurance.

xxxvi *Forewords*

Without exception, his colleagues are impressed with his professionalism, his cheerful manner, and the strength of his leadership contributions.

I find Dr. Medani Prasad Bhandari to be among the brightest individuals whom I have had the good fortune to meet in my thirty years in higher education. He brings to graduate study a genuine thirst for knowledge and a strong intellect. He demonstrates academic strengths in several areas of higher education. His empathy and caring attitude toward others, maturity, strong interpersonal traits, and cheerful outlook are among his core assets.

Prof. Bhandari thrives on social empowerment and social change. His focus is on how society can be inclusive and cohesive. Prof. Bhandari's many papers and books on climate change, biodiversity conservation, education transformations, sustainable development, the role of an international organization, inequality, social theories and practices, etc., are the evidence of his involvement in social and environmental policy paradigm.

Prof. Medani P. Bhandari is a globally well-known environmentalist, and humanitarian, and "Perspectives on Sociological Theories, Methodological Debate, and Organizational Sociology" also presents how an understanding of humanity and social science can help to identify the societal problems and provide the pathways to solve them. This will be a valuable resource to those who like to understand and learn about sociological research and methodologies and international organizational behaviors and their impact on societies.

Thank you.
Prof. Douglass Lee Capogrossi, Ph.D.
President Emeritus
Akamai University, USA

The social theories, methods, and applications presented in the book by Prof. M. Bhandari "**Perspectives on Sociological Theories, Methodological Debates, and Organizational Sociology**" is timeless, with a clearly emphasized role of social scientists analyzing the varieties of complex social, cultural, religious, political, and economic systems. The importance of the discussion is intensified by globalization processes and dependencies of world economies. Globalization has been an important direction of research in social sciences since the 1990s. The area of international relations started to be analyzed under the pretext of far-reaching qualitative changes and the fact that the classical theoretical and methodological tools used so far were no longer sufficient. Sociology, for most of its history, did not problematize the relationship between society and the nation-state, and the borders of the state were determined by the horizon of its theoretical research. The international phenomena were monopolized by the science of international relations, which recognized the thesis about the absolute nature of nation-states as the reason and justification for their existence. The growing number of phenomena that did not fit within the boundaries of the nation-state made the essence of the problems visible. This led to the uprising of proposals to create a new sub-discipline related to the study of international phenomena, regarding the creation of international sociology, world-historical sociology, the sociology of international relations, global sociology, and the sociology of globalization. As a result, there has been a shift in the methodological perspective from methodological nationalism to methodological cosmopolitanism.

Despite numerous criticisms pointing to the crisis of sociological theory, it should be stated that it not only keeps up with the changing world but also participates in the ongoing evolution by providing the necessary tools to interpret and shape social processes.

The book by Prof. Medani P. Bhandari is a presentation of scientific achievements of Western theories of social sciences, referring to the development of organizational theory and the way the organizational theorists are responding to the emergence of challenges to the traditional rational approaches to understanding organizations in the historical context. It also addresses the issues of quantitative and qualitative methods used to describe phenomena and explains the importance of qualitative methods to understand the phenomenology and hermeneutical phenomenology and linkages of the principles of the "symbolic interaction." It also provides a general overview of how international organizations were formed, for what purposes, and how their structure has been changed.

In his book, Prof. M. Bhandari also tries to answer the question of how the theories and perspectives of organizational sociology can better serve the study of international organizations.

Due to its content, the book can be recommended for those readers who are interested in the subject of social sciences, social theories, and their practical application and/or for those involved in the elimination of strong social imbalances. It can also be treated as a sourcebook for an undergraduate to doctoral students.

xxxviii   *Forewords*

Prof. Jacek Piotr Binda, Ph.D.
Rector of the International Affairs, Bielsko-Biala School of Finance and Law,
Poland

СУМСЬКИЙ ДЕРЖАВНИЙ УНІВЕРСИТЕТ	SUMY STATE UNIVERSITY
Навчально-науковий інститут бізнесу, економіки та менеджменту	**Education and Research Institute for Business, Economics, and Management**
вул. Римського-Корсакова, 2, м. Суми, 40007 тел.(0542) 33-54-75 e-mail: info@biem.sumdu.edu.ua	2, Rymsky-Korsakov, St. Sumy, 40007, Ukraine tel. +38 (0542) 33-54-75 e-mail: info@biem.sumdu.edu.ua

Sumy state university 2, R.-Korsakov, Str.
Sumy, 40007, Ukraine
Phone: +38 (0542) 33-53-83
e-mail: vn.boronos@finance.sumdu.edu.ua

I am proud to write a forward for the book titled "Perspectives on Sociological Theories, Methodological Debates, and Organizational Sociology" by Prof. Medani P. Bhandari, Akamai University, Hawaii, USA, and Sumy State University, Ukraine.

Prof. Medani P. Bhandari is a globally well-known environmentalist, humanitarian, and a scholar of social science theories, methods, and application as well as climate science, sustainable development, and a trainer of life sciences (Bashudaiva Kutumbakkam – all living beings are relative and neighbors for human). Prof. Bhandari is also a poet, essayist, philosopher of peace living, and a true educator, who advocates that education should not be only for education sake and for employment. He is an author, editor, and co-editor of several books, and an author of hundreds of scholarly papers on social and environmental sciences.

Prof. Bhandari holds extended experience in scientific and pedagogical work: organizing academic seminars, conducting panel discussions and seminars with the scholars of the world, as well as with the students and teacher at the international level, and supervising doctoral and master's students' dissertations and theses and publication activity. Moreover, Prof. Bhandari is known worldwide for his valuable investigations into sociological and environmental issues, in particular, its policy making, climate change problems, and sustainable development. He takes an active part in international conferences and forums on the development and practical implementation of social models in society's lifestyle.

In the book, "Perspectives on Sociological Theories, Methodological Debates, and Organizational Sociology," Prof. Bhandari provides a summary of the contribution of the western social sciences theorists beginning from Karl Marx to contemporary theorists and, second, provides the root of the research method and the ontology and epistemology of qualitative and quantitative method and gives the overview of debates on research methods. Third, the book provides the theoretical root of international organization formation, and its functions. In each section, Prof. Bhandari provides a critical view of social problems and the ways to manage them. The ideas set out in the work embrace crucial aspects of the current methodical basis and practical recommendations on social aspects. The book helps its readers to choose and implement the relevant social model according to the peculiarities of the social type and problem aspects within it. Each chapter is worth hundreds of pages of books within the social science domain.

To sum up, the book covers three fundamental aspects of social sciences, theory, method, application, and the chosen field of studies organizational sociology. The book can be helpful to researchers, students, graduates, practitioners, public officers and policymakers, public organizations, or anyone who thrive to understand the core concept of social sciences, research method, and application.

I would like to thank Prof. Medani for bringing and adding new knowledge and insightful thoughts on the fundamentals of social sciences, the theory, methods, and application. This book is a masterpiece of social science, where Prof. Bhandari provides a summary of western social thinkers' works, their theories, and how those theories are still providing the knowledge base for all new epistemologies. This book can be useful to all scholars and general readers who thrive on the knowledge of social science, research method, and application of acquired knowledge in the practical world.

xl *Forewords*

I am thankful for this groundbreaking work and wish you all success. I expect more such knowledge from Prof. Bhandari in the coming years as well.

Thank you,
Володимир М. Боронос
Prof. Volodymyr M. Boronos,
Head of the Department of Finance and Entrepreneurship
Sumy State University, Sumy, Ukraine

This book "Perspectives on Sociological Theories, Methodological Debates, and Organizational Sociology" authored by Prof. Medani P. Bhandari encapsulates in words the many years of experience and contemplation of the author's academic and professional learning. It covers three major fields – social science theories, qualitative and quantitative methodologies, and the foundation of organizational sociology. The book provides some examples of the sociology of selected international organizations and analyzes how they function as institutions serving the public.

Human societies evolved from tribal hunter-gathering bands culminating in the modern cosmopolitan and global civilization. While we retain many of our evolutionary characteristics making us the successful survival machines, our sociological character has changed vastly to make us a highly advanced species. Our invention of a sophisticated language, the proficiency in science and technology, and the use of expanded mobility have put us solidly apart from the humble origins of ape-like animals. The study of sociology helps us understand how we have come such a long way, and how we live our modern lives. In addition, sociology also helps us understand our group behavior, our ambitions, dreams, and challenges, and how we can make our lives even better.

The author elaborates on the contribution of the founding writers of western sociology, with a focus on how some of them addressed the sociology of organizations. He deals with several topics in this area such as international organizations, international relations, organizational sociology, organizational theory, and contemporary theories in sociology. To benefit the readers who are new to the field, he also reviews and critiques the theories of classical sociology.

Prof. Bhandari carefully discusses how sociology researchers employ qualitative and quantitative methods to understand, analyze, and dissect sociological issues. The book also highlights how philosophical commitments and political and ethical considerations shape the use and benefits of qualitative and quantitative approaches in research. By providing examples of some textbooks in the field, the author makes it easy for the readers to understand this topic better. Prof. Bhandari reviews the contributions of some of the pioneers and luminaries of sociology such as Karl Marx, Emile Durkheim, Max Weber, Henri Fayol, Frederick Taylor, Luther Halsey Gulick, Herbert A. Simon, and Berton H. Kaplan.

The book provides a general overview of the sociology of international organizations by discussing how they are formed, what purposes they serve, and how their structure evolves to better fulfill their mission. As the world becomes increasingly dependent on institutional actors, understanding the sociology of organization becomes even more important. This is a topic of keen interest for the especially many professionals who work on global issues such as climate change, environmental management, biodiversity, and human rights. The book provides an overview of international organizations with their origin, historical account, and their roles and effectiveness in solving international challenges. The analysis and theoretical background provided in the book in this regard is another useful element for a variety of readers.

The book also helps in understanding the notion of justice, fairness, and equity among individuals and countries. It is designed to fill the knowledge gap especially in using sociological models to appreciate international organizations and their work. As the contemporary society becomes more sensitive to the issues of race, equality, class, and the limits of the concept of meritocracy, discussion of fairness and equity become critical to advance the goals of enabling every individual to reach his or her full intrinsic potential.

In authoring this book, Prof. Medani P. Bhandari has utilized his extensive background in this field as a student, educator, and practitioner in the area of social and environmental development. He started his education and a career in the environmental and development field in the rural and small-town setting in Nepal. His childhood and young adult life in Nepal were spent in a poor but cohesive and community-oriented environment, where it was everybody's business to know about the private life of their neighbors. It was a quintessential traditional and agrarian society. He later moved to the USA to obtain his doctorate and now teaches in several countries. The society in the USA compared to that of Nepal is individual-centered, cosmopolitan, privacy-sensitive, and materialistic. His experience in such different environments has provided him with a comparative perspective on how societies function and how organizations help advance important objectives in shaping the lives of individuals and the character of the community. Societal

xlii *Forewords*

values and experiences also affect how one can deal with larger issues such as biodiversity conservation, global warming mitigation, and the reduction in social inequalities. Bhandari's life journey has enabled him to gain and then share deep insights into the problems of contemporary society and the ways to solve the many existing challenges.

To author this book, Prof. Bhandari has undertaken extensive research covering a vast area of sociology-related history, practice, and outcomes and has cleverly distilled them for the benefit of the readers. His challenging work has produced a book that can be a valuable reference to the beginner as well as professional sociologists and the students of sociology, environment, and social justice.

This book will be important reading for students, academics, researchers, policymakers, and laypeople who are interested to understand sociological theories and especially the sociology of international organizations.

Dr. Ambika P. Adhikari, Ph.D.
Urban Planner, and International Development Professional
Phoenix, Arizona, USA
March 2022

People's perceptions and mindset about the existence of individuals as well as the society as a whole is critical in fostering social harmony. In eastern philosophy, *Bashudaiva Kutumbakkam*, meaning, "the world is one family," is a common and powerful phrase from the Hindu Upanishad that is commonly cited while expressing views on the global harmony and it is the strongest value that Hindus have developed from their scriptures in terms of their outlook to the world.

It promotes social harmony, recognizes everybody in the world as equal, and motivates everybody to work together for the betterment of individuals and the entire world. Prof. Medani P. Bhandari has written extensively on *Bashudaiva Kutumbakkam* in his several books and articles. Learning is a complex process, and the main objective of any learning is to promote behavioral changes, enhance cognitive development, raise personal motivation, and increase the ability of the learner's observe and interact with various processes and activities in the social context. Values, cultures, traditions, and norms that society imparts on young individuals shape the future of society.

Forewords xliii

Similarly, factors such as economics, international environment, politics, and socioeconomic and environmental conditions also impact the behavioral and cognitive development of the individuals in a society. Therefore, an understanding of these complex cognitive, behavioral, humanistic, and socio-situational orientations of individuals including their linkages and consequences in the social environment is critical for appropriate policy development and making necessary transformations in the society.

Prof. Medani P. Bhandari, in this book, presents a plethora of theories and practices about understanding behavior and practices in societies. Prof. Bhandari has very powerfully presented the values and relevancy of both qualitative and quantitative research and studies in a social environment. He has reviewed the works of world scholars on qualitative and quantitative research in the social context and has established the fact that qualitative research can play a powerful role in understanding the social environment of inequalities, discrimination, and differences inherent in the society and minds and perceptions of the people through a qualitative approach.

In this highly globalized world, we all are dependent on each other, and one's activities affect others. Many issues that we currently face is transboundary matter such as trade, export, and imports, climate change, global peace and security, pandemic, research and innovation, education, resource sharing, etc. Globalization has resulted in the development of many international organizations with diverse goals and perspectives. These organizational goals and perspectives are so powerful that they heavily affect the perspective and outlook of common individuals in society. Therefore, an understanding of the culture, perspective, behavior, norms, and values of these international organizations is also critical while studying the socioeconomic environment of a society. In this book, Prof. Medani P. Bhandari has successfully connected this issue of international organizations, societal perceptions, and the impacts, in studying the sociological behavior of our societies. Prof. Medani P. Bhandari has done an excellent job in bringing up this issue of theoretical perspectives and research in the context of social inclusion and international organizations. This book will be a valuable resource to those who like to understand and learn about sociological research and methodologies and international organizational behaviors and their impact on societies.

Prof. Durga D. Poudel, Ph.D., The Founder of Asta-Ja Framework, the University of Louisiana at Lafayette, Lafayette, LA, USA

----

xliv *Forewords*

The four-chaptered book, *Perspectives on Social Theories, Methodological Debates, and Organizational Sociology*, starts with the basic concepts of sociological theories and applications of qualitative and quantitative research methods. The author makes attempts to explain why and how qualitative and quantitative information documentable phenomena started to find out the causes of consequences of certain human behaviors and the structures and processes they create in contemporary society. Further, providing numerous examples, this book explains how inequalities are experienced by female individuals in different social settings. The author also investigates power relations in a society with the notion of the purpose of sociology as a discipline or the feminist epistemological framework that seeks to eliminate gender inequality. The author has realized that gender inequality cannot be eradicated by amassing voluminous descriptions of women's lives based on their standpoint, location in the matrix of domination, or documentation of how their social location reflects oppressions. The author explains how western scholars have postulated a theoretical framework purporting to eliminate gender inequality within the framework of sociological theory. The author provides several examples where men do less housework than women because society believes women are being held morally accountable for the well-being of men. The author further explains how society believes that it is being held morally accountable to a gender category and provides examples of how society behaves toward women as per the contemporary cultural norms. The author then fits these human behaviors within the sociological theory that it is potentially falsifiable and gender biased. In many places, the author asks for an apology to women folks for the norms of his moral accountability as a part of the cultural ideology that develops different behaviors for women and men in institutional settings. The author further explains how individuals are being held accountable to culturally constructed norms of behavior tied to gender categories even in situations when gender-bias should have been irrelevant.

The author elaborates how despite the production of a voluminous body of scholarship on inequality, still gender inequality prevails in contemporary society. He argues that understanding the lives of men and women is important in different social contexts. The author while exemplifying his rural livelihood warns that we cannot ignore how social location impacts lives, and how oppression and domination prevail in the Hindu society where a well-privileged society exploits others based on their social hierarchy. The author explains how interlocking axes of domination mask the underlying processes that reproduce gender inequality structurally. As a sociologist, he emphasizes that the label of feminist must be first understood by conducting

Forewords xlv

systematic research. He urges us to invoke the reality of science and our social composition and to understand the importance of women folks in society by providing examples of menstrual cycles and the reclusion of women folks from certain chores.

The author presents inequality theories from historical perspectives and critically analyzes multiple issues that the global society confronts today. The first part gives the overall scenario of theories, the second part provides the pathway to the research destination, the research method, and the third and the final part is the destination of the substantive field of study and the roles of international organizations on social, political, economic, and environmental regimes. It intertwines political sciences, sociology, and political economies to address the roles and issues of international organizations and explains the concepts of international relations. It also discusses how despite different overlapping theories and making efforts to fulfilling knowledge gaps in inequality theories, some vacuum still exists, and the author claims that this book tries to bridge such knowledge gaps by utilizing scholars' deep insights into the sociological theories.

Analyzing the social structure of contemporary society, the book presents contrasting cases and explores several conciliatory approaches despite the prevalence of different caste hierarchies where someone is ranked on the higher level and not on a meritorious basis but based on castes and ethnicity and get favorable environment at workplaces. This book also talks about societies that are in "haves" and "have-nots" situations. Using their own experiences, the author explains why some people have access to education and other resources while others do not. Using his sociological skills, the author examines the activities of social actors and explains how western scholars have postulated many social theories to address the underlying causes such as social conflicts and inequalities; yet, no perfect theory has been found. In this endeavor, the author traces the development of sociological theories starting from the work of Plato and Aristotle. The book also explains how the research was done in the 19th and 20th centuries. Then the author presents the contributions of Karl Marx, Ferdinand Tönnies, Émile Durkheim, Ludwig Gumplovicz, Vilfredo Pareto, Max Weber, and Talcott Parsons attempting to build sociological theories to address various forms of inequalities. The author discusses how western sociologists crafted organizational theory to answer the traditional rational approaches. The author further elaborates on the role of western sociological theorist and ties these theories to the seminar work of Karl Marx, Emile Durkheim, and Max Weber.

After dovetailing sociological theories with the seminal works of western philosophers and theories, the author elaborates on the development of

xlvi *Forewords*

organizational theory, philosophical approaches, and the emerging challenges to the traditional rational approaches. Then the author advances these ideas with the contributions of Talcott Parsons, Henri Fayol, Frederick Taylor, Luther Halsey Gulick, Herbert A. Simon, Berton H. Kaplan, Michel Foucault, Jurgen Habermas, Jacques Derrida, and Jurgen Habermas. Furthermore, contemporary theories are tied with the seminal work of Philip Selznick, Peter Blau, James David Thompson, Charles Perrow, Paul DiMaggio, and Walter W. Powell. Eventually, these ideas are blended with the feminist approach in social sciences to explain the gender-based inequalities while elaborating on the contributions of Arlene Daniels, Dorothy Smith, Marjorie DeVault, Gisela Bock, Susan James, Martha Calas, and Linda Smircich. The author then explains how these findings can be evaluated using quantitative and qualitative methodological approaches to ameliorate inequalities.

Overall, the book binds many contemporary issues within the sociological theory. This book will be useful to understand the basic theoretical framework of inequality.

Keshav Bhattarai, Ph.D.   March 27, 2022
University of Central Missouri
Warrensburg, MO 64093 USA
bhattarai@ucmo.edu

Many scholars have tried to conceptualize the idea of happiness. However, no one has been able to define it concretely. For me, when a friend from humble beginnings goes on to achieve remarkable things in academia and asks to write the foreword for his book, that is happiness. It is my immense pleasure to write a foreword note for the social scientist who has been publishing numerous academic books and journal articles relentlessly. Dr. Medani P. Bhandari and I met as master's degree students at Tribhuvan University and have known each other for a little over three decades.

This book is a byproduct of the author's long-term engagement in social sciences. He has gained an enormous grasp of the subject matter through teaching and research in leading global institutions. Going through the biography of Prof. Medani, it can be said that one can indeed achieve a higher academic position abroad despite growing up in a small village in Nepal. Dr. Bhandari was not the brightest of minds when I first met him as a student; however, he made a radical transition, and after 30 years of absolute dedication and challenging work later, his academic merit speaks for itself. He has published hundreds of journal articles and books from reputed institutions of the world with credible findings. Dr. Bhandari can be a good example for scholars and students to look up to.

As I mentioned above, Dr. Bhandari has made several contributions to publishing books and journal articles from abroad. One day over a telephone conversation, he mentioned his desire to publish a book from Nepal. I suggested that he write a textbook targeting the graduate-level social science students who are pursuing their degrees in Nepal. He accepted my request and authored the book "Perspectives on Sociological Theories, Methodological Debates, and Organizational Sociology."

This book is divided into four clusters. The first section of the book focuses on sociological theories in general and Marx, Weber, and Durkheim in particular. He has nicely exhibited the epistemological and ontological similarities and differences between the previously mentioned scholars. While talking about the theoretical perspective, the author has critically scrutinized their contribution in the present context. The author has synthesized the complex theoretical models in comprehensible form. I have an impression that he internalized the complex ideas of Marx, Weber, and Durkheim's contributions.

The author has nicely shown the basic differences between quantitative and qualitative approaches in social sciences. He stresses more on qualitative epistemology and ontology more and shows how qualitative paradigms have shifted over the years. Exemplary evidence is provided while talking about the paradigms under the qualitative research. In my experience of teaching, the graduate students in Nepal find difficulty in linking their research work with ontology and epistemology. I hope that this section will help the students to link their empirical works with the branches of philosophy.

Section III is all about organizational theories. Understanding organizational sociology is a new concept in the context of Nepal. Some ethnographic studies of organizations have been conducted by native and foreign scholars in Nepal. Conventionally, international organization is the area of inquiry for political science. In recent years, the study of formal

xlviii *Forewords*

organizations has been popular among Tribhuvan University departments and donor agencies working in Nepal. This section is very fruitful for the graduate and undergraduate students of the world. This book will help the students to understand the global processes through theoretical perspectives.

Finally, this book will be a milestone for the students and faculty of the university who are pursuing their academic degrees. I hope that this book will be a basic textbook for graduate-level students.

Binod Pokharel, Ph.D.
Professor
Central Department of Anthropology
Tribhuvan University, Nepal

"The ethos of social science is the search for "objective" truth. The faith of the student is his conviction that truth is wholesome and that illusions are damaging especially opportunistic ones." – Gunnar Myrdal (1969). Objectivity in Social Research: The 1967 Wimmer Lecture. New York: Pantheon House.

I am honored to write this foreword for the book "**Perspectives on Sociological Theories, Methodological Debates, and Organizational Sociology**" by Prof. Dr. Medani P. Bhandari. Many congratulations to the author for the timely publication of this book intended for Nepali social science scholars. I also congratulate the readers of this book for whom this is an opportunity to gain experience theories, methodological debates, and their applications in social science written by a Nepali scholar who has the deepest knowledge and strong background in the context. I am confident that everyone who delves into this book will undoubtedly benefit from its juicy and fleshy matter. Let me share my experiences and observations of the author.

About the author

I have personally known Prof. Bhandari since very recently. However, this name has been familiar to me since I first became a listserv member of the Environmental Sociology group, a forum of the American Sociological Association (ASA) about 12 years ago and I regularly saw postings and contributions to the forum. Now, I am in touch with him almost every day or every week and we have been collaborating on several chapters in *four* books

Forewords xlix

in which he is on the editorial team. Not only this, but we also worked together on a short course in social research methods that was offered to Nepali social science scholars recently through a virtual platform due to COVID-19. I enjoy working with him and I feel fortunate to have this opportunity to write my thoughts. Thank you, Prof. Bhandari, for the opportunity.

To me, Prof. Bhandari is a highly intellectual person with versatility. He is a person with multiple talents and is one among the productive and highly prolific contributors as a social scientist who thus far has published *eight* books on social science that are closely linked to the environment and climate change and inequality and over 100 scientific papers published in the international peer-reviewed journals. More books including this one are lined up for publication. Prof. Bhandari does not have a specific regional boundary in academia. His work has focused on issues spanning Asia, Africa, North America, Western Europe, Australia, Japan, and the Middle East (to mention a few are – Kenya, Australia, Japan, Canada, USA, UK, Switzerland, Thailand, India, Nepal, Bangladesh, Pakistan, Middle Eastern countries, Ukraine, the Netherlands, Poland, Hungary, and Greece).

Similarly, Prof. Bhandari does not have a specific boundary in academia. His areas of scholarship focus on a wide range of disciplines including social innovation; sociological theories; environmental sustainability; social inclusion, climate change mitigation, and adaptation; environmental health hazard; environmental management; social innovation; global and international environmental politics, environmental institutions, and natural resources governance; climate change policy and implementation, environmental justice, and sustainable development; impact evaluation of rural livelihoods; international organizations; public/social policy; the non-profit sector; low carbon mechanism; good governance; climate change adaptation; REDD-plus; carbon financing; green economy and renewable energy; nature, culture, and power.

He is now serving as the editorial board member of 22 international journals, Editor-in-Chief of the highly prestigious journal "The Strategic Planning for Energy and the Environment (SPEE)" and Managing Editor of Asia Environment Daily. His scientific papers *"**Bashudaiva Kutumbakkam**"* and *"**Live and let others live**"* and over a hundred other scientific papers are powerful scientific contributions to the global academia with a message to unite them and work for the common goal of nature (environmental) protection and conservation. Moreover, his contributions extend beyond academia and have contributed as a poet (in English and Nepali language – who has written two volumes of poems with Prajita Bhandari), and several literary journals.

l *Forewords*

He is a real change-maker and a true giver as a voluntary academician, a researcher, and a teacher. As the social change-maker, Prof. Bhandari began nature conservation work in Nepal at the age of nine and continues as such. Thus, he has over 50 years of contribution to society. On top of this, he is a real giver to society who has been serving and voluntarily offering courses to universities, NGOs, and other social organizations. He is a great teacher and a mentor. His motto of life is to give back to society to the fullest, which is reflected in his papers such as *"Bashudaiva Kutumbakkam"* and *"Live and let others live"* as well as in other more than 25 papers. He strongly believes in collectivism. Despite these, he always loves to remain on a low profile but keeps contributing to the world in all possible ways. Thus, I strongly feel honored and fortunate to write this piece on his behalf.

About the book

Now, I turn to the book itself. *Why should I read this book?* In this book, Prof. Bhandari provides a brief description of major sociological theories that provide the important groundwork for understanding and explaining various sociological problems. This book further offers existing methodological debates on qualitative vs. quantitative social research methods that are used to understand the "objective reality" of the problems. Moreover, this book discusses the applications of state-of-the-art research methods primarily focusing on qualitative research methods. Prof. Bhandari further attempts to answer the following question: "why the study of an international organization is a subject of sociological study?" To answer this question, this book presents the perspectives of organizational sociology in a way a scholarly reader can view the interlink among political sciences, sociology, and economics in addressing the roles and issues of the international organization.

Divided into three broad chapters, the first chapter entitled, "**The Major Theorists of Sociology, Theories, and Contemporary Development of Organizational Perspectives in Social Sciences**," elaborates on the contributions of founding theorists of western sociology with a focus on how they addressed (or did not address) organizations. This discussion proceeds with the development of organizational theory and how organizational theorists respond to the emerging challenges of the traditional rational approaches to understanding organizations. This chapter is also devoted to the application of various theories in understanding societal problems and society at large. In my view, this chapter helps shape the theoretical grounding of scholars and strengthens their capacity to apply these theories in explaining and solving real-world societal problems. This chapter, however, teaches readers to examine societal problems through the eyes of western sociological theories. However, the author believes and advocates for the need for a context-specific theoretical lens in understanding problems designed, crafted, and assessed in our Nepali or South Asian society to examine or explain our problems.

In chapter 2, "**Debates Between Quantitative and Qualitative Method: An Ontology and Epistemology of Qualitative Method**," the author attempts to elucidate the superiority vs. inferiority of qualitative and quantitative methodological debates – the debate commonly referred to as the qualitative–quantitative debate – between the two major social science paradigms or models – *positivists/empiricists* approach vs. *constructivists/phenomenological* approach – that guide researchers to understand or examine existing societal problems. Specifically, these two approaches or orientations represent quantitative vs. qualitative research methods – with that, the positivists/empiricists look at problems through the lens of quantitative methods, whereas the constructivists look at problems through the qualitative methods lens. The chapter further highlights the features of successful and exemplary qualitative-based works of William Foote Whyte, Erving Goffman, and Robert J. Thomas and reveals the root of qualitative ontology and epistemology and presents why the debate is still unsolved. This chapter attempts to bridge the gap between the two approaches and provides the pathways to choosing the right research method based on the research topic. This chapter further leads to the discussion of the end of the war or the emergence of the middle ground path – the mixed methods lens, to which scholars refer to the *pragmatism* or *pragmatic* approach to understanding the problems of society.

In the concluding chapter, "**International Organization and Organizational Sociology Theories and Perspectives**," Prof. Bhandari describes the foundation, the basis of formation of an international organization, perspectives, history, growth, and the applicability of theories of social sciences to understand the roles of international organizations. Overall, the chapter summarizes the existing theories and readings that focus on the study of international organizations. This chapter provides a general overview of how international organizations were formed, for what purposes, and how their structure has been changed. The chapter also unveils the relationships between organizational sociology and international organizations and the application of institutional theory in the study of international organizations. Overall, in this book, Prof. Bhandari attempts to bridge the knowledge gap in social science theories and their applications to understand the roles of organizations, particularly the international organizations.

lii   *Forewords*

In summary, this book is a comprehensive collection of the understanding of the western theories of social sciences to explain or answer questions about a larger society. The author himself is not satisfied with the book; he believes that we need to search for our social theories to understand that the reality of our social problems are grounded in the ethical, traditional, spiritual, and harmonious structures of our society. He adds that our ancestors have already shown the path to understanding our society and solving the societal problems through the lens of *"**Bashudaiva Kutumbakkam**"* and/or **"Live and let others live,"** – the wealth of knowledge that has the thousands of years of history of epistemology. According to the author, "this book could provide pathways to begin to search for a theorist who built our society and whom we never recognized."

Overall, I found this a highly informative and timely published book full of knowledge in social science research methods that will be important in understanding and explaining larger societal problems in Nepal and the whole South Asia region. Enriched with the prominent level of expertise and experiences of the author, this is an important contribution to the field. This book provides an important link between theory, research methods, and the role of international organizations in a rapidly changing and fast-growing society. I am confident that this book will serve as a coursebook in social research methods and the region. *It deserves special space in every library and on my shelf as well – a must-read book.*

Prem B. Bhandari, Ph.D.
Social Researcher and Demographer
Adjunct Professor, Agriculture and Forestry University, Nepal
Managing Director, South Asia Research Consult, Inc, Michigan, USA.
Former Assistant Research Scientist, Institute for Social Research,
University of Michigan, USA
April 2, 2022

It is my immense pleasure to write a foreword for the book entitled, **"Perspectives on Sociological Theories, Methodological Debates, and Organizational Sociology,"** written by Prof. Dr. Medani P. Bhandari. I thank Dr. Bhandari for these many opportunities. Dr. Bhandari dedicated to his field. I must acknowledge and thank Dr. Prem Bhandari who introduced me to Dr. Medani P. Bhandari. I was familiar with Dr. Prem Bhandari for more than a decade as a learner of research and publication. First, I became Facebook friends with Dr. Medani P. Bhandari and had the opportunity to read a paper by Govinda Luitel about Dr. Medani P. Bhandari's ambition, devotion, and sacrifice toward higher education in the USA. I could read his poem and status on Facebook; by analyzing the contents, I found them more patriotic and loving indigenous ideas of Nepal that have great learning to the world like "Bashudaiva Kutumbakkam." I was motivated by what Dr. Medani P. Bhandari was doing as an academician. He has been doing meditation in writing and publications. He is a professor at Akamai University, Hawaii, USA, and Sumy State University, Ukraine. He takes responsibility for editing reputed international journals, like Editor-in-Chief of "Strategic Planning for Energy and the Environment" and Managing Editor of "The Asia Environment Daily." I found him a good literary writer both in Nepali and in English. I also had the opportunity to invite him to a zoom online seminar organized by NAPA, where he presented the simplest way and the complex mechanisms of authoring a scientific paper. When he posted on Facebook his publication by an international publisher, I had a general remark that we do not have access to those books; so how can we make them accessible in Nepal? I wholeheartedly requested him to publish some works from Nepal, which certainly visualize his sincere work and contribution among the Nepali scholars that might inspire and enhance their passion for sincerity in academic contribution.

This present book is comprehensive that presents how sociology is theoretically and methodologically founded in time and space contexts. Furthermore, this book highlights sociological works and understanding of international organizations. He traced the historical roots of an international organization as well as the birth of modern international organizations. He has focused on the distinctiveness of sociological contribution compared with the role of other social sciences. This book is useful for students and professionals who wished to learn about the dynamic in sociological knowledge. I wish him every success in all his endeavors.

Dr. Man Bahadur Khattri, Ph.D.
Lecturer in Anthropology, Tribhuvan University, Kirtipur, Kathmandu, Nepal
Central Department of Anthropology, Tribhuvan University, Kathmandu, Nepal

----

Міністерство освіти та науки України Сумський державний університет	Ministry of Education and Science of Ukraine Sumy State University
КАФЕДРА УПРАВЛІННЯ ІМЕНІ ОЛЕГА БАЛАЦЬКОГО	OLEG BALATSKYI DEPARTMENT OF MANAGEMENT
40007, Україна, м.Суми, вул. Римського-Корсакова, 2 тел. (0542) 68-78-78, 68-78-79 факс: (0542) 334-058	R-Korsakova St., Sumy, Ukraine, 40007 Phone: +38-0542- 68-78-78, 68-78-79 Fax: 380-542-334-058

I am pleased to write a foreword for the book titled "Perspectives on Sociological Theories, Methodological Debates, and Organizational Sociology" by Prof. Medani P. Bhandari, affiliated with Akamai University, Hawaii, USA, and Sumy State University, Ukraine.

Prof. Medani P. Bhandari is one of the most devoted activists who spent his life and effort to prove that environmental, social, and economic development are interconnected and inter-influenced. His human-centric approach is widely presented in his poems, essays, and interviews. His advocacy campaigns in the sphere of protection of human rights led him to all continents. Prof. Bhandari is well-known as a talented educator, for he has been the supervisor of undergraduates and graduates.

Most of the papers and books by Prof. Bhandari are in the field of climate changes, sustainable development, and social challenges, but this new work "Perspectives on Sociological Theories, Methodological Debates, and Organizational Sociology" may enlighten scholars, practitioners, businessmen, undergraduates, public officers and policymakers, NGOs, and activists on the matter of evolution of social sciences theory from Marxism to modern theories with the detailed analysis of the roots, causes, and consequences of social changes along the way. Organizational sociology is another big segment of the book, where the author provided a critical view of the formation and management of social processes.

The book is divided into sections, and each of them represents a certain model of social processes, implemented in different societies. Three main dimensions of the work are reflected in the title of the book – theories, methodology and its application, and the link with organizational sociology.

This work is the culmination of Prof. Bhandari who accumulated the findings in social theories and provided new epistemology and new paradigms. The book is the result of the theoretical and practical work of Prof. Bhandari as a social theorist and change-maker who is a well-known influencer in environmental sciences.

I would like to thank Prof. Bhandari for his endless energy in bringing new knowledge to relevant fields, and for his efforts and contributions to the development of a new generation of thinkers.

Sincerely,

Shvindina Hanna, Ph.D., Dr.Sc., Head of the Department of Management, Associate Professor, Fulbright Alumna 2018–2019, tel: +380502603995, e-mail: shvindina@management.sumdu.edu.ua

----

This is an important book that aims to provide students of social sciences and enthusiastic readers with a fundamental understanding of the basics of social, economic, and political ontology. It could provoke epistemology of the situations which are intriguing in Nepal's societal environment. The dominant social science theories will evoke scholars and academics as well as independent freethinkers who have witnessed transformations in the socio-political and economic domain, particularly during the past decades. Prof. Bhandari's transformative personal experience is quite provocative and elucidates the dominant societal environment in rural Nepal. This is compelling, beyond just storytelling. I must confess that this will invoke many others' consciousness, like me, too serious contemplation on historical epistemology and methodology, triggering the study of self-consciousness of experience and reality – impacting intellectual and philosophical biases that influence social prejudices, perspectives, and concept of enlightenment in life.

The book is a collection of masterpieces of various theories on sociology, starting from methods of general phenomenology to complex hermeneutic interpretations of the linkages in modern sociological literature, be that in the social, economic, or political sphere. The study of the social science theories will revolutionize the understanding of knowledge that influences societal paradigm to provoke more research on "what," "how," and "why." This will enhance students', enthusiastic readers', and other novelty-seekers' deep lvi *Forewords*

understanding of nuances in social sciences to examine theories critically, and articulate surrounding societal norms, behaviors, and practices in an environment where they live and grow, and what and how we get influenced.

It is important also to recognize the everlasting impact of advancing technologies that are rapidly evolving in our social and cultural landscape, unseen in human history. The digitally interconnected new fiction-like materiality is unprecedented in a borderless global village where social, political, and economic behavior is bound to transform because of the expanse of irresistible and powerful social media. The impact of mobile technology on human behavior is unavoidable and forceful, beyond the inventor's comprehension. Social scientists and philosophers would be debating endlessly on qualitative and quantitative effects, and future trends.

Let us not be ignorant of developing scenarios and the impact of social phenomena which will have a profound legacy on contemporary sociological theories and perspectives, more prominently when increased use of *artificial intelligence* will replace all repetitive human activities. Future generations may then confront the new challenges and discover hard to grasp the relevancy of the past social premises. It is difficult to foresee the objectively full impact of transformative surroundings in a completely digitized environment. By that time, human behavior would have adjusted qualitatively to evolving dictates, emerging societal norms, and concomitant values. This could shatter established societal norms, behavior, and beliefs. This phenomenon would be an enthusiastic subject for future debate. Would this not be an interesting era for philosopher's delight and social scientists' quagmire?

Kedar Neupane, retired UN's international staff and Executive Board Member of Nepal Policy Institute, is an independent global think tank.

I am so happy to get a chance to write a few words on the book, "Perspectives on Sociological Theories, Methodological Debates, and Organizational Sociology" by an eminent global scholar of social, environmental, and climate scientist Prof. Medani P. Bhandari, Ph.D., whose motive of life is to give back to the society in fullest through education.

Nowadays, the issues related to organization and management theory have become "a daily bread" for specialists in sociology, economics, business, management, and even representatives of humanities such as philosophy, literary studies, film studies, etc. However, the multi-faceted view of the situation of the structures and a certain organic layer of the various organizations deserves appreciation because it encourages practical and scientific reflection. Forging an innovative approach in the minds of the public to the analysis of classical and contemporary schools of organization science not only causes scientific progress but is also an important determinant for

Forewords lvii

sustainable economic development. Promoting new forms of organizations that can face the expectations of the future, especially in terms of flexibility in the implementation of innovative solutions, requires a structured knowledge of organizations.

Prof. Medani P. Bhandari, as a specialist in analyzing various contemporary theories about organizations presented by Karl Marx, Émile Durkheim, Max Weber, Henri Fayol, Frederick Taylor, Luther Halsey Gulick, Herbert A. Simon, Berton H. Kaplan, Michel Foucault, Jurgen Habermas, Jacques Derrida, Jurgen Habermas, Philip Selznick, Peter Blau, James David Thompson, Charles Perrow, Paul J. DiMaggio, Walter W. Powell, Arlene Daniels, Dorothy Smith, Marjorie DeVault, Gisela Bock, Susan James, Martha Calas, Linda Smircich, and which he has described in numerous articles in several countries of the world, presents a position in which knowledge is not only systematized but also urges the reader to understand the essence of cultural realities about organizations as a living organism formed by people. The lack of understanding and respect for the culture of the place, as well as the culture of the employees of transnational organizations, is therefore becoming a key element in the success of any business today. The inclusion of pedagogical elements and at times even political science in the content gives the discussion of organizational sociology and international relations based on green business, which teaches the creation of a platform for micro and macro partnerships, an even greater value and shows new paths in scientific reflection. In every book written by Prof. Bhandari, we can see a piece of the author's soul in addition to a detailed scientific analysis. The same is also true in this book, whose undisputed richness lies in the methodology chosen by Prof. Medani P. Bhandari to compile the materials and the way they are interpreted. Thanks to it, the contents presented in the book also contain the message of the author's life wisdom, which combines the cultural interpretation of two great civilizations in terms of looking at the issues of organization and human relations. I am delighted that Prof. Medani P. Bhandari, with whom I have the immense pleasure of working for yet another year, continues to enrich the world of science and the world of economic practice with his publications that promote the message of the world as our common home, where we must live in peace for our own and others' sake. This message is a tremendous contribution of Eastern philosophy to the world of western civilizations in developed countries, and it may well provide interesting new insights into the field of organizational sociology for other scholars around the world.

Aleksander Łukasz Sapi ski, Bielsko-Biala School of Finance and Law (Poland), CEO of NGO – Beskid Association of Ecological Production and Tourism "BEST PROEKO."

Acknowledgment

Informally, this book holds a long educational trajectory from the date my memory begins, and I remember the social events from my primary schooling days to date. As usual, as part of my socialization, at home, my parents, grandparents, relatives, siblings, neighbors, my playmates, and the surroundings tried to teach me how to live in the stratified, classified, caste, race, and ethnically divided unequal society.

Here, I would also like to note that the role of social scientists is crucial and important because we belong to the varieties of complicated social, cultural, religious, economic, political, traditional, etc., systems and our role is to reveal the positive and negative realities of this system and contribute for the betterment of the society directly or indirectly. Therefore, we must accept and acknowledge that many heads have worked extremely hard to bring us as sensible and responsible humans. We should not feel ashamed to tell the truth and should not be scared to find the truth and produce the truth. Social scientists are those who understand the societal trajectory and thrive for social justice, well-being, inclusive and equitable society, and rational social change. Therefore, social scientists need to understand the social theories, applicable methods, and actual systems of the society as the body of knowledge – the mind (theories), methods (the pathways of research), and the heart part (the knowledge itself of the society). Until or unless we do not find our niche and the grounded reality of our surroundings, the sociological knowledge we possess cannot contribute to a meaningful social change and cannot reveal the underlined facts of the social system. Here, I would like to acknowledge the contributions of social scientists who provided the pathways to understand society through theories, methods, and their uses.

It took me years to complete this book, and there are many people to be acknowledged.

First of all, I would like to thank Dr. Prem Bhandari, Dr. Man Bahadur Khattri, and Prof. Binod Pokhrel for encouraging me to complete and publish this book. I accept and acknowledge that this is the product of your involvement and your support. Without your tireless efforts, this book would not have been possible. Thanks to both of you and congratulations. Your efforts are in the hands of readers, scholars of social sciences, and everyone interested in theories and methods of social sciences. I would also like to acknowledge and thank my childhood friend Mr. Kshitij Raj Prasai, who has

lx *Acknowledgment*

been always insisting me for the continuation of my research and writing. Your encouragement, support, motivation, and love provide me with the pathways of knowledge creation. Thank you.

I would like to thank Dr. Krishna Prasad Oli, Ph.D.; Prof. Mary Jo Bulbrook, Ph.D.; Prof. Ganesh Man Gurung, Ph.D.; Prof. Lekhnath Sharma, Ph.D.; Dr. Subash Shree Pokhrel, Ph.D.; Prof. Douglas Capogrossi, Ph.D.; Prof. Jacek Piotr Binda, Ph.D.; Prof. Volodymyr Boronos, Ph.D.; Dr. Ambika Adhikari, Ph.D.; Prof. Durga Poudel, Ph.D.; Prof. Keshav Bhattarai, Ph.D.; Prof. Bishwa Kalyan Parajuli, Ph.D.; Prof. Naba Raj Devkota, Ph.D.; Dr. Kailash Timalsina, Ph.D.; Dr. Kapil Adhikari, Ph.D.; Dr. Prem Bhandari, Ph.D.; Dr. Man Bahadur Khatri, Ph.D.; Dr. Shvindina Hanna, Ph.D.; Dr.Sc; Mr. Kedar Neupane; Dr. Aleksander Łukasz Sapi ski; and others for your valuable forewords/endorsements, inputs, commencements, and encouragements. Each of your inputs indicates why we need to know the theories, methods, and applications in the academic trajectories and why all academic stakeholders need to work together.

I would like to thank Prof. Steven R. Brechin, Prof. Cecilia Green, Dr. Rishi Shah, Mr. Govinda Luitel (Mama), Mr. Ananda Bhandari, Mr. Hikmat Basnet, Prof. Dhan Pandit, Dr. Nabin Khanal, Dr. Bijaya Kattel, Mr. Medini Adhikari, and many other scholars for your valuable input directly or indirectly. I would also thank my friends Rajan Adhikari, Govinda Luitel, Tirtha Koirala, Prof. Sanjay Mishra, Dhir Prasad Bhandari, Prof. Bishwa Kalyan Parajuli, Ph.D., Prof. Naba Raj Devkota, Ph.D., Dr. Kailash Timalsina, Ph.D., Dr. Kapil Adhikari, Ph.D., and all of my Facebook and LinkedIn friends, who have always been encouraging us to give back to the society through knowledge sharing.

I must acknowledge and state that some texts of this book's chapters are taken from my previously published scientific papers in the international journals (within my copyrights) (in Scientific Journal of Bielsko-Biala School of Finance and Law, ISSN: 2543-9103, Educational Transformation – ISBN-13: 978-1796048957 and Advance Journal of Agriculture and Environmental Sciences, respectively). I would also like to declare and state that these three chapters were based on my three Ph.D. comprehensive exam questions (theory, method, and comprehensive field of study). And these chapters are answers to the broader questions; chapter 1 is "what are the major theorists of sociology, theories, and how contemporary development of organizational perspectives in social sciences have developed?"; chapter 2 is "what are the debates between quantitative and qualitative method: and what is the ontology and epistemology of qualitative method?," and chapter three is "what is the foundation of international organization and organizational sociology theories and perspectives and why this field of scholarships is important?" given by Prof. Marjory DeVault, Prof. Peter Ibarra, and Prof. Steven R. Brechin, respectively (of Syracuse University, New York, USA).

I acknowledge the input of Ms. Prajita Bhandari for creating a peaceful environment to complete this book and for insightful comments and language editing. Without your efforts, support, and contributions, this book as well as all other books and papers would have been impossible. Thank you.

I would also like to thank Prameya, Kelsey, Manaslu, Abhimanyu, Uma, and Mahesh for their insightful comments and support in a tough time of life trajectory. I would also like to thank Neena and Neelok (our granddaughter and grandson who brought joy to the family so that I was able to concentrate on my job). I would also like to thank all my family members, all my friends, playmates, and all of you; without your support, blessings, encouragement, and empowerment, none of my books and other writings were and would be possible.

Thanks to all readers.

List of Figures

Figure 3.1 The exponential growth of publications indexed by Sociological Abstracts containing "social network" in the abstract or title. Source: S.P. Borgatti, P.C. Foster / Journal of Management 2003 29(6) 991–1013.. 149

Figure 3.2 The visual of the complexity of institutionalism. Source: Theret (2000), adopted by Klaus Nielsen (2001).. 158

Figure 4.1 The semantics of sustainable development (as in Lele 1991, page 608).. 201

Flowchart 1 Organizational complexity. 219

List of Tables

Table 4.1 The chronological overview of the meaning of sustainable development in the period 1980–2018. 204

Table 4.2 The development trend – the worrisome of environmental damage and mainstreaming of sustainability. 206

Table 4.3 Planetary boundaries and quantification. 214

Table 4.4 Examples of factors facilitating creativity for sustainability. 223

Table 4.5 Different phases of creativity. 225

Table 4.6 Definitions. 231

List of Abbreviations

ASA	American Sociological Association
CE	Creative Economy
CITES	Convention on International Trade in Endangered Species
CSD	Commission on Sustainable Development
GE	Green Economy
IGO	Intergovernmental organization
INGO	international non-governmental organization
IPCC	Intergovernmental Panel on Climate Change
IR	International relation
IUCN	International Union of Conservation of Nature
LDC	Less developed country
MCN	mediated-conflict neo-institutionalism
MDGs	millennium development goals
MNC	multinational corporation
NGOs	Non-governmental organizations
OR	Organization
RAN	Rational-action neo-institutionalism
SCN	Social-constructivist neo-institutionalism
SD	Sustainable development
SDG	Sustainable development goal
SPEE	Strategic Planning for Energy and the Environment
UIA	Union of International Associations
UN	United Nations
UNCED	UN Conference on Environment and Development
UNCLOS	United Nations Convention on Law of the Sea
UNEP	United Nation Environment Program

1

The Major Theories of Sociology, and Contemporary Development of Organizational Perspectives in Social Sciences

Outline

This chapter elaborates on the contribution of the founding writers of Western sociology, with a focus on how they addressed (or did not address) organizations. Then, it discusses (in brief) the development of organizational theory and how organizational theorists are responding to the emergence of challenges to the traditional rational approaches to understanding organizations.

This chapter is purely theoretical in which I illustrate the contributions of the founding theorists of Western sociology, by focusing on how they addressed (or did not address) organizations. Then, I discuss (in brief) the development of organizational theory and how organizational theorists are responding to the emergence of challenges to the traditional rational approaches to understanding organizations. These analyses are situated in historical contexts and include the major contributions of each theorist. This research is solely based on secondary information. The chapter contains four sections. The first is the work of the three founding theorists of Western sociology, Karl Marx, Émile Durkheim, and Max Weber. Second, I have illustrated the development of organizational theory and the emergence of challenges to the traditional rational approaches to understanding the organization, where I have analyzed the work of classical theorists: Max Weber, Henri Fayol, Frederick Taylor, Luther Halsey Gulick, Herbert A. Simon, Berton H. Kaplan, Michel Foucault, Jurgen Habermas, Jacques Derrida, Jurgen Habermas, etc. The third section covers contemporary theories and perspectives. In this section, I have exemplified how Philip Selznick, Peter Blau, James David Thompson, and Charles Perrow

1

2 *The Major Theories of Sociology, and Contemporary Development*

incorporated the Weber notion of bureaucracy followed by Paul J. DiMaggio, Walter W. Powell, etc. The fourth section covers the feminist approach in theory building with the focus of organizational analysis (with the focus of works of Arlene Daniels, Dorothy Smith, Marjorie DeVault, Gisela Bock, Susan James, Martha Calas, Linda Smircich, etc.). This chapter has detailed footnotes and contains useful references to the sociological theory and practices.

Introduction
Founders of Sociology – Theory and Perspectives

Sociology examines social actors' activities in society and social problems. Western scholars have developed many social theories which address the underlying causes such as social conflicts and inequalities, and the many formal and informal social organization texts involved in those issues. The study of social organizations is a new phenomenon in sociology. Broadly, its historical roots can be traced to Greek civilization (Plato and Aristotle), and it has mostly flourished since the Enlightenment era. However, empirical studies show that the scientific study of organizations begins only in the 19th and 20th centuries. Among the scholars of these centuries, the contributions of Karl Marx, Ferdinand Tönnies, Émile Durkheim, Ludwig Gumplovicz, Vilfredo Pareto, Max Weber, and Talcott Parsons are considered the pillars of sociology. To answer the first question (founding writers of Western sociology), I will only focus mainly on three classical sociologists: Max Weber (1864–1920), who introduced the concept of bureaucracy, and Karl Marx (1818–1883) and Emile Durkheim (1858–1917) who developed the concept of division of labor as the founding concept of formal ground for organization sociology, respectively. Likewise, to answer the second question "development of organizational theory and how organizational theorists are responding to the emergence of challenges to the traditional rational approaches to understanding organizations," first, I will briefly revisit the contribution of major classical organizational theorists such as Max Weber, Henri Fayol, and Frederic Taylor followed by Luther Halsey Gulick and Herbert A. Simon. Several authors (Moore 2003; O'Connor 1993; Wallerstein 1974, 1998, 2000) illustrate that Weber was a rational theorist. Wallerstein (1998) in his article "The Ecology and the Economy: What is Rational" (online publication[1]) states that "Rationality is; more than we admit, in the eye of the beholder. It has something to do with the optimal means to achieve a goal, any goal, what Weber called "formal rationality." And it has something to do with the relative wisdom of the goal that is given priority, what Weber called "substantive rationality" (*Rationalität material*" (Wallerstein 1998). Second, I will illustrate the contribution of Berton H. Kaplan, who followed the rational approach of organizational analysis in the context of social dynamism and social development. Mainstream organizational sociologists rarely illustrate Kaplan. Third, I will briefly describe the contemporary theoretical perspectives developed on the ground of the traditional rational approaches. This section will demonstrate the contribution of Philip Selznick and Peter Blau who are considered the founders of organizational sociology, followed by Charles Perrow, Paul J. DiMaggio, and Walter W. Powell. In the last section (of the second section), I will briefly examine the feminist approaches to organizational study, which follow both rational and natural system perspectives of organizational analysis but challenge the traditional Weberian notion of bureaucracy. They follow Foucault's postmodern perspectives to analyze formal organizations. In this (final) section, I will illustrate the contributions of Arlene Daniel, Martha Calas, Linda Smircich, and Jana Brewis whom I consider challengers of traditional perspectives of organizational study.

In the following paragraphs, I will first discuss the major contributions of Marx followed by Durkheim and Weber.

First Section

The Founding Writers of Western Sociology

Karl Marx

Karl Marx is one of the popular and evergreen philosophers of the 19th century. His philosophical contributions have been important to the modern world since the beginning of the 20th century to formulate a new vision, especially in global politics and anthropogenic socio-economic environments. Marx developed several epistemologies and also examined notions of established theories. His major focus was to examine how political and economic histories were grounded and to what extent they reveal the social reality. Based on historical studies, he developed his new theories on the dialectical materialistic ground. He authored several books solely and several together with Fredric Angels. There are hundreds of books and journal articles for and against his materialist theory of history, means, mode, and forces of production[2], laws of historical development, and particularly his theory of ideology. His earlier writings were on political economy. The Capital[3] was the extended version

4 The Major Theories of Sociology, and Contemporary Development

of his economy writings, where he extensively discussed capital, commodity, exchange, exchange and social relation, labor (useful and abstract), values, forms of values, the relationship between economy and society, theory of surplus (labor and wage), and capitalism (primitive accumulation and division of labor). He sharply criticized religion (*"the opium of the people"*). In addition to economy and religion, he extensively engaged in political writings (actually most of his writings can be considered political and economic writings). In his political writings, Marx examines political history on the dialectical paradigm and provides new ground in politics (*communist manifesto, contribution to the critique of political economy, the historical origin of the modern state, a critique of Hegel's philosophy of rights, etc.*).

His new epistemology[4] of reasoning (on the dialectic ground) has been always crucial and problematic to the western feudalistic society. Marx was mostly influenced by Hegel in his early life. However, there are clear differences between Hegel's epistemology of dialectic and Marx's dialectic materialism[5]. Hegel focused on how ideas and concepts can be dialectic and how logical ground can be identical. Hegel states that all things are in a continuous state of motion and change and that general laws of motion are intrinsic to the development of the individual and history. Hegel examined the world as an interconnected process. This doctrine was viewed as dialectic as the principle of contradiction is identifiable in three phases, i.e., affirmation or thesis, negation, or antithesis, and "negation of the negation or synthesis."

In contrast to Hegel, Marx developed a different doctrine named materialistic dialectic to indicate the shift from the dominance of ideas to the dominance of economic conditions (Morrison 1995, page 312). Marx states *"My dialectic method, is not only different from the Hegelian but is its direct opposite. To Hegel, the life-process of the human brain, i.e., the process of thinking, which, under the name of 'the Idea,' he even transforms into an independent subject, is the demiurges of the real world, and the real world is only the external, phenomenal form of 'the Idea.' With me, on the contrary, the ideal is nothing else than the material world reflected by the human minds and translated into forms of thought"* (Capital Afterward 1887). This narrative provides the basis of how Marx developed the epistemology of dialectic materialism. Hegel, through his dialectic approach, visualized world development as an interconnected process. Hegel did not separate person and things, and things around the person.

On the other hand, Marx examined how the principle of contradiction manifested itself in the form of coercive class structure, where socio-economic history was the process of class struggle, "For Marx stages of development were related to economic production and the system of social classes"

(Morrison 1995, page 312). Marx analyzed the historical development of socio-economy in four stages, i.e., "primitive community": where class relations were not developed and private ownership was not established; ancient society: a system of ownership developed, where relations were based on the dominance of one class over the others; feudal society: class relations were embedded in property relations when the class of producers emerged; finally, "the Capitalism" classes which are in direct opposition, leading to the class struggle between capitalists and those who produce the capital (the working class)[6]. Marx did not write directly under the heading of sociology or considered himself a sociologist. However, Marx examined society in a dialectical way, which resulted in fellow theorists placing him as one of the pillars of sociological thought. His social, political, and economic equations have been applied in both hard sciences and social sciences. In Capital, Karl Marx examines how capital dominates and influences production and produces a surplus-value in monetary form. He states, *"Although we come across the first beginnings of capitalist production as early as the 14th or 15th century, sporadically, in certain towns of the Mediterranean, the capitalistic era dates from the 16th century"* (Capital, page 715). Marx argues that market expansion is not an effortless process but could be a forceful and difficult one. According to Marx, primitive accumulation is the historical process of separating labor from product and production[7]. He argues that a simple production is also a reproduction of the capital–labor social relationship; however, it does not act reciprocally on the capitalist social system.

When Marx wrote The Capital, the social structure was quite different, and he might not have imagined the future of the world as it is now. When he wrote The Capital, the slavery system existed and there was competition among European nations for colonization and extreme European influence on the Marx known deprived world. As a socially progressive thinker and activist, what he visualized was true and relevant to that time. His philosophy was applied and is still in use in many parts of the world as a model. Many poor people in the developing world still think Marxism is the best model which can free them from bourgeois feudalism.

It is hard to summarize what major theoretical contributions Marx made in sociological theory building. He pointed out that whatever he is doing is in the society and for the society *"Even when I conduct scientific work.......I perform a social because human act. It is only the material of my activity-----like the language itself which the thinker uses-----which is given to me as a social product. My existence is a social product"* (as cited by Tucker 1969, page 89). His presence can be found in most of the subject matter of sociological epistemology. His notion of dialecticism[8] provides new ways to

6 *The Major Theories of Sociology, and Contemporary Development*

examine society. Marx first examines the sociological reality through critical perspectives and proposes the optimal solution to resolve the underlying social problems. His critical reasoning on social development gave others the ground to oppose the positivist basis of social inquiry. In terms of his contribution to the sub-fields of sociology, such as political sociology, historical sociology, organizational sociology, feminist sociology, etc., he gave the insights to examine society on logical grounds. *"Marx's work has been the inspiration and constant touchstone for radical critiques of management under conditions of capitalist industrial development as exemplified in debates concerning the nature of the labor process under capitalism"* (Braverman 1974 as cited by Starkey 1992, page 1). His writings on class struggle and conflict provide the basis to explore how important power dynamism is, the relationships between the social elite and the working class, and how capital formation occurs in feudalistic and capitalist societies. In general terms, Marxist notions can be applied to examine critically how organizations are formed, for whom, and with what purpose. Further, his notions allow us to explore organizational conflict and how capital is formatted to run the organization. Marx introduced the concept of greed in the possession or consumption of goods and services.

Marxist epistemology was seldom taken into consideration in the North American political, economic, and sociological inquiry. I am not arguing that Marxist thought was ignored in the Western world; however, there were only a few American sociologists who considered Marx as a sociologist before the Second World War. American sociologists mostly criticized Marx as an ideologist, and rejection of Marx in sociology reflected ideological differences of American sociologists (Ritzer 2000). Organizational sociology as a discipline began in America in the 1950s among those who did not consider Marx's notion of division of labor, people's alienation from power and class, and power struggle, which could suggest a way of analyzing the organization. Instead, they gave more emphasis to other western theorists who leaned toward the capitalist mode of economy. However, this trend changed after the Second World War in American academia. Various scholars began to use Marx's epistemological position to examine social movements (civil rights movements, feminist movements, etc.). Most importantly, feminist scholars have been incorporating a Marxist approach to critical reasoning from the first wave[9] to date. Within sociology, scholars (e.g., Simone de Beauvoir, Kate Millett, Shulamith Firestone, Gayatri Spivak, Ann Oakley, Juliet Mitchell, Sheila Rowbotham, Dorothy Smith, etc.) began to see society deeply through Marxist perspectives. In organizational sociology, new perspectives developed (rational, natural, and open system (primarily) and environmental, demographic, ecological, etc., more recently). The women scholars began to inquire with the application of critical perspectives on where women stand in the organization in every sector of social life, including formal and informal social organizations, and scholars began to see the women's role in organizational structure. Several feminist authors have contributed to organizational theory development. Likewise, organizational sociologists also began to examine formal organizations through the application of critical and dialectical approaches. In the last section of this essay, I will summarize how the Marxist approach incorporated in evaluating the organization, especially by feminist scholars Dorothy Smith, Chandra Talpade Mohanty, Joanna Brewis, Marta B. Calás, Linda Smircich, Judith Stacey, Barrie Thorne, and Marjorie DeVault.

Emile Durkheim

Emile Durkheim is another founding writer of Western sociology. His major writings were Division of Labor in Society (1893), Rules of Sociological Method (1894), Suicide (1897), and Elementary Forms of Religious Life (1912). In 1896, he began a journal "Annee Sociologique"; through this journal, he published many articles. Durkheim's stand was opposite to Marx's. He followed and developed the functionalist approach embedded in positivism. The functionalist approach was constructed under an epistemology that allows us to evaluate society as organisms. In other words, the complexity of social systems is similar to the way different organisms act in the human body or the lives of any living creature. This notion of society as a function which Hegel described *"as a continuous state of motion and change, and those general laws of motion are intrinsic to the development"* fits with Durkheim's grounds for sociological theory building. While Hegel provided an idealistic view that society runs as an interconnected process, Durkheim followed the same track and examined the social problems with the application of Comtenian positivist philosophy. Durkheim accepted the positivistic thesis with the assumption that society can be examined as facts and that facts can be observed only through the scientific method. Furthermore, he also accepted Comte's idea of sociology, that *"sociology as the science of society could be validly constituted only when it was stripped of its metaphysical abstraction and philosophical speculation"* (Morrison 1995, page 123). Durkheim's use of scientific methods to study society was unchallenged until the Second World War.

Durkheim tried to examine social functions from individual to the group level. He believed that social realities exist in the form of social rules, customs, and beliefs; therefore, these phenomena can be studied by

8   *The Major Theories of Sociology, and Contemporary Development*

focusing on social facts rather than on individuals. He thought that focusing on the individual is ignoring the larger system of social rules which forms the basis of society (Morrison 1995). Durkheim's contribution to sociology was important because he was the first author who considered himself a sociologist and developed sociology as a different discipline. Durkheim defined sociology as a moral science. His theses are (1) society comes before the individual; (2) society as ideal; (3) production of collective conscience: individual and collective conscience will differ; (4) society is greater than the sum of its parts – this is unique to social organization; and (5) sociology is to study moral rules as part of the social organization (Morrison 1995; Ritzer 2000). Durkheim saw society as a social fact (society as a function), introduced scientific approaches to study social phenomena, and examined how social order exists in several types of society. He studied social organizations in the context of division of labor and compared traditional and modern society. He states that *"the bulk of the population is no longer divided according to relations of consanguinity, real or fictive, but according to the division of territory.... All peoples who have passed beyond the clan stage organized in territorial districts (counties, communes, etc.) which ... connected themselves with other districts of a similar nature ... which, in their turn, are often enveloped by others still more extensive (shire, province, department) whose union formed the society"* (Durkheim 1893, pages185–186). He reexamined the earlier predecessors such as Herbert Spencer or Otto von Gierke, who had argued that societies evolved like living organisms (based on the Darwinism concept). Earlier sociologists such as Goldenweiser (1917), Barnes (1920), Bellah (1959), and Lammers (1978) have extensively advocated the usefulness of Durkheim in social sciences theory building. In this context, Barnes's examination of "Durkheim's contribution to the reconstruction of political theory" provides a good outline of to what extent Durkheim was successful in examining social and political organizations[10]. However, Durkheim saw organization just as a functionary of the social system, which was criticized by his successors. In this regard, Charles Tilly (1981) authored a book named "Useless Durkheim"; however, Durkheim is not useless. As Emirbayer (1996) points out, his moral sociology has something to contribute to contractual organizational relationships[11].

Durkheim examined religion more deeply. He states, *"A religion is a unified system of beliefs and practices relative to sacred things, which is to say, things set apart and forbidden--beliefs and practices which unite in one single moral community called a Church, all those who adhere to them"* (Durkheim 1912). In the context of organization management, Durkheim sees similarities with religion in the relevance of discipline (forcing or administering discipline), cohesion (bringing people together), a strong bond (vitalizing, making more lively or vigorous, to boost spirit), and euphoria (a good feeling, happiness, confidence, and well-being) (Durkheim 1912).

These notions were important in maintaining social order when society was influenced and guided by religious norms. In differentiating between the collective and individual consciousness, Durkheim introduced a key notion of individualism which Foucault has discussed a lot (but has not acknowledged Durkheim). These ideas also show the similarities between Durkheim and Weber about a free society. Legal and administrative authorities were based on the biblical myth or the spiritual aspect of the society or backed by the religious body. Marx carefully internalized this notion of the social system, pointing out that the major cause of social classification was due to religious institutions, and developed his thesis against the existing social system. Marx indicted religion as an evil phenomenon of society and social organizations. In the following paragraphs, I will write on Max Weber who is commonly considered the founder of organizational sociology.

Max Weber

Max Weber is one of the most important sociological theorists who followed the rational ground of social reality, with the influence of Kantian's and Hegelian's thoughts. Like Marx and Durkheim, Max Weber had various interests such as politics, history, language, religion, law, and administration. There are several similarities and differences between Weber and Marx. In some cases, Weber superseded Marx in his explanation of religion, ideas, values, and meaning of social action: "Weber spent his life having a posthumous dialogue with the ghost of Karl Marx" (Cuff 1979). Weber's analysis refers first to economic determinism and the extent to which developments are rooted in the material base and, second, the extent to which economic factors alone can be considered to be the root of social structure. Weber's thought has similarities to that of Marx because he came from the same economic, social, and intellectual environment as Marx; Weber analyzes history, politics, and economics on a structural basis. They both consider space and time in changing sequence, which is important and applicable all the time. The acceptance of timing sequence and space specification shows their long-lasting influence on the discipline. One way or another, Marx's thought deals with one side of the coin while Weber covers another part of it. One talks about collectivism and the other talks about individualism. Marx sees everything under the collective scenario and from the economic viewpoint,

10   *The Major Theories of Sociology, and Contemporary Development*

while Weber, on the other hand, looks from the individual's perspective. Both offer valid insights for me, one way or another.

For Max Weber, the economic order was paramount in determining the precise position of various communities; however, other structures such as religion, ideas, status, and bureaucracy are determining factors. He showed that the importance of people's actions does not always exert influence only through economic interests. Weber argued that national bureaucracy is significant to society and the individual rather than the class struggle. According to Weber, basic characteristics of bureaucracy are (1) officeholders personally free and subject to authority only within the scope of their impersonal official obligations; (2) hierarchy of offices; (3) spheres of competence; (4) free selection into office, filled by free contractual relationships – always free to resign; (5) candidates appointed, not elected, on the basis of technical qualifications; (6) remuneration is by fixed salaries of $$; (7) office is the sole or primary occupation of the incumbent; (8) constitutes a career – system of promotion; (9) official cannot own means or appropriate position; (10) official subject to strict and systematic discipline and control in the conduct of office (Scott 2003). There can be several disagreements in terms of the current world situation; however, these are still significant characteristics of sound bureaucracy. Weber emphasized the historical[12] evidence, which he examined carefully to frame the bureaucratic order.

Max Weber addresses Capitalism as historically embedded in the religious movement of Protestantism with a focus on Calvinism (The Protestant Ethic and the Spirit of Capitalism), where religious followers internally guided by religious thought and where individuals do not accept blame for right or unethical conduct themselves but blame their God and convince themselves that it was their God's wish. He elaborates on the idea that rationalism is based on calculations of the return. Weber capitalism supposes the free markets for production and labor[13]. A similar argument is found in Durkheim's elaboration of moral religious life, and opposite arguments in Marx's writings.

Marx, Durkheim, and Weber had a strong influence on Hegelian philosophy. They all deal with common social problems: *"The theoretical origins of the conflict, functionalist and organizational paradigms in sociology are usually seen as distinct. Common elements in the social theories of Marx, Durkheim, and Weber are usually seen as common responses to the development of industrial, capitalist, democratic, bureaucratic structures"* (Knapp 1986, page 586). Marx and Weber analyzed social problems on the common rational ground and Durkheim examined society as a function of the living organism. Their focuses were on how history was developed and on what criteria and what can be learned from history to manage contemporary society. Marx directly used the dialectic paradigm of Hegel with contradiction; Durkheim did not mention Hegel but applied positivism as Hegel noted that society runs as a process. All three founding authors pointed to labor as the main force for socio-economic development. Marx and Durkheim went in opposite directions, but Weber followed the middle path in analyzing an organization[14]. Knapp (1986) summarizes each of these three authors' similarities and differences and also gives an account of the extent to which Hegel influenced them. Organizational sociological literature is mostly silent on the root philosophy of the organization. Among these three major writers of sociology, organization sociology is based most notably on Weber's rational notion of bureaucracy. In the following section, I will briefly describe other influential writers and note how organizational sociology has developed.

Second Section

The Development of Organizational Theory and the Emergence of Challenges to the Traditional Rational Approaches to Understanding the Organization

Organizational theory has a long history associated with major fields of social sciences such as sociology, economics, political science, public administration, anthropology, and social psychology. The organizational study covers multiple viewpoints, methods, and levels of analysis. It ranges from micro-level individual behavior of organizations to macro-level organizations, where one can analyze a variety of organizational settings and their behavior, such as why they were founded, how they developed, in what structures they build, and what their functions are. It also covers which strategy they use to function, and what procedure they apply to sustain the organization. Further organizational study covers the broader ground of their productivity (knowledge, power, wealth, and services) and studies their products based on their respective niches. Several scholars (classical Weber, Foyal, and Taylor to contemporary Scott, Smircich, etc.) have examined organizational forms at formal and informal levels. The unit of analysis of an organization varies from micro-, macro-, and meso-level according to the organization's size and its connections.

There are several paradigms to examine organizations such as in terms of power dynamism, culture, networks (within organizations and with individuals), or population or ecological perspectives with the application

12 *The Major Theories of Sociology, and Contemporary Development*

of both qualitative and quantitative methods. The organizational theory also examines the bureaucratic order within the organization and evaluates how individuals interact in or with organizations and maintain their role to administrate the organization. It also analyzes the control mechanism, and its model (particularly bureaucratic), and explains how such modality works in terms of product and production delivery to the society. Therefore, the organizational study is multi-dimensional and can be examined from various perspectives. Many scholars have been working in this field. Most important are the founders of sociology such as Karl Marx, Ferdinand Tönnies, Émile Durkheim, Ludwig Gumplovicz, Vilfredo Pareto, Max Weber, Talcott Parsons, and many others who have discussed formal and informal forms of social organizations (Ritzer 2000). Among the classical sociologists, especially, Max Weber (1864–1920) introduced the concept of bureaucracy, and Karl Marx (1818–1883) and Emile Durkheim (1858–1917) developed the concept of division of labor as a founding concept of the formal basis for organizational sociology. Organizational sociology is rooted in the sociological canon but is not limited to it. Organizational sociology is also influenced by public administration and business management studies, political science, and psychology. In another word, organizational analysis is complex and is not limited to sociological epistemology only.

Classical Theorists

Significant authors of three major classical epistemologies in organizational theory-building include:

Max Weber[15] and his concept of rational bureaucracy (an ideal, rational form of organization, organizational structure based on rationalization of collective activities, based on formal rules and regulations, impersonal relationships, and employment based entirely on technical competence).

Henri Fayol (French industrialist and general administration theorist who was contemporary to Weber) developed five basic grounds for organization management, i.e., planning, organizing, commanding, coordinating, and controlling. He further developed 14 principles of administrative management of organizations, i.e., division of labor, authority and disciple, unity of command and direction, subordination of individual interests to the general interests, remuneration and centralization, scalar chain, order, equity stability of tenure of personnel, initiative, and esprit de corps.

Frederick Taylor, another important organizational theorist, developed the scientific management theory of organizations. Taylor described four major principles: (1) scientific job analysis (observation, data gathering, and careful measurement to determine "the one best way" to perform each job); (2) selection of personnel (scientifically select and then train, teach, and develop workers); (3) management cooperation (managers should cooperate with workers to ensure that all work is done by the principles of the science that developed the plan), and (4) functional supervising (managers assume planning, organizing, and decision-making activities, and workers perform jobs) (Scott 2003; Fincham and Rhodes 1999).

In addition to these major classical organization theorists, **Luther Halsey Gulick** (1892–1992) was another who followed the Fayol theoretical path and developed a new organizational management theory. Gulick proposed planning, organizing, staffing, directing, coordinating, controlling, and budgeting as key principles for good organization management. Another most influential organizational theorist was **Herbert A. Simon** (1916–2001) who extensively contributed to large areas of social sciences and technological fields (cognitive psychology, computer science, public administration, economics, management, philosophy of science, and sociology). He was critical of Fayol and Taylor's organizational theory (Scott 2003). He examined organizational behavior on the rational ground, as proposed by Max Weber, and added work on how rationality fits the management of the organization. Simon analyzed organization in six major categories, i.e., objectively, subjectively, consciously, deliberately, and organizationally rational.[16] Simon presented a series of five contradictions in organizational behavior, nicely summarized by Brown (2004), i.e., "the prime importance of the scientific paradigm, which is crucial to the legitimacy of his proposition; the view of administrative science from the logical positivist position; the positing of an objective world for the organization; the inclusion of psychology, allowing room for speculation about the decision-maker in terms of "motivation" rather than "drive"; and the provision of "space" for the complexity of subjective intent and voluntarism." Simon's book "Administrative Behavior" was published in 1947. According to him, the aim of the book was to show how organizations can be understood in terms of their decision processes (Simon, 76, pages ix & xxv). Simon treats decision-making as the heart of administrative behavior. He states that administration must be based on the logic and psychology of human choice, i.e., economic theory and psychology (Bakka and Fivesdal 1986, page 168). Simon provides the practical ground to explain his organizational theory[17].

14 *The Major Theories of Sociology, and Contemporary Development*

Like Simon, **Berton H. Kaplan** (1968) deals with bureaucracy in the context of social dynamism and social development. Kaplan proposes six alternatives: (1) that the organization is theoretically oriented; (2) that the organization is designed to provide latent structures to meet the changing contingencies of the development process; (3) that the organization is client-centered and is consequently designed to work with the entire social system(s); (4) that the organization is designed to perform a socialization or socialization function; (5) that social development organizations are ideally committed to a norm emphasizing experimental design as the primary consideration in program design; (6) and that the organization for social development is constrained by the limited alternatives for change available at any given time (Kaplan 1968, page 471). Kaplan's list does not reject the seven parameters of the good bureaucracy of Weber but provides a refined way to see the system in the changing social situation. He provides an alternative definition based on the current demand of organizations which focuses on the problem solving and program design approaches. The author states that "a development bureaucracy is assumed to involve the following elements: (1) the management of change, that is, the direction of efforts to alter the basic pattern(s) of a way of life; (2) the *design* of structures to plan change, that is, the specification of workable criteria of organizational structure to affect and direct a change process; and (3) the focus on the goal of altering the whole "way of life" or parts of it, to increase the adaptive capacities of individuals and groups" (page 472). The basis of problems in organizations, Kaplan (1968) points out, are to be found in the basic values and structural features of development bureaucracies, the range of structures, transactions between bureaucracy and environment, and the input–output system (page 472).

Kaplan (1968) suggests that the bureaucracy model needs to consider the changing sociological phenomena. His notion is practical and insists that organizational sociologists should reexamine the organizational status with consideration of the socio-political and economic demands of the time.

However, all the classical theorists have been heavily criticized by the contemporary organizational theorists, particularly since the late 1950s. As Argyris (1957) objects, classical organizational theorists did not consider the worker's perspectives. He states that workers have minimal control over their working lives. Likewise, Graeme Salaman states that "a genuine sociology of organizations is not assisted by the efforts of some organization analysts to develop hypotheses about organizations in general, lumping together such diverse examples as voluntary organizations, charities, and political organizations ... It also obstructs the analysis of those structural elements which dramatically revealed in employing organizations, but not necessarily in all forms of organization" (Salaman 1979, page 33, as cited by Thompson and McHugh 2002, page 6). Zey-Ferrell (1981) has summarized the major criticisms of organizational theories[18] mostly concerning the comparative structural and structural contingency approaches.

Third Section
Contemporary Theories and Perspectives

To address the criticisms of organizational theories, various system perspectives have been developed particularly from the late 1950s. These system perspectives examine organization in terms of rational (embedded through the work of classical organizational theorists, Taylor, Fayol, Weber and Simon, March, and others), natural (including conflict approach, functionalist analysis of organization Durkheim, Malinowski, Radcliffe-Brown, and Parson) Barnard's cooperative system, Selznick, Perrow, and Mayer: institutional approach, Mayo: Hawthorne effect, and open system (based on social movements: Bertalanffy, Boulding: Systems, Simon and March 1958, etc.) (cf., Scott 2003). According to Kuhn (1983), all three – the natural, rational, and open systems perspectives – are functional and they do not need to be verified. All three have importance and co-exist and have different methodologies. Each of them has a different value and each is based on a different rhetoric. Kuhn's summary captures the notion of system perspectives because they interlinked one way or another. Similar notions can be found in the works of Granovetter (1985), Weick (1976), Buckley (1967), Pondy and Mid-off (1979) as well as Guillen (1994), Pfeffer (1982), Burrell and Morgan (1979), and Beniger (1986) who analyze organizational theory with the combined perspectives. Furthermore, based on Weber's bureaucratic principles, sociologists view organizations as social systems, as negotiated orders, as structures of power and domination, as symbolic constructions, as social practices, as well as power structures and power struggles, the nature of social practices, and ideology and culture. In other words, most of the social science epistemologies have been applied to study organizations on different grounds, economic (Williamson 1975: transaction cost approach), market and labor (Pfeffer and Cohen 1984; Uzzi 1993), ecology (Carroll 1984; Hannan and Freeman 1977), environment (Tushman and Anderson 1986), the organization as networks (Fligstein 1985; Davis and Stout 1992; Chandler 1962; Uzzi 1996; Powell 1990), and so on.

In terms of organization theories, there are wide ranges of applications such as contingency theory (Lawrence and Lorsch 1967; Galbraith 1974; Ness

16   *The Major Theories of Sociology, and Contemporary Development*

and Brechin 1988), cultural theory (Louis 1985; Weick 1985), critical and conflict (Marxist) theory (Burawoy 1979), and by the feminist organizational sociologists. Likewise, institutional theory (Meyer and Rowan 1977; Zucker 1983; Selznick 1984; DiMaggio and Powell 1983), management theory (Hackman 1975, 1995; Kerr 1975), network theory (Granovetter 1973; Powell 1990), organizational learning (March and Olsen 1975; Baum and Jintendra 1994; Cohen and Levinthal 1990), and population ecology theory (Astley1985; Carrol and Hannan 1989) have been applied to conduct organizational analysis.

The application of postmodern approaches in an organizational study is a recent phenomenon. Most importantly, since the 1990s, the application of Foucault's perspectives to the study of the organization is growing. Feminist organizational sociologists such as Joanna Brewis, Marta B. Calás, and Linda Smircich are extensively utilizing this approach (see the concluding section of this essay). Other theoretical approaches most commonly in practice in the organizational analysis are resource dependency theory (Salancik 1978; Pfeffer 1982, 1992), sense-making (Weick 1976), work and technology (Perrow 1983; Ness and Brechin 1988), and socialization theory (Maanen 1977; Maanen and Barley 1984; Maanen and Schein 1979). In addition to the above-mentioned theories in the organization, there is also a radical theory that is likely to change the critical and conflict theory (Mansfield and Warner 1975; Clegg and Dunkerley 1980). Perrow's complex organization and Goffman's Asylum also considered radically viewed theories (as noted by Bradley and Wilkie 1980). These lists of works give a general scenario of how multidisciplinary organization theories are changing and how broadly this subfield of sociology is growing. Each of the above-mentioned paradigms has its paths and methods, though mainstream organizational sociology is mostly interwoven in and around Weber's theory of bureaucracy and confined in his bureaucratic iron cage.

Most of the authors have highlighted the effectiveness of the systems perspective is an emphasis on setting specific goals, prescribing the behavioral expectations of organizational participants through the formalization of rules and roles, and monitoring conformance to these expectations. These concepts originated with Weber, Taylor, and Simon. The concept of management control came from Frederick Taylor, who explored the notion of scientific management. New models are emerging. However, a critical attribute model, a cause-and-effect model, and strategy models are still in use, but the networking model is the emerging and logical rational perspective, for which logic was based on the natural, open perspective and, most recently, a new logic environment-oriented, network system. Modern technologies,

Third Section 17

particularly computer-generated models, are providing new paths of analysis of social organizations.

In the following paragraphs, I will note how Philip Selznick, Peter Blau, James David Thompson, and Charles Perrow incorporated the Weber notion of bureaucracy followed by Paul J. DiMaggio, and Walter W. Powell. In the concluding section of this writing, I will note the feminist contribution to organizational theory building.

Philip Selznick follows Weber's principles of bureaucracy. He states that from the last decade of the 19th century, Max Weber's notion of bureaucracy has a strong influence in the academic field, particularly in Europe, and from the second decade of the 20th century in United States academia (Philip Selznick 1943). In addition to appreciating Weber's works, Selznick has provided a different frame of the organization as structure. Philip Selznick (1943)[19] proves his four hypotheses, i.e., "every organization creates an informal structure, in every organization, the goals of the organization are modified (abandoned, deflected, or elaborated) by processes within it and the process of modification affected through the informal structure" (page 47) and "The actual procedures of every organization tend to be molded by action toward those goals which provide operationally relevant solutions for the daily problems of the organization as such" (page 49). He examines the research work conducted by Barnard (1940) and Roethlisberger and Dickson (1941) and shows that even smaller organizations have structures and frameworks for their operation[20]. The beauty of Selznick's article is that he thinks that it is necessary to investigate the iron cage of organizational structure for the achievement of group goals, which creates the paradox to which we have referred (page 48). I see the certain type of boundary Selznick is advocating for a successful organization. In this context, Max Weber's metaphor can have an optimistic connotation, because Selznick is illustrating (and acknowledging) Weber's notion of bureaucracy to provide empirical evidence for his thesis.

Selznick (1943) examines bureaucracy in the organization from a sociological point of view. He distinguishes the large organization, small organization, formal organization, and informal organization; he states that each type of organization has a certain type of structure guided by the nature of the organization. Selznick examines bureaucratization as a process and identifies the criteria, i.e., co-operative effort, a delegation of functions and activities through agents, bifurcation of interest, control mechanism, internal and external relevancy, etc. He identifies the problems in such processes but also offers recommendations. Selznick gives importance to hierarchy and power dynamics, abstractions, and organizational patterns. His notion of

18 *The Major Theories of Sociology, and Contemporary Development*

knowledge production follows the same path. Selznick (1948) provides links to organizational theory, i.e., the organization as an action system, as a formal system, concrete organization as the economy in an adaptive structure, as a cooperative system, and as an organism. He explains how organizations can be analyzed from the structural and functional points of view. For the formal organizations, the "maintenance of the system," Selznick (1948) proposes the following points to consider. In my opinion, these are still applicable, namely (1) the security of the organization as a whole about social forces in its environment; (2) the stability of the lines of authority and communication; (3) the stability of informal relations within the organization; (4) the continuity of policy and the sources of its determination; and (5) a homogeneity of outlook concerning the meaning and role of the organization (Selznick 1948, pages 29–32). He proposes selective process principles: "Our frame of reference is to select out those needs which cannot be fulfilled within approved avenues of expression and thus must have recourse to such adaptive mechanisms as ideology and the manipulation of formal processes and structures in terms of informal goals" (page 32). This account provides the linkages of organizational theory to the political structure of the society where power dynamics act to maintain the socio-political system. Selznick, Blau, Thompson, Perrow, DiMaggio, and Powell also developed their organizational theory from Weber's iron cage paradigm.

Peter Blau (1918–2002) is considered one of the founders of organizational sociology with Coleman, Gouldner, Lipset, and Selznick (W. Richard Scott and Craig Calhoun's memory note). Blau's major works include "The Dynamics of Bureaucracy" (1955), "A Formal Theory of Differentiation in Organizations" (1970), "The Organization of Academic Work" (1973), "Parameters of Social Structure" (1974), "Inequality and Heterogeneity: A Primitive Theory of Social Structure" (1977), "Structural Contexts of Opportunities" (1994), and "A Circuitous Path to Macro-structural Theory" (1995) solely and many books and journal articles with several other authors. As Scott notes, Blau focused on behavior within white-collar, administrative systems rather than blue-collar settings. As one of the victims of the Second World War, Blau captured the notion of changing world and focused on the system of interrelated elements that characterize the organization as a whole (Blau 1965, page 325). "The focus......is the system of interrelated elements that characterize the organization as a whole, not its parts" (Blau 1965, page 326). As did Selznick, Kaplan, Simon, and other organizational theorists, Blau also refined Weber's theory of bureaucracy (Argyris 1972). Through his book "Exchange and Power in Social Life" (1964), he explained Merton's concept of middle-range theory, and by microeconomic analysis and utility

Third Section 19

theory, Blau offered a micro-sociology of strategic interaction that anticipated and influenced the later rise of rational choice theory (Coleman, 1990; Cook, 1990 as noted by W. Richard Scott and Craig Calhoun's memory notes). Blau examined organizations with an integrated approach. He proposed that organization needs to be examined with close perspectives. He states that differentiation makes the organization more complex, and complexity generates problems in communication and coordination. In a critique, Argyris (1972) states that Blau lacks providing concrete definition and also questions the decentralization concept developed by Blau. However, in organizational theory development, Blau applied a macro-sociological theory of social structure, stratification, and a theory of social exchange which laid new ground to analyze formal organizations.

James Thompson applied a similar notion to identify the distinctive properties of an organization. **James David Thompson** (1920–1973) examines the new ground of organizations with environmental perspectives. He focuses on uncertainty in the organization because of changing technology and external environment and these changes affect the transactions within the organization; therefore, there is uncertainty in the organization. Charles Perrow's works match Thompson's thesis that technology is a significant external factor for organizational change.

Charles Perrow is one of the leading scholars of organizational sociology; his major works are "The Radical Attack on Business" (1972), "Organizational Analysis: A Sociological View" (1970), "Complex Organizations: A Critical Essay" (1972; 3rd ed., 1986), "Normal Accidents: Living with High-risk Technologies" (1984; revised, 1999), and "The AIDS Disaster: The Failure of Organizations in New York and the Nation" (1990) with Mauro Guillen's, "Organizing America: Wealth, Power, and the Origins of American Capitalism" (2002) and many journal articles. Perrow considers technology as the defining factor of an organization. It can be an independent variable and arrangements to get things done can be dependent variables; so organizations should be studied as a "whole" (as Blau and Thompson proposed), rather than by dealing with specific processes or subsections; technology is a better basis for comparing organizations than the several schemes that now exist (Perrow 1967, pages 194–195, as cited by Argyris 1972, page 35). Thompson was uncertain about the implication of technology in defining the characteristics of the organization; however, Perrow asserts that technology is the major factor in analyzing organizational performance.

DiMaggio and Powell (1983) began their visit to Weberian bureaucracy with the citation to Weber: "it is primarily the capitalist market economy which demands that the official business of administration discharged

20 *The Major Theories of Sociology, and Contemporary Development*

precisely, unambiguously, continuously, and with as much speed as possible. Normally, the large, modern capitalist enterprises are themselves unequaled models of the strict bureaucratic organization" (Weber 1968, page 974 as cited by DiMaggio and Powell 1983). Weber reveals the competitive marketplace as the most important force encouraging bureaucratization, arguing that market pressures toward efficiency required the institution of bureaucratic structure because (Weber argued) this is the most precise and efficient administrative form. DiMaggio and Powell argue that the mode of organization has changed since Weber developed his theory of bureaucracy. They revisit the iron cage in the sense of multiple situations. They argue that "Organizational structure, which used to arise from the rules of efficiency in the marketplace, now arises from the institutional constraints imposed by the state and the professions. The efforts to achieve rationality with uncertainty and constraint lead to homogeneity of structure (institutional isomorphism)." They use the term isomorphism (a mathematical term meaning "constraining process that forces one unit in a population to resemble other units that face the same set of environmental conditions") and divide isomorphism into two categories, competitive and institutional. Further, they examine isomorphism as coercive isomorphism, mimetic processes, and normative pressure categories where coercive refers to the pressures from other organizations, governments, or other agencies; mimetic processes refer to the uncertainty that leads the organization to imitate what other organizations are doing: this can be diffused through shifting employees from one organization to another; normative pressure comes from the professionals. They cite Alchian (1950) whose statement clarifies what the mimetic process is: "while there certainly are those who consciously innovate, there are those who, in their imperfect attempts to imitate others, unconsciously innovate by unwittingly acquiring some unexpected or unsought unique attributes which under the prevailing circumstances prove partly responsible for the success. Others, in turn, will attempt to copy the uniqueness, and the innovation-imitation process continues" (as cited by DiMaggio and Powell 1983, page 151).

To clarify these processes, they state that "Each of the institutional isomorphic processes can be expected to proceed in the absence of evidence that it increases internal organizational efficiency. To the extent that organizational effectiveness enhanced, the reason is often that organizations for their similarity to other organizations in their fields. This similarity can make it rewarded easier for organizations to transact with other organizations, to attract career-minded staff, to be acknowledged as legitimate and reputable, and to fit into administrative categories that define eligibility for public and private grants and contracts" (page 154). This explanation provides a new way to evaluate the bureaucracy and presents different perspectives. It is a valid proposition that every organization has its strength and approaches and also problems and ways to minimize them. However, the changing process mentioned by DiMaggio and Powell is not clear in the sense that they do not explain how this process occurs. In terms of application in my research context, DiMaggio, and Powell's (1983) findings are worthwhile to consider.

Fourth Section

The Feminist Approach to Organizational Analysis

Arlene Daniels (1975, page 349) states that "The women's movement contributes far more to sociology than a passing interest would. The development of a feminist perspective in sociology offers an important contribution to the sociology of knowledge. And through this contribution, we are forced to rethink the structure and organization of sociological theory in all the traditional fields of theory and empirical research" (as cited by Stacey and Thorne 1985). Daniels captures the notion of feminist movements, which I think presents a major turn, not only to change the directions women face in the 20th century onwards but also to provide a ground for the development of feminist scholarship. Adding to this notion, Tracy and Thorne (1985) bring an important account of how sociology developed by the privileged western, white, upper-middle-class, straight men (page 306). This hegemony of the male began to be challenged; however, it was not a strong stand until the feminist movements began at an organized level. The foundation developed through the first wave of feminist movements. The first wave had influence on the women's stand to some extent; however, formally, this stand became more visible only in the 1960s. Since then, various feminist scholars have challenged the one-sided view of society (privileged western, white, upper-middle-class, straight men), including postmodern thinkers.

This challenge brought a new way to examine society. Academicians began to examine society more openly and flexibly, which helped to develop new thoughts and theories relating to feminism, racism, etc. Within sociology, scholars began to see society deeply through feminist perspectives[21] (Dorothy Smith, Marjorie DeVault, Gisela Bock, and Susan James). In organizational sociology, new perspectives developed (rational, natural, and open system (primarily) and environmental, demographic, ecological, etc., more recently). At first, the women's standpoint in the organization was not much focused upon, as discourse dealt more often with women's freedom as individuals as the feminism's movement began to examine the women's stand in every sector

22   *The Major Theories of Sociology, and Contemporary Development*

of social life including formal and informal social organizations, scholars began to see the women's role in organizational structure. Several authors in feminist scholars have contributed to organizational theory development. In this essay, I will only focus on Martha Calas and Linda Smircich's contribution to organizational theory building. They primarily examine women's standing in organizational management and apply a postmodern perspective to analyze the organization based on the perspectives developed by Michel Foucault, Jurgen Habermas, Jacques Derrida, Jurgen Habermas, etc.

Martha Calas and Linda Smircich state that organization theories – once they are presented as knowledge – guide organizational participants in their efforts to understand and control organizations. "In this sense, organizational scientists make organizations as much as we study them; thus, having a socially conscious organizational practice may depend first on having a more socially conscious organizational scholarship" (Calás and Smircich 1992b, pages 223, 234).

These authors' approach to organization study is particularly based on postmodern notions of thought. They analyze organizations from various perspectives and provide a detailed account of the functionalist liberal way to postmodern power dynamism. I think Foucault's notion of power politics and social change through knowledge is a relevant ground for them to examine organizational dynamism. Because of the changing faces of organizations within modern neo-liberal socio-economic scenarios, it is hard to develop universal principles for organizational management. Calás and Smircich's analysis goes beyond traditional sociological scholarship which was silent about women's standing and roles in the organization and elaborates on how women are ignored, or at least passed over, in organizational power politics. Another aspect they have analyzed is the impact of colonialism on the developing world's organizations. In the following paragraphs, I will examine how these two authors view feminism in organizational management and what they have contributed to organizational theory development.

Calás and Smircich (1996) state that the word "feminism" cannot contain the notion of the strength of the feminist theory, because it includes several perspectives; hence, it should be "feminisms." This minute correction encapsulates the seriousness of their stand. Another point they state is that "feminist theories go beyond "women's issues" where they examine feminisms as critical and political issues, which have been embedded in society since earliest times and can be seen in every aspect of social, economic, and political spheres. They argue that feminist theorists should situate themselves as a part of any project "in research" to articulate the real grounds of tension. Feminist authors are not satisfied with the existing theory of feminism which according to them is not necessarily in sequential order. They state that theories of feminism built on, responded to, and changed as a result of different dialogues – boundaries between them are "blurry and blurring." They look into existing organizational theories through feminist perspectives and evaluate how feminisms contribute to organization theory building in the context of existing liberal, radical, psychoanalytic, Marxist, socialist, poststructuralist/ postmodern, and third world/(post) colonial perspectives.

Calás and Smircich (1996) explain each of these categories, which provide an important basis for how organizations can be analyzed and explained. The following paragraphs give a brief account of such points, developed by Calás and Smircich, which can be used in studying social organizations. Similarly, their liberal perspective is based on the functionalist/ positivist approach, which mostly examines sex and gender as a variable, not a framework for organizational analysis. At the *individual and psychological level*, this approach examines the sex and gender differences in leadership, power, job stress, satisfaction, organizational commitment, sex stereotypes, androgyny, recruitment, selection, and performance appraisal. It also examines the glass ceiling, organizational demography, career building, and social networks and evaluates whether organizations provide equal opportunity and take affirmative action without discrimination against the women workers in the organizations. Calás and Smircich are analyzing the situation of women in organizational management around 1996, and where women stand more than ten years later is not presently clear.

Likewise, the radical feminist approach uses case studies and ethnographies to examine organizations and search for innovative ideas of alternative organizations that may arise for the creation of "woman space." Calás and Smircich (1996) illustrate Koen's five alternatives to increase women's role in organizations such as participatory decision making, rotating leadership, flexible and interactive job designs, and equitable distribution of income, interpersonal, and political accountability. However, the question is whether it is possible in the real ground to apply these principles or not. Here, questions arise, such as who heads the organization for whose interest? While most organizations still operate with the traditional functional system of governance, whether this new radical approach can take a forward step? These authors are silent about the implementation part. Another approach they reveal is psychoanalytic. Here, they state that organizational study should examine whether women have equal advantages in the organization or not, in terms of leadership and teamwork capabilities. This approach "considers the consequences of women's different psychosexual development for their roles in organization and management" (Calás and Smircich 1996, page 224). The

24 *The Major Theories of Sociology, and Contemporary Development*

psychoanalytic aspects of the organizational study have been little considered in practice. Many scholars have analyzed organizational behavior; however, they have seldom adequately represented the essential differences governing women's standpoint and roles.

Calás and Smircich (1996) next elaborate on the Marxist approach, where they criticize capitalism and patriarchy together: "work organizations are important sites for analyzing the ongoing reproduction of sex/gender inequality as they expose the intersections of patriarchy and capitalism" (Calás and Smircich 1996, page 226). They state that the socialist approach to organizational research examines the case studies of "women in the organization." In this approach, organization studies do not distinguish individuals from private and public life: "families and societies are mutually constituted through gender relations" (Calás and Smircich 1996, page 227). This approach is opposite to Max Weber's notion of the bureaucratic model. As Kilduff and Mehra (1997) note: "Feminist postmodern researchers seek to represent women as subjects rather than objects and to give voice to the narratives of those who violate what". Cassell (1996, page 46) referred to as the "principles of the incarnate social order" (Kilduff and Mehra 1997, page 472). However, traditional bureaucratic expositions reject this notion. Feminist scholars criticize the traditional organizational model because it focuses on power in the hierarchical order which is silent about the women's stand in the decision-making process. I think an alternative model can be proposed based on dialectical classification (in terms of gender, sex, race, ethnicity, and country of origin) and where organizations can be analyzed in the context of sex/gender, north, and south, or as a power struggle.

Calás and Smircich further explore the subject from the poststructuralist/ postmodern perspective. This approach is based on power relationships (as Foucault illustrates). They state that postmodern feminist ethnography "subverts many images about what it is to be a gendered self belonging to particular ethnic groups within particular life circumstances; as well as what counts as theory and where the boundary is between the empirical and the theoretical" (Calás and Smircich 1996, page 231) and note poststructuralist study of "secretaries as a social group and their discursive constructions in the day-to-day relationships of power" (Calás and Smircich 1996, page 231). Calás and Smircich's postmodern approach examines women's role in the organization in terms of power politics. In the bureaucratic web, power considered a major aspect to manage the operation of the organization. In this context, to study organizations from any perspective, it is important to see how the organization is structured and who makes the decisions. The final approach they propose is the study of the third world's perspective, which is

Fourth Section 25

still an innovative approach that focuses on how the organization or agency formed and how knowledge is created within it. The organizational study is dominated by western scholars. Scholars are silent about the developing world situation on "how organizations are created, operated, and how they function."

Another silent feature is the changing face of the developing world's organizations in the postcolonialism condition. Calás and Smircich highlight this issue and state that knowledge developed by third-world women is still not for them (as I have observed, too often, the benefits of financial and another aid benefit disproportionally the donor country rather than the recipient). Chandra Mohanty (1988) examines how western eyes see women of color in the United States. She states "I would like to suggest that the feminist writings I analyze here discursively colonize the material and historical heterogeneities of the lives of women in the third world, thereby producing/ representing a composite, singular 'third-world woman' - an image which appears arbitrarily constructed but carries with it the authorizing signature of western humanist discourse" (Mohanty 1988, page 63). Her focus was to see how third-world women are examined from western eyes. She argues that the third world is facing western hegemony in many ways. Mohanty's notion is valid even to propose alternatives in the feminist discourses. This sector needs to be examined more deeply through a comparative study of how southern women are changing their stand in society. Women's participation in the decision-making process is limited. Calás and Smircich insist that the western world needs to explore more about women's role in the southern context.

Calás and Smircich are considered feminist and postmodern organizational theorists (Joanna Brewis 2005). They examine organizations in two major frames: (1) feminisms and (2) modernism and postmodernism. From the feminisms perspective, they bring the notion of how identity makes difference in organizations[22] due to sex, class, and culture. The identity issue not only applies in the organizational setting but equally works with other social behavior. In the organizational setting, Calás and Smircich bring three basic points about identity, i.e., (1) it constitutes a racial term and condition of employment, (2) it is a form of race-plus discrimination, (3) and it reflects racial stereotyping. The question arises then as to how to address such an issue. Here, the authors lack clarity.

It is worthwhile to evaluate what Calás and Smircich have added to organizational theory. In this context, Joanna Brewis's (2005) summary of Calás and Smircich's organizational theory is useful to quote[23]. Calás and Smircich present a valid argument to apply postmodern perspectives in the

26 *The Major Theories of Sociology, and Contemporary Development*

organizational study (see endnote xxiii). I am not a fan of the postmodern approach, but in researching the place where women stand in organizations, their points provide some assistance.

In the context of the postmodern approach to organizational research, Foucault's power dynamism is the major ground for Calás and Smircich. However, the postmodern approach[24] itself is not universally accepted in organizational research. Calás and Smircich (1999) advocate postmodern thought, in their words: "Insofar as postmodern perspectives allow for questioning conventional approaches to theory development, the argument goes; they provide incisive analyses showing the inner workings and assumptive basis of those theories. At the same time, however, the elusiveness of theory under postmodern premises prevents those who articulate postmodern perspectives from theorizing other, alternative views, because they do not have any "solid ground" from which to speak" (Calás and Smircich 1999, page 649).

These accounts of postmodern thought provide a ground to go for the application of postmodern perspectives in sociological research (in my case, organizational research). In institutional research, the application of the reflexive perspective exists (e.g., Erving Goffman's Asylum, etc.). Nevertheless, formal organizations are still operating with a basis on the traditional bureaucratic system. It is possible to use the postmodern perspective, but until there is wider adoption and documentation of organizations operating in new ways, it is certain to be difficult for me to find the appropriate information.

Conclusion

Organizational sociology is one of the recent subfields that founded based on the philosophy developed by western authors Durkheim, Marx, and Weber. Marx provides the procedure to manage the organizational labor based on dialectical materialism (socialism). Durkheim, as a functionalist, discusses the division of labor as a normal social mechanism (social ethics and religion) and Weber focuses on the trend of rationalization in organizational governance in both the public and private sectors of modern societies (rationalism and capitalism). The theories of Marx and Weber focus on how society can produce more goods and services to fulfill social needs through formal forms of organizations. Marx talks about the statelessness situation through the labor movement, while Weber says this is shallow imagination. Among these three major sociologists, Weber is considered as one of the founding fathers of organizational sociology; he developed the rational approach to the analysis of bureaucracy. According to Collins (1986, page 286), "there is nothing better known in the field of organizations, in all of sociology, than Weber's model of bureaucracy. It also happens that there is no more complete misunderstanding of major sociological theory than the way Weber's organizational theory treated in American Sociology" (re-cited from Scott 2003, page 43). It is needless to state that Weber's contribution is paramount in organizational sociology. Weber focuses on the standard interpretation of society and examines sociology as a comprehensive science of social action. Weber provides a model of the bureaucracy that services the organization. In addition to Max Weber, organization sociology is also influenced by classical organizational theorists such as Frederick W. Taylor (scientific management or organization), Henri Fayol (administrative theory of organization), and Herbert A. Simon (administrative behavior) (Scott 2003, pages 38–53). The major contemporary authors of organizational sociology (Philip Selznick, Peter Blau to Charles Perrow, Paul DiMaggio, Walter Powell, etc.) follow the Weberian rational philosophy (including Taylor, Fayol, and Simon) to analyze the formal organizations one way or another. Organizational sociology has three major perspectives – rational, natural, and open systems. Based on these major perspectives, contemporary sociologists have developed several theories and methods grounded in the classical roots but with new models (Kuhn 1962; Burrell and Morgan 1979; Morgan 1980; Ness and Brechin 1988; Taylor 2002; Scott 2003).

Organizations are formed by the contexts or environments in which they are established. Modern organizations replicate the impact of their historical origins in societies characterized by growing privileged circumstances and conflicts over the control and distribution of products and services. Organizations come in many puzzling forms because they have been designed to deal with a wide range of social, cultural, economic, and political problems. Because they have emerged under widely varying environmental conditions, they have to deal with complexity within and emerging externalities. Therefore, there is no limitation on theoretical approaches and their applications in organizational analysis. There is a range of paradigms (ontology, epistemology, and methods as well as the positivism to constructivism) used to examine organizations such as in terms of power dynamism, culture, networks (within organizations and with individuals), or population or ecological perspectives with the application of both qualitative and quantitative methods. The organizational theory also examines the bureaucratic order within the organization and evaluates how individuals interact in or with organizations and maintain their role to

28 *The Major Theories of Sociology, and Contemporary Development*

administer the organization. It also analyzes the control mechanism, and its model (particularly bureaucratic), and explains how such modality works in terms of product and production delivery to the society. Therefore, the organizational study deals with multi-dimensional and complex phenomena, and it is not possible to capture the complete social environment where they originate, operate, and function. Postmodern, Marxist, and feminist authors have been challenging this western notion of organizational theory. They argue that classical and rational organizational theories are not complete because, first, they hold mostly western white male perspectives, and, second, they only minimally consider the workers' perspectives (and I agree with this criticism).

Feminist approaches to organizational study, which follow the rational, natural, and open system perspectives of organizational analysis, challenge the traditional Weberian notion of bureaucracy. They follow Foucault's postmodern perspectives to analyze formal organizations. The contributions of Arlene Daniel, Martha Calas, Linda Smircich, Jana Brewis, and others are exemplary works of this kind illustrated in this essay. I think the concept of formal organization is not only a western product, however, but also southern perspectives marginally included in the organizational studies (Chandra Mohanty 1986; Gayatri Spivak 1990). "There are overlaps of theories and paradigms among international relations theory, sociological theory, organizational theory, and international organization theory. Literature is silent on bridging such gaps. Ness and Brechin (1988) have initiated studies to bridge this gap, but there has been no continuation of this effort from the sociological point of view" (Bhandari 2019).

In this connection, Bhandari (2012, 2018, 2019) tried to add a new web to the organizational theory, by using multidisciplinary approaches to study the role of the International Union of Conservation of Nature (IUCN) and Intergovernmental Panel on Climate Change (IPCC). It is noticed that there are no collaborative approaches among the organizational sociologist, between the USA and Europe as well as with the scholars of the rest of the world. The egoism or I supremacy has divided social scientists, and, as much as possible, individual scholars are trying to create their niche. As society is moving from collectivism to individualistic paradigms, scholarships also boast this narrative. As a sociologist, I follow the principle of "live and let others live – the harmony with nature/living beings" and "Bashudaiva Kutumbakkam – the entire world is our home, and all living beings are our relatives." All scholars need to acknowledge their fellow scholars' proof, support, and rejection but should not ignore the built knowledge. This paper is honoring all pillars of social thoughts by briefly analyzing the knowledge they have provided. There is a strong need for a more detailed study about the contributions of these world GURUS and the need for utilization of their MANTRAS for social harmony and development.

I have provided only a glimmer of understanding about the founding authors of western sociological theories and how organizational theories have been developed, but I have given a general scenario of the available literature and theory, as I have found it. There is a need for extensive research on how the western notion of formal organization is viewed in the developing world and of how western hegemony has contributed to or dismantled the traditionally formed and functioning formal organizations of the developing world.

Endnotes

1   "The Ecology and the Economy: What is Rational" by Immanuel Wallerstein (published in 1998) http://www.binghamton.edu/fbc/iwecoratl.htm (downloaded on May 19, 2008).
2   Quite apart from the analysis so far given, it was, in general, a mistake to make a fuss about the so-called distribution and put the principal stress on it. Any distribution whatsoever of the means of consumption is only a consequence of the distribution of the conditions of production themselves. The latter distribution, however, is a feature of the mode of production itself. The capitalist mode of production, for example, rests on the fact that the material conditions of production are in the hands of non-workers in the form of capital and land ownership, while the masses are only owners of the personal condition of production, of labor power. If the elements of production are so distributed, then the present-day distribution of the means of consumption results automatically. If the material conditions of production are the collective property of the workers themselves, then there likewise results a distribution of the means of consumption different from the present one. The vulgar socialists (and from them, in turn, a section of the democrats) have taken over from the bourgeois economists the consideration and treatment of distribution as independent of the mode of production and hence the presentation of socialism as turning principally on distribution. After the real relation has long been made clear, why retrogress again? (Critique of the Gotha Programme; MECW 1958, 24:87–88, Marx-Engels Collected Works. New York: International Publishers. http://www.marxists.org/archive/marx/works/cw/index.htm).

30 *The Major Theories of Sociology, and Contemporary Development*

3 "From the standpoint of a higher socio-economic formation, the private property of particular individuals in the earth will appear just as absurd as the private property of one man in other men. Even an entire society, a nation, or all simultaneously existing societies taken together, are not owners of the earth, they are simply its possessors, its beneficiaries, and have to bequeath it in an improved state to succeeding generations, as boni patres familias [good heads of the household]" (Capital, vol. 3, page 911.

4 Since matter determines consciousness, knowledge must be conceived in a realistic fashion; the subject does not create the object, for the object exists independently of the subject; knowledge results from the fact that copies, reflections, or photographs of matter are present in the mind. The world is not unknowable but is thoroughly knowable. Naturally, the true method of knowing consists solely of science combined with technical practice; technical progress shows well enough the degeneracy of all agnosticism. Though knowledge is essentially sense knowledge, rational thought is necessary to organize these experiential data. Positivism is "bourgeois charlatanry" and "idealism," because we do actually grasp the essences of things through phenomena. So far, Marxist epistemology sets itself up as absolute naive realism of the usual empiricist type. The peculiarity of Marxist materialism lies in the fact that it combines this realistic outlook with another one, the pragmatic. From the notion that all contents of our consciousness are determined by our economic needs, it follows equally that each social class has its own science and its own philosophy. Independent, nonparty science is impossible; the truth is whatever leads to success, and practice alone constitutes the criterion of truth. Both these theories of knowledge are found side by side in Marxism without anyone trying very hard to harmonize them. The most they will concede is that our knowledge is a striving for the absolute truth, but that, for the moment, it is simply relative, answering to our needs. Here the theory seems to fall into contradiction, for if the truth were relative to our needs, then knowledge would never be a copy of reality – not even a partial copy. The Philosophy of Karl Marx and Friedrich Engels (Marx and Engels Collected Works, vol. 5, pages 41–43). http://www.faculty.rsu.edu/~felwell/Theorists/Marx/Words.htm

5 "The first premise of all human existence and, therefore, of all history… that men must be in a position to live in order to be able to 'make history.' But life involves before everything else eating and drinking, housing, clothing, and various other things. The first historical act is thus the production of the means to satisfy these needs, the production of material

Endnotes 31

life itself. And indeed this is a historical act, a fundamental condition of all history, which today, as thousands of years ago, must daily and hourly be fulfilled merely in order to sustain human life…the production of life, both of one's own in labor and of fresh life in procreation…appears as a twofold relation: on the one hand as a natural, on the other hand as a social relation" (Marx and Engels Collected Works, vol. 5, pages 41–43). http://www.faculty.rsu.edu/~felwell/Theorists/Marx/Words.htm

6 Stages of development of the division of labor: (1) tribal: elementary division of labor; extension of natural d of l existing in family, (2) ancient communal: an urban system of masters and slaves; communal private property, (3) feudal state: a rural system of lords and serfs; little d of l; feudal organization of trades into guilds. Marx emphasizes the need to look at different societies and see how the social and political structure of each is connected to production (http://ssr1.uchicago.edu/PRELIMS/Theory/marx.html 2/09/2008).

7 Marx explains, in terms of money, that "converts all capital into accumulated capital, or capitalized surplus-value…value appropriated without its equivalent" (page 715). He says acquired money surplus is an unequal nature of capitalist because they do not pay fairly to the labor ("the unpaid labor of others," page 715) and capitalist can be unfair to the labor. He states "capitalist produces the worker as a wage-laborer" (page 716) and "the production and reproduction of the capitalist's indispensable means of production: the worker" (page 718), "how money is transformed into capital" (page 873), "lazy rascals spending their substance, and more, in riotous living" (page 873), "free from, unencumbered by, any means of production of their own" (page 874), and "in actual history, it is a notorious fact that conquest, enslavement, robbery, murder, in short, force play the greatest part" (page 874).

8 "According to the materialist conception of history, the ultimate determinant element in history is the production and reproduction of real life…. Hence if somebody twists this into saying that the economic element is the only determining one, he transforms that proposition into a meaningless, abstract, and senseless phrase. The economic situation is the basis, but the various elements of the superstructure … also exercise their influence upon the course of the historical struggle and in many cases preponderate in determining their form" (1962, II, page 488).

9 The first wave refers to the feminism movement of the 19th through early 20th centuries, which dealt mainly with the suffrage movement. The second wave (1960s–1980s) dealt with the inequality of laws, as well as cultural inequalities. The third wave of feminism (1990s–current)

32 *The Major Theories of Sociology, and Contemporary Development*

is seen as both a continuation and a response to the perceived failures of the second wave (from Krolokke, Charlotte, and Anne Scott Sorensen, (2005), "From Suffragettes to Grrls' in Gender Communication Theories and Analyses: From Silence to Performance, Sage, 2005).

10 "Durkheim states the problem which constitutes the most pressing necessity for political reform. It is to be found in the need for providing some remedy for the present anarchical conditions which exist in economic affairs, particularly in the industrial relations between employer and employee. While there is at least a rudimentary professional morality among lawyers, magistrates, soldiers, professors, clergymen and physicians, there is practically no semblance of fixed customs or a moral code to guide the vast mass of industrial activities and relations of the present time. The rights and relations of employer and employee and of both with the public, when not regulated in an arbitrary manner by the state, are settled, without any attempt at uniformity of procedure or any regard for equity of principle, according to the relative strength in each instance of the parties involved and the methods best adapted to any particular case. The party that is vanquished by force is filled with resentment and awaits the opportunity for revenge. Modern industrial life is thus, in reality, what Hobbes imagined the state of nature to be, namely, a condition of economic warfare." The modern occupational group is the only organization that fulfills or has the potentiality of fulfilling these conditions. These secondary groups, interpolated between the individual and the state, are, on the one hand, general enough to allow their policy to be regulated intelligently by the state, and, on the other hand, possess the detailed knowledge and the flexibility which enables them to comprehend the diverse needs of specialized industrial interests and to minister to these needs in an expert manner.

Durkheim gives a brief sketch of the history of corporations to show their past services and the necessary changes which their organization would have to undergo to adapt it to modern conditions. In Rome, the occupational groups were under distinct disadvantages. They had no legal standing and shared in the general prejudice of the Romans toward any type of industry save agriculture. In the medieval period, conditions were different, for corporate occupational groups were then not only possessed of almost monopolistic control of all industry but also, as a rule, controlled the government of the towns. They were the real cornerstone of medieval society. Their one defect was that being a product of a narrowly local and exclusive economy, they were unable to adjust themselves to the national economy which followed the Commercial Revolution, and, as a result, they became a barrier to industrial and social progress Barnes (1920: 242–245).

11 "One substantive example of this emotional binding together of institutions can be found in Professional Ethics and Civic Morals, where Durkheim investigates the religious and sacred foundations of contractual relationships. ("New institutions," he observes, "begin as a rule by taking the old as their model and only split off from these by degrees in order to develop their own pattern in freedom" (Durkheim 1992, page 1791).) Durkheim speaks of several historical stages in the evolution of contract, culminating in the partially normative ideal of "the just contract, objective and equitable" (Durkheim 1992, page 208). The origins of this history, he claims, lie in emotionally charged ritual experiences – "blood covenants" 1 that allow "two different individuals or groups, between whom no natural ties exist, [to1 agree to be associated in some common aim: in order that this covenant should be binding, they … bring about the physical blood relationship considered to be the source of all obligations. They mingle their blood" (Durkheim 1992, page180). Later stages in the evolution of contract represent merely the humidification and objectification of essentially this same ritual process. Even latter-day contractual relationships (within the economy as well as civil society e.g., the marital bond) thus retain an emotional, solidaristic dimension" (Emirbayer 1996, page 120).

12 As Ritzer (1996) states, "Sociology seeks to formulate type concepts and generalized uniformities of empirical processes. This distinguishes it from history, which is oriented to the causal analysis and explanation of the individual actions, structures, and personalities possessing cultural significance. The ideal procedure is to make sure imputation of individual concrete events occurring in historical reality to concrete, historically given causes through the study of precise empirical data which have been selected from specific points of view (page 15)"; in this situation, we can refer Weber as a historical sociologist.

13 Weber's last book is *The General Economic History*. Randall Collins refers to *American Sociological Review* 45 (1980) Weber's Last Theory of Capitalism that capitalism is "rational."

14 "Hegel wrote at the time of the French and the industrial revolutions. The idea that both sociology in general and the theories of Marx, Durkheim, and Weber were generated by the attempt to describe and explain this transformation is hardly new (Nisbet 1966; Giddens 1971). Rural,

34 *The Major Theories of Sociology, and Contemporary Development*

agricultural, local, monarchical, peasant, and feudal social structures coexisted with urbanization, industrialization, bureaucratization, the development of national states, the democratic revolution, and the growth of literacy. Some contrasts and changes leaped to the eye. Marx analyzed these changes in terms of alienation, expropriation, and the development of capitalism. The rise of capitalism and the world market leads to the destruction of self-employment, local boundaries, and the creation of an international working class. Durkheim analyzed the same changes in terms of the weakening of normative integration and then the formation of new normative integration on a new basis. Mechanical solidarity is replaced by organic solidarity in which greater individual differences are integrated by increasingly abstract, general norms concerning human dignity. Weber analyzed the changes as a process of rationalization" (Knapp 1986, page 588).

15 Weber does not define bureaucracy directly but provides identified special characteristics administrative forms: Jurisdictional form: duty areas clearly specified; principle of hierarchy: lower department controlled and supervised by higher rank officials; wide set of rules to handle bureaucracy, to govern official decisions and actions; means of production or administration (belong to the department, not to the employee); employees' selection based on technical qualifications (work for a salary); and employment means a career.

16 "Objectively rational – if, in fact, it is the correct behavior for maximizing given values in a given situation. Subjectively rational – if it maximizes attainment relative to the actual knowledge of the subject. Consciously rational – to the degree that the adjustment of means to ends is a conscious process. Deliberately rational – to the degree that the adjustment of means to ends has been deliberately brought about (by the individual or the organization). Organizationally rational – if it is oriented to the organization's goals and personally rational – if it is oriented to the individual's goals" (Reva Brown 2004).

17 [I]f there were no limits to human rationality, administrative theory would be barren. It would consist of the single precept: always select that alternative, among those available, which will lead to the most complete achievement of your goals. The need for an administrative theory resides in the fact that there are practical limits to human rationality, and that these limits are not static but depend on the organizational environment in which the individual's decisions take place. The task of administration is so to design this environment that the individual will approach as close as practicable to rationality (judged in terms of the organization's

goals) in his decisions (Simon, 76, page 240f). The central concern of administrative theory is with the boundary between rational and nonrational aspects of human social behavior (Simon, 76, page xxviii).

18 "Criticisms of the comparative structural and structural contingency approaches: (1) hold an overly rational image of the functioning of organizations; (2) construct theory which reifies organizational goals; (3) generate ideologically conservative assumptions and methods of analysis; (4) view organizational systems as integrated through the value consensus and common interests of its employees/members; (5) conduct a historical analysis of organizations; (6) emphasize only the static aspects of organizations; (7) de-emphasize power in organizational analysis; (8) hold images of organizations which are overly constrained; (9) hold images of humans as nonvolitional; and (10) view organizations as the exclusive unit of analysis" Mary Zey-Ferrell (1981, page 182).

19 On his article on "An Approach to a Theory of Bureaucracy" published on American Sociological Review.

20 "The structure consisted of a set of procedures (binging, sarcasm, ridicule) by means of which control over members of the group was exercised, the formation of cliques which functioned as instruments of control, and the establishment of informal leadership. "The men had elaborated, spontaneously and quite unconsciously an intricate social organization around their collective beliefs and sentiments" (F. J. Roethlisberger and W. J. Dickson 1941 as cited by Selznick (1943) on page 47). Selznick defines bureaucracy as "If the ideas developed above have been clear, it will be readily evident that the approach which identifies bureaucracy with any administrative system based on professionalization and on hierarchical subordination is not accepted here." He further clarifies that "Such a point of view is maintained in the work of Friedrich and Coles on the Swiss Civil Service; the interest of the authors is clearly in the formal structure of the administrative apparatus as a mechanism of, in this case, popular government. The structure is related to the asserted, professed purposes of the administration; and bureaucratization is conceived of as the tendency toward the complete achievement of the formal system" (page 49). And "Bureaucratization is in a sense the process of transforming this set of procedures from a minor aspect of the organization into a leading consideration in the behavior of the leadership" (page 53).

21 "A vision of feminist social justice emerges in the writings of contemporary American women writers Toni Morrison, Joy Harjo, Barbara Kingsolver, and Adrienne Rich. Their collective bodies of work envision a world

36 *The Major Theories of Sociology, and Contemporary Development*

that does not devalue and separate people, a world connected to ideals of justice grounded in the interrelationships of words and deeds. These writers argue that we need to create a new way of seeing and interacting with the world around us, recognizing our individual responsibilities for creating better communities, questioning government actions, and seeking, above all, a society that sustains people regardless of gender, race, class, ethnicity, sexuality, or access to resources. As such, these writers variously articulate what we propose as a feminist vision of justice--one which asserts that interdependence, responsibility, respect for and relationship with the environment, and an ethics of care are the foundation for a more reasoned and reasonable practice of justice" (Riley Jeannette, Torrens Kathleen, and Krumholz Susan, 2005, Contemporary feminist writers: envisioning a just world, Contemporary Justice Review, Volume 8, Number 1, March 2005, pp. 91–106(16)).

22 In their article "Identity Performance," Calás and Smircich state that "A person's experiences with and vulnerability to discrimination is based not just on a status marker or difference (call this a person's status identity) but also on the choices that person makes about how to present her difference (call this a person's performance identity)." "Everyone performs identity. Though we may not recognize that we are doing it, by making choices about what we wear, how we talk, how we walk, and how we structure a conversation…we are performing identity(ies). Different intersections of identities can bring varying amounts of privilege and oppression. It isn't addictive but is contextual, relational, and historical. For instance, we don't try to determine who is oppressed more: an able-bodied upper-class, black gay man or a working-class white woman that uses a wheelchair…" (page 71).

23 Joanna Brewis states that "(1) revealing 'the inner workings and assumptive basis' (1999, page 649) of existing organization theory, identifying the arbitrary discursive limitations within which it operates; (2) focusing on the fixing of meaning in organization theory and therefore on how our scholarship represents some phenomena, interests, and groups and marginalizes others (while implicitly or explicitly making much more universalist claims); (3) seeking to make space for non-traditional voices in organization theory, whilst being aware of the difficulties in attempting to speak for the others; (4) disavowing notions of enduring truths about organizations; (5) acknowledging the 'real-world' power of organization theory and considering how it might best be undertaken; (6) creating localized, temporary, and subjective accounts of organizations which are sensitive to how they 'realize' their subject matter; and (7)

acknowledging that writing on organizations exists to be read, and that the author is 'just one interpreter among other readers'" (1999, page 653 as cited from Brewis 2005, page 80).

24 Kilduff and Mehra (1997) state that "Within the social sciences in general, the specter of postmodernism has aroused widespread anxiety". Postmodernism has been viewed as an enterprise that calls for the death of all scientific inquiry; the end of all new knowledge; the dissolution of any standards that may be used to judge one theory against another; a banishment into utter relativism wherein a clamor of fragmented and contentious voices reigns (see Pauline Rosenau's 1992 balanced review of these concerns and Stanley Fish's [1961 - recent discussion of misunderstandings of postmodernism) (page 454). Calás and Smircich (1999) have a slightly different perspective than what Kilduff and Mehra (1997) have highlighted.

References

Adler, P. S. (1993), "Time and Motion Regained." Harvard Business Review, 97-108.

Adib, A. and V. Guerrier (2003), "The Interlocking of Gender with Nationality, Race, Ethnicity, and Class: The Narratives of Women in the Hotel Work." Gender, Work and Organizations Vol.10, No. 4 (August)

Alchian, A. (1950), "Uncertainty, Evolution, and Economic Theory," Journal of Political Economy, 58, 211–221.

Allen, N., and J. Meyer (1990), "Organizational Socialization Tactics: A Longitudinal Analysis of Links to Newcomer's Commitment and Role Orientation." Academy of Management Journal, 33(48): 847-858.

Allen, T. J. (1977), Managing the flow of technology, Cambridge, MA, MIT Press.

Alter, C. (2007), Bureaucracy and democracy in organizations: Revisiting Feminist Organizations, The Sociology of Organizations, Wharton A.S. editor, Roxbury Publication Company

Argyris, C. (1957, Personality and organization: The conflict between system and the individual, Harper.

Arensberg, C. (1951), Behavior and organization: Industrial studies. In Social Psychology at the Crossroads, eds. J. H. Rohrer and M. Sherif, pp. 324-352. New York: Harper.

38 *The Major Theories of Sociology, and Contemporary Development*

Astley, W. G. (1985), "The two ecologies: population and community perspectives on organizational evolution." Administrative Science Quarterly, 30: 224-241.

Bakka, Jørgen Frode Og Fivelsdal, Egil (1986), Organisationsteori. Struktur, kultur, processer. Handelshøjskolens Forla.

Barker, J., R. (1993), "Tightening the iron cage: concertize control in self-managing teams." Administrative Science Quarterly, 38: 408-437.

Baker, W. (1984), "The Social Structure of a National Securities Market." American Journal of Sociology (Jan.): 775-811.

Barley, S. R. (1992), "Design and Devotion: Surges of Rational and Normative Ideologies of Control in Managerial Discourse." Administrative Science Quarterly, 37: 363-399.

Baran, B. (1987), "The technological transformation of white-collar work: a case study of the insurance industry" in H. I. Hartman, Computer Chips and Paper Clips, National Academy Press.

Barley, S. (1986), "Technology as an occasion for structuring: Evidence from observations of CT scanners and the social order of radiology departments." Administrative Science Quarterly, 31: 78-108.

Baum, J. A. C., and V. S. Jintendra (1994), "Organization-Environment Coevolution" in J. Baum and V. S. Jitendra. The Evolutionary Dynamics of Organizations. New York, Oxford University Press: 379-402

Barnard C. I. (1940), The Functions of the Executive, Cambridge: Harvard University Press, 1940, p. 115.

Barnes, Harry E. (1920), Durkheim's Contribution to the Reconstruction of Political Theory, Political Science Quarterly, Vol. 35, No. 2. (Jun. 1920), pp. 236-254.

Beauvoir, Simone de (1993), All Said and Done. Translated by Patrick O'Brian. New York: Paragon House, English translation of Tout Compte fait (Paris: Gallimard, 1972).

Beauvoir, Simone de (1992), All Men are Mortal, Translated by Leonard M. Friedman. New York: W. W. Norton & Co. English translation of Tous les Hommes sont Mortels (Paris: Gallimard, 1946).

Beauvoir, Simone de (1990), America Day by Day, Translated by Carol Cosman. Berkeley: University of California Press, English translation of L'Amérique au jour le jour (Paris: Gallimard, 1954).

Beauvoir, Simone de (1948), The Blood of Others. Translated by Roger Senhouse and Yvonne Moyse, New York: Pantheon Books, English translation of Le sang des autres (Paris: Gallimard, 1945).

Benny, Hjern, Chris Hull (1984), Going Interorganizational: Weber Meets Durkheim

Scandinavian Political Studies 7 (3), 197–212. doi:10.1111/j.1467-9477.1984. tb00301.x

Bellah, Robert N. (1959), Durkheim and History, American Sociological Review, Vol. 24, 4. 447-461.

Beniger, J. R. (1986), The Control Revolution: Technological and Economic Origins of the Information Society, Cambridge, MA, Harvard University Press.

Bhandari, Medani P. (2019), The Development of the International Organization and Organizational Sociology Theories and Perspectives. Scientific Journal of Bielsko-Biala School of Finance and Law, ASEJ 2019; 23 (3): 5-29

DOI: 10.5604/01.3001.0013.6523 ISSN: 2543-9103 | E-ISSN: 2543-411X | ICV: 100 | MNiSW: 7 - https://asej.eu/resources/html/article/details?id=196026

Bhandari, Medani P. (2019), Sustainable Development: Is This Paradigm the Remedy of All Challenges? Do Its Goals Capture the Essence of Real Development and Sustainability? With Reference to Discourses, Creativeness, Boundaries, and Institutional Architecture, Socioeconomic Challenges, Volume 3, Issue 4, 97-128 ISSN (print) – 2520-6621, ISSN (online) – 2520-6214 https://doi.org/10.21272/sec.3(4).97-128.2019, http://armgpublishing.sumdu.edu.ua/wp-content/uploads/2020/01/9.pdf

Bhandari, Medani P. (2019). The Debates between Quantitative and Qualitative Method: An Ontology and Epistemology of Qualitative Method- the Pedagogical Development, in Douglass Capogrossi (Ed.) Educational Transformation: The University as Catalyst for Human Advancement, Xlibris Corporation, USA ISBN-10: 179604895X; ISBN-13: 978-1796048957

Bhandari, Medani P, (2019). Live and let others live- the harmony with nature /living beings-in reference to sustainable development (SD)- is contemporary world's economic and social phenomena is favorable for the sustainability of the planet in reference to India, Nepal, Bangladesh,

and Pakistan? Adv Agr Environ Sci. (2019);2(1): 37–57. DOI: 10.30881/
aaeoa.00020 http://ologyjournals.com/aaeoa/aaeoa_00020.pdf

Bhandari Medani P. (2019). "Bashudaiva Kutumbakkam"- The entire world
is our home and all living beings are our relatives. Why do we need to
worry about climate change, with reference to pollution problems in the
major cities of India, Nepal, Bangladesh, and Pakistan? Adv Agr Environ
Sci. (2019);2(1): 8–35. DOI: 10.30881/aaeoa.00019 (second part) http://
ologyjournals.com/aaeoa/aaeoa_00019.pdf

Bhandari, Medani P. (2020), Getting the Climate Science Facts Right:
The Role of the IPCC (Forthcoming), River Publishers, Denmark / the
Netherlands- ISBN: 9788770221863 e-ISBN: 9788770221856

Bhandari, Medani P. (2018) Green Web-II: Standards and Perspectives from
the IUCN, River Publishers, Denmark / the Netherlands ISBN: 978-87-
70220-12-5 (Hardback) 978-87-70220-11-8 (eBook).

Bimber, B. (1994), "Three Faces of Technological Determinism" in M. R.
Smith and L. Marx. Does Technology Drive History. Cambridge, MA,
MIT Press.

Blau, P. M. (1995), A circuitous path to macro-structural theory. Annual. Rev.
Social. 21:1-19.

Blau, P. M. (1994), Structural Contexts of Opportunities, Chicago: University
of Chicago Press.

Blau, P. M. (1977), Inequality and Heterogeneity: A Primitive Theory of
Social Structure. New York: Free Press.

Blau, P. M. (1974), Parameters of social structure. Am. Social. Rev.
39:615-635.

Blau, P. M. (1973), The Organization of Academic Work. New York: Wiley.

Blau, P. M. (1970), A formal theory of differentiation in organizations. Am.
Social. Rev. 35:201-218.

Blau, P. M. (1964), Exchange and Power in Social Life. New York: Wiley.

Blau, P. M. (1955), The Dynamics of Bureaucracy. Chicago: University of
Chicago Press.

Bock, Gisela (1989), "Women's History and Gender History: Aspects of an
International Debate" pages 7-30 from Gender and History, Volume 1,
1989.

References 41

Bowen, D. E., G. E. J. Ledford, et al. (1991), "Hiring for the Organization, Not the Job" Academy of Management Executive, 5(4): 35-51.

Bradley, David A., and Roy Wilkie (1980), Radical Organization Theory - A Critical Comment, The British Journal of Sociology, Vol. 31, No. 4-574-579.

Braverman, Harry (1974), Labor and Monopoly Capital: The Degradation of Work in the Twentieth Century. New York: Monthly Review Press.

Brewis, Joanna (2005), Othering Organization Theory: Marta Calas and Linda Smircich, The Editorial Board of the Sociological Review, 2005, Blackwell Publishing, Ltd.

Brown, Reva (2004), Consideration of the origin of Herbert Simon's theory of "satisficing? (1933-1947) Management Decision, Volume 42 Number 10 2004 pp. 1240-1256

Bruno G. (1987), "Pareto, Vilfredo" The New Palgrave: A Dictionary of Economics, v. 5, pp. 799-804.

Buckley, Walter (1967), Sociology and Modern Systems Theory. Englewood Cliffs, NJ: Prentice-Hall.

Burawoy, Michael (2003), For a Sociological Marxism: The Complementary Convergence of Antonio Gramsci and Karl Polanyi, Politics Society 2003; 31; 193

Burawoy, M. (1979), Manufactured Consent, Chicago, University of Chicago Press.

Burrell, G., and G. Morgan (1979), Sociological Paradigms and Organizational Analysis, Heinemann.

Calas, M.B. and L. Smircich (1996), "From 'The Woman's Point of View: Feminist Approaches to Organizational Studies" Handbook of Organizational Studies, Sage Publications.

Calás, Marta B. and Linda Smirch (1992a), "Using the 'F' Word: Feminist Theories and the Social Consequences of Organizational Research." In Albert J. Mills and Peta Tancred (eds), Gendering Organizational Analysis: 222-234. Newbury Park, CA: Sage.

Calás, Marta B. and Linda Smirich (1992b), "Re-writing Gender into Organizational Theorizing: Directions from Feminist Perspectives." In Michael Reed and Michael Hughes (eds), Rethinking Organization: New Directions in Organization Theory and Analysis: 227-253. London: Sage.

42 *The Major Theories of Sociology, and Contemporary Development*

Calas, M.B., Smircich, L. (1991), "Using the F word: feminist theories and the social consequences of organizational research", in Mills, A.J., Tancred, P. (Eds), Gendering Organizational Theory, Sage, Newbury Park, CA.

Calas, M.B., Smircich, L. (1990), "Re-writing gender into organizational theorizing: directions from feminist perspectives", in Reed, M.I., Hughes, M.D. (Eds), Re-thinking Organization: New Directions in Organizational Research and Analysis, Sage, London.

Carroll, G R (1984), Organizational Ecology, Annual Review of Sociology, Vol. 10: 71-93

Carrol, G. R., and M. T. Hannan (1989), "Density dependence in the evolution of populations of newspaper organizations." American Sociological Review, 54: 524-548.

Chris Argyris (1972), The Applicability of Organizational Sociology, London, Cambridge University Press.

Cassell, J. (1996), "Feminist Approaches to Software Design: Building Interactive Story Systems for Girls." Small Computers in the Arts Network'96 (Nov 1996).

Chandler, A. (1984), "The Emergence of Market Capitalism." Business History Review, 58(Winter): 473-503.

Chandler, A. (1962), Strategy and Structure, Cambridge, MA: M.I.T. Press.

Chapnis, A. (1983), "Engineering Psychology" in M. D. Dunnette. The Handbook of Industrial and Organizational Psychology, New York, Wiley: 697-744.

Clegg, Stewart R. (1981), Organization and control, Administrative Science Quarterly, 26: 545-562.

Clegg, Stewart, and David Dunkerley (1980), Organization, Class and Control, London: Routledge and Kegan Paul.

Cohen, W. M., and D. A. Levinthal (1990), "Absorptive Capacity: A New Perspective on Learning and Innovation." Administrative Science Quarterly, 35: 128-152.

Coleman, J.S. (1990), Foundations of Social Theory, Belknap Press of Harvard University Press.

Collins, R. (1980), "Weber's Last Theory of Capitalism: A Systematization." American Sociological Review, 45(December): 925-942.

References 43

Collins, R. (1979), The Credential Society: An Historical Sociology of Education and Stratification, Orlando, FL, Academic Press.

Collins, Patricia Hill (1986), Learning from the Outsider Within: The Sociological Significance of Black Feminist Thought, Social Problems, Vol. 33, No. 6, Special Theory Issue (Oct. - Dec. 1986), pp. S14-S32

Cook, K. S. (1990), Linking actors and structures: an exchange network perspective. In Structures of Power and Constraint, ed. C. Calhoun, M. W. Meyer, W. R. Scott. Cambridge: Cambridge Univ. Press

Cuff, E.C. (1979), Perspectives in Sociology, Taylor & Francis Group.

Cusumano, M. (1989), Japanese Automobile Industry, Boston, Harvard University Press.

Davis, Gerald F and Suzanne K. Stout (1992), Organization Theory and the Market for Corporate Control: A Dynamic Analysis of the Characteristics of Large Takeover Targets, 1980-1990, Administrative Science Quarterly, Vol. 37, No. 4. 605-633.

Dalton, M. (1959), "Men Who Manage" in M. Granovetter and R. Swedberg, The Sociology of Economic Life, Boulder, CO, West-view Press.

DeVault, Marjorie (2004), What is Description? (One Ethnographer's View), Perspectives (ASA Theory Section Newsletter), 27 (#1): 4

DeVault, Marjorie, (1999), Liberating Method: Feminism and Social Research, Philadelphia: Temple University Press.

DeVault, Marjorie (1996), Talking Back to Sociology: Distinctive Contributions of Feminist Methodology. Annual Review of Sociology 22: 29-50, 1996.

DiMaggio, P. (2001), Making sense of the contemporary firm and prefiguring its future. In DiMaggio, P. (Ed.), The Twenty-First-Century Firm: Changing Economic Organization in International Perspective. Princeton: Princeton University Press.

DiMaggio, P. (1988), "Interest and agency in institutional theory", in Zucker, L.G. (Eds), Institutional Patterns and Organizations, Ballinger, Cambridge, MA.

DiMaggio, Paul, J., and Walter W. Powell (1983), "The iron cage revisited: Institutional isomorphism and collective rationality in organizational fields," American Sociological Review 48: 147-160.

44 *The Major Theories of Sociology, and Contemporary Development*

DiMaggio, P. & Powell, W. W. (1983), The iron cage revisited: Institutional isomorphism and collective rationality in organizational fields. American Sociological Review, 48:147-160.

Dore, R. (1983) "Goodwill and the Spirit of Market Capitalism." British Journal of Sociology, 34: 459-482.

Durkheim, Emile [1893/ 1964), The Division of Labor in Society. Tr. George Simpson. New York: Free Press.

Durkheim, Emile (1982), Rules of Sociological Method, Simon & Schuster (June 1982).

Durkheim, Emile. (1915), The Elementary Forms of the Religious Life: A Study in Religious Sociology, Translated by Joseph Ward Swain, New York: Macmillan.

Durkheim, Emile. [1897 /1951], Suicide: A Study in Sociology: Tr. John A. Spaulding and George Simpson. Glencoe, IL: Free Press.

Eccles, R., and N. Nohria (1992), Beyond the Hype, Cambridge, Harvard Business School Press.

Eller Shafritz, J. M., J. Steven Ott, and Yong Suk Jang (2005), Classics of Organization Theory, 6th Edition, Thompson/Wadsworth

Engels, F. (1958 [1894]), "The Peasant Question in France and Germany." In: Karl Marx and Frederick Engels: Selected Works, II, pp. 420–440. Moscow: Foreign Languages Publishing House.

Emirbayer, Mustafa (1996), Useful Durkheim, Sociological Theory, Vol. 14, No. 2.109-130.

Faunce, W. A. (1965), "Automation and the Division of Labor." Social Problems, 13: 147-160.

Fisher, C. D. (1986), "Organizational Socialization: An Integrative View." Research in Personnel and Human Resources Management, 4: 101-145.

Fincham R and Rhodes, P (1999), 'Principles of Organizational Behavior', Oxford University Press.

Firestone, Shulamith (1970), The Dialectic of Sex, The Women's Press.

Fligstein Neil (1985), The Spread of the Multidivisional Form Among Large Firms, 1919-1979, American Sociological Review, Vol. 50, No. 3 -377-391.

Frank, R. (1985), Choosing the Right Pond: Human Behavior and the Quest for Status, New York, Oxford University Press.

Friedman, M. (1953), "The Methodology of Positive Economics" in M. Friedman. Essays in Positive Economics. Chicago, University of Chicago Press.

Foucault, M. (1972), The Archaeology of Knowledge. Translated by A. M. Sheridan-Smith. New York: Pantheon Books, c1972.

Frost, P. J., L. F. Moore, et al., Ed. Eds. (1985), Organizational Culture. Beverly Hills, Sage.

Galbraith, J. R. (1974), "Organization Design: An Information Processing View." Interfaces, 4: 28-36.

Gergen, K. J. (1992), "Organizational Theory in the Post-Modern Era" in M. Reed and M. Hughes. Rethinking Organizations: new directions in organization theory and analysis, Sage Publications: 207-226.

Geertz, C. (1978), "The Bazaar Economy: Information and Searching Peasant Marketing." American Economic Review, 68(May): 28-32.

Gerschenkron, A. (1952), "Economic Backwardness in Historical Perspective" in M. Granovetter and R. Swedberg, The Sociology of Economic Life, Boulder, CO, West-view Press.

Giddens, A. (1979), "Agency, Structure" in A. Giddens, Central Problems in Social Theory. Berkeley, University of California Press.

Goldenweiser A. (1917), Religion and Society: A Critique of Émile Durkheim's Theory of the Origin and Nature of Religion, The Journal of Philosophy, Psychology and Scientific Methods, Vol. 14, No. 5. 113-124.

Granovetter, M. (1995), Getting a Job: A Study of Contacts and Careers, Chicago, University of Chicago Press.

Granovetter, M. (1985), "Economic Action and Social Structure: The Problem of embeddedness" American Journal of Sociology, 91: 481-510.

Gregory, K. L. (1983), "Native-View Paradigms: Multiple Cultures and Culture Conflicts in Organizations." Administrative Science Quarterly, 28: 359-376.

Goffman, Erving (1963), Behavior in Public Places: Notes on the Social Organization of Gatherings, New York, Free Press.

Goffman, Erving (1961), Asylums: Essays on the Social Situation of Mental Patients and Other Inmates. New York, Doubleday.

46 *The Major Theories of Sociology, and Contemporary Development*

Goldenweiser, Alexander A. (1917), The autonomy of the social. American Anthropologist 19:441-47.

Guillen, Mauro F. (1994), Models of Management: Work Authority, and Organization in a Comparative Perspective. Chicago: The University of Chicago Press.

Hackman, J. R., and R. Wagemen (1995), "Total Quality Management: Empirical, Conceptual and Practical Issues." Administrative Science Quarterly, 40: 309-342.

Hackman, J. R. (1985), "Designing work for individuals and for groups" in J. R. Hackman, E. E. Lawler, and L. W. Porter. Perspectives on behavior in organizations. New York, McGraw-Hill Book Company: 242-258.

Hackman, J. R. (1975), "On the Coming Demise of Job Enrichment" in E. L. Cass and F. G. Zimmer. Men and Work in Society. New York, Van Nostrand Reinhold Company: 97-115.

Hannan, M. T. and J. Freeman (1989), Organizational Ecology, Cambridge, Harvard University Press.

Hamilton, G., and N. W. Biggart (1988), "Market, Culture, and Authority: A Comparative Analysis of Management and Organization in the Far East." American Journal of Sociology, 94 (Supplement): S52-S94.

Hamilton, G. (1994), "Civilizations and the Organization of Economics" in N. Smelser and R. Swedberg, Handbook of Economic Sociology: 183-205.

Hardin, G. (1968), "The Tragedy of the Commons," Science, 162(December): 1243-1248.

Higgins, T.E. (1996) "Anti-Essentialism, Relativism, and Human Rights" Harvard Women's Law Journal

Hill, L. A. (1992), Becoming a Manager, Boston, Harvard Business School Press.

Hirschman, A. (1982), "Rival Interpretations of Market Society: Civilizing, Destructive, or Feeble?" Journal of Economic Literature, 20(Dec.): 1463-1484.

Hirsch, P. M. (1972), "Processing Fads and Fashions" American Journal of Sociology, 77: 639-659.

Hopp, W. and M. L. Spearman (1996), Manufacturing in America" in Factory Physics. Chicago, Irwin.

Hounshell, D. A. (1984), From the American System to Mass Production -- 1800-1932, Baltimore, Johns Hopkins University Press.

Hutchins, E. (1990), "The Technology of Team Navigation" in J. Galegher, R. E. Kraut and C. Egido. Intellectual Teamwork: Social and Technological Foundations of Cooperative Work. Hillsdale, NJ, Lawrence Erlbaum Associates: 191-221

James, Susan (2000), "Feminism in Philosophy of Mind: The Question of Personal Identity." In The Cambridge Companion to Feminism in Philosophy, ed., Miranda Fricker and Jennifer Hornsby, Oxford: Oxford University Press.

Kaplan, Berton H. (1968), Notes on a Non-Weberian Model of Bureaucracy: The Case of Development Bureaucracy, Administrative Science Quarterly, Vol. 13, No. 3, Special Issue on Organizations and Social Development 471-483.

Kaufman, Herbert (1964), Organization Theory and Political Theory, The American Political Science Review, Vol. 58, No. 1. 5-14

Keating Anne B. (1995), A Farm', Kate Millett's Feminist Art Colony, 1978-1994" (Ph.D. Dissertation, University of Maryland.

Keating, Anne B. and Kate Millett." (1993), "Contemporary Lesbian Writers of the United States: A Biobibliographical Critical Sourcebook" 361-369. eds. Denise C. Knight and Sandra Pollack. Westport,CT: Greenwood Press

Kerr, S. (1975), "On the Folly of Rewarding A, While Hoping for B." Academy of Management Journal, 18(4): 769-783.

Kiesler, S., and T. Finholt (1988), "The Mystery of RSI." American Psychologist, 43(12): 1004-1015.

Kilduff, Martin and Ajay Mehra (1997), Postmodernism and Organizational Research, The Academy of Management Review, Vol. 22, No. 2 - 453-481

Knapp, Peter (1986), Hegel's Universal in Marx, Durkheim, and Weber: The Role of Hegelian Ideas in the Origin of Sociology, Sociological Forum, Vol. 1, No. 4. (Autumn, 1986), pp. 586-609.

Knowles, M. (1984), The Adult Learner: A Neglected Species (3rd Ed.). Houston, TX: Gulf Publishing.

Kolb, D. A. (1984), Experiential learning: Experience as the source of learning and development, Englewood Cliffs, New Jersey, Prentice-Hall, Inc.

48 *The Major Theories of Sociology, and Contemporary Development*

Kuhn, Thomas (1983b), "Rationality and Theory Choice", Journal of Philosophy 80: 563-70.

Lammers, C. J. (1978), 'The Comparative Sociology of Organizations', Annual Review of Sociology 4, 485–510.

Lawrence, P., and J. Lorsch (1967), "Differentiation and Integration in Complex Organizations." Administrative Science Quarterly, 12: 1-30.

Lawler, E. E. I., and S. A. Morhman (1985), "Quality Circles After the Fad." Harvard Business Review, (January-February): 65-71.

Levinthal, D. A. and J. G. March (1993), "The Myopia of Learning." Strategic Management Journal, 14: 95-112.

Levinthal, D. A. and J. G. March (1981), "A Model of Adaptive Organizational Search." Journal of Economic Behavior and Organization, 2: 307-333.

Louis, M. R. (1985), "Perspectives on Organizational Culture" in P. J. Frost, L. F. Moore, M. R. Louis, C. C. Lundberg and J. Martin, Organizational Culture. Beverly Hills, Sage: 27-29.

Louis, M. R. (1985), "An Investigator's Guide to Workplace Culture" in P. J. Frost, L. F. Moore, M. R. Louis, C. C. Lundberg, and J. Martin. Organizational CLouis - Investigators Guide to Workplace Cultureulture. Beverly Hills, Sage: 73-93.

Louis, M. R. (1980), "Suprise and Sensemaking: What Newcomers Experience Entering Unfamiliar Organizational Settings." Administrative Science Quarterly, 25: 226-251.

Maanen Van, J. and S. R. Barley (1985), "Cultural Organization: Fragments of a Theory" in P. J. Frost, L. F. Moore, M. R. Louis, C. C. Lundberg, and J. Martin. OrVan Maanen & Barley - Cultural Orgs Fragments of a Theory Organizational Culture. Beverly Hills, Sage: 31-53.

Maanen, Van J. and S. Barley (1984), "Occupational Communities: Culture and control in organizations." Research in Organizational Behavior, 6: 287-365.

Maanen, Van J. and E. H. Schein (1979), "Toward of Theory of Organizational Socialization." Research in Organizational Behavior, 1: 209-264.

Maanen, Van J. (1977), "Experiencing Organization: Notes on the Meaning of Careers and Socialization" in J. Van Maanen. Organizational Careers: Some New Perspectives.

Macaulay, S. (1963), "Non-Contractual Relations in Business: A Preliminary Study." American Sociological Review, 28: 55-67.

Manning, P. K. (1977), "Talking and Becoming: A View of Organizational Socialization" in R. L. Blankenship. Colleagues in Organization: The Social Construction of Professional Work. London, Wiley & Sons: 181-205.

Mansfield, Pugh, D.S., R., and M. Warner (1975), Research in Organizational Behavior: A British Survey (London: Heinemann Educational Books, 1975).

March, J. G. (1996), "Learning to Be Risk Averse." Psychological Review, 103:22, 309-319

March, J. G. (1995), "The future, disposable organizations and the rigidities of imagination." Organization, 2: 427-440.

March, J. G. (1994), A Primer on Decision Making, New York, The Free Press.

March, J. G. (1994), Three Lectures on Efficiency and Adaptiveness in Organizations. Helsingfors, Sweden, Swedish School of Economics and Business Administration.

March, J. G. (1991), "Exploration and Exploitation" Organization Science, 21(February): 71-87.

March, J. G. (1991), "Organizational Consultants and Organizational Research, J of Applied Communication Research" Journal of Applied Communication Research, 19: 20-31.

March, J. G., and Z. Shapira (1971), Managerial Perspectives on Risk and risk Taking, Management Science, 33(11): 1404-1418.

March, J. G., and J. P. Olsen (1975), "The Uncertainty of the Past: Organizational Learning Under Ambiguity." European Journal of Political Research, 3: 147-171.

March, J. G., L. S. Sproull, et al. (1991), "Learning from Samples of One or Fewer." Organization Science, 2: 1-13.

March, J. G., and Z. Shapira (1992), "Variable Risk Preferences and the Focus of Attention." Psychological Review, 99(1): 172-183.

March, J. G., and J. P. Olsen (1995), Democratic Governance, New York, The Free Press.

50 *The Major Theories of Sociology, and Contemporary Development*

Marcson, S. (1960), The Scientist in American Industry: Some Organizational Determinants in Manpower Utilization, Princeton, NJ, Industrial Relations Section, Princeton University.

Martin, J. (1990), "Deconstructing organizational behavior taboos: The suppression of gender conflict in organizations." Organization Science, 1: 339-359.

Marx, Karl. (1964), Selected Writings in Sociology and Social Philosophy (translated by T.B. Bottomore). London: McGraw-Hill.

Marx, Karl. (1959), Toward the Critique of Hegel's Philosophy of right, in Marx and Engels, Basic Writings, Lewis S. Feuer (ed). New York: Doubleday & Co., Anchor Books.

Marx, Karl, and Friedrich Engels (1962), Selected Works, 2 vols. Moscow: Foreign Language Publishing House.

Merton, Robert K (1968), Social Theory and Social Structure. New York: Free Press.

Meyer, J. W., and B. Rowan (1977), "Institutional organizations: formal structure as myth and ceremony." American Journal of Sociology, 83: 340-363.

Meyer, J.W. (1980), The World Polity and the Authority of the Nation-State." In Studies of the Modern World-System, edited by A. Bergesen. New York: Academic Press.

Miller, V. D. and F. M. Jablin (1991), Information seeking during organizational entry: Influences, tactics, and a model of the process." Academy of Management Review, 16(1): 92-120.

Mills, A.J. (2002), "Studying the Gendering of Organizational Culture Over Time: Concerns, Issues and Strategies." Gender, Work, and Organizations. Vol. 9, No. 3 (June).

Mintz, B., and M. Schwartz (1985), The Power Structure of American Business, Chicago, University of Chicago Press.

Mitchell, Juliet (2000), Psychoanalysis and Feminism. Freud, Reich, Laing, and Women, 1974, reissued as Psychoanalysis and Feminism: A Radical Reassessment of Freudian Psychoanalysis, Basic Books.

Mitchell, Juliet (1987 editor), Selected Melanie Klein, The Free Press Mitchell, Juliet (1984) Women: The Longest Revolution, Virago Press.

References 51

Mitchell, Juliet (1985 editor), Feminine Sexuality. Jacques Lacan and the école freudienne, W. W. Norton & Company.

Mitchell, Juliet (1971), Woman's Estate, Harmondsworth, Penguin.

Millett, Kate (1969), Theory of Sexual Politics, Granada Publishing.

Mohanty, C.T. (1984), "Under Western Eyes: Feminist Scholarship and Colonial Discourses" boundary 2, Vol. 12, No. 3 On Humanism and the University I: The Discourse of Humanism. (Spring-Autumn): 333-358

Morgan, Gareth (1980), Paradigms, Metaphors, and Puzzle Solving in Organization Theory, Administrative Science Quarterly, Vol. 25, No. 4. 605-622

Moore, M. (2003), "The New Fiscal Sociology in Developing Countries" Paper presented at the annual meeting of the American Political Science Association, Philadelphia Marriott Hotel, Philadelphia, PA Online <.PDF> Retrieved 2008-04-21 from http://www.allacademic.com/meta/p64000_index.html

Morrison, Ken (1995), Marx, Durkheim, Weber: Formations of Modern Social Thought, London: Sage.

Mumby, D.K. and L.L. Putman (1992), "The Politics of Emotion: A Feminist Reading of Bounded Rationality." The Academy of Management Review, Vol. 17, No.3: 465-486.

Ness, Gayl D., and Steven R. Brechin (1988), Bridging the Gap: International Organizations as Organizations, International Organization, Vol. 42, No. 2. 245-273

Noble, D. F. (1979), "Social choice in machine design: The case of automatically controlled machine tools" in A. Zimbalist, Case Studies in the Labor Process. New York, Monthly Review Press.

Oakley, Ann (1997a), 'The Gendering of Methodology: An Experiment in Knowing', Paper given at the Swedish Collegium for Advanced Study in the Social Sciences, April.

Oakley, Ann (1998), Gender, Methodology and People's Ways of Knowing: Some Problems with Feminism and The Paradigm Debate in Social Science, Sociology (1998), 32: 707-731 Cambridge University Press doi:10.1177/0038038598032004005

52 *The Major Theories of Sociology, and Contemporary Development*

Orlikowski, W. J. (1991), "Integrated Information Environment or Matrix of Control? The Contradictory Implications of Information Technology." Accounting Management and Information, 1: 9-42.

O'Connor, Timothy (1993), Indeterminism and Free Agency: Three Recent Views, Philosophy and Phenomenological Research, Vol. 53, No. 3. 499-526

Orlikowski, W. J. (1996), "Improvising Organizational Transformation over Time: A Situated Change Perspective." Information Systems Research,

Orr, J. (1996), "About Copier Technicians" in Talking About Machines: An Ethnography of a Modern Job. Ithica, NY, ILR Press.

Padgett, J. F. (1995), "The emergence of simple ecologies of skill: a hypercycle approach to the economic organization" in B. Arthur, S. Durlauf and D. Lane. The Economy as a Complex Evolving System.

Parente, D. H. (1998), Across the manufacturing-marketing interface: Classification of significant

research. International Journal of Operations & Production Management, 18 (12), 1205.

Parker, M. (2002), "Queering Management and Organization" Gender, Work and Organization. Vol. 9. No.2 p. 146-166.

Parsons, Talcott (1971), The System of Modern Societies. Englewood Cliffs, NJ: Prentice-Hall.

Parsons, Talcott (1951), The Social System. Glencoe, IL: Free Press.

Perin, C. (1991), "The moral fabric of the office: Panopticon Discourse and Schedule Flexibilities" in P. S. Tolbert and S. Barley. Organizations and Professions, Volume 8, Research in the Sociology of Organizations. Greenwich, CT, JAI Press.

Perrow, C. (1983), "The Organizational Context of Human Factors Engineering." Administrative Science Quarterly, 28: 521-541.

Pfeffer, J. (1992), Managing with Power: Politics and Influence in Organizations, Boston, Harvard Business School Press.

Pfeffer, J. (1982), Organizations and Organization Theory, Pittman.

Pfeffer, J. and G. Salancik (1978), The External Control of Organizations, Harper & Row.

References 53

Pickering, J. M., and J. King (1995), "Hardwiring Weak Ties: Interorganizational Computer-Mediated Communication, Occupational Communities, and Organizational Change." Organization Science, 6(4): 479-486.

Polanyi, K. (1957), "The Economy as Instituted Process" in m. Granovetter and R. Swedberg. The Sociology of Economic Life. Boulder, CO, Westview Press.

Polanyi (1944), The Great Transformation, Boston, Beacon Press.

Pondy, Louis, R., and Ian 1. Mitroff (1979), "Beyond open system models of organization." Research in Organizational Behavior, 1: 3-39. Greenwich, CT: JAI Press.

Ritzer George (2000), Classical Sociological Theory, 3rd edition. New York: McGraw-Hill

Ritzer George (2000), Modern Sociological Theory, McGraw-Hill Humanities/Social Sciences/Languages, 5th edition

Ritzer George (2000), The McDonaldization Thesis: Extensions and Explorations, London: SAGE

Robbins, L. (1932), An Essay on the Nature and Significance of Economic Science, New York, New York University Press.

Rohlen, T. (1973), "The Education of a Japanese Banker" in Unknown, The Future of Organization Design: 526-534.

Roethlisberger F. J. and Dickson W. J. (1941), Management and the Worker, Cambridge: Harvard University Press, 1941, p. 524.

Roloff, M. E. (1981), Interpersonal Communication: The Social Exchange Approach, Beverly Hills, CA, Sage.

Rowan, B. (1982), "Organizational Structure and the institutional environment: the case of public schools." Administrative Science Quarterly, 27: 259-279.

Rowbotham, Sheila (1975), Hidden from History. 300 Years of Women's Oppression and the Fight against It, Pluto Press, 1975

Roy, D. F. (1959), "Banana Time: Job Satisfaction and Informal Interaction." Human Organization, 18: 158-168.

Salaman, Graeme, and Kenneth Thompson (1980 eds.), Control and Ideology in Organizations Milton Keynes: The Open University Press.

Salaman, Graeme (1979), Organizations, resistance and control, Longman.

54 *The Major Theories of Sociology, and Contemporary Development*

Scarselletta, M. (1996), "The infamous lab error: education, skill, and quality in medical technician's work" in S. Barley and J. Orr. Between craft and science: technical work in US settings, Ithaca, NY, ILR Press.

Schein, E. (1996), "Culture: The Missing Concept in Organization Studies." Administrative Science Quarterly, 41(2): 229-240.

Scott, W. R. (2004), Institutional Theory: Contributing to a Theoretical Research Program, Great Minds in Management: The Process of Theory Development, Ken G. Smith and Michael A. Hitt, eds. Oxford UK: Oxford University Press.

Scott W.R. (2004), Reflections on a Half-Century of Organizational Sociology, Annual Review of Sociology, 30:1–21.

Scott, W. R. (2003), Organizations: Rational, Natural & Open Systems (5th Edition).

Scott, W. R. (1995), Institutions and organizations. Thousand Oaks, CA: Sage.

Scott, W. R. (1991), Unpacking institutional arguments. In P. J. DiMaggio & W. W. Powell (Eds.), The new institutionalism in organizational analysis (pp. 164-182). Chicago: University of Chicago Press.

Scott, W. R. and John W. Meyer (1983), "The organization of societal sectors." In John W. Meyer and W. Richard Scott, Organizational Environments: Ritual and Rationality: 129-153. Beverly Hills, CA: Sage.

Seidman, S. (1994), "Queering Sociology, Socializing Queer Theory: An Introduction." Sociological Theory, Vol. 12, No.2: 166-177.

Selznick, P. (1984), "Guiding Principles and Interpretation: A Summary" in. TVA and the Grass Roots. Berkeley, UC Berkeley Press: 249-266.

Selznick, Philip (1948), Foundations of the Theory of Organization, American Sociological Review, Vol. 13, No. 1. 25-35

Selznick, Philip (1943), An Approach to a Theory of Bureaucracy, American Sociological Review, Vol. 8, No. 1. 47-54.

Shafritz, J.M., Ott, J.S. (Eds.2001), "Classics of Organization Theory", 5th Ed., Harcourt, 2001

Shea, G. F. (1994), Mentoring: Helping Employees Reach their Full Potential, American Management Association.

References 55

Simon, Herbert A. (1976), Administrative Behavior. A Study of Decision-Making Processes in Administrative Organization, Third Edition, The Free Press, Collier Macmillan Publishers, London, UK, 1976.

Simon, Herbert A. (1973), "Applying Information Technology to Organizational Design", in Public Administration Review, Vol. 33, No. 3, May/June 1973, pp. 268-278.

Simon, Herbert A (1969), The Sciences of the Artificial, The Massachusetts Institute of Technology, The Murray Printing Company, USA, 1969.

Smith, A. (1776), Wealth of Nations, Chicago, University of Chicago Press.

Smith, Dorothy E. (2005), Institutional ethnography: A sociology for people, Rowman Altamira Publisher.

Smith, M. R. (1994), "Technological Determinism in American Culture" in M. R. Smith and L. Marx. Does Technology Drive History? Cambridge, MA, MIT Press: 1-35.

Smith, Dorothy E, (1987), The Everyday World as Problematic: A Feminist Sociology, Toronto: University of Toronto Press.

Smith, Dorothy E, (1984), The Renaissance of Women Knowledge Reconsidered: A Feminist Overview, Ursula Franklin, et al. (eds.), Ottawa: Canadian Research Institute for the Advancement of Women, 3-14.

Smith, Dorothy E., (1977), Feminism and Marxism: A Place to Begin, A Way to Go, Vancouver: New Star Books.

Smircich, L. (1983), "Concepts of Culture and Organizational Analysis" Administrative Science Quarterly, 28(3): 339-358.

Spivak, Gayatri C (1999), A Critique of Post-Colonial Reason: Toward a History of the Vanishing Present (Harvard UP, 1999).

Spivak, Gayatri C (1990), The Post-Colonial Critic: Interviews, Strategies, Dialogues. Ed. Sarah Harasym. (London: Routledge, 1990).

Spivak, Gayatri C (1988), "Can the Subaltern Speak?" in Cary Nelson and Larry Grossberg, eds. Marxism and the interpretation of Culture (Chicago: University of Illinois Press, p.271-313.

Spivak, Gayatri C (1988), Selected Subaltern Studies. Ed. with Ranajit Guha, Oxford.

Strauss, G. (1955), "Group Dynamics and Intergroup Relations" in W. Whyte, F. Money, and Mot. New York, Harper & Row.

56 *The Major Theories of Sociology, and Contemporary Development*

Starkey P. (1992), The early development of numerical reasoning, Congnition,43(2):93-126.

Stacey, J. (1996), In the Name of the Family: rethinking family values in the postmodern age. Boston: Beacon Press.

Stacey, J. (1990), Brave New Families: Stories of Domestic Upheaval in Late Twentieth-Century America. Basic Books.

Stacey, J. (1983), Patriarchy and Socialist Revolution in China. University of California Press.

Stacey, J., Bereaud, S. & Daniels, J. (Eds.) (1974), And Jill Came Tumbling After: Sexism in American Eduction. Dell.

Stinchcombe, A. L. (1959), "Bureaucrats and Craft Administration of Production: A Comparative Study." Administrative Science Quarterly, 4(2): 168:187.

Taylor, Ralph (2003), Fear of crime, social ties, and collective efficacy: Maybe masquerading measurement, maybe déj`a vu all over again, Justice Quarterly 19:4, 773-792.

Terry, Maley (2004), Max Weber and the Iron Cage of Technology, Bulletin of Science Technology Society 2004; 24; 69

Tilly, Charles (1981), "Useless Durkheim." Pp. 95-108 in As Sociology Meets History New York: Academic Press.

Tilly, Charles (1978), From Mobilization to Revolution. Reading, MA: Addison-Wesley.

Tiryakian, E.A. (1981), The sociological import of a metaphor: tracking the source of Max Weber's 'iron cage' Sociological inquiry 51,1: 27-33

Thompson, P. and McHugh, D. (2002), Work Organizations, 3rd edition, Palgrave.

Thompson, James D. (1967/ 2003), Organizations in Action: Social Science Bases of Administrative Theory, with a new preface by Mayer N. Zald and a new introduction by W. Richard Scott, New Brunswick, New Jersey: Transaction Publishers.

Thorne, Barrie (1984), "Nomenclature, Gender, and the 1984 Election," Women and Language VIII, No. 1/2 39-40.

Thorne, Barrie, Virginia Powell, Beverly Purrington, Regi Teasley, and Carol Wharton, (1984), "Teaching the Sociology of Sex and Gender," American Sociological Association Teaching Newsletter, 1(4), August 1984, pp. 2-7.

Thorne, Barrie (1982),"Guidelines for Introductory Sociology," in Sex and Gender in the Social Sciences: Reassessing the Introductory Course (Judith M. Gappa and Janice Pearce). Washington, D.C.: American Sociological Association Teaching Resources Center, 1982.

Tolbert, P. S., and L. G. Zucker (1983), "Institutional sources of change in the formal structure of organizations: the diffusion of civil service reform, 1880-1935." Administrative Science Quarterly, 28: 22-39.

Trist, E. L., and K. W. Bamforth (1951), "Some social and psychological consequences of the longwall method of coal getting" Human Relations, Vol. 4, No. 1, 3-38 (1951).

Trist, E. L. (1978), "On socio-technical systems" in W. A. Pasmore and J. J. Sherwood. Socio-technical Systems. La Jolla, CA, University Associates.

Tönnies Ferdinand Gesamtausgabe (1998), Tönnies› Complete Works 24 vols., since 1998, critically edited by Lars Clausen, Alexander Deichsel, Cornelius Bickel, Carsten Schlüter-Knauer, and Uwe Carstens; Publisher: Walter de Gruyter, Berlin/New York)

Tucker, Francis (1969), White-Nonwhite Age Differences and the Accurate Assessment of the "Cost of Being Negro" Social Forces, Vol. 47, No. 3 .343-345

Tushman, M. L., and P. Anderson (1986), "Technological discontinuities and organizational environments." Administrative Science Quarterly, 31: 439-465.

Turkle, S. (1985), The Second Self: Computers and the Human Spirit, New York, Simon & Schuster.

Turner J. H. (1990) Emile Durkheim's Theory of Social Organization, Social Forces, Vol. 68, No. 4. 1089-1103.

Uzzi, Brian (1996), The Sources and Consequences of Embeddedness for the Economic Performance of Organizations: The Network Effect, American Sociological Review, Vol. 61, No. 4. 674-698

Uzzi, Brian. (1993), "The Dynamics of Inter-organizational Networks: Embeddedness and Economic Action." Ph.D. Dissertation, Sociology Department, State University of New York, Stony Brook, NY.

58 *The Major Theories of Sociology, and Contemporary Development*

Wallerstein, Immanuel (online 2007), The Ecology and the Economy: what is rational" http://www.binghamton.edu/fbc/iwecoratl.htm

Wallerstein, Immanuel (2000), The Essential Wallerstein. The New York Press. New York.

Wallerstein, Immanuel (1974), The Modern World-System I: Capitalist Agriculture and the

Origins of the European World-Economy in the Sixteenth Century. New York: Academic Press.

Weber, Max (1946), "Science as a Vocation" in H.H. Gerth and C. Wright Mills (Translated and edited), From Max Weber: Essays in Sociology, pp. 129-156, New York: Oxford University Press, 1946.

Weber, Max (1949), "Objectivity in social science and social policy" in the methodology of the social sciences, translated by Edward a Shils and Henry A Finch, New York: Free Press 1949.

Weber, Max (1904-05/1992), The Protestant Ethic and the Spirit of Capitalism. trans. T. Parsons/intro. A. Giddens. London: Routledge.

Weber, Max 1903-1917 (1949), The Methodology of the Social Sciences. Edward Shils and Henry Finch (eds.). New York: Free Press.

Weber, Max (1962), Basic Concepts in Sociology by Max Weber. Translated & with an introduction by H.P. Secher. New York: The Citadel Press.

Weber, Max. (1904/1930), The Protestant Ethic and the Spirit of Capitalism, Translated by Talcott Parson, New York: Charles Scribner's Sons.

Weber, Max. (1946/1958), From Max Weber. Translated and edited by H. H. Gerth and C. Wright Mills. New York: Galaxy.

Weick, K. (1985), "The Significance of Corporate Culture" in P. J. Frost, L. F. Moore, M. R. Louis, C. C. Lundberg, and J. Martin. Organizational Culture. Beverly Hills, Sage: 381-389.

Wieland, George F. (1974), The Contributions of Organizational Sociology to the Practice of Management: A Book Review Essay, The Academy of Management Journal, Vol. 17, No. 2. (Jun. 1974), pp. 318-333.

Williamson, O. (1985), "Contractual Man" in the Economic Institutions of Capitalism, The Free Press: 43-63.

Williamson, O. (1981), "The Economics of Organization: The Transaction Cost Approach." American Journal of Sociology, 87(3): 548-577.

Williamson, O. (1975), Markets and Hierarchies, The Free Press.

Wiggenhorn, W. (1990), "Motorola U: When Training Becomes an Education." Harvard Business Review, 5(4): 35-51.

Zelizer, V. A. (1978), "Human Values and the Market: The Case of Life Insurance and Death in 19th-Century America." American Journal of Sociology, 84: 591-610.

Zey-Ferrell, Mary (1981), Criticisms of the Dominant Perspective on Organizations, The Sociological Quarterly 22:181-205

Zuboff, S. (1984), In the Age of the Smart Machine, New York, Basic Books.

Zucker, Lynne G. (1983), "Organizations as institutions In Samuel B. Bacharach (ed), Perspectives in Organizational Sociology Theory and Research ASA Series, Vol 2 Greenwich, CT JAI Press (forthcoming).

Zucker, Lynne G. (1977), The Role of Institutionalization in Cultural Persistence, American Sociological Review, Vol. 42, No. 5:726-743

2

The Debates Between the Quantitative and Qualitative Methods: An Ontology and Epistemology of the Qualitative Method

Outline

This chapter discusses how we see the divide in sociology between researchers employing qualitative versus quantitative methods.· First, the chapter highlights, from a historical perspective, the philosophical commitments and political and/or ethical considerations that have shaped how social scientists approach or think about the problem of "qualitative versus quantitative." Second, it highlights the features of successful qualitative-based work by discussing three exemplary texts." The chapter also points out what we see as indicative of a core commitment to qualitative methodological principles in these works.

Finally, the chapter discusses three researchers' works that follow the tradition, pinpointing which aspects of the tradition they wish to build upon, and making the case for how knowledge in their expected field of research would be advanced by proceeding in a qualitative vein, whether in a "pure" way or as part of a "mixed methods" approach.

Introduction

The debates between quantitative and qualitative methods are essential for and against positivism and interpretive perspectives of social inquiry. Methods associated with positivism are grounded in the work of Comte, Mill, and Durkheim in social sciences, who believed that the social world can be viewed in the same way as natural sciences. In contrast, philosophers like Dilthey, Rickert, and Weber who followed the Kantian tradition challenged the positivist philosophy and developed the interpretive approach (Smith 1983). The positivist tradition of social inquiry has been followed by quantitative scholars and the interpretive path by qualitative scholars. In my literature search, I found engagement in debates from both quantitative and

62 *The Debates Between the Quantitative and Qualitative Methods*

qualitative scholars. However, as a qualitative sociologist, I did not focus very much on what quantitative scholars say; therefore, most of the authors I have cited in this chapter are from qualitative disciplines. In this chapter, I will first explore why there is a debate and the fundamental differences between qualitative and quantitative methods in sociology. To understand this, I will explain the major theoretical ground of debates between qualitative and quantitative methodologies in terms of their origin from major classical sociological authors Durkheim and Weber. I think to understand the root cause of debate; it is essential to understand its historical root, its ontological and epistemological position, as well as its paradigms and methodological approaches. There is a debate between quantitative and qualitative scholars from the epistemological level. However, there are no debates on the objectives of research because both methods have been trying to capture the social reality and investigate the causes of social problems. To explore this situation, I will discuss the ontological, epistemological, and theoretical grounds and paradigms of the qualitative method. Quantitative scholars follow the positivist approach and qualitative scholars follow the constructivist and interpretive approaches. At the epistemological level, debates are about the application of knowledge. Quantitative scholars follow the established notion (deductive) to explore the social reality and qualitative scholars construct the knowledge by doing inductive research. In the second section, I will briefly reexamine the development of interpretive philosophy in social science and note the three best exemplary works of qualitative sociologists, followed by how researchers apply the qualitative method in their research in the third section of this essay.

Section 1

Debates on Quantitative Versus Qualitative Historical Perspective

There has been a long debate between qualitative and quantitative sociologists. These debates in social sciences are linked directly to the assumptions about ontology, epistemology, and human nature (Morgan and Smircich 1986). Rudra and Peter J. Katzenstein (2005) state that most scholars think of the theoretical universe as divided between different schools of thought. What most consistently divide these schools are not their substantive claims but the metatheoretical *cognitive structures* within which such claims are formulated. These structures shape what phenomena are considered important and explainable, how research questions about such phenomena are posed, what concepts and methods are most suited for investigating these questions, whether the objectives of the investigation are to confirm axiomatic laws or engender an interpretive understanding of contexts, and what standards are reasonable for evaluating specific research products. The necessarily abstract responses these questions elicit reflect enduring ontological and epistemological, metatheoretical, assumptions shared by members of some research communities but not others. Social scientific disciplines and subfields are often characterized by the emergence of, competition between, and evolution or degeneration of discrete traditions of scholarly research. These traditions distinguish themselves based on programmatic understandings that provide the foundation for the construction, communication, and evaluation of various forms of models or narratives (Sil and Katzenstein 2005, page 4). I agree with Sil and Katzenstein's arguments. The debates between quantitative and qualitative are embedded from the origin of the practice of the social investigation, which firstly assumes that social reality can be quantified and secondly assumes that social reality cannot be explained with the application of mathematics but can be interpreted in the words.

The Distinction Between Qualitative and Quantitative

There is a fundamental distinction between qualitative and quantitative studies. Both have different epistemological positions. Quantitative methodology is associated with positivist epistemology and qualitative method with interpretive epistemology. The quantitative method refers to the collection of numerical data and analysis through using statistical tools, with an emphasis on facts. On the other hand, qualitative methodologies refer to the forms of field data collection that emphasize and rely on understanding (Marshall 1998). Quantitative and qualitative methods have different assumptions, purposes, and approaches to researchers' roles. For example, quantitative researchers assume that social facts have objective reality and can be separated into variables. Those identified variables can be measured with fixed methods and observed from outside (Lincoln and Guba 1985). In contrast, qualitative researchers assume that social reality is socially constructed and that variables can be complex, interwoven, and difficult to measure. They assume that to understand social reality, the researcher needs to be in the field physically, mentally, and emotionally (Goffman 1959). The quantitative method is embedded through positivist paradigms and the qualitative method is grounded on interpretive paradigms. Qualitative research tends to start with the what, how, and why type of inquiry, and quantitative tends to investigate how much or how many (Draper 2004).

64 *The Debates Between the Quantitative and Qualitative Methods*

Further, Draper (2004) notes that "qualitative research can thus be broadly described as interpretive and naturalistic; in that, it seeks to understand and explain belief and behaviors within the context that they occur" (page 642). Qualitative researchers contextualize the problem from the root; they interpret the situation with personal involvement. They are flexible and believe that researchers should have the freedom to acquire information in their way, which provides a way to generate new epistemology.

On the other hand, the quantitative methodology is based on the positivist approach, which has, as a fundamental limit, the extent to which the methods and procedures of the natural sciences could be applied to the social world (Devers 1999). There has been a canonical tradition of positivist approaches to investigating social facts. In sociology, this approach was developed and used by Emile Durkheim (1858–1917), who examined social behavior as social facts. The primary task of sociology was the description and observation of social facts. According to Durkheim, the study of social facts is the first step in the program of scientific sociology because they: (1) identify collective phenomena separate from individuals; (2) they are not part of individual psychological motivations; (3) they are the subject matter of observation; (4) they are diffused throughout the society; and (5) they exist in their own right independent of the individual (Durkheim 1938, pages 2, 10, 13, as cited by Morrison 1995, page 334). Durkheim advocated that social facts should be considered as things. To do so, Durkheim provided the three characteristics of social facts: (1) they are "general throughout society" and "diffused within the group"; (2) they are "external to individuals" and exist independently of their will; and (3) they exercise external constraint over individuals, which is recognized by the power of external coercion, by the existence of some sanction, or by the resistance offered against individual efforts to violate them (Durkheim 1938, pages 55–56 as cited by Mission 1995, page 334). According to this approach, social realities are different from ideas, and ideas should be considered as things. For Durkheim, idea has no reality. He distinguished sociology from philosophy and other social sciences disciplines. Durkheim's sociology is empirical and investigates causes. The sociological method is objective; social facts are things and are studied as such, and the sociological method is unique to sociology because social facts are social (Morrison 1995). Durkheim was trying to relate the sociological phenomena with the natural sciences where facts remain unchanged in a specified period and can be replicated in other environments. His major objective was to establish the compatibility of sociological events with the natural sciences. The positivist social scientists still follow the same traditions.

Durkheimian Notion

Based on the Durkheimian notion, quantitative sociologists claim that the qualitative method produces a scientific result that can be assessed and validated with the application of statistical tools. They state that the quantitative method can be replicable and generalized in a broader arena. They criticize the qualitative method and question the representation, reliability, and validation of the research outcome. Further, they argue that the qualitative method is impressionistic, piecemeal, and idiosyncratic and this method cannot be replicable and comparable and cannot capture the notion of social problems in the holistic approach (Bryman 1984). Another criticism they pose about the qualitative method is the researcher's relationships with the population and the possibility of human bias because of the close relationships. These claims of quantitative sociologists about the qualitative method are rooted in positivism, based on the social situation as a natural environment and concern for research criteria such as internal and external validities, reliability, and objectivity. In this perspective, their focus is on how to define and measure concepts. They believe that concepts must be made observable because, if the concept cannot be observed and measured, it does not exist (Lin 1998). Such prescriptions of making science have been challenged and methodological pluralism has been developed through multiple and diverse research procedures (Jessor 1996). This notion was first challenged by Max Weber (1864–1920), who developed the interpretive approach to investigate social events and the social environment.

Ontological Assumptions

Max Weber

The ontological assumptions of the qualitative sociologist differ from positivist arguments because the social world is seen as more dynamic, contextual, complex, and socially constructed. Qualitative sociologists do not agree that society can be examined as the natural environment. This notion was primarily explained by Max Weber, who stated that there are fundamental differences between natural and social sciences such as (1) the subject matter of natural sciences and social sciences are different, where physical science studies natural events and social science studies social events; (2) each seeks to obtain different kinds of knowledge, i.e., in natural sciences, knowledge is of the external world which can be explained in terms of valid laws – in the social science, knowledge must be "internal" or "subjective" in the sense that human beings have an inner nature that must be understood to explain

66 *The Debates Between the Quantitative and Qualitative Methods*

outward events; and (3) in natural sciences, it is sufficient to observe events in the natural world and to report relationships between things observed. On the contrary, in social sciences, investigations must go beyond observation to look at how individuals act on their understanding, and how this "understanding" may be related to their social action (Weber 1978, Economy and Society, pages 3–26, as noted by Morrison 1995, page 274). Weber focused on social action and the role of individual actors. He did not provide rules for social inquiry (as Durkheim had established rules to investigate social facts) but focused on how social action can be understood (*verstehen*).

Weber focused on social action which involves four central concepts: the concept of understanding or *verstehen*; the concept of interpretive understanding; the concept of subjective meaning; and the concept of social action (Morrison 1995). Weber looked at sociology as an interpretive science. In his own words, "Sociology is a science which attempts the interpretive understanding of social action to arrive at a causal explanation of its course and effects. Inaction is included in all human behavior when and as far as the acting individual attaches a subjective meaning to it. Action in this sense may be either overt or purely inward or subjective; it may consist of positive intervention in a situation or of deliberately refraining from such intervention or passively acquiescing in the situation. Action is social as far as, by the subjective meaning attached to it by the acting individual, it takes account of the behavior of others and is thereby oriented in its course" (Weber 1978, page 4, as cited by Morrison 1995, page 274). This definition provides a ground to argue that social events can only be understood with the application of interpretive paradigms because social events are not fixed and cannot be explained as things (which was proposed by Durkheim and other positivist theorists). The social environment is complex and changeable and human actors act meaningfully. To reveal the social reality, the investigator needs to understand the meaning of social action. *Verstehen* is seen as a concept and a method central to a rejection of positivistic social science. It refers to understanding the meaning of social action from the actor's point of view.

Weber's notion accepts that human beings think, have feelings, communicate through language, attribute meaning to their environment, and have different beliefs and characters. Because of this reality, social science theories are unlikely to apply across time and place. They cannot be the sole source of hypotheses or cannot be judged only through a deductive approach. Therefore, to reveal the social truth, qualitative inquiry (inductive approach) has been widely used in the social sciences. The notion of the qualitative method is to find out the social truth through in-depth inquiry. In other words, qualitative research is a broad umbrella term for research that describes and explains persons' experiences, behaviors, interactions, and social context (Fossey et al. 2002) through inductive inquiry.

My objective in this chapter is to examine the debates of quantitative and qualitative methods historically. The qualitative method was developed as a counter to the positivist approach; therefore, it is important to know how qualitative methods were developed and who the major figures to bring in the current situation were. Many institutions have contributed to the development of the qualitative method in the United States such as Columbia University, Harvard University, Michigan University, and so on. However, the Chicago School is considering the original institution for sociological knowledge production, particularly the qualitative method.

I think there is a major contribution of Max Weber in the development of the qualitative method; however, the documents do not illustrate his direct influence. I tried to trace the date when the *verstehen* was written and how it was adopted in sociological research. I did not find any illustration of Max Weber in the historical documents. Supporting the opposite viewpoint, Jennifer Platt (1985) has provided evidence stating that there was no Max Weber's *verstehen* influence in the early American sociology. According to her, "interviews and documentary sources show that he was not influential in the American sociology generally or in qualitative research before First World War" (page 448). She gives an outline of the historical account of qualitative method development in the United States and universally acknowledges the contribution of the Chicago School.

The Chicago School

"Crucial steps in the emergence of qualitative research methods are generally agreed to have taken place at the University of Chicago in the 1920 and 1930, and then more specifically in the elaboration of participant observation as a distinct method in the decade following World War II and classic exemplars were produced there; the argument will, therefore, focus mainly on that bodywork, and on the extent to which Weber's Verstehede Soziologie was known to those producing it, drawn on by them in their thinking about it, and was necessary to produce the research outcomes" (page 449). However, the development of the qualitative research method was not solely the production of American sociologists. Even in the United States, scholars from Germany applied the qualitative method in the United States. However, there is no traceable record of whether they were influenced by Max Weber or not. Most importantly, Platt (1985) states that even Parson (Talcott Parsons was an American sociologist of the classical tradition, best known for his social

68 *The Debates Between the Quantitative and Qualitative Methods*

action theory and structural functionalism. Parsons is considered one of the most influential figures in sociology in the 20th century) was not aware of Max Weber when he went to Heidelberg in 1925. If so, then it raises a more interesting point about Weber. His influence came late but became dominant in a brief period. Emerson (2001), who provides an outline of qualitative method history, cites Platt (1985) to show the importance of the Chicago School but does not illustrate her argument about Max Weber. However, one cannot deny that the University of Chicago's sociology department was the first to challenge the positivism tradition of research design and significantly contributed to the development and diffusion of the qualitative method. The Chicago tradition was diffused to Western Europe and Western European influence was similarly diffused to the United States.

Transmission of knowledge has been occurring throughout the history of civilization; however, this process was more accelerated since the "tracing back to the SOCIETAS CIVILIS in Aristotelian tradition" (Kocka 2004). Particularly in Europe, it has a long association with politics and society. Kocka (2004) states that the modern interpretation of society began in the 17th and 18th centuries through the writers of enlightenment such as John Locke, Adam Ferguson, Montesquieu, the Encyclopedists, Immanuel Kant, etc. Sociological research has a positive connotation with the Enlightenment process. Sociological research history is essential to understand the production and circulation of knowledge. History gives the idea to categorize contemporary thoughts and make judgments about the process of knowledge production throughout. Further historical accounts provide the experiences faced by the authors, explain their relationship to contemporary society, explore their research method and analysis, and also provide information about the debates and explanation within their context as well as with the previous authors, predecessors, allies, and rival connections (Jean-Michel Chapoulie 2004).

The Positivist Research Paradigms

Bronislaw Malinowski

As a supportive argument about the historical challenges to the positivist research paradigms, Robert Emerson (2001) provides extensive evidence of empirical research conducted by British anthropologists. He takes the example of Bronislaw Malinowski's extensive fieldwork as a "model of fieldwork as a means for direct observation requiring intensive, prolonged stay amid the daily life of those studied, proclaimed and promoted by the publication of Argonauts of the Western Pacific 1922" (Emerson 2001, page 6). Malinowski provides the importance of being in the field. Malinowski's

Section 1 69

description provides two aspects of the extensive field method: the first is how important it is to be in the field, and the second is the historical value of participant observation, which equally implies in the current context a major challenge for the quantitative research design.

In sociology according to Emerson (2001), "the roots of sociological fieldwork extended back in late 19th-century social reform movements, in which observers sought to describe the living conditions of the urban poor to change and better them. Particularly significant for later sociological fieldwork was the social survey movement. Charles Booth's Life and Labor of the People in London (1902) remains the best known of these massive surveys, one more systematic form of the "social exploration" (Keating 1976:11ff) following the dramatic changes produced by rapid industrialization and urbanization" (page 9). This survey conducted by Booth and others (Life and other) was applied by DuBois in the study of the Philadelphia Negro (1899). In the United States, the classic Chicago School Sociology Department dominated academic research during the first century of the 20th century.

Jean-Michel Chapoulie (2004) notes that Chicago sociology was paramount to diffuse the western modality of research sequences, particularly the ethnic relation to white, protestant Anglo-Saxons. Nigel Fielding (2005) states that "with the quantitative approach growing alongside the general march of positivism and the budding discipline of statistics, the Chicago School is usually seen as the champion of the qualitative method during sociology's childhood" (Fine 1995; Platt 1995, 1996; Abbott 1990; Becker 1999). We know the school for its declaration that the city offered a vast natural laboratory for exploring social phenomena, using ethnographic methods. This was the stance of the first Chicago School and then regarded as the top US sociology department and associated with the empirical approach of figures like W. I. Thomas (appointed in 1895) and Robert Park. But in 1927, William Ogburn was appointed to bring in "scientific" sociology based on statistics, and by the 1940s, with Parsons' rise at Harvard and Columbia's growing dominance in survey research and opinion polling, the US sociology had shifted to a quantitative paradigm. In the 1950s, a group of quantitative sociologists came to Chicago from Columbia and Everett Hughes stood virtually alone as a representative of the earlier tradition (Fielding 2005).

Robert E. Park

The leadership of Robert E. Park who joined Chicago University in 1913 helped to explore the city area's problems associated with the anonymous rooming dwellers, occupational institution forms, and development change (Emerson 2001). Park emphasized the value of the fieldwork, its importance,

70 *The Debates Between the Quantitative and Qualitative Methods*

and its application. Emerson quotes McKinney (1966, page 71) to illustrate that Park's focus on fieldwork is much more relevant in this context: "you have been told to go grubbing in the library, thereby accumulating a mass of notes and a liberal coating of grime. You have been told to choose a problem wherever you can find musty stakes of routine records based on trivial schedules prepared by tired bureaucrats and filled out by reluctant applicants for aid or fuzzy do-gooders or indifferent clerks. This is called "getting your hands dirty in real research." Those who counsel you are wise and honorable, the reasons they offer are of immense value. But one more thing is needful, firsthand observation. Go and sit on the luxury hotels and the doorsteps of the flophouses; sit on Gold Coast settees and the slum shakedowns; sit in Orchestra Hall and the Star and Garter Burlesque. In short, gentleman, get the seat of your pants dirty in real research" (page 11). Park provides insights into the real settings which cannot be achieved without "being in the real field." Park with Burgess developed the multi-method approach. Emerson (2001) notes the contribution of Thomas and Znaniecki through a monograph on the Polish immigrants (The Polish Peasant in Europe and America 1917).

This was based on a diary, a life history written by ordinary people. These combinations of field research methods show that case study, life history, participant observation, interviews, and autobiography analysis were considered a multi-method approach. A case study was based on direct observation and informal interviews. The observation method was used by Nels Anderson's "the Hobo 1923," Paul G. Cressey's "the taxi dance hall 1932," and Fredric Thrasher's "Gang 1927." This research was done without formal information about the "subject, the research population" (Emerson 2001). In the early Chicago School research, case study was not achieved by the investigator's systematic participation role (Platt 1996). Emerson (2001) notes that in the early time of the Chicago School research, "the case study had tended to separate observation, on the one hand, understanding the point of view of those studied through personal documents on the other, participant observation displaced this dichotomy, transforming the prior heavily naturalistic conception of observation into a more experiential one emphasizing empathetic involvement as a means for grasping local and subjective meaning" (page 13). Anderson, Cressey, and Thrasher used the observation method but did not describe it as participant observation (Emerson 2001). I think that it clearly shows that the Chicago School was the pioneer in developing (qualitative) observation method in the United States, which later on diffused back to Europe (first it was initiated in Europe and then diffused to the USA) and diffused to the rest of the world.

Section 1 71

Likewise, the Chicago School was also a pioneer in the development of field interview techniques in the United States. The interview tool is a major data collection technique in contemporary sociological research. However, up to the second decade of the 20th century, in-depth interview method was not developed in sociological research. There was a "verbatim interview" where researchers were conducting unstructured interviews which often relied on the mood of the interviewee. Cavan (1929, page 107) states that "It represented instead an attempt to obtain as nearly as possible a 'report of the interview, in anecdotal form, including gestures, facial expressions, questions, and remarks of the interviewer'" (recited from Lee 2004). According to Lee (2004), "In much of the writing associated with the Chicago School the term 'interview' is scarcely differentiated from the term 'life history.'"

Life history was a form of autobiography usually written by a research subject. Like more modern versions of the unstructured interview, it involved a degree of sustained interaction between the researcher and research participant and was unstructured in form and focused on subjective elements of the interviewee's life. "This last aspect reflected the importance to early writers in the Chicago tradition of the concept of "personality" (something overshadowed by the attention later writers have paid to the work of George Herbert Mead)" (page 4). However, the historical account of the Chicago school in the academic debate is not fully out of criticism. David Nock's article "The myth about "myths of the Chicago School": Evidence from Floyd Nelson house," in The American Sociologist, Volume 35, Number 1/March 2004, raises the questions on the reliability of authorship of the Chicago School in the qualitative method development: "Some important work (Bulmer, Harvey) in the history of sociology questions whether the Chicago School should be identified with qualitative as opposed to more quantitative, statistical, and correlation methods. This paper will examine whether *this* characterization is a "myth" or whether there was some factual basis for this association of Chicago sociology with qualitative research and a broader epistemological stance critical of radical neo-positivism" (from the abstract). Although I do not think it makes any difference whether Chicago School was the pioneer or not, its contribution to the qualitative method of knowledge production cannot be avoided.

The above paragraph provides a general overview of how the qualitative method was developed. In this context, one can state that qualitative methods originated in anthropology and diffused to sociological research. The historical context of the qualitative method was not a planned phenomenon, but methodological knowledge was developed by learning by doing. Emerson's (2001) "Contemporary Field Research, Perspective, and Formulations"

72   *The Debates Between the Quantitative and Qualitative Methods*

provides a nice explanation of this development trend. Likewise, other authors such as Norman K. Denzin and Yvonna S. Lincoln (2000) also provide a historical account of qualitative research method development and the Chicago School's contribution. According to them, the history of qualitative research in the human disciplines consists of seven moments, which are the traditional (1900–1950); the modernist or golden age (1950–1970); blurred genres (1970–1986); the crisis of representation (1986–1990); the postmodern, a period of experimental and new ethnographies (1990–1995); post-experimental inquiry (1995–2000); and the future (2000–) (re-cited from Pertti Alasuutari, 2004, page 565). This notion shows that there is a shift in the use of qualitative methods since 1960, because of the modern technology development (use of tape recorders, shorthand writing, etc.). Raymond M. Lee (2004) provides a historical account of recording technologies and the interview in sociology, from 1920 to 2000, which is significant in terms of method development to track the debates between qualitative and quantitative methods.

The above historical account presents qualitative method development, particularly in the United States, and British, German, and French scholars' influence on the United States or the United States or vice versa. The literature is silent about the rest of the world's contribution to sociological knowledge formation. This seems a field of new research. Whatever is the case qualitative method has a long history of applicability in researching society in both the action and the academic fields, which challenges the positivist approaches to research? Why qualitative research? Why ethnographic theory? Richard A. Shweder (1996) has the following answer: "ethnographic theories will tell us what it means to be differently situated—what it is like to have different preferences (values, goals, tastes, desires, ideas of personal well-being and developmental competence) and/or what it is like to live with different constraints (information, causal beliefs, abilities, dispositions, resources, technology, systems of domination or control). Its methods make use of the things people say and do to each other in everyday life, as well as the things they strategically and deliberately say and do to us on special "scientific" occasions (for example, when we ask them to answer questions in an interview or to narrate a life history), to construct a plausible and intelligible account about what it is like to be someone else. Yet true ethnography also aims to deepen our understanding of "otherness" and to move us beyond the cover stories, idealized self-representations, well-rehearsed verbal modes of public image management, and strategic manipulations of those whose lives we seek to understand" (pages 17–18). The qualitative method covers many methods such as participant-observation, ethnography, photography, ethnomethodology, dramaturgical interviewing, sociometry, natural experiment, case study, unobtrusive measures, content analysis, historiography, secondary analysis of data, and others. The application of the qualitative method is a global phenomenon. Pertti Alasuutari (2004) and many others have explained the qualitative method and its relevance in the modern neo-liberal globalized world as a counter to quantitative (positivist) research design.

Related to the historical connection between quantitative and qualitative debates, there is also a compelling argument in favor of the qualitative method from feminist scholars (Oakley 1998). They argue that traditional social science ignores or marginalizes women and that all the major social theories explain the public world of labor but not the private world of work and the home and the areas of social life. Traditional social science research based on the quantitative method often implicitly supports sexist values; female subjects are excluded or marginalized; relations between researcher and researched are intrinsically exploitative; the resulting data are superficial and over-generalized; and quantitative research is not used to overcome social problems (Jayaratne and Stewart 1991; Jayaratne 1983). Oakley (1998) adds more points to this notion. She states that there are three major problems of a quantitative method such as three Ps, i.e., positivism (objectivity is male subjectivity), power (hierarchy, valid/invalid through male judgment), and padded value (the quantitative method is ideologically linked with men's desire to dominate, to exert power over people as well as nature; in other words, it is a veritable "exercise in masculinity" (pages 709–711).

The Qualitative Inquiry Accepts the Notion of Social Variation

Qualitative inquiry searches for the causal effects of social problems from individual to the group level. Qualitative methodologists believe that each individual can reveal the social environment differently as they have perceived it; therefore, there are no fixed rules and regulations in the qualitative method (Sofaer 1999). Qualitative sociologists prefer open perspectives in social inquiry, and, therefore, they believe that predesigned structure in an investigation may not be able to capture the complexity and dynamism of social questions. To capture the social complexity, qualitative sociologists have developed various epistemologies.

Qualitative Ontology and Epistemology

The sociological ontological question searches for the answer of what the form and nature of reality are, and, therefore, what is there that can be known about it (Guba and Lincoln 1994, page 108). D. Snape and L. Spencer

74 *The Debates Between the Quantitative and Qualitative Methods*

(2003) note that "Within social research key ontological questions concern: whether or not social reality exists independently of human conceptions and interpretations; whether there is a common, shared, social reality or just multiple context-specific realities; and whether or not social behavior is governed by 'laws' that can be seen as immutable or generalizable" (Snape and Spencer 2003, page 20). There are three positions on whether there is a captive social reality and how this reality is constructed: they are realism, materialism, and idealism (Anneline 2003), where realism accepts the notion that there is an external reality that is independent of people's perspective, materialism accepts that there is a real-world but holds only material features, and idealism differs with these two and asserts that reality can be understood through human interpretation and socially constructed meanings. Only idealism can fit with qualitative epistemology.

Social sciences have various epistemologies to understand the social world. These epistemologies attempt to specify how we can learn about social reality and which form of knowledge is appropriate to investigate social problems. The major problem of qualitative epistemology is the way of exploring the relationship between researchers and researched (population) (Taylor and Bogdan 1998). In quantitative research, researchers are independent of the phenomena being studied; therefore, quantitative scholars argue that they can produce value-free research outcomes. However, qualitative scholars do not agree with this notion, because in the social world, the research process itself affects the people. According to qualitative epistemological understanding, the relationship between researchers and social phenomena is an interactive process. Qualitative scholars believe that social environments cannot be fully understood without this interactive process between researchers and the population. Howard Baker (1996) states that epistemology has characteristically concerned itself with "ought" rather than "is" and settles its questions by reasoning from first principles rather than by empirical investigation. In explaining qualitative epistemology, Becker (1996), with the illustration of exemplary works of Erving Goffman, Clifford Geertz, and William Foote White (and others), notes that the epistemology of qualitative research is "being there," "taking the point of view of the other," and "think description." There are few studies available that directly discuss the epistemology of qualitative sociology (Bryman 1984; Denzin 1994; Chin Lin 1998; Sofaer 1999; Michelle et al. 2000). Denzin (1994) states that the epistemological question is "What is the nature of the relationship between the knower or would-be knower and what can be known? The answer that can be given to this question is constrained by the answer already given to the

Section 1 75

ontological question; that is, "not just any relationship can now be postulated" (Denzin 1994, page 108).

Qualitative researchers try to gain knowledge of social reality, with their interpretation and with their deep understanding of the social context embedded in it. Taylor and Bogdan (1998), in the introduction of their book "Introduction to Qualitative Methods," provide several examples of qualitative knowledge. They note that "As qualitative researchers, we develop social constructions of social constructions (and sometimes others come along and deconstruct our social constructions)" (Taylor and Bogdan 1998, page 19). This account gives a sense that through qualitative methods, we discover our knowledge while doing fieldwork. Taylor and Bogdan (1998) make clearer the nature of qualitative knowledge with the citation of Laurel Richardson (1990b). "Sociological discovery happens through finding out about people's lives from the people themselves - listening to how people experience their lives and frame their worlds, working inductively, rather than deductively. Quantitative researchers learn about other people through interaction in specified roles, such as participant-observer/informant, interviewee/ interviewer, and so on. As a result, their knowledge of people's lives is always historically and temporally grounded. Most ethnographers are keenly aware that knowledge of the world they enter is partial, situated, and subjective knowledge" (Richardson 1990b, cited by Taylor and Bogdan 1998, page 19). This thesis shows that qualitative knowledge formation occurs with the interaction of the researched population. As qualitative researchers, we need an established epistemology to produce new knowledge. I agree with Taylor and Bogdan (1998) who state that "qualitative research is a craft that can only be learned and appreciated through experience. It requires skills and a devotion that must be developed and nurtured in the real world" (Taylor and Bogdan 1998, page 259).

I think research skills can be learned through reading and practicing; however, devotion can be generated only when the researcher fully embraces and enjoys the fieldwork. Qualitative inquiry assumes that reality is socially constructed by every unique individual from within their unique contextual interpretation (Joniak 2003, page 5); therefore, the knowledge formation differs according to the social context of the researcher and research. James A. Holstein (2000) nicely summarizes this situation. He notes that "If we are to study lives, including selves in social interaction, we must study them from within the social contexts they unfold, not separate from them. ... Human beings do not settle their affairs with meaning once and for all. Rather, they continually engage in the interpretive process, including the interpretation of what they mean to themselves....The methodological directive here is

76 *The Debates Between the Quantitative and Qualitative Methods*

to document the articulation and emergence of meaning in rich detail as it unfolds, not in lifeless analytic categories and statistical tables" (Holstein 2000, page 33). Therefore, qualitative epistemology development occurs through the in-depth investigation of social context. It requires both the application of researcher skills to investigate the social reality and the interpretation of learned knowledge from the social phenomena (Bhandari 2010, 2011, 2012, 2014).

Qualitative and Quantitative Debate is Still There

Relating to the debate on qualitative and quantitative methods, there is not much argument, because both inquiries are "to explore the social reality and truth." "Qualitative and quantitative research is not merely diverse ways of doing research, but diverse ways of thinking" (Joniak 2003, page 3). When the debate is about exploring social reality, both methods can be valid for specific purposes. There may be disagreement on whether these methods of qualitative research hold different epistemology or not. Denzin (1997), with the debates with Huber, states that there is a clear debate. He states that the research field is divided into two camps: the non-positivists and the positivists. This division creates another, those who believe in science and who also hold to a conception of a disciplinary core consisting of demography, social organization, and stratification (Denzin 1997, page 1418). This explanation clearly shows that the positivist line differs not only at the methodological level but is rooted in the ontological and epistemological levels. Each of these methods has a certain epistemology and can be the subject matter of further investigations (Bhandari 2010, 2011, 2012, 2014). The qualitative inquiry examines social reality with inductive reasoning which involves various processes. There are diverse ontological and epistemological perspectives within qualitative traditions.

The Paradigms of Qualitative Methods

Following the inductive inquiry process in knowledge building, the qualitative method has various paradigms. Denzin (1994) notes that a "paradigm may be viewed as a set of basic beliefs (or metaphysics) that deals with ultimate or first principles. It represents a worldview that defines, for its holder, the nature of the "world," the individual's place in it, and the range of relationships to that world and its parts, as, for example, cosmologies and theologies do. The beliefs are basic in the sense that they must be accepted simply on faith (however well-argued); there is no way to establish their ultimate truthfulness. If there were, the philosophical debates reflected in these pages would have been resolved millennia ago" (Denzin 1994, page 107). Denzin's explanation gives an overview of what paradigms are and why there is no end to theoretical debates in social science. Sociologists need to be knowledgeable about the multiple paradigms and perspectives to understand the social actors' activities in the society and to understand the social problems (Ellie Fossey, Harvey, McDermott, and Davidson 2002). They also need to know the interactive pattern of social behavior to understand social conflicts, social dynamism, and social inequality, which is the major subject to be addressed by social scientists. By nature, human beings are sensitive to their niche as well as familiar with its phenomena. Many scholars have tried to address sensitive issues through qualitative methods (Riley and Love 2000; Lincoln and Guba 1985; Schwartz and Ogilvy 1979). Addressing sensitive issues raised in qualitative inquiry is not that simple. Because of the complexity of the social environment, fixed rules or knowledge may not explicitly address social problems; therefore, new paradigms have been developed to address the problems.

These frameworks or paradigms are not static. Paradigms are shifting (Guba 1990; Denzin and Lincoln 1994) and alternative paradigms have been developed in terms of ontology and epistemology in qualitative methodology. Guba and Lincoln (1994) examine paradigms in four major categories such as positivism, post-positivism, critical theory, and constructivism. They explain these categories in three major questions, i.e., ontological, epistemological, and methodological, which help to explore the root cause of debates between qualitative and quantitative sociology. Gareth Morgan and Linda Smircich (1980) suggest that this ontological and epistemological difference is crucial. They devised a spectrum from subjectivist to objectivist which embodies ontological stances of reality as a project of human imagination/ socially constructed to reality as a concrete process or structure; and the epistemic stances of knowledge for revelation and the understanding of social construction to knowledge for the construction of a positivist science (Bhandari 2010, 2011, 2012, 2014). The manifestation of these two sets of assumptions is the relation between the knowing subject and the studied object.

Norman K. Denzin (2008) explains why paradigms are related to debates between quantitative and qualitative sociology. In his paper presented at the (QSE/QR/1,01; 12-6, 7, 10, 11, 17, 18/07; 2-11-08—Israeli conference) in the heading of The New Paradigm Dialogs and Qualitative Inquiry, he cites Amos Hatch's (2006) work to illustrate that the paradigms war is not over. According to Hatch, "Let us engage in the paradigm wars. Let us defend

78 *The Debates Between the Quantitative and Qualitative Methods*

ourselves against those who would impose their modern notions of science on us by exposing the flaws in what they call scientifically based research. Let us mount a strong offense by generating qualitative studies that are so powerful they cannot be dismissed" (Hatch 2006, page 407). Hatch's and Denzin's argument is true because debates between qualitative and quantitative are in the same position as they were in the 1980s. As Hatch (2006) notes, "let us open up the publishing possibilities for qualitative researchers working within a variety of qualitative paradigms. If we do not fight back, qualitative education research could become self-absorbed, fragmented, and ineffectual. And the neo-conservative dream of a return to scientific modernity will have come true" (page 407). This notion equally applies to research in sociology. The strength of qualitative paradigms can only be established with the application of the qualitative methods as broadly as possible.

Theories and Approaches of Qualitative Method

The qualitative method searches for the answers to questions unanswered by pure (hardliner) scientific research, with the development of new theory. "Theory is about starting points. Research usually relies on theory to justify starting with pre-commitments to independent variables, background factors, or structural conditions that will explain historically and geographically varying phenomena, which are treated as dependent, fungible, superficial upshots, or otherwise secondary and inferior. I propose that we start by trying to describe the phenomena to be explained as they exist for the people living them. For this, we need a theory of another sort, a theory of social ontology that indicates the lines of inquiry required to produce a complete description. If we start research by describing the nature of social phenomena as they are experienced, it will be effective in structuring data gathering; developing a research craft capable of seeing practice, interaction maneuvers, and tacit embodiment; shaping a research agenda; and in where we end substantively" (Katz 2002, page 255). In this connection, Jack Katz (2002) provides an answer to what theory is, why theoretical approaches are needed, and how theory can be constructed. More concisely, Meleis (1997) explains that "Theory is defined as a symbolic depiction of aspects of reality that are discovered or invented for describing, explaining, predicting, or prescribing responses, events, situations, conditions, or relationships" (Meleis 1997, page 12). The following approaches of qualitative methods fulfill the objectives of the theory postulated by Katz and Meleis.

There are several theories/approaches in qualitative research. The methodological frameworks (paradigms) help to address the ontological question: to find the nature of social reality and the way to discover knowledge through which the emerging social problems can be tackled. The epistemological inquiry arouses debates in qualitative research because the relationship between researchers and their subject matter (population) cannot fix the problem. It is also difficult to answer how much knowledge is sufficient to resolve such issues or what the saturation stage of information is. The major qualitative approaches are interviewing (open-ended, semi-structured, and narrative), single-case study, action research, conversation analysis, discourse analysis, narrative analysis, protocol analysis, interpersonal process (recall), interpretative analysis, IPA, hermeneutic, biographical methods, q methodology, feminist research, cooperative inquiry, participative inquiry, human inquiry groups, focus groups, grounded theory, phenomenological inquiry, heuristic inquiry, diary, diary-in-group, ethnomethodology, naturalistic/field study, lived inquiry, integral inquiry, intuitive inquiry, organic inquiry, transpersonal–phenomenological inquiry, exceptional experience, etc. In the following paragraphs, I will only very briefly discuss phenomenology, ethnography, grounded theory, ethnomethodology, symbolic interaction, and hermeneutical phenomenology which use most of the tools of qualitative data collection. These approaches are fundamentally different from qualitative techniques of data collection.

Phenomenology

Phenomenology views human behavior and examines how people say and act and how people define their world. In other words, it studies how people construct their realities (Taylor and Bogdan 1998). Social phenomena are complex and associated with multilayered events and so are not easy to understand. Qualitative inquiry searches the meaning of individual events and texts and helps us to understand the underlying situation within the social environment. In other words, the qualitative method provides a basis for "thick description" (Ryle 1971; Geertz 1973; Bogdan and Biklen 2003; Creswell 1998; Denzin 1989; Denzin and Lincoln 2005; Lincoln and Guba 1985; Marshall and Rossman 1999; Patton 1990), which is not possible in quantitative research method. I think as phenomenology, ethnomethodology, and symbolic interactions are common concepts in the qualitative method, "thick description" adds new strength to the qualitative epistemology. Ryne (1971) first coined the term "thick description" to explain golfing (Geertz 1973), which was used to interpret culture. Clifford Geertz interpreted "thick description" as a philosophical term to describe the work of ethnography. He states "From one point of view, that of the textbook, doing ethnography

80 *The Debates Between the Quantitative and Qualitative Methods*

is establishing rapport, selecting informants, transcribing texts, taking genealogies, mapping fields, keeping a diary, and so on. But it is not these things, techniques, and received procedures that define the enterprise. What defines it is the kind of intellectual effort it is: an elaborate venture in, to borrow a notion from Gilbert Ryle, thick description" (Geertz 1973, page 6, as cited by Ponterotto 2006, page 539). This notion enables authors to interpret the contextual situation of how and under which conditions data were collected.

Norman K. Denzin nicely explains this strength of the qualitative method. He states that "A thick description ... does more than record what a person is doing. It goes beyond mere fact and surface appearances. It presents detail, context, emotion, and the webs of social relationships that join persons to one another. Thick description evokes emotionality and self-feelings. It inserts history into the experience. It establishes the significance of an experience, or the sequence of events, for the person or persons in question. In the thick description, the voices, feelings, actions, and meanings of interacting individuals are heard" (Denzin 1989, page 83 as cited by Ponterotto 2006, page 540). The quantitative method has no provision for investigators to describe the situation nor do they provide the interpretations of the situation. In other words, "think description" articulates or helps to interpret the "insider" or "native" perspectives through external eyes (to describe the perspective of those experiencing the phenomena under investigation: emic perspectives). On the contrary, a *"thin description"* simply reports facts, independent of intentions or the circumstances that surround an action (Denzin 1989), what normally qualitative researchers do (etic observation).

Other widely used qualitative methods are ethnography and grounded theory, which also invites major criticisms from non-qualitative scholars (bias, time-consuming, chances to be native, etc.). However, these are the major approaches qualitative scholars use. According to Katz, "the ethnographic method is distinctively committed to displaying social realities as they are lived" (Katz 361). According to Duneier and Back (2006), "I think that ethnography is one of the sub-set of cases where those kinds of transcendent connections and recognitions of the humanity of others are possible, where it is possible to gain access to the humanity of 'others' despite the normal barriers that are there" (Voices from the sidewalk, pages 548–549). This argument is similar to what Kathy Charmaz (2000) has stated in explaining the grounded theory. She states that the grounded theorist's analysis tells a story about people, social processes, and situations. The researcher composes the story; it does not simply unfold before the eyes of an objective viewer. The story reflects the viewer as well as the viewed. Furthermore, she states that "grounded theory research might limit understanding because grounded theorists aim for analysis rather than the portrayal of the subject's experience in its fullness ... fracturing the data imply that grounded theory methods lead to separating the experience from the experiencing subject, the meaning from the story, and the viewer from the viewed. Grounded theory limits entry into the subjects' worlds and thus reduces the understanding of their experience" (page 335 in Emerson edited Book 2001). Ethnography opens a totality of circumstances and produces accounts of everyone who is involved during the study process. Katz focuses on the stand and warrant of ethnography. He asks, "Assuming your argument is empirically sound, so what?" Ethnographers are especially vulnerable to this question. Their warrants are commonly diffused throughout their texts because they aim to describe what is obvious to their subjects and because such rude questions usually are raised only silently. "The most common warrant for ethnography is a claim that social forces have created a moralized ignorance that separates research subjects and the research audience" (Katz 1997, page 391). The warrant concept in ethnographic research is complicated. The basic problem is to link "warrant" with empirical illumination. How can it be publicly visible and generalizable? How can qualitative research warrant the research outcome?

My problem of understanding is more basic, such as how to link the research with the accessible methods and theory development? I am having a tough time understanding how a particular social setting can be claimed to be sound or unquestionable. Social circumstances change according to time and spatiality. Most probably, qualitative information represents the particular time and mood of the researcher and respondent. However, the information which the researcher gets presents the truth of that time and spatiality and also the social setting. As Goffman (1989) suggested, "Embodied presence in the daily lives of those who host the research" (page 157 in Emerson edited Book), the ethnographer reveals the observed and unseen reality of particular social settings. The research outcomes of ethnographic research are not only as Katz states "projections of readers of the researcher's imagination" (Katz 1997, page 361). Doing ethnographic research is not an easy task, as most qualitative research methodologists acknowledge (Ibarra, DeVault and McCoy, Emersion, Goffman, Katz, Kathy Charmas, Dorothy Smith, etc.). However, the richness and thickness of qualitative research and the success of research depend on the understanding of the audience. "What is obvious to the subjects has been kept systematically beyond the cognitive reach of the ethnographer's audience because of the moral character of the social life under investigation" (Katz, page 361). In this respect I think there will be differences in understanding between audiences too. The *in-situ* audiences

82 *The Debates Between the Quantitative and Qualitative Methods*

may find the narratives shallow; yet, the same narratives can be very thick and rich to the *ex-situ* audiences.

Hermeneutical Phenomenology

Another important approach that the qualitative methodologist uses is hermeneutical phenomenology, developed by Wilhelm Dilthey (1833–1911), with the influence of Emmanuel Kant's ideas. Qualitative method tries to be attentive to both terms of its methodology: it is a descriptive (phenomenological) methodology because it wants to be attentive to how things appear; it wants to let things speak for themselves; it is an interpretive (hermeneutic) methodology because it claims that there are no such things as un-interpreted phenomena (Van Manen 1991, page 180). Likewise, the ethnomethodology approach developed by Harold Garfinkel (1960) states that "Ethnomethodological studies analyze everyday activities as members' methods for making those same activities visibly-rational-and reportable-for-all-practical-purposes, i.e., "accountable," as organizations of commonplace everyday activities. The reflexivity of that phenomenon is a singular feature of practical actions, practical circumstances, common-sense knowledge of social structures, and practical sociological reasoning. By permitting us to locate and examine their occurrence the reflexivity of that phenomenon establishes their study" (page vii). Garfinkel (1960) focuses on commonplace activities and practical action as a key element of ethnomethodology.

Symbolic Interaction

Similarly, another important approach is symbolic interaction perspectives in the qualitative method developed by Herbert Blumer (1900–1987), for which there is a remote influence from Weber and close influence from George Herbert Mead of the Chicago School. According to Blumer, "The term "symbolic interaction" refers, of course, to the peculiar and distinctive character of interaction as it takes place between human beings. The peculiarity consists in the fact that human beings interpret or "define" each other's actions instead of merely reacting to each other's actions. Their "response" is not made directly to the actions of one another but instead is based on the meaning which they attach to such actions. Thus, human interaction is mediated by the use of symbols, by interpretation, or by ascertaining the meaning of one another's actions. This mediation is equivalent to inserting a process of interpretation between stimulus and response in the case of human behavior" (Blumer 1963, page 180). Blumer focuses on (in symbolic interaction) human interaction, interpretation, or definition rather than mere reaction, response based on meaning, use of symbols, and interpretation between stimulus and response. His approach is based on human beings acting toward things based on the meanings that things have for them, while the meaning of things arises out of the social interaction one has with one's fellows and the meanings of things that are handled in and modified through an interpretive process used by the person in dealing with things he encounters (Ruth A. Wallace and Alison Wolf 1995). I think there is a close association between pragmatic thought and ethnomethodology, particularly the practicality of qualitative method application. Having clear influence from George Hebert Mead, qualitative methodologists such as William Foote Whyte, Herbert Blumer, Harold Garfinkel, and Erving Goffman have focused on the notion of being in the field "in reality" to show the practicality of the field. The pragmatic approach asserts that if there is a problem, then there is a practical way to figure out that problem.

So far, I have explained the major theoretical ground of debates between qualitative and quantitative in terms of their origin from major sociological canons of Durkheim and Weber. Further, I discussed the ontological, epistemological, and theoretical grounds of the qualitative method. Quantitative scholars follow the positivist approach and qualitative scholars follow the constructivist and interpretive approaches. At the epistemological level, debate is about the application of knowledge. Quantitative scholars follow the established notion (deductive) to explore the social reality and qualitative scholars construct the knowledge by doing inductive research (Bhandari 2010, 2011, 2012, 2014). However, at the objective level, there are no debates because both try to reach a better understanding of social reality. "Considering the facts, it is argued that each approach should be evaluated in terms of its particular merits and limitations, in the light of the particular research question under study" (Duffy 1987). However, this implies that there are only technical differences between the two: those of research strategies and data collection procedures (Bryman 1988) (as cited by L. T. Carr 1994, page 720). There is also a similarity in applications of research tools. For example, both quantitative and qualitative researchers heavily use the interview method, through which they first convert acquired information into numbers and use statistical tools to analyze the data. On the other hand, qualitative scholars interpret the information in language. For the qualitative scholars, the social environment, respondents' situation, the way respondents respond, what their body language tells, and their other gestures, all of which have a greater meaning than exactly what they are saying, but for the quantitative researcher, there is no such room in their analysis.

84 *The Debates Between the Quantitative and Qualitative Methods*

Bridging the Gap Between the Two Methods

There is also a tendency for researchers to bridge the gap between the two methods such as the application of both methods simultaneously (mixed method) or application of statistical tools to analyze qualitative data through coding with new software programming, etc. This is particularly relevant to environmental and sustainability research in which people's social conditioning and behavior, studied using qualitative methods, are likely to influence environmental or socioeconomic outcomes that are measurable and hence investigated by quantitative methods. However, at the paradigm level, the distance between qualitative and quantitative is increasing (J. Amos Hatch 2006; Denzin 2008). As Hatch (2006) argues and Denzin (2008) supports ("*I agree with Amos Hatch. Let us re-engage the paradigm disputes of the 1980s (Gage, 1989). But after Guba (1990a, b), I call for a paradigm dialog, not a new war" Denzin*), there is a need of more quality research and publications to win the paradigms war with quantitative paradigms (positivism).

At the beginning of this section, I also noted that the quantitative method is by nature superficial in many ways because quantitative scholars commonly do research with preset questionnaires and there is usually little room for the researcher to include any interpretation about the social settings. Normally, such data cannot be applicable in statistical testing for sociological interpretation. In other words, the quantitative researcher goes out with a half-filled pot or preoccupied mind so that they can fill in a little more in the field, but the qualitative researcher goes to the field mostly with an open bag and open mind; therefore, they generate new epistemology through learning by doing. The quantitative method has no such options to allow the researcher to interpret the field situation and investigate the unseen social environment. More strongly, Pauly (1991) explains the beauty of the qualitative method: "The 'something' that qualitative research understands is not some set of truisms about communication, but the awful difficulties groups face in mapping reality. The qualitative researcher is an explorer, not a tourist. Rather than speeding down the interstate, the qualitative researcher ambles along the circuitous back roads of public discourse and social practice. In reporting on that journey, the researcher may conclude that some of those paths were, in fact, wider and more foot-worn than others, that some branched off in myriad directions, some narrowed along the way, some rambled endlessly while others ran straight and long, and some ended at the precipice, in the brambles, or back at their origin" (Pauly 1991, page 7). This explanation illustrates the major strength of the qualitative method. In other words, there

Section 1   85

is no such option (of learning by doing) in deductive research paradigms which purport to reveal the grounded social reality.

I also note that outsiders' (positivist/quantitative methodologists) major criticisms of qualitative methods are about the nature of data collection techniques (i.e., open-ended questions, participant observation, content analysis, subjectivity, and time and space). Quantitative sociologists assume that reality is single and tangible, that the investigator and social population are independent, and that social facts can be time and context-free. They claim that such inquiry goes beyond the context or objective of the research (which excludes the meaning and purpose) (Fossey et al. 2002). This criticism is valid for those who believe that social issues can only be understood through quantitative measurement (positivist). In contrast, qualitative sociologists oppose this thesis and argue that realities are multiple, constructed, and holistic and that researchers and research population are interactive. Further, qualitative sociologists argue that human social systems are complex, socially constructed, and dynamic; therefore, revealing the social facts in in-depth knowledge is essential, which cannot be captured through a positivist approach. In addition to debates between qualitative and quantitative methods, there are also debates within the methods of qualitative sociologists (Merriam 1988; Creswell 1994).

These debates particularly concern procedures relating to researcher identity issues and research population. However, the qualitative method has various approaches and there is no universal standard of data collection. Therefore, even within teams of colleagues, there is debate on the qualitative method. These debates are mostly on the interpretation of the meaning of subject matter (conflict and problems), and the problem of generalization, because every individual case can be different from other individual cases. These debates are particularly related to the paradigms and nature of qualitative inquiry. Furthermore, such debates relate to the identity of the researcher and the research populations. In other words, insiders' debates are about the identity of the researcher and research populations in terms of sex/gender, race/ethnicity, insider/outsider, black and white, Northern and Southern, etc. (DeVault 1990; Lois 2005; Michelle et al. 2000; Bryman 1984; Devers 1999; Sanday 1979). However, debates are helpful for knowledge building and framing new ways to examine social issues. In the following section, I will briefly re-examine the development of interpretive philosophy in social science and note the three best exemplary works of qualitative sociologists.

86 *The Debates Between the Quantitative and Qualitative Methods*

Section 2

Features of Successful Qualitative-based Work by Discussing Three Exemplary Texts

In the first section of this essay, I briefly illustrated the major debates, ontology, epistemology and paradigms, and approaches of the qualitative method. In this section, I will briefly illustrate the works of William Foote Whyte, Erving Goffman, and Robert J. Thomas, who have successfully applied the qualitative method in their research.

Three Successful Examples of Qualitative Research

1. William Foote Whyte

For the development of the qualitative method, the publication of "Street Corner Society," written by **William Foote Whyte** in 1943 was a milestone in sociology. It provided a way of application of participant observation and helped to popularize ethnographic fieldwork in sociological research. Street Corner Society is one of the best examples of the development of qualitative epistemology. Whyte in the appendix notes that "when I began my work, I had had no training in sociology or anthropology. I thought of myself as an economist and naturally looked first toward the matters that we had taken up in economics courses, such as the economics of slum housing" (Whyte 1943, page 288). This account of Whyte's experience shows that if there is wish and devotion, the researcher can learn the way to conduct research. Being in the field, Whyte invented his interpretive style and own way of participant observation, which is not admissible in the positivist approach to social research. Whyte was for the creation of one's knowledge and he insisted that society should create its knowledge to resolve its social problems. He notes that "I emphasize the autonomous creation of social invention to suggest that human beings have enormous resources of creativity that permit them to devise their social inventions, without waiting for an outsider to intervene and invent what the community or organization needs" (Whyte 1982, page 1). Whyte's following statement provides the conditionality of being a real participant observer. "I also had to learn that the fieldworker cannot afford to think only of learning to live with others in the field. He has to continue living with himself. If the participant-observer finds himself engaging in behavior that he has learned to think of as immoral, then he is likely to begin to wonder what sort of person he is unless the field worker can carry with him a consistent picture of himself, he is likely to run into difficulties" (Whyte 1943, page 317). This account gives the idea of how much the qualitative researcher needs to be sensitive to the field situation. However, quantitative scholars criticize ethnographic field studies as very time-consuming and sometimes the researcher may not be able to generate the desired outcome in the time available. Whyte accepts this. He states that "In describing Connersville study, I have often said I was eighteen months in the field before I knew where my research was going. In a sense, this is true" (Whyte 1943, page 321) – eighteen months in the fieldwork but no idea about what a researcher is doing can be frustrating. However, it also indicates that qualitative research, ethnographic fieldwork, and interpretation are not easy, piecemeal or story writing as quantitative scholars suggest.

In addition to "Street Corner Society," William Foote Whyte (June 27, 1914 to July 16, 2000) authored or co-authored 22 books and hundreds of journal articles, ranging from the study of slums to multinational corporations such as oil companies in Oklahoma and Venezuela, restaurants in Chicago, worker cooperatives in Spain, factories in New York State, and villages in Peru. I consider Whyte to be one of the pioneer qualitative sociologists who applied participant observation and in-depth interview methods to the study of formal organizations.

Another exemplary work of William Foote Whyte that I would like to illustrate here is his research article "Social Inventions for Solving Human Problems" published in 1982 in *American Sociological Review*, Vol. 47, No. 1. In this article, Whyte states that "a social invention can be: - a new element in organizational structure, or inter-organizational relations, - new sets of procedures for shaping human interactions and activities and the relations of humans to the natural and social environment, - a new policy in action (that is, not just on paper), or - a new role or a new set of roles" (page 1). This approach is relevant to the conduct of research in organizational sociology. He explores *the legal and financial structure* of the Mondragon firm, *Caja Laboral Popular* (cooperative bank), and coordination and cooperation between agriculture firms. He points out how research in agriculture was not coping with the contemporary social setting. He examines research and development systems in agricultural research with an example from Peru and notes that there was no coordination among researchers. In addition to an interpretation of field outcomes, Whyte also provides an outline of what fieldwork is and how the researcher should conduct the research. He states that "In the research strategy required for the study of social inventions, you do not start with a pre-established research design. Of course, you do not start with a blank mind either. You consult the research literature, but you refuse to be bound by it. In the first place, you assume that the published literature is likely to be a decade behind the most interesting things happening in the

88 *The Debates Between the Quantitative and Qualitative Methods*

field. Furthermore, while the literature may illuminate a problem, it may also impose intellectual blinders that guide you along traditional pathways. In many cases, it is less important to gather new data than to develop a new way of organizing and interpreting data. For example, few problems in sociology have received more research attention than the diffusion of innovation, yet, as I have pointed out, researchers on changes in agriculture in developing countries have followed a conceptual scheme based on a misdiagnosis of the problem and have therefore provided findings that are worse than useless" (Whyte 1982, page 10). This account clearly shows that Whyte was not in favor of the positivist research paradigms and approaches for which some contemporary qualitative scholars have blamed him (such as Denzin, Taylor, Bogdan, etc.).

Whyte was much interested in multidisciplinary approaches and did not ignore the quantitative form of research. The following passage reveals how much he enjoyed working in a multidisciplinary team. Whyte states that "For each day in the field, the members of this joint team went out in pairs, a social scientist with a plant scientist, and each evening the team got together to discuss results and to raise questions for further checking. Each day also the composition of the pairs was changed so that each social scientist gained experience with each plant scientist, and vice versa. This strategy gave each team member a broad range of interdisciplinary and inter-personal experiences. As the new methodology came into widespread use, we found plant scientists increasingly basing their experimental strategies upon information provided by the field farming system surveys" (Whyte 1982, pages 7–8). For his comprehensive approach to research design, he faced several criticisms from authors like Norman Denzin and others (Taylor and Bogdan 1998). His record of excellent work in the multidisciplinary team offers a basic guideline for new scholars of qualitative methods. He extensively utilizes teamwork to conduct open-ended interviews, and participant observations and to collect the secondary information needed to examine cooperative forms of organization. I favor the multidisciplinary approach for large-scale research. Anyone can extensively use his approach as one of the GURU MANTRAS in their research.

2. Erving Goffman

A prominent scholar of qualitative method **Erving Goffman** in "On Fieldwork" (1989) asks us to internalize the field situation, observe every aspect of ongoing processes during fieldwork, and ask us to reveal the underlying facts during the observation. According to him, the overall phenomena to be described need to incorporate all these aspects during the field observation. Goffman asks the researcher to internalize the field situation, capture untold or unanswered questions, and visualize in such a way that research can reveal the reality.

The contribution of Erving Goffman is nicely summarized in the Book titled "Erving Goffman" (edited by Gary Alan Fine and Gregory W. H. Smith, in four volumes published by SAGE in 2000). They state that "Goffman fundamentally revised how we think of social life. After him, the study of social encounters, behavior in public, the construction and deconstruction of the self, stigma, and forms of everyday communication, were never the same again. Without being attached to any discrete research tradition, Goffman drew from the best thought on social interaction, applied it in his fieldwork, and produced a richly satisfying and extraordinarily influential approach to making sense of social life. He was a sociological virtuoso, producing unmatched insights into how life with others is sustained and why forms of interaction break down or cause personal damage" (from the back-cover page of the book). I agree with Fine and Smith (2000). Goffman particularly concentrated and developed two major concepts in sociological theory, i.e., the dramaturgical approach and symbolic interactionist perspective. In developing the idea of the dramaturgical approach, Goffman thinks that the most meaningful individual behavior occurs in the chance, intimate encounters of each day. These encounters include greeting people, appearing in public, and reacting to the physical appearance of others (Goffman 1959). For me, all works of Goffman are exemplary. His epistemology of "be in the field physically, emotionally, and mentally" is the key factor of the qualitative method, especially for those who want to apply the participant observation approach in their fieldwork.

Asylums were published in 1961, as a collection of four essays. The book explores the mental patients' condition, their behaviors, perceptions of selves, dramatic actions, and interactions with the hospital staff and with other people who visit them. Mental hospitals are prisons for mental patients, where mental asylums seek transformation from their prison-like situations into socially accepted conditions. Goffman sees mental hospitals as institutions, where patients and staff interact according to their positions. His research describes the experience of the inmates and staff within the institution, and he explains the institutional system as a problematic situation for mental patients. His central focus is the study of society, and the relationship between society and the individual is like a voluntary agreement, which is permanent and cannot be discarded. He states that mental illness is a byproduct of the lack of individual capacity to cope with the individual as well as a societal problem. He sees society as a bond. Most importantly, he

90 *The Debates Between the Quantitative and Qualitative Methods*

examines organizational interaction as social or individual interaction and applies his "face-to-face" method to analyze the social organization. His perspective on the study of the organization is "observation of participants." He gives the example of a musician tuning as prescribed activities before the beginning of the music. This account also values the ethical and moral obligations of other participants in the organization and accepts that the individual is not free in managing the self.

In the chapter *"The Underline of a Public Institution: A Study of Ways of Making Out in a Mental Hospital,"* he explores how mental patients deal with the under-control situation of the mental hospital. He examines the free-space behavior of inmates, under-observation behavior, and coping strategy of inmates and hospital staff. The most valuable aspect of this research for me is his minute study of the inmates' behavior. Goffman not only examines the inmates' condition but also analyzes the institutional condition and strategy within the institution. He finds several drawbacks within the institution which were not favorable to the mental patients. The most important aspect of the book is his theorizing of institution: "the total Institution." He deals with five types of such institutions: (1) homes for the aged, blind, orphans, or poor; (2) mental asylums, TB sanitariums, and leprosy camps; (3) jails, prisons, POW camps, and concentration camps; (4) army barracks, ships, military bases, and boarding schools; and (5) abbeys, monasteries, convents, and retreats. This notion of the total institution provides not only the institutional functions, the institution's role, and its structure but also gives a general idea of societal interaction with institutions.

Goffman further clarifies how total institutions are related to modern organizational form and explores the in-depth situation of individuals and society. In Asylums, he has provided two frames. The first is the theory of the institution and the second is the application of the qualitative method to study the organization. Goffman explains bureaucracy within the institution, power dynamism, and social interactions. I found that Goffman has built an institutional theory but has been ignored by the mainstream organizational theorists. My examination of an institution explores similar notions in terms of power dynamism and interaction with the individual and group, not in an analogous situation to that which Goffman is talking about, but in a national or international context. Goffman's research and approach have considerable relevance to my study.

His work has also helped in finding a new way of analyzing social problems, although there are some complications in the application. I prefer to choose Goffman's approach which I think leaves sufficient room to examine the organization's connectedness. My approach and focus on my research will be more open and flexible toward Goffman's and Whyte's findings on the open nature of fieldwork and learning by doing. These two authors are both qualitative theorists and researchers whose works are considered forerunners in the application of the qualitative method. Several other authors and researchers have been following Goffman and Whyte's approach in the organizational study. In the following paragraph, I will note how **Robert J. Thomas** studies various industries with the application of the qualitative method.

3. Robert J. Thomas

Every industry or manufacturing company tries to improve its machinery and plan for advancement. In other words, manufacturing companies try to adopt "automatic forms of machinery" to boost their production cycle. However, Robert J. Thomas' book "Machines Can't Do (Politics and Technology in the Industrial Enterprise)" reveals that advancing machinery was not only the ground for industrial revival.

His research is based on organizational sociological theory. He states that "Organizations are composed of social and technical systems; that these systems are interdependent; and that changes in one usually occasion adaptation in the order" (page 1). In the elaboration of the power process perspectives, he argues that power affects the process, as well as the outcomes of technological change (page 10). He says that history is important for industrial advancement due to varied reasons. "Most important, the choice of temporal context has serious implications for how we define "process" and therefore, for how attentive we are to the variety of activities associated with technological change in organizations" (page 11). He highlights the chain of relationships in the organization that he finds most important for industrial advancement.

He uses case study methods, in-depth interview techniques, and observation approaches. He focuses on information from individuals although he also compiles case studies and observes groups and managers, officials, and worker communities. His emphasis is on individual information. To get in-depth information on the relationship between production organization and workers, he used in-depth interviews. He was able to get detailed information from industry personnel because he had established incredibly good relationships with both high-level officials and workers.

Another most important technique Thomas used to draw samples was the investigation of official records through company library research. He states that his reputation as a faculty member at MIT helped him to get into the companies and access the official documents. Through the

92 *The Debates Between the Quantitative and Qualitative Methods*

official records, he was able to figure out what is happening inside the organization, and this allowed him to investigate influencing events inside the organization. He states that this helped him to understand current events rather than intervening to change future events. He also recorded individual accounts. He states that recording individual accounts aimed to give power to people and influence strategy while making them more noticeable. In this book, he attempts to integrate qualitative research for human empowerment and strategy advancement for humanity. This leads him to conclude what machines cannot do but humans can do.

Thomas focuses on an integrated approach, where he tries to clarify industrial enhancement or development. He has evaluated development as an interconnected process with two different dimensions in terms of high-tech and worker inter-relationships. Using an integrated approach, Thomas investigates different dimensions separating the economic and social impacts of technology implementation in the factories. He tries to recognize the interlinkages and tensions between the owners and workers. Thomas evaluates the complexity of an aircraft company, a computer company, an aluminum company, and the auto industry, and he tries to figure out the inter-relationship between politics and technology. Through this evaluation, he gets an accurate reflection of reality based on recognition of multiple realities where realism is seen as essentially subjective. He uses his expert knowledge to differentiate stakeholders' attitudes (owners, managers, and workers) and usually finds different perceptions of power relations within organizations. Thomas is flexible, open in many ways, and has nicely used qualitative methods. Thomas identifies the power struggles between owners, managers, workers, and the ultimate effects of the political environment. He treats these complexities and differences both hierarchically as well as in parallel to conclude that human empowerment is more important than implementing higher technology. This conclusion is not without criticism; however, the narrative presentation of the situation is well structured.

Thomas offers a comprehensive discussion of the guidelines, strong points, and dissimilarities in fundamental linkages between organizational patterns and technologies employed in private sector organizations. He recognizes that upper-management control cannot be assumed, for "choices of technology could be influenced as much by efforts to alter structure and power relations as they could by efforts to reinforce or reproduce existing relations" (page 229). He further elaborates on the point (in Chapter 3) that computer information technology does not always have the outcomes intended by its designers or implementers. This is a central finding of the community of researchers focused on social issues of computing over the past 30–40 years. This finding has been stable across all periods, every sort of information technology, and in many social contexts. He recommends that this should be taken into consideration, not only the possibility but also the likelihood, that there will be many and various unintended consequences in our individual and collective actions (pages 253–254). The author provides in-depth information about technological innovation and shows the relationships between workers' work and workers' life. He explains more about the integration, reflection, openly or perfectly achieved combination, and effect of management judgments about hi-tech implementation on industries. This account shows how workers respond to managerial decisions. The author describes challenging scenarios that are more than the operation of tools. This tends to focus on managerial interests' incompetence and control. He emphasizes the importance of managerial statements regarding what expertise can and should do, concerning enhancing outputs.

These three illustrated works show how the qualitative method can explore the organizational problem. Without the application of qualitative methods, such in-depth investigation was impossible. In other words, there is no way in the quantitative method which can provide such a vivid interpretation of the living environment. I do not think that the complexities that Whyte, Goffman, and Thomas have explored through qualitative inquiry could be as effectively investigated with the application of the quantitative method. There are critics of the Whyte approach of research method (for example, no women's participation in the entire research: Denzin 1992). However, in Goffman's case, he is well accepted. There is a limited citation of Thomas' work; however, in my case, Thomas' work is more appropriate because he directly addresses the organizational problems based on organizational theory. In the following section, I will explain why and how I have been applying the qualitative method in my research.

Section 3

Application of the Qualitative Method

In the first two parts of this essay, I noted that methodological paradigms are shifting as challenges emerge because the notion of the qualitative method is to accept the changing social environment and induce appropriate skills to reveal the social reality. In the second part, I illustrated the development scenario of the qualitative method and its application in organizational research from three prominent authors, i.e., Whyte, Goffman, and Thomas. These accounts clearly show that the qualitative method has its strengths.

94 *The Debates Between the Quantitative and Qualitative Methods*

The debates between quantitative and qualitative methods are about epistemology. Knowledge can be acquired with prescribed methodology, measurements, and mindset; however, there is a limitation. I think predesigned measurable procedures, which are the major ground of positivist paradigms, cannot be perfect to investigate complex, dynamic, and socially constructed social facts. Therefore, the interpretive open and knowledge-driven investigation is necessary to investigate the social reality. In this position, the qualitative method is more appropriate to reveal the social reality.

I do not mean that the qualitative method is perfect. This method has room for error. It can be very time-consuming, confusing, and sometimes overly subjective. It needs the inner capacity of the researcher to recognize record and interpret the interplay between the observed and the observer. Sometimes, what I hear and see, and feel, may not be true of the individuals or groups I am researching. All research is value-laden, and my observations and conclusions may reflect my background and influences. Qualitative research sometimes faces questions of reliability, validity, generalizability, and applicability because normally it is not based on the situation of controlled or semi-controlled data-gathering, which normally is possible in quantitative research. Furthermore, some researchers raise the questions of credibility – internal validity, transferability – external validity, dependability-reliability, and conformability – objectivity (LeCompte and Schensul 1999). These can be valid criticisms; however, we can pose similar types of questions to both qualitative and quantitative methods. The most crucial point is that each method has its limitations and strengths. The choice and application of methods depend on the purpose of the study.

Both qualitative and quantitative paths need equal energy to travel, and the main difference is that the qualitative way allows travelers to change the way during their journey as they feel appropriate, but the quantitative route does not to the same extent. Qualitative pilgrims have the right to change their faith and can assess the existence of a superpower in an incarnated form of deity, but the quantitative devotee has only one God, which may not be omnipresent. Therefore, qualitative is flexible, open, and appropriate to investigate human behavior which always changes direction and never remains in a motionless situation.

Conclusion

Why Qualitative Method?

The qualitative method has a long history of applicability in sociological research in both action and academic fields. Why qualitative research? Why

Conclusion 95

ethnographic theory? Many qualitative sociologists (Shweder 1996; Devers 1999; Fossey et al. 2002; Emerson 2001; Denzin and Yvonna 2000; Marcus 1998; Taylor and Bogdan 1998, and many more to note) and the exemplary authors I noted in the second section of this essay (Whyte, Goffman, and Thomas) have provided answers. The qualitative method produces descriptive data, people's own written or spoken words, and observable behavior (Taylor and Bogdan 1998). Taylor and Bogdan (1998) note that qualitative researchers (1) are concerned with the meanings people attach to things in their lives, (2) use an inductive approach, (3) look at settings and people holistically, (4) examine how people think and act in their everyday life, (5) consider all perspectives are worthy of study: the goal of qualitative research is to examine how things look from different vantage points, (6) emphasize the meaningfulness of research, (7) believe that there is something to be learned in all settings and groups, and (8) trust that qualitative research is a craft (cf., from Taylor and Bogdan 1998, pages 7–10). Furthermore, qualitative methods help us (1) to understand what is happening in my case in a large international organization.

The qualitative method helps to make the selection of criteria and indicators for how organizations are functioning, and what the limitations are or complexities with the application of interviews and observation methods. The qualitative method is appropriate to investigate the complex and sensitive impact of how the organization is functioning at headquarters and regional and national levels, which is not possible to quantify. (2) This method contributes to the understanding of who is affected and in which ways. In my case, how bureaucracy is structured, how executive officials treat the program level staff, and how the bureaucratic culture is diffused to the field level offices. The qualitative method helps to investigate who the most advantaged and most disadvantaged groups of people through observations are, which is impossible to quantify. (3) Qualitative method can only be able to capture why a particular impact is occurring in certain phenomena. This method will help me to investigate the context and development process through interaction with the executive officers to the field-level staff. A series of interactions will allow me to understand the interactions between the contexts, strategies, and institutional intervention at the global to national levels. (4) Finally, this method will enable me to investigate the ongoing policy (through archival review) and its impact at the global as well as national level, which will further enable me to make recommendations for the policy improvement which will be one of the major contributions of my research. These are the mantras of the qualitative method. In other words, this is the main reason scholars use the qualitative method. The qualitative

96 *The Debates Between the Quantitative and Qualitative Methods*

method allows us to use expert knowledge and is appropriate to develop our epistemology through learning by doing.

References

Abbott, Andrew (1990) A Primer on Sequence Methods, *Organization Science*, Vol. 1, No. 4, 375-392

Anderson, Nels (1923) *The Hobo: The Sociology of the Homeless Man.* University of Chicago Press, Chicago (reprinted in 1961, 1965, and 1967).

Alasuutari, Pertti (2004) The Globalization of Qualitative Research. In: Clive Seale et al.: Qualitative Research Practice, London: Sage 2004, 595-608.

Atkinson, Paul (1992) Understanding ethnographic texts. Newbury Park, CA: Sage.

Becker, Howard S. (1996) "The Epistemology of Qualitative Research," in Richard Jessor, Anne Colby, and Richard Schweder, edit., Essays on Ethnography and Human Development (Chicago: University of Chicago Press, 53-71.

Becker Howard S. (1999) The Chicago School, So-Called, *Qualitative Sociology, Vol. 22, No. 1.*

Bhandari, Medani P. (2002) Interview Techniques in Field Research, APEC-Nepal.

Bhandari, Medani P. (2019). The Debates between Quantitative and Qualitative Method: An Ontology and Epistemology of Qualitative Method- the Pedagogical Development, in Douglass Capogrossi (Ed.) Educational Transformation: The University as Catalyst for Human Advancement, Xlibris Corporation, USA ISBN-10: 179604895X; ISBN-13: 978-1796048957

---- (2012) Environmental Performance and Vulnerability to Climate Change: A Case Study of India, Nepal, Bangladesh, and Pakistan, "Climate Change and Disaster Risk Management" Series: Climate Change Management, Springer, New York / Heidelberg, ISBN 978-3-642-31109-3

---- (2012) Centre for Integrated Mountain Development (ICIMOD) [for conservation and management of the Hindu Kush-Himalayas – Afghanistan, Bangladesh, Bhutan, China, India, Myanmar, Nepal, and Pakistan Environment], in Ritzer, George (Ed.) Blackwell Encyclopedia of Globalization, Wiley-Blackwell Publication Volume 3, 1076-1078.

References 97

---- (2012) International Union for Conservation of Nature (IUCN) [Implication of the global conservation policies and its contribution for biodiversity conservation in the developing world], in Ritzer, George (Ed.) Blackwell Encyclopedia of Globalization, Wiley-Blackwell Publication Volume 3, 1086-1088.

---- (2012) The Intergovernmental Panel on Climate Change (IPCC) [The fourth assessment reports on climate change: a factual truth of contemporary world], in Ritzer, George (Ed.) Blackwell Encyclopedia of Globalization, Wiley-Blackwell Publication Volume 3, 1063-1067.

---- (2012) South Asian Association for Regional Cooperation (SAARC) [Problems and opportunities in improving the livelihood of its member countries: Sri Lanka, India, Pakistan, Afghanistan, Bhutan, Maldives, Bangladesh, and Nepal], in Ritzer, George (Ed.) Blackwell Encyclopedia of Globalization, Wiley-Blackwell Publication, Volume 4, 1891-1898.

---- (2011) "Viewpoints: What do you think should be the two or three highest priority political outcomes of the United Nations Conference on Sustainable Development (Rio+20), scheduled for Rio de Janeiro in June 2012? Natural Resources Forum 36, 251-252 (Wiley-Blackwell)

---- (2011) The conceptual problems of Green Economy and Sustainable Development and the Theoretical Route of Green Economy Initiatives, Applicability, and the Future, Compilation Document - Rio+20 - United Nations Conference on Sustainable Development, United Nations, New York, (Major groups), 141-153 http://www.uncsd2012.org/rio20/content/ documents/compilationdocument/MajorGroups.pdf

http://www.uncsd2012.org/rio20/index.php?page=view&type=510&nr=138 &menu=20 http://www.uncsd2012.org/rio20/content/documents/ 138apec. pdf

Brechin, Steven R., and Bhandari, Medani P. (2011) Perceptions of climate change worldwide, *WIREs Climate Change* 2011, Volume 2:871–885.

Mathiason, John, and Bhandari, Medani P. (2010) Getting the Facts Right: The Intergovernmental Panel on Climate Change and the New Climate Regime, Journal of International Organization Studies, Volume 1, Number 1, (September 2010) 58-71 http://www.journal-iostudies.org/sites/journal-iostudies.org/files/JIOS1014.pdf

Mathiason, John, and Bhandari, Medani P. (2010) Governance of Climate Change Science: The Intergovernmental Panel on Climate Change and the

98 *The Debates Between the Quantitative and Qualitative Methods*

New Climate Change Management Regime, the UNITAR-Yale, Geneva, USA, 2nd Issue.

Bhandari, Medani P. (2004) An Assessment of Environmental Education Programs in Nepal, Environmental Awareness, *International Journal of Society of Naturalist, Vol.27, No.1. (ISSN 0254-8798)*

Blumer, H. (1963) "Society as Symbolic Interaction," in Arnold Rose, editor, Human Behavior and Social Processes: An Interactionist Approach, Boston, Houghton Mifflin, 179-192.

Boas, Franz (2007) In Encyclopedia Britannica. Retrieved October 4, 2007, from Encyclopedia Britannica Online: http://www.britannica.com/eb/article-9015808

Boelen, W.A.M. (1992): Street corner society: Connersville revisited. Journal of Contemporary Ethnography, 21, 1, 11-51

Bogdan, R. & Biklen, S. (2003). Qualitative education research: An introduction to theory and methods. Needam, MA: Allyn and Bacon.

Bruce, L. Berg. (1995) Qualitative Research Methods for the Social Sciences, 2nd edition. Allyn and Bacon Boston, MA.

Bryman, A. (1984) The Debate about Quantitative and Qualitative Research: A Question of Method or Epistemology? The British Journal of Sociology, Vol. 35, No. 1.

Bryman, A. (1988) Quality and Quantity in Social Research, London: Unwin Hyman.

Campbell, Marie (2008) Dorothy Smith and knowing the world we live in" Journal of Sociology and Social Welfare. March 2003. FindArticles.com. 15 May. 2008.

Carr, Linda T. (1994) The strengths and weaknesses of quantitative and qualitative research: what nursing method? *Journal of Advanced Nursing,* 1994, 20, 716-721.

Charmaz, K. (2000). Grounded theory: Objectivist and constructivist methods. In Denzin, N.K. & Lincoln, Y.S. (Eds.), Handbook of qualitative research (2nd ed., 509-35), Thousand Oaks, CA

Charmaz, K. (2001) Grounded Theory. In Contemporary Field Research: Perspectives and Formulations, edited by Robert M. Emerson, Prospect Heights: Waveland Press. . 335-352.

Charmaz K. (2004) Premises, Principles, and Practices in Qualitative Research: Revisiting the Foundations Keynote Address: Fifth International Advances in Qualitative Methods Conference, Qualitative Health Research, Vol. 14 No. 7, Sage Publications.

Chase, Susan (2003) Taking Narrative Seriously: Consequences for Method and Theory in Interview Studies, in Turning Points in Qualitative Research: tying knots in a handkerchief (edited by Yvonna S. Lincoln, Norman K. Denzin) 2003 Rowman Altamira publisher.

Chapoulie, Jean-Michel (2004) Being here and being there, Field Work Encounters and Ethnographic Discourses, The Annals of the American Academy of Political and Social Sciences, Vol. 595, 2004.

Clifford, James (1997) "Traveling Cultures," in Routes. Travel and Translation in the Late Twentieth Century (Cambridge/London: Harvard University Press, 1997): 25.

Cook, Judith A., (1991 Editor), Beyond methodology: Feminist scholarship as lived research, Indiana University Press, Bloomington, IN (1991), 85–106.

Cockburn J. (2004) Interviewing as a Research Method, The Research and Development, Vol. 2: 3

Cockburn, J. (1984) The Use of Interviewing in Social Science Research. Unpublished Ph.D. Thesis. Centre for Applied Research in Education, University of East Anglia.

Coser, Lewis A. (1977) Masters of Sociological Thought: Ideas in a historical and social context (second edition), Harcourt Brace Jovanovich, Inc.

Cressey, Paul G. (1932) *The Taxi-Dance Hall: A Sociological Study in Commercialized Recreation and City Life*. Chicago, IL: University of Chicago Press.

Creswell, J. (1994) Research design: Qualitative and quantitative approaches. Thousand Oaks: Sage.

Du Bois W. E. B. (1899) The Philadelphia Negro a Social Study, Introduction by Elijah Anderson (paper edition publication on 1995), University of Pennsylvania Press,

Devers, K.J. (1999) "How Will We Know "Good" Qualitative Research When We See It? Health Services Research, December 1999, v.34, no. 5, Part II, S1153-1188

100   *The Debates Between the Quantitative and Qualitative Methods*

Denzin, N. (1994) The Qualitative Paradigm: An Overview of Some basic Concepts, Assumptions, and Theories of Qualitative Research. [Available On-Line] HTTP:// http://www.unf.edu/dept/cirt/workshops/joniak/qual_par.pdf (17/4/2008, 5.00AM)

Denzin, N. (2008) The New Paradigm Dialogs and Qualitative Inquiry, paper presented at the (QSE/QR/1, 01; 12-6, 7, 10, 11, 17, 18/07; 2-11-08— Israeli conference)

Denzin, Norman K., and Lincoln, Yvonna S. (2000) 'Introduction: the discipline and practice of qualitative research, in Norman K. Denzin and Yvonna S. Lincoln (eds), Handbook of Qualitative Research (2nd ed.). Thousand Oaks, CA: Sage 1–28.

Denzin N. (1997) Interpretive Anthropology: Ethnographic Practices for the 21st Century. Norman K. Denzin. Thousand Oaks, CA: Sage.

Denzin N. (1997) Whose Sociology, is it? Comment on Huber Author(s): The American Journal of Sociology, Vol. 102, No. 5, (Mar. 1997), 1416-1423

DeVault, Marjorie (2004) What is Description? (One Ethnographer's View), Perspectives (ASA Theory Section Newsletter), 27 (#1): 4, January 2004.

DeVault, Marjorie (1996) Talking Back to Sociology: Distinctive Contributions of Feminist Methodology. Annual Review of Sociology 22: 29-50.

DeVault, Marjorie, (1999) Liberating Method: Feminism and Social Research, Philadelphia: Temple University Press.

DeVault, Marjorie, and Liza McCoy, (2002) Institutional Ethnography: Using Interviews to Investigate Ruling Relations, 751-776, Handbook of Interview Research: Context and Method, J. Gubrium and J. Holstein (eds.), Thousand Oaks, CA: Sage Publications.

Draper, Alizon K. (2004) The principles and application of qualitative research, Proceedings of the Nutrition Society 63:641-646 Cambridge University Press

Duffy M. (1987) Methodological triangulation: a vehicle for merging qualitative & quantitative research methods. IMAGE: Journal of Nursing Scholarship 19(3), 130-133.

Duneier, Mitchell (1999) Sidewalk, New York: Farrar, Straus, and Giroux.

Duneier Mitchell in conversation with Les Back (photographs by Ovie Carter) (2006) Voices from the sidewalk: Ethnography and writing race, Ethnic and Racial Studies Vol. 29 No. 3 May 2006 pp. 543_/565

References 101

Durkheim, Emile (1997) Division of Labor in Society, by, (Introduction by Lewis Coser), (Translator W.D.Halls), publisher Simon & Schuster.

Durkheim, Emile (1979) Suicide: A Study in Sociology, Simon & Schuster

Durkheim, Emile (1982) Rules of Sociological Method, Simon & Schuster

Elwell, Frank, 1996, The Sociology of Max Weber, Retrieved June 1, 1999 (retrieved on May 21, 2008), http://www.faculty.rsu.edu/~felwell/Theorists/Weber/Whome.htm

Emerson, M Robert (2001) Contemporary Field Research, Perspective, and formulations (second Addition) Waveland Press Inc. IL.

Emerson, Robert, Rachel Fretz, and Linda Shaw (1995) Writing Ethnographic Field Notes. Chicago: University of Chicago Press.

Fielding,Nigel(2005).TheResurgence,Legitimization,andInstitutionalization of Qualitative Methods Forum Qualitative Sozialforschung / Forum: Qualitative Social Research [On-line Journal], 6(2), Art. 32. Available at: http://www.qualitative-research.net/fqs-texte/2-05/05-2-32-e.htm [Date of Access: 04/04/2008)

Fine,Michelle,etal. 2000. "ForWhom?QualitativeResearch,Representations, and Social Responsibilities." 107-132 in Norman K. Denzin and Yvonna Lincoln (Eds.), Handbook of Qualitative Research (2nd ed). Thousand Oaks: Sage.

Fine, Gary and Greg Smith (Editors). 2000. Erving Goffman. V.1-4. London: Sage Publications.

Fossey, Ellie, Carol Harvey, Fiona McDermott, Larry Davidson. (2002) Understanding and evaluating qualitative research, Australian and New Zealand Journal of Psychiatry 36:6, 717–732

Gage, N. L. 1989. "The Paradigm Wars and Their Aftermath: A 'Historical' Sketch of Research and Teaching since 1989." Educational Researcher, 18, 7: 4-10.

Garfinkel, Harold (1984) Studies in Ethnomethodology. Malden MA: Polity Press/Blackwell Publishing. (ISBN 0-7456-0005-0) (First published in 1967).

Geertz, Clifford (1988) Works and Lives the anthropologist as an author, Stanford, Stanford University Press.

102 *The Debates Between the Quantitative and Qualitative Methods*

Geertz, Clifford (1973) "Thick Description: Toward an Interpretive Theory of Culture". In The Interpretation of Cultures: Selected Essays. (New York: Basic Books, 3-30.

Gerth, Hans and C. Wright Mills (1946 [1958] (translators and editors). *From Max Weber: Essays in Sociology.* New York: Galaxy Books.

Gobo, Giampietro (2005, September). The Renaissance of Qualitative Methods [22 paragraphs]. Forum Qualitative Sozialforschung / Forum: Qualitative Social Research [On-line Journal], 6(3), Art. 42. Available at: http://www.qualitative-research.net/fqs-texte/3-05/05-3-42-e.htm [Date of Access: 05/17/2008].

Goffman Erving (1959) The Presentation of Self in Everyday Life, University of Edinburgh Social Sciences Research Centre.

Goffman, Erving (1961) Asylums: Essays on the Social Situation of Mental Patients and Other Inmates. New York, Doubleday.

Goffman, Erving (1963) Behavior in Public Places: Notes on the Social Organization of Gatherings, New York, Free Press

Goffman, Erving (1961) Encounters Two Studies in the Sociology of Interaction, Indianapolis, Bobbs-Merrill, HM291 G58

Goffman, Erving (1967) Interaction Ritual, Chicago, Aldine, HM 291 G59

Goffman, Erving (1969) Strategic Interaction, Philadelphia, University of Pennsylvania,

Goffman, Erving (1989) On fieldwork. Journal of Contemporary Ethnography 18:123-32.

Gobo, Giampietro (2005) the Renaissance of Qualitative Methods, Qualitative Social Research (ISSN 1438-5627) Volume 6, No. 3, Art. 42

Guba, E.G. & Lincoln, Y.S. (1994) Competing paradigms in qualitative research. Chapter 6 in N.K. Denzin & Y.S. Lincoln (Eds) Handbook of Qualitative Research. Sage.

Guba, Egon G. & Yvonna S. Lincoln. (2005). Paradigmatic controversies, contradictions, and emerging confluences. In Denzin & Lincoln (2005), 191–215. The Sage Book of Qualitative Research. 3rd ed. Thousand Oaks, Calif: Sage.

Hatch, Amos. 2006. "Qualitative Studies in the Era of Scientifically-based Research: Musings of a Former QSE Editor." International Journal of Qualitative Studies in Education, 19, 4 (July-August): 403-409.

References 103

Holstein, James (2000) The Self We Live By. (With J. Gubrium). 2000. Oxford University Press.

Holstein, James (2000) "An Interpretive Analytics for Social Problems." (With J. Gubrium), Japanese Journal of Sociological Criminology 25:29-48.

Holstein, James (2000) "Analyzing Interpretive Practice." (With J. Gubrium). 487-508 in Handbook of Qualitative Research, 2nd Edition, edited by N. Denzin and Y. Lincoln. Newbury Park, CA: Sage.

Ibarra, P.R. and J.I. Kitsuse (2003), "Claims-making discourse and vernacular resources." Constructionist Challenges, edited by James A. Holstein and Gale Miller, 17-50. Hawthorne, NY: Aldine de Gruyter.

Ibarra, P.R., and M. Kusenbach (2001), "Feeling the field: Tracking shifts in ethnographic research." Studies in Symbolic Interaction 24: 193-219.

Platt, Jennifer (1996). A History of Sociological Research Methods in America 1920-1960. Cambridge: Cambridge University Press.

Platt, Jennifer (1995). Research Methods and the Second Chicago School. In Gary Fine (Ed.), A Second Chicago School? (82-107). Chicago: University of Chicago Press.

Platt Jennifer (1985) Weber's Verstehen and the History of Qualitative Research: The Missing Link, The British Journal of Sociology, Vol. 36, No. 3 -448-466

Jayaratne, Toby Epstein and Abigail Stewart (1991), Quantitative and qualitative methods in the social sciences: Current feminist issues and practical strategies. In: Mary Margaret Follow and

Jayaratne, T. E. 1983. 'The Value of Quantitative Methodology for Feminist Research, 140–61 in Bowles and Duelli Klein (eds.).

Jessor, R. (1996) Ethnographic methods in contemporary perspective. In R. Jessor, R., Colby, A., and Shweder, R.A. (eds.). Ethnography and Human Development: Context and Meaning in Social Inquiry. Chicago, Illinois: University of Chicago Press.

Jessor, Richard., Anne Colby, and Richard A. Shweder (1996) Ethnography and Human Development: Context and Meaning in Social Inquiry. Richard Jessor, Anne Colby, and Richard A. Shweder, eds. Chicago: University of Chicago Press

104 *The Debates Between the Quantitative and Qualitative Methods*

Joniak, E. (2003) "How Staff Create, Sustain and Escalate Conflict at a Drop-in Center for Street Kids." Annual Meetings of the American Sociological Association, Atlanta, GA.

Johnson, Sherrill (2001) "Strengthening the Generational Chain: Engaging the Next Generation of Social and Civic Leaders in Canada." Paper produced for the Canadian Centre for Social Entrepreneurship (10).

Johnson, Sherrill (2002) "Social Entrepreneurship Literature Review." Paper produced for the Canadian Centre for Social Entrepreneurship (18)

Johnson, Sherrill (2003) Young Social Entrepreneurs in Canada, Project Paper of Canadian Centre for Social Entrepreneurship School of Business, University of Alberta.

Kahn, Joel S (2001) "Anthropology and Modernity", Current Anthropology 42. 5: 651–664.

Katz, Jack (1983) A theory of Qualitative methodology, Social System and Analytical fieldwork, In Contemporary Field Research. Robert Emerson, ed. (Boston: Little-Brown). 127-148.

Katz, Jack (1997) Ethnography's Warrants, Sociological Methods & Research, 25 (4, May): 391-423.

Keating, P. (1976) Into Unknown England 1866–1951: Reflections from the Social Explorers. Glasgow: Fontana/Collins.

Kocka, Jurgen (2004), Civil Society from a historical perspective, European Review, Vol 12, no.1.

Kusenbach, Margarethe (2005). Across the Atlantic: Current Issues and Debates in US Ethnography. Forum Qualitative Sozialforschung / Forum: Qualitative Social Research [On-line Journal], 6(3), Art. 47. Available at: http://www.qualitative-research.net/fqs-texte/3-05/05-3-47-e.htm [Date of Access: 09/22/07].

Lee, Allen S. (1991) Integrating Positivist and Interpretive Approaches to Organizational Research, Organization Science, Vol. 2, No. 4. 342-365.

Lee, Raymond M. (2004) Recording Technologies and the Interview in Sociology, 1920–2000, Sociology, Volume 38(5): 869–889, SAGE Publications

LeCompte, Margaret and Jean Schensul (1999) Designing and Conducting Ethnographic Research, Roman & Littlefield Publisher, USA

Lemert, Charles and Ann Branaman (1997) The Goffman Reader, Oxford, Blackwell Publishers, 1997.

Lincoln, Y., & Guba, E. (1985) Naturalistic inquiry, New York: Sage.

Lincoln, Yvonna S.; Guba, Egon G (1985) Naturalistic inquiry, Sage Publishing, Thousand Oaks

Lincoln, Y.S. (Ed.) (1985) Organizational Theory and inquiry: The paradigm revolution. Beverly Hills, CA: Sage.

Lin, Ann Chin (1998) Bridging positivist and interpretive approaches to qualitative methods, Policy study journal, vol 26, No 1.

McKinney, John C (1966) Constructive typology of social theory, Appleton Century Crofts, New York.

Marshall, C. and Rossman, G.B. (1999) Designing qualitative research (3rd ed.), Thousand Oaks: Sage Publications.

Malinowski, Bronislaw (1967) A diary in the strict sense of the term. London: Routledge & Kegan Paul.

Marcus, George E. (1998) Ethnography through Thick and Thin, Princeton: Princeton University Press.

Marcus, George E. (1995) Ethnography In/Of the World System: The Emergence of Multi-sited Ethnography, "Annual Review of Anthropology 24: 95.

Mariampolski, H.Y. (2006) Ethnography for Marketers: A Guide to Consumer Immersion, 2006 Sage Publications Inc.

McCoy, Norma L. (1998) Methodological problems in the study of sexuality and menopause. Maturitas, 29(1), 51-60.

Meleis, A. I. (1997) Theoretical nursing: development and progress (3rd ed.). Philadelphia, PA: Lippincott-Raven.

Morgan, Gareth, and Linda Smircich (1980) The Case for Qualitative Research, The Academy of Management Review, Vol. 5, No. 4. 491-500

Merriam, S. B. (1998). Qualitative research and case study applications in education. San Francisco: Jossey-Bass. Stage, F. (Ed.).

Morrison, Ken (1995) Marx, Durkheim, Weber: Formations of Modern Social Thought, London: Sage, 1995.

106 *The Debates Between the Quantitative and Qualitative Methods*

Northcutt, N. And D.McCoy (2004) Interactive Qualitative Analysis: A Systems Method for Qualitative Research, Thousand Oaks, CA: Sage

Nock, David (2004) The Myth about "Myths of the Chicago School ". Evidence from Floyd Nelson House, The American Sociologist / Spring

Oakley, Ann (1998) Gender, Methodology and People's Ways of Knowing: Some Problems with Feminism and the Paradigm Debate in Social Science, Sociology 32: 707-731

Oakley, Ann (1997a) 'The Gendering of Methodology: An Experiment in Knowing', Paper given at the Swedish Collegium for Advanced Study in the Social Sciences,

Patton, M. Q. (1990). Qualitative evaluation and research methods (2nd ed.). Newbury Park, CA: Sage.

Pauly, John J. (1991) `A Beginner's Guide to Doing Qualitative Research in Mass Communication', Journalism Monographs 125 (February). Columbia, SC: Association for Education in Journalism and Mass Communication.

Pauly, John J. (1999) `Journalism and the Sociology of Public Life', in Theodore L. Glasser (ed.) The Idea of Public Journalism. New York: Guilford.

Platt, Jennifer (1996). A History of Sociological Research Methods in America 1920-1960. Cambridge: Cambridge University Press.

Platt, Jennifer (1995). Research Methods and the Second Chicago School. In Gary Fine (Ed.), A Second Chicago School? (82-107). Chicago: University of Chicago Press.

Ponterotto, Joseph G. (2006) Brief Note on the Origins, Evolution, and Meaning of the Qualitative Research Concept "Thick Description" The Qualitative Report Volume 11 Number 3 538-549

Polkinghorne, D.E. (1982) What makes research humanistic? Journal of Humanistic Psychology 47-54.

Polkinghorne, D.E. (1983) Methodology for the Human Sciences: Systems of inquiry. SUNY.

Reetley, Anneline (2003), A literature review on grounded theory, Master thesis, Rand Afrikaans University, South Africa.

Richardson, L. (1990a) 'Narrative and sociology', Journal of Contemporary Ethnography, 19:116-35.

Richardson, L. (1990b) Writing Strategies: reaching diverse audiences, Newbury Park, Sage.

Richardson, L. (1992) 'Trash on the Corner: ethics and technography', Journal of Contemporary Ethnography, 21, 1, 103-119.

Ritzer, George (1996) Sociological Theory (fourth edition), McGraw-Hill

Ryle, G. (1971) Collected papers. Volume II collected essays, 1929-1968. London: Hutchinson.

Sanday, Peggy Reeves (1979), "The ethnographic paradigm(s)", Administrative Science Quarterly, Vol. 24 No.4, 527-38.

Schwartz P, Ogilvy J. (1979) The Emergent Paradigm: Changing Patterns of Thought and Belief.Values and Lifestyles Program. VALS Report 7. Menlo Park, CA: SRI International.

Sharrock, Wes (1989) Ethnomethodology, The British Journal of Sociology, Vol. 40, No. 4. 657-677.

Sil, Rudra and Peter J. Katzenstein (2005) What is Analytic Eclecticism and Why Do We Need it? A Pragmatist Perspective on Problems and Mechanisms in the Study of World Politics, Paper presented at the Annual Meeting of the American Political Science Association,

Smith, J.K. (1983). Quantitative Versus Qualitative Research: An Attempt to Clarify the Issue. Educational Researcher, 12(3), 6-13.

Smith, Dorothy E., (1977) Feminism and Marxism: A Place to Begin, A Way to Go, Vancouver: New Star Books.

Smith, Dorothy E, (1984) The Renaissance of Women Knowledge Reconsidered: A Feminist Overview, Ursula Franklin, et al. (eds.), Ottawa: Canadian Research Institute for the Advancement of Women, 3-14.

Smith, Dorothy E, (1987) The Everyday World as Problematic: A Feminist Sociology, Toronto: University of Toronto Press.

Smith, Dorothy E. (2005) Institutional ethnography: A sociology for people, Rowman Altamira Publisher.

Snape, D., and Spencer, L. (2003), 'The foundations of qualitative research, in J. Ritchie and J. Lewis (eds), Qualitative Research Practice, London: Sage, 1–23.

Sofaer, S. (1999) Qualitative Methods: What Are They and Why Use Them? Health Services Research3 4(5): 1102-18.

108 *The Debates Between the Quantitative and Qualitative Methods*

Sofaer, S, and R.C. Myrtle (1991) Interorganizational Theory and Research: Implications for Health Care Management, Policy, and Research. Medical Care Review 48(4):371-409.

Taylor, Steven & Robert Bogdan (1984), Introduction to Qualitative Research Methods: The Search for Meanings. Second Edition. New York: John Wiley and Sons.

Thomas, Robert J. (1994) What Machines Cannot Do: Politics and Technology in the Industrial Enterprise, University of California Press

Thrasher, Frederic M. (1927) The *Gang: A Study of 1,313 Gangs in Chicago,* University of Chicago Press.

Turner, Jonathan H. (1991) The Structure of Sociological Theory, fifth edition, Belmont, CA Wadsworth.

Van Maanen (1979) The Fact of Fiction in Organizational Ethnography, Administrative Science Quarterly, Vol. 24, No. 4, Qualitative Methodology. 539-550.

Van Maanen (1979) Reclaiming Qualitative Methods for Organizational Research: A Preface, Administrative Science Quarterly, Vol. 24, No. 4, Qualitative Methodology.520-526

Van Maanen, J. (1983) The moral fix: On the ethics of fieldwork. In Contemporary field research: A collection of readings, edited by R.M. Emerson. Boston: Little, Brown

Van Manen, M. (1990) Researching Lived Experience: Human Science for an Action Sensitive Pedagogy. Albany, New York: State University of New York Press.

Van Manen (1991). The tact of teaching: The meaning of pedagogical thoughtfulness, Albany, New York: State University of New York Press.

Wallace, Ruth A., and Alison Wolf (1995) Contemporary Sociological Theory: Continuing the Classical Tradition, fourth edition, Englewood Cliffs, New Jersey, Prentice-Hall.

Welz, Gisela (2002) "Sitting Ethnography, some observations on a Cypriot highland village," in Shifting Grounds. Experiments in Doing Ethnography. eds. Ina-Maria Greverus, Sharon Macdonald, Regina Römhild, Gisela Welz and Helena Wulff. Anthropological Journal on European Cultures 11 137–158.

References 109

Weber, Max (2002) The Protestant Ethic and the 'Spirit' of Capitalism and Other Writings, Edited by Peter R. Baehr, Gordon C. Wells, Penguin USA

Weber, Max 1903-1917 (1949) The Methodology of the Social Sciences. Edward Shils and Henry Finch (eds.). New York: Free Press.

Weber, Max (1962) Basic Concepts in Sociology by Max Weber. Translated & with an introduction by H.P. Stecher. New York: The Citadel Press.

Weber, Max. (1904/1930) The Protestant Ethic and the Spirit of Capitalism, Translated by Talcott Parson, New York: Charles Scribner's Sons.

Weber, Max. (1946/1958) From Max Weber. Translated and edited by H. H. Gerth and C. Wright Mills. New York: Galaxy.

Whyte, William Foote, (1943) Street Corner Society: The Social Structure of an Italian Slum University of Chicago Press.

Whyte, William Foote (1982), "Social Inventions for Solving Human Problems," 1981 Presidential Address, American Sociological Association], American Sociological Review, 47:1-13.

Whyte, William Foote, Davydd Greenwood, and Peter Lazes (1989), "Participatory Action Research: Through Practice to Science in Social-Research," American Behavioral Scientist, 32:5, 513-551.

Whyte, William Foote, and Kathleen King Whyte (1988, 1991), Making Mondragon: The Growth and Dynamics of the Worker Cooperative Complex, Ithaca, New York: Cornell University Press,

Whyte, William Foote (1994), Participant Observer: An Autobiography, Cornell University Press.

3

International Organization and Organizational Sociology Theories and Perspectives

Outline

This chapter summarizes the current literature [key theories and readings] that focuses on the study of international organizations and answers on how the theories and perspectives of organizational sociology might better inform the study of international organizations.

This chapter provides a general overview of how international organizations formed, for what purpose, and how their structure changed. The distinction between formal organizational studies and studies of international organizations is minimal because both help to widen the idea of creating an original position for better combinations of favorable circumstances or situations in human affairs. The chapter will explain the origin of the term international organization (OR); the historical roots of studies; define or analyze the types of ORs in the contemporary world; reveal the relationship between the international relation (IR) and regime theories application in the OR's studies; and the impact of globalization. The chapter also unveils the relationships between organizational sociology and ORs, and, finally, it gives a general outline of the application of institutional theory in the study of ORs following a summary. Organizations bring people in concert to achieve combined goals. They are accountable for determining the intelligence needed to meet their goals. This chapter provides a glimmer of international organizations theory, origin, historical account, definitions, and utilization of the contemporary academic world intertwined with the international relations, regime, and globalization as well as organizational sociological theories and perspectives that can be utilized to study international organizations. This chapter will help understand the historical account of international organizations, pedagogical development, and contemporary theories and practices of international organizations and organizational sociology.

111

112 *International Organization and Organizational Sociology*

Introduction

How Were International Organizations Formed?

There is not much historical literature available on how international organizations were formed and how their expansion occurred beyond state borders before 1900. However, we do know that the internationalization or formalization of organizations beyond state borders was aimed primarily at securing the political and legal security of the state (Bernard 1868; Burns 1917; Calvo 1896; Dickinson 1920; Potter 1922, 1935). Another aim of formalizing organizations was to build cooperation between nations' citizens for their welfare and the exchange of business commodities. According to Potter (1922), "Among nations of the world the first and basic type of relationship and activity to develop is that of interchange of commodities and cultural contributions in general which we call international intercourse. This activity leads into forms of an international organization, which is private or unofficial, and into that form of worldwide culture and activity which we call cosmopolitanism" and "The principal element in modern cosmopolitanism, as it has developed since 1850, is a common economic and scientific culture" (Potter 1922, pages 36, 50). Potter's account highlights how (between 1900 and 1920) cosmopolitanism paved new ground for the establishment of international organizations related to travel, communication, industry, and commerce, how finance was developing and establishing control over the international relations of the world (Potter 1922, page 51), and how imperialism was adopted in the western world.

Traditionally, international organizations have been mostly established by the states to fulfill political goals (Archer 1991). The study of international organizations is fully developed as a subfield of political science, and we as sociologists have much to learn about the dynamism of politically embedded international organizations. Therefore, from the sociological viewpoint, we know only a little about international organizations. On the other hand, both organizational sociological theories and international organization theories follow the same historical route of theory building in that there are ontological similarities between international organizations and organizational theory. In this context, it is necessary to understand what a theory is and how theories come into practice. Broadly, theories are developed through critical thinking and knowledge building reasoning. According to Robert Cox, "Theory is always for someone's random purpose. All theories have a perspective. Perspectives derive from a position

Introduction 113

in time and space, especially social and political time, and space. The world is seen from a standpoint definable in terms of nation or social class, dominance, or subordination, of declining power, of a sense of immobility or present crisis, experience, and hopes and expectations for the future" (Cox 1981, page 128). Cox's notion of theory provides the legitimate ground to understand the theories in social sciences (in the context of this paper, organizational sociological theories examine the social context of organizations and international organization theories deal with the political context of organizations in time and space).

As sociologists, we believe that all forms of organizations follow certain norms, values, social order, legal and social rules, and regulations; they are established with a vision and mission and try to attain certain goals. The ultimate goal of any national or international organization is to help maintain and fulfill societal demands (which could be political, economic, or social). In this context as sociologists, we know some basic grounds of international organizations, their foundations, their bureaucratic functions, and roles in society. There is a large body of sociological knowledge which sits as a background to international organizational research, but little in the way of specific contributions. For the international organizations of the future, however, particularly those that will attempt to address global environmental concerns as they affect communities, there is a body of sociological knowledge poised to inform international organizations (Bhandari 2011, 2012, 2014, 2017, 2018, 2019, 2010).

There are hundreds of scholars (political scientists) who have evaluated international organizations from combined perspectives (Cook 1992; Lash 1971; Norton 1998; Otto 1996; Archer 1983, 1992; Barnett and Finnemore 2004, and so many to note). On the other hand, only a few sociologists (Philip Selznick 1949; William Foote Whyte 1943; Ness and Brechin 1988; Brechin 1997, for example) have tried to examine international organizations through a combined perspective (via the application of international relations and regime as well as sociological theories). Through the close examination of the available literature on organizational theory and international organizations, there is an overlap of relevant theories. There is also a close relationship between international relations, regime formation and development, globalization, global transformation and internationalization of social movements, and organization and international organizations theories. Historically, sociological epistemologies have been developed to tackle social problems and formal and informal organizations have been formed to address social issues as they appeared. When socioeconomic and political problems

114 *International Organization and Organizational Sociology*

crossed the borders, international organizations were formed to tackle those issues on an international scale.

In this short essay, first, I will briefly explain what the international organizations are, their origin, and the relationship between international relations, regime formation and development, globalization, and global transformation. And, second, I will note how organizational sociological perspectives can be understood through the study of international organizations. The field of organizational sociology as an academic discipline is new. As Scott (2004) notes, "the overall history (organizational sociology) is, I believe, a positive one, beginning from a barren landscape and developing into one of the most vigorous intellectual areas of the second half of the twentieth century" (page 1). Scott's statement provides a basis to compare organizational sociology with international organizations' history. Organizational sociology was mostly developed as a substantive field of study from 1970, whereas international organization textbooks for graduate classes can be found as early as 1922 (Potter's introduction to international organizations was published in 1922). However, the epistemology of social sciences has the same historical roots (Cox 1981) that apply in the context of organizational sociology and international organization theory-building. Organizational sociology examines organizations from three major perspectives: rational, natural, and open systems. According to the rational perspective, organizations are instruments designed to attain specified goals. These perspectives are developed based on major classical organizational theories (e.g., Fredrick W. Taylor's scientific management theory, Henri Fayol's administrative theory, and Max and Weber's theory of bureaucracy). Natural system perspectives disagree with the rational system and add the view that organizations are collectivities; they were developed by the post-modern and modern theorists (who incorporated the classical theorist's concept and added more contemporary thoughts) (e.g., Elton Mayo, Chester I. Bernard, and Philip Selznick). Open system perspectives view "organizations as systems of interdependent activities linking shifting coalitions of participants. The systems are embedded independent on continuing exchanges with and constituted by- the environment in which they operate" (Scott 2003, page 30). The open systems perspective is the most recent phenomenon of organizational analysis. This perspective is backed by the contingency theorists such as James Q. Wilson, Jay Galbraiand Paul Lawrence, Jay Lorsch, and the proponent of the organization as odea l, on Karl Weick (Scott 2003). Various organizational thought can be classified according to micro and macro levels of organizational analysis including system-structural, strategic choice, natural selection, and collective-action

Introduction 115

views of organizations (Astley and Van de Ven 1983). Based on these major perspectives, organizational sociologists have developed various approaches to analyzing the function of organizations in social environments.

Some of the scholars of international organizations have used such thoughts and perspectives (Oran Young 2002; Martha Finnemore 1993, 1996; Martha Finnemore and Kathryn Sikkink 2005; Michael Barnett and Martha Finnemore 2003; Kenneth W. Abbott and Duncan Snidal 1998). However, there is no extensive utilization of this solid sociological knowledge in international organizations' literature. Likewise, sociologists also have not pointed out which organizational theory mostly fits the study of international organizations. Only a few organizational sociologists have attempted to utilize organizational theory to study international organizations (Elton Mayo's Hawthorne Studies 1932; Selznick 1949 (his examination of Tennessee Valley Authority and grassroots organizations must be the earliest complete sociological study of organizations); Jonsson 1986; Ness and Brechin 1988; Kahn and Zald 1990; Goldman 2005). Kahn and Zald (1990) apply Graham Allision's (1971) essence of the decision method to understand how international organizations work to foster international relations. They argue that both nations and organizations face parallel problems, including the need to manage conflict and enable cooperation. They focus on the dynamic of international organizations and international relations in terms of decision-making and the condition of uncertainty. Kahn and Zald (1990) illustrate organizations as a model for national states and the importance of understanding the organizational character of international relations. Goldman (2005) studies World Bank work procedure partly as an insider and partly as an external observer; his study examines the bureaucratic hegemony of the World Bank, which (despite the World Bank's mission statement) is not necessarily useful or productive in the development of the developing world. These organizational sociological approaches can serve as models in the study of international organizations. Such perspectives could inform the international organizational disciple of sociology.

In the following paragraphs, I will briefly note the origin of international organizations; their development followed by the definitions and roles of IOs, and their focus and relationships with the international relations, regime, and globalization theories. As I noted in the above paragraphs, most of the organizational sociological perspectives (rational, natural, and open) and approaches (organization as complex phenomena, network, institutional, transaction cost, ecological, etc.) could be utilized as models for the study of international organizations. However, in this essay, I will discuss major organizational sociological perspectives and explain how they could

116 *International Organization and Organizational Sociology*

contribute to understanding international organizations in very general terms. Finally, I will illustrate how sociological organization as complex phenomena and institutional theory can be applied to study international organizations and conclude this essay followed by the endnotes.

The Origin of the Term International Organization

Historically, the study of an international organization examines the formal organizations and their roles to address issue areas of international cooperation from a political perspective. According to Archer (1991), the term international organization was first used by Professor James Lorimer of England in 1867. Archer does not give any detail about how and in which context Lorimer used the term "international organizations." In this respect, Pitman Potter (1945) has done extensive research about the origin of the term, confirming that James Lorimer was the first lawyer who used the term international organization in his lecture before the Royal Academy in Edinburgh on May 18, 1867, on the heading of "On the application of the principle of relative or proportional, equity to the international organization." According to Potter, Lorimer again used the term international organization in his publication in 1971. Following Lorimer, Thomas Willing Balch used the term international organization in 1874 (Potter 1945, page 805). However, Potter assures us that until 1920, the term was not familiar to the American academicians. Pitman Potter, in his article entitled "Origin of the Term International Organization" published in 1945, notes that "when thinking out the application of the general principles of political science and the art of the government to the international field in the years 1914-1920, and composing a general text on the subject, the present writer employed the phrase has been employed previously or not" (Potter 1945, page 803). Potter in his book "Introduction to the study of international organization," published in 1922, randomly uses the term "international organization" without any definition of the term. He begins "I have tried to show that international organization is not a new thing in world history, nor a reform proposed for the future, but a political system of long-standing which deserves to be studied as such" (Potter 1922, vii in the preface). He further notes that "I have tried to show how this standing system of international organization has expanded and developed, particularly in the past century, to set forth the cases which will probably lead to a continuation and intensification of that process in future................finally I have expressed the conviction that such a process is salutary, in that it meets a real need of the world today, and have attempted to make some suggestions regarding steps which

Introduction 117

might profitably be taken in the improvement and development of existing institutions of international governments." Potter's publication of 1922, which is already a historical document (in the current context), focuses on two major historical accounts of international organizations: (1) international organizations were not new phenomena even at the beginning of the 20th century; (2) the expansion of international organizations was accelerating even during 1900–1922. Potter's (1922) account also asserts that the study of international organizations involved a major field examination of world politics and international relations.

Potter's (1922) prime motive was to establish international organizations as a separate field of study under the political science discipline. He does not oppose the application of an integrated approach to the study of international organizations and thinks that international organizational study can benefit from a broader approach. Most importantly, Potter searches other disciplines such as sociology and psychology and explains how researchers other than political scientists examine the state. He states that "sociologists have traced the origin of the state to the primitive tribe or clan or even to the elementary human family" (page 24). Classical examples of such a search for human political life can be seen in the research by Weber and Durkheim in sociology and Malinowski's research in anthropology. To answer the questions of what we know about the international organization, I think we should understand how the study of international organizations became an academic discipline. In this context, Potter's book "Introduction to the Study of International Organizations," published in 1922, provides a basis. Potter does not explicitly define what the meaning of international organization is but tries to explain it, in terms of international intercourse, cosmopolitanism, international politics, laws, treatises, negotiations, conferences, the international bureaucracy (administration), and international control with the concrete example of the "League of Nations," its role, and its formation. Another critical point I would like to illustrate from Potter is an acknowledgment of the roles of non-state actors. He states that "decades and even centuries, before the national states were willing to join in common governmental action, private persons were ready and eager to associate their activities and their interests across the national frontiers. Private international financial, scientific, and commercial organizations date back to the early days of modern Europe, not to mention, for the movement, the great religious orders and trading companies of a still earlier period" (page 37). However, in my survey of literature on international organizations, I found only limited illustrations of Potter's contributions to the foundation of international organization studies by contemporary scholars. This seems an area for investigation.

Historical Roots of International Organization Studies

International organizations (IO) are not new phenomena. Broadly, international organizations' historical roots can be traced to Greek civilization (Plato and Aristotle), although they have mostly flourished since the Enlightenment era. However, empirical studies show that the scientific study of IOs begins only in the 19th century. Political scientists examine international organizations in terms of international relations, governance, and power dynamics. To examine society, they use various historical perspectives (developed by ancient and classical social thinkers) such as power and authority (rewards and punishment) and the political community (including nationalism). Power and authority notions were developed first by Plato and further explanations developed by Bodin continued to be built upon by the classical organizational theorists (Weber, Taylor, Simon, etc.). Likewise, another perspective is to see the world in terms of mathematical order (quantitative approach) (Lucas 1977, 1980, 1981). Archer (1991) examines these perspectives in two major classifications, i.e., (1) traditional and (2) revisionist. The traditional perspective considers the international organization as a part of the institutionalized relationship between states and governments. This perspective is state-centric and only focuses on governmental international organizations. The traditional school of thought (which covers both realist and neo-realist schools of thought) is mostly developed by the lawyers who primarily study organizations such as the League of Nations and United Nations, NATO, European Union, etc., who contribute to the formation of international government. They examine international organizations' role in global legal policy formation. Likewise, revisionists also focus on the state-centric approach to studying international organizations; however, they do not discard the roles of non-governmental international organizations in world politics (Archer 1991).

Scholars in the social sciences have developed many social theories that address the underlying causes such as social, political, and cultural conflicts and inequalities (through various paradigms: positivist, constructivist, functionalist, interpretive, radical-humanist, radical-structuralist, etc.; (Kuhn 1970, 1974, 1977, 1979). To address such issues, there is a long history of establishing many formal and informal organizations in national and international contexts (Potter 1922). There is no empirical evidence to state when international organizations began their formal roles. According to Archer (1992), the rise of modern international organizations began in 1919 at the Versailles Peace Conference. The participants at Versailles were the representatives of victorious powers ready to write a peace treaty, including many national interest groups and international non-governmental organizations (INGOs) wanting to advance public health, a lot of workers, the cause of peace, or the laws of war (Archer 1992, page 3). This conference was influenced by the previous Hague Conferences in 1899 and 1907 which formed the grounds for the creation of the League of Nations. The League of Nations could not generate a consensus on world politics, which was the example of the Second World War. Therefore, world leaders were looking for a new international organization that could bring the world's nations together to manage permanent peace across the globe. The foundation of the United Nations was the outcome of that effort. There have been debates about the role of the United Nations, its usefulness, and its power dynamics (Pangle and Ahrensdorf 1999; Grant 2001). However, the role of the United Nations to bring international society to resolve global geo-politico-socioeconomic problems is unavoidable (Archer 1983). One of the United Nations' roles is also to bridge the gap between the states and non-governmental organizations.

Definition of International Organizations

Traditionally, the study of international organizations was a field of political science that examined international organizations along with international relations. Political perspectives assume that states have military and economic power, but other institutions or individuals do not (Barkin 2006). International relations theory sees world politics as a struggle for power among sovereign states. According to Barkin (2006, page 3), IOs can be seen as the agents of forces for globalization because the roles of international organizations change due to technological changes and lead to more interdependency among states. IOs can be seen as regime as well as institution creators. In this context, international organizations are understood to be intergovernmental organizations, or those organizations created by agreement among the states. The international organizations established by a political group or non-affiliated individuals and groups are part of the international political system, but they are not considered IOs in traditional political science literature (Barkin 2006). However, the trend and field of IOs have been becoming broader since the First World War. As Kratochwil (2006) states, international organizations can be conceived of as the investigation of the various organizational forms that populate the international arena. This leads to the conclusion that the study of IOs does not just cover the IOs but includes all forms of organizations that have international influences or relationships. Based on Kratochwil's notion, the study of international organizations covers NGOs, nation-states, international regimes, security

120 *International Organization and Organizational Sociology*

alliances, multinational corporations, economic classes, democratic forms of governance, nationalisms, ethnicities, and cultures (Kratochwil 1994). In this context, international organizations cannot be the sole concern of political science but become matters for multidisciplinary investigation.

Theoretically, organizational research broadly examines (1) producing units and what factors determine organizational effectiveness or productivity and (2) sets of individuals whose well-being is affected by the terms of organizational membership and whose motivation to continue that membership depends on their assessment of its comparative contribution to their well-being (Kahn 1990, page 3). This notion can be applied to investigating the role of international organizations because they follow more complex formalities than domestic formal organizations. The roles of organizations depend upon the motives behind why, how, and for what purpose organizations were formed.

To understand international organizations, it is essential to investigate what criteria make an organization international. The Yearbook of International Organizations (1976/1977), published by the Union of International Associations (UIA), broadly states eight major criteria. (1) The aims must be genuinely international to cover at least three states. (2) Membership must be individual or involve collective participation, with full voting rights, from at least three states and must be open to any individual or entity appropriately qualified in the organization's area of operations. Voting must be arranged so that no one national group can control the organization. (3) The constitution must provide for a formal structure giving members the right to periodically elect governing bodies and officers. Provision should be made for continuity of operation with a permanent headquarters. (4) Officers should not all be of the same nationality for more than a given period. (5) There should be a substantial contribution to the budget from at least three states and there should be no attempt to make profits for distribution to members. (6) Those with an organic relationship with other organizations must show that they can exist independently and elect their officials. (7) Evidence of current activities must be available. (8) There are some negative criteria: size, politics, ideology, fields of activity, geographical location of headquarters, and nomenclature are irrelevant in deciding whether a set-up is an "international organization" or not (as cited by Archer 1992, pages 33–34). UIA provides a clear picture of how organizations should be categorized and evaluated.

Several authors have tried to define international organizations along the same lines as those suggested by the Union of International Associations (UIA1976/1977) (Archer 1983, 1992, 2001); however, they depend on disciplinary orientations (political science, law, sociology, business,

Introduction 121

administration, religion, etc.). An example from a legal perspective is as follows: "Any contemporary international organization (intergovernmental) is created by states using a concluding an international treaty for the purpose…A constituent instrument of an international organization provides for certain rights and capabilities of the organization and possesses a certain degree of international legal personality" (Osaka 1972, pages 24–30, as cited by Archer 1992, page 35). Another definition from a socialist perspective is "in its most general form…a stable, clearly structured instrument of international co-operation, freely established by its members for the joint solution of common problems and the pooling of efforts within the limits laid down by its statute….[Such organizations] have a rule of at least three member countries. These may be governments, official organizations, or non-governmental organizations. International organizations have agreed on aims, organs with appropriate terms of reference, and specific institutional features such as statutes, rules of procedure, membership, etc. The aims and activity of an international organization must be in keeping with universally accepted principles of international law embodied in the Charter of the United Nations and must not have a commercial character or purpose of profit-making" (Morozove 1977, page 30, cited by Archer 1992, page 35). Authors like Reuter (1958) see an IO as permanently expressing a juristic will distinct from that of its members, and Pentland (1976) sees it as a legal body of the bureaucratic structure. Archer (1992) actually provides a comparative list of definitions and confirms that there is no homogeneity in the definitions.

These definitions give a fuzzy picture of "what international organizations" are. The UIA (1976/1977) outline is widely accepted. Authors like Pierre Gerbet (1977), Plano and Riggs (1967), Wallage and Singer (1970), and Virraly (1977) have also tried to capture the notion of IOs' basic nature. Among them, Gerbet's definition is most convincing. He states that "The idea of an international organization is the outcome of an attempt to bring order into international relations by establishing lasting bonds across frontiers between governments or social groups wishing to defend their common interests within the context of permanent bodies, distinct from national institutions, having their characteristics, capable of expressing their own will and whose role it is to perform certain functions of international importance" (Gerbet 1977, page 7, cited in Archer 1992, page 36). Based on these common criteria, Archer states that an "IO is a formal, continuous structure established by agreement between members (governmental and/or non-governmental) from two or more sovereign states to pursue the common interest of membership" (Archer 1992, page 37). It is a common concept that

122 *International Organization and Organizational Sociology*

international organizations should have international memberships, aim to serve common interests, and have a certain structure of operation.

In the contemporary world, the impact of international organizations can be found in every sphere of the political, social, economic, and environmental arenas. The political function of IOs is to provide the means of cooperation among states in areas in which cooperation provides advantages for all or a large number of nations. Their social function is to try to reduce social inequality. Their economic function can be to reduce inequality on a global scale, and their environmental function can be to make collaborative efforts to overcome global environmental problems (Young 1999; Bennett 1982; Ness and Bechin 1988; Archer 1992). As Selznick (1957) notes, international organizations represent a form of institution that refers to a formal system of rules and objectives and are a rationalized administrative instrument. Likewise, Duverger (1972) states that a formal technical and material organization includes a constitution, local chapters, physical equipment, mechanics, emblems, letterhead stationery, a staff, an administrative hierarchy, and so forth (as cited by Archer 1992, page 2). As noted above, international organizations form to attain certain goals and have specified rules and regulations at both local and global levels. They hold the authority (granted by the respected governments) to spread their products and services beyond any one country's borders and therefore assist globalization. International organizations are also defined as a process; international organizations are representative aspects of the phase of that process that has been reached at a given time (Claude 1964, page 4, as cited by Archer 1992, page 2). These accounts show the relationships between globalization and the spread of international organizations in various categories.

Types of International Organizations

International organizations can be grouped according to their objectives and their functions. There are three major categories of organizations: intergovernmental organizations (IGOs), international non-governmental organizations (INGOs), and multinational enterprises or multinational corporations (MNCs). Intergovernmental organizations are based on a formal instrument of agreement between the governments of nation-states including three or more nation-states as parties to the agreement, possessing a permanent secretariat performing ongoing tasks. INGOs are defined and classified as in the ECOSOC definition of INGOs; they should be international NGOs in terms of aims, members, structure, officers, finance, autonomy, and activities, all of them taking place in three or more countries. To be

Introduction 123

considered multinational enterprises, organizations should have the products and services in more than three countries. In this paper, my focus will be on INGOs, those established to attain certain goals, and their relationship with certain organizational theories, according to niche and demands. These INGOs are considered non-state actors and have a considerable influence role on socioeconomic and human services delivery (education, health, human rights, and women's rights), economic development (agriculture, microcredit, and infrastructures), and environmental conservation and world politics. There are many varieties of INGOs, and they have a long history of their products and service delivery. For example, the International Red Cross Society is one of the oldest INGOs and was established in February 1863 in Geneva, Switzerland, to treat war victims and deliver health services. Fauna & Flora International was established in 1903 as the world's first international conservation organization with the purpose of control conserves instrumental in establishing much of today's global and local conservation infrastructure, including organizations such as the World Wide Fund for Nature, IUCN, The World Conservation Union, the Convention on International Trade in Endangered Species of Wild Fauna & Flora, and conservation instruments such as the Red List of endangered species.

There are thousands of international organizations working in various sectors. Each of them has varieties of identical roles and contributions to the conservation of nature, social development, human rights, economic development, governance, health, infrastructure development, crisis management, etc. In other words, the contemporary world in which there are no international organizations creating rules, monitoring behavior, or promoting cooperation (Barkin 2006). These organizations are also key actors in socio-political and economic transformation. It is important to explore the contribution of international organizations to understand how international social orders are created, connected, maintained, and changed through complex formal organizations (Avant 2004) in the contemporary world.

International Organizations in the Contemporary World

Contemporary scholars in the social sciences are fascinated by international organizations. Traditionally, many social scientists, particularly from political science, have long been engaged in analyzing international organizations, primarily in terms of power and security. However, there was a gradual shift in their focus in the first decades of the 19th century. In the contemporary arena, political scientists look farther afield as they study international affairs, political economy, policy studies and analysis, comparative

124 *International Organization and Organizational Sociology*

politics, international relations, and international organizations. In studying international organizations, they focus on the problem of cooperation in world politics. Political scientists examine international organizations by asking fundamental political questions, including those about the nature of political authority and political rights, the relationship between power and values, variation in the role and quality of government, the origins of political institutions, and the dynamics of international politics. There is a distinction between political scientists' and sociologists' approaches to the study of international organizations. Sociologists examine the social actors' activities, i.e., society and social problems. The purpose of social science is to find better options for a better society. Paul Taylor notes: "In the 20th-centuryventional social science developed as a trilogy of disciplines -- economics, sociology, and political sciences -- which purport, between them, to cover all social behavior" (Taylor, 2000, page 1106). There is a common notion of economic, political, and sociological theory that began with the same goal and purpose to benefit society. Robert Cox notes that "Social and political theory is history-bounded at its origin, since it is always traceable to a historically-conditioned awareness of certain problems and issues, a problematic, while at the same time it attempts to transcend the particularity of its historical origins to place them within the framework of some general propositions or laws" (Cox 1981, page 128).

The study of international organizations in the contemporary world is a common agenda. However, as noted earlier, the formation of international organizations was for political purposes, which is why political science has included the study of international organizations from the very beginning of its disciplinary development. Political scientists began to examine international organizations before the rise of the League of Nations. They also evaluate international organizations as means of global interaction. Archer (1992) illustrates Keohane and Nye's (1971, page xii) proposition of global interaction as occurring through (1) communication – the movement of information, including the transmission of belief; (2) transportation – the movement of physical objects, including war material and personal property, as well as merchandise; (3) finance – the movement of money and instruments of credits; and (4) travel – the movement of persons (Archer 1992, page 29). This notion of interaction resulted in the growth of international organizations. In other words, a favorable political environment is one of the causes of the exponential growth of international governmental, non-governmental, and multinational corporations. The examples can be drawn from the formal Soviet Union or other communist regimes on one hand and the proliferation of international organizations in the democratic republics of the developing world such as

India, Bangladesh, Nepal, etc., on the other. However, for decades in sociology, researchers have failed to fully apply sociological imagination to the study of international organizations. As the world becomes more interconnected and these types of social structures become more important, the need for critical analyses becomes more urgent (Brechin 1997). Ness and Brechin (1988) made an early attempt to bridge the gap between the study of international organizations and the sociology of organizations. In terms of bridging the gap, they first argue that international organizations are different according to their roles and functions. They reject the functionalist notion and argue that contingency theory is more suitable to understand international organizations which are alike. Following the Galbraith's (1973) principles of contingency theory (– there is no one best way to organize and any way to organizing is not equally effective, page 2), they state that "contingency theory argues that there is no one best way to organizing anything; the best structure and process is contingent upon such things as the environment and technology" (Ness and Brechin 1988, page 249). Theoretically, the contingency approach allows us to examine external and internal constraints in the organization. Ness and Brechin attempt to focus on how technological enhancement can be effective in global organizational settings. They state that "technology links the organization with its environment, creating a conduit through which influence, power, and materials pass. Relationships also exist between technology and other organizational element-structure...... Technology contributes to international organizations" (Ness and Brechin, 1988, pages 256–257). The organizational environment does not need to always remain placid; it can be turbulent and complex. However, contingency theory allows us to examine international and external environments to fit with complex situations. I see a clear link between technology organization and international organization as proposed by Ness and Brechin. Because of technological development, the contemporary world became more interconnected, and the role of international organizations is becoming increasingly significant, and, importantly for international policymaking, the process accelerates with the globalization of world politics.

International organizations, even the well-known and influential ones involved in economic development, have rarely been studied from a sociological perspective (Brechin 1989, 1997; Le Prestre 1985; Ness and Brechin 1988). Political scientists, particularly neo-realists, have historically seen international organizations as relatively insignificant players in international politics and affairs, at best as little more than the simple extensions of powerful states (Brechin 1997). More recently, Finnemore (1996, 2004) and several other authors representing political science, international relations,

126 *International Organization and Organizational Sociology*

public administration, and law have argued that international organizations are provocative institutions of power, especially in the developing world (Finnemore and Sikkink 1998; Barnett and Finnemore 1999). Barnett and Finnemore utilize sociological theory in explaining how social norms and values impact international organizations in terms of international relations. They argue that international relations (IR) scholars have not considered how IOs behave. Finnemore (1994) has applied the sociological perspective to study the extending role of UNESCO; however, her leaning is more toward political theory rather than sociological theory.

This important new realization in the literature, however, does not fully utilize sociological insights to examine complex formal organizations. Sociology views complex organizations with greater nuance. With legitimate authority, resources, and goals, complex organizations attempt to promote their professionalized missions and themselves while negotiating various institutional and technical environmental demands. The outcomes of these negotiations allow for greater or lesser organizational autonomy depending on actual conditions and politics from local to international levels. Sociology also views how technology and resource make the differences in organizational functions (Pfeffer and Salancik 1978). Pfeffer and Salancik (1978) argue that none of the organizations can be self-sufficient and so they have to obtain resources from their environment. Obtaining resources depends on power, which originates in social and economic exchanges, under uncertain conditions, when organizations seek to acquire vital resources but avoid dependence on organizations that supply those resources. This power dynamism equally applies in the case of international organizations when particular states hegemonize the authority of another state. In this context, as Bernett and Finnemore (1999, page 699) note, the rational-legal authority that IOs embody gives them power independent of states that created them and channels that power in particular directions. From a review of the political science literature related to international organizations, it is clear that political scientists have tended to examine international organizations through the theories related to international relations and regimes (Bhandari 2010, 2011, 2012, 2014).

International Relation (IR) Theory and International Organizations

Political scientists study political philosophy and governmental forms as well as the political behaviors and social interactions involved in the process of government. In this context of globalized world order, the study of

Introduction 127

intergovernmental relations has been the most important subject matter for the discipline since the First World War. Stephen Walt (1998) states that we need international relations theories because "there is an inescapable link between the abstract world of theory and the real world of policy." Furthermore, he notes that "We need theories to make sense of the blizzard of information that bombards us daily" and that "It is hard to make good policy if one's basic organizing principles are flawed, just as it is hard to construct good theories without knowing a lot about the real world" (Watt 1998, page 29). Robert Cox (1981) states that IR studies foreign affairs and global issues among states within the international system. Furthermore, IR theorists try to understand why war occurs – due to nationalism? Due to ideological class? And due to lack of government? Due to misperception among states? – and why there is inequality between different regions of the world (Viotti and Kaupppi 1999). It covers the roles of states, intergovernmental organizations (IGOs), non-governmental organizations (NGOs), and multinational corporations (MNCs). It is both an academic and public policy field and can be either positivist or normativism as it seeks to both analyze and formulate the foreign policy of particular states. There are many perspectives and theories to studying international relations. Different perspectives on international relations have been developed according to changes in the global political environment. In the 1930s, realist and idealist perspectives were in focus, with attention paid to the nature of international politics and the prospect of peaceful change. In the 1960s, traditionalists and behaviorists had debates about the application of appropriate methods to studying international relations (Viotti and Kauppi 1999). In this era, IR theorists began to apply dialectical approaches drawing from the historical epistemology of dialectical materialism coined by Hegel and applied by Marx, followed by positivism, realism, neo-realism, constructivism, critical, Marxism, neo-Marxian, Gramscian, feminism, post-colonialism, relativism, etc. As Robert Cox (1981) notes in terms of social forces of world order, dialectic materialism examines three categories of forces such as ideas, material capabilities, and institutions, which interact with each other. Likewise, international relations concepts have been developed on the grounds of power dynamics (Clifford 2005; Cooley and Ron 2002; Risse, Ropp, and Sikkink 1999; Keck and Sikkink 1998; Barnett and Finnemore 2004). However, in the contemporary world, most authors analyze IR from the perspectives of realism, pluralism, and globalism. According to Viotti and Kauppi (1999), realism has four key assumptions: (1) states are the principal or most important actors; (2) states are viewed as unitary actors; (3) the state is a rational actor (game theory and deterrence theory); and (4) using military force for national security can attain international stability. Further realist

128 *International Organization and Organizational Sociology*

approaches consider the consistency with power dynamism (world must be perceived as interwoven, with an established notion of power) as universally applicable policy sustainability (policy must command support from public opinion and the international community) and contextuality (action must take account of socio-cultural historical contexts) (Kissinger 2001).

Likewise, pluralism (also referred to as liberalism) has different assumptions, wherein (1) non-state actors are important entities in international relations and cannot be ignored. Pluralists assume that international organizations can be independent actors in their own right and can act to maintain the world order. Another challenge pluralists pose to realists is that for them, (2) the state is not a unitary actor; (3) they also challenge the realist notion that "the state is essentially a rational actor." They believe that individual actors, and international and national organizations, are more influential in maintaining the law and order of any single around the globe. The last point in the pluralists' argument is (4) that the agenda of international politics is extensive. Pluralists focus more on welfare than warfare. Furthermore, the neo-liberal approach cossid of proportionality (wise use of force), complementarity (consideration of both national and international interests), and clarity in terms and restraint (Nye 1999).

Another mostly used IR approach is constructivism. Realism and liberalism focus on the material factor of power and trade, while constructivism gives attention to the impact of ideas. Ted Hopf (1998) states that constructivism offers alternative understandings of a number of the central themes in international relations theory, including the meaning of anarchy and balance of power, the relationship between state identity and interest, an elaboration of power, and the prospects for change in world politics. "Constructivism itself should be understood in its conventional and critical variants, the latter being more closely tied to the critical social theory" (Hopf 1998, page 172). This approach considers IR policy as dependent on historical, cultural, political, and social contexts.

Likewise, globalism is another comparatively new phenomenon in IR theory. "Globalists typically assume that the starting point of analysis for international relations is the global context within which states and other entities interact." Globalists (1) emphasize the overall structure of the international system or, more colloquially, the "big picture" (Viotti and Kauppi 1999, page 9). Globalists (2) view international relations from a historical perspective. They analyze international relations through Marxist and neo-Marxist perspectives and hold that the defining characteristic of the international system is that it is capitalist. Globalists (3) emphasize how international organizations, transnational actors, and coalitions work in the

Introduction 129

mechanism of domination by which some states, classes, or elites manage to benefit from this capitalist system at the expense of others. "More specifically, globalists are typically concerned with the development and maintenance of dependency relations among northern, industrialized states (in North America, Europe, and Japan) and the poor, underdeveloped, or industrially backward Third World or less developed countries (LDCs) of Latin America, Africa, and Asia" (page 9). Globalists (4) emphasize the importance of economic factors when it comes to explaining the dynamics of the international system (Viotti and Kauppi 1999, pages 6–12).

In addition to major realism, neo-realism, constructivism, liberal and neo-liberal, or pluralism perspectives, international relations theory also applies multidisciplinary approaches such as behaviorism (psychological), world system (sociological), critical (sociological based on Marxist and neo-Marxist notion), and feminism (which mostly criticizes the realist approach: it is seen as a male-dominated theory about the aggressive world of states controlled by aggressive men) (Tickner 1992). These various approaches to international relations examine how organizational processes and bureaucratic politics are associated. It draws on the Weber notion of bureaucracy to create a world view of international organizations (pluralist paradigm). Its focus is on transnationalism, which emphasizes ties between societies that include much more than state-to-state relations. Transnationalism can be understood as an extension of pluralist politics beyond the borders of any state. "Transnationalism is the processes whereby international relations conducted by governments have been supplemented by relations among private individuals, groups and societies that can and do have important consequences for the course of events" (James Rosenau 1969, as cited by Viotti and Kauppi 1999, page 211). The transition to transnationalism occurs through modernization, integration (regional integration downplays the state as the unit of analysis; decision making and power make a significant difference and allow other forms of political organization aside from territoriality-based national states to become possible), interdependence, regime, and multilateralism (Viotti and Kauppi 1999, pages 212–215). Social science scholars need to understand the fuzziness of global social and political environments. Walt (2005) examines the complexities of current world politics and explains the importance of IR theories the policymaking.

There are overlaps of theories and paradigms among international relations theory, sociological theory, organizational theory, and international organization theory. Literature is silent on bridging such gaps. Ness and Brechin (1988) have initiated studies to bridge this gap, but there has been no continuation of this effort from the sociological point of view. In contrast,

130   *International Organization and Organizational Sociology*

political scientists have been engaged in developing several paradigms based on this notion (Young 1989; Barnett and Finnemore 2004). I think sociological theories can offer more to the study of international relations, particularly through contingency, networks, and systems and agency theories, because the purposes of those theories match with international relations theory-building. Equally, organizational sociologists can learn from IR, particularly through the epistemologies of pluralism and globalism. However, to examine the common ground of epistemology, extensive multidisciplinary research is needed. Another major approach to the study of international organizations is highly influenced by the international regime theory (Bhandari 2010, 2011, 2012, 2014). There is an established notion that international organizations create their niches and standards and diffuse those through their programs, networks, and program implementation procedures.

Regime Theory and International Organizations

As international relations theories are closely interlinked with the IOs, IOs create regimes. "Regime is sets of implicit or explicit principles, norms, rules and decision-making procedures around which actors expectations converge in a given area of international relations" (Krasner 1983; Krasner's approach to international regimes defines them as (1) principles and values; (2) norms; (3) rules; and (4) enforcement mechanisms; as cited by Cogburn 2003, page 136). Keohane and Nye (1983) state that regimes are sets of governing arrangements [that include] networks of rules, norms, and procedures that regularize behavior and control its effects. Viotti and Kauppi (1999) clarify, stating that regimes are sets of rules which may have international and non-governmental organizations associated with them (page 215). International regimes are structures designed to foster international cooperation among participants' countries. Every country needs help to solve transnational problems. Examples to be seen in the current environment are global terrorism and the fight against the transnational drug problem, and the fight to minimize HIV and AIDS, which cannot be resolved by a single state. International organizations can create powerful tools to solve a particular problem, which helps to increase their power, access, and authority through collaborative efforts, mutual agreements, and policy formation. This situation creates a favorable environment for formulating new regimes, where solutions can be contemplated. This is one aspect of international regimes. The second aspect focuses on the implementation of formulated policy through the institutionalization of rules and international agreements that devise and

Introduction   131

control solutions to the initial problem(s) (Krasner 1983; Young 1989; Rittberger 1993; Cogburn 2003).

Power-based realist theorists emphasize the role of anarchy and the impact of the relative distribution of capabilities. In this type of realist regime, the guiding idea is hegemonic stability; the argument is that regimes are established and maintained when a state holds a preponderance of power resources, as the United States did after the Second World War and continues to do. Another type of regime is interest-based, which makes claims that international regimes can play a role in helping states to realize their common interests. Similarly, knowledge-based theorists argue that state interests are not given but created. Knowledge is shared by decision-makers through the influence of transnational epistemic communities. A knowledge-based regime can be formed through social construction (Viotti and Kaupppi 1999). This knowledge of regime can equally be applied to the study of international organizations from an organizational sociological approach to examining the effectiveness and contribution to social well-being.

Regime studies use similar epistemology to international relations. The major approaches of regime studies are liberal and neo-liberal, realist (classical realism and defensive realism), neo-realist and Marxist, neo-Marxist (Western or Hegelian Marxism, such as neo-Gramscian theory), and post-modernist (Cogburn 2003). However, there are several other approaches in use embedded within these epistemologies, such as the balance of power (Paul, Wirtz, and Fortmann 2004), behaviorism (Viotti and Kauppi 1987), complex interdependence (Keohane and Nye 1977), constitutive theory and constructivism (Wendt 1992), cosmopolitanism (Cheah and Robbins 1998), dependency, feminism, game theory (Viotti and Kauppi 1987), globalization (Gill 1998), globalism developed through Marxist and dependency theory (Viotti and Kauppi 1987; Cogburn 2003), conflict prevention (Friedman 2000), hegemony (Gramsci 1971; DuBoff 2003; Chomsky 2003), imperialism (Morgenthau 1948), intergovernmental (Moravcsik 1993), normative theory (Viotti and Kauppi1987), and so on. These approaches are equally important and commonly used approaches by organizational sociologists. The only difference is that political scientists examine these approaches as political power dynamics. They put the state first and social dynamism comes later. On the other side for the sociologist is that society or social environment is given priority. Both regime and international relations theories follow the same basic theories and principles, equally support the importance of international organizations, and are equally influenced by development theory and globalization. Except for Ness and Brechin, sociologists have

132 *International Organization and Organizational Sociology*

mostly not examined how international relations and the regime concept can be applied to study social problems. Ness and Brechin (1988, page 258) state that "international relations can be enhanced if we pay greater attention to how modern international organizations emerged and what they do in action - in short if we pay greater attention to organizational performance." They argue that technology is the prime factor in organizational change. I see a clear link between technology organization and international regime as proposed by Ness and Brechin. Technology produced both world consensus and conflict (in the case of the condom distribution); however, external technology has benefited the organization (Ness and Brechin 1988, page 258). This account can be related to contemporary regime formation through technology. Another example is the expansion of information technology to the regime generated by the Mcdonald's fast-food corporation. However, the incremental formation of such regimes will not necessarily solve associated political or social problems (Bhandari 2018, 2019, 2010).

Social problems have been increasing on a global scale (HIV, AIDS, inequality, transnational migration, terrorism, and environmental problems), and these problems themselves create certain types of regimes and format their networks and relationships (Bhandari 2010, 2011, 2012, 2014). In this context, sociologists can inform international relations theorists and regime theorists about how knowledge forms in local contexts (social collaboration) and how this knowledge can be transferred to the international context.

Globalization, Organizations, and International Organizations

Sociological analysis of national societies utilizing sociological perspectives centers on social organization, power, conflict, and culture at the global level (Evans 2005). Various organizational sociologists have explained the impact of globalization on organizational theory building and have defined globalization as the diffusion of capitalistic paradigms in the global social system. The importance of organizations must be acknowledged in the present world. As Daft (2003) notes, organizations (both national and international) bring together resources to achieve desired goals and outcomes, produce goods and services efficiently, facilitate innovation, use modern manufacturing and information technologies, adapt to and influence a changing environment, create value for owners, customers, and employees, and accommodate ongoing challenges of diversity, ethics, and the motivation and coordination of employees. However, the globalized world has also brought various challenges to these organizations such as global competition, ethics and

Introduction 133

social responsibility, speed of responsiveness, the digital workplace, and diversity (Daft 2003).

The process of globalization has intensified the global interconnections of world societies. This process has made it a routine to discuss social life in a global frame rather than a national or a local one. This trend of globalization has also helped the standardization of organizational structures, organizational quality maintenance, and the regulation of organization management practices. Thus, standardized homogeneity can be seen in organizations in the form of education, business, social enterprises (hospitals and charity organizations), government agencies, and national and international development agencies (Drori, Mayer, and Hwang 2006). Globalization is not only an economic, political, and social process but also a cultural process, which is expanding and intensifying worldwide interdependencies. Organizational networks analyze these interdependencies, which are weakening national boundaries and classical bureaucracies. "World society models shape nation-state identities, structures, and behavior via worldwide cultural and associational processes .... As creatures of exogenous world culture states are ritualized actors marked by intensive decoupling and a good deal more structuration than would occur if they were responsive only to local, cultural, functional, or power processes" (Meyer et al. 1997, page 173). The trend of globalization process is leading the world society toward becoming a stateless society and helping to build the networks' purposive organizations. This is a shift from a power-centralized, traditional, and authoritative structure. Meyer et al. (1997) examine this globalization process as a shift of organizational roles in terms of social and cultural dynamism, "the dynamism that is generated by the rampant inconsistencies and conflicts within world culture itself," especially "contradictions inherent in widely varied cultural goods: equality versus liberty, progress versus justice," and the like (Meyer et al 1997, page 172).

The globalized neo-liberal world economy has also influenced organizational strategy and structure. New administrative systems have been developed and traditional/classical hierarchical, top-down bureaucracy has been challenged by flexible administrative design. This environment has also changed the organizational culture in terms of its values, attitudes, and behaviors (which were guided by the Western hegemonic (American) power system) (Daft 2003; Held 2004). In addition to changes in organizational settings, globalization has influenced the global economic system and its relationship with the natural environment; various perspectives have emerged for analyzing the role of transnational corporations. New global trade regimes have formed. Globalization has also changed the earlier perspectives on biophysical environmental change, which has helped

134 *International Organization and Organizational Sociology*

policymakers to formulate new agreements for environmental management. International organizations, as well as governments, have been forced to update their agendas to address global environmental degradation issues such as freshwater scarcity, renewable resource management, food supply, forest loss, biodiversity loss, and climate change, along with their ability to analyze and evaluate the conflicting perspectives.

Globalization has not only had positive impacts on global socio-political, economic, and environmental management but also has strong negative connotations, foremost among them, broadly, discarding the role and voice of the marginalized world. However, as I noted earlier, globalization is a continuous process embedded throughout the long history of the development of the western world. The notion of globalization is closely interlinked with development theory. Development theory dates from the 13th-century history, which reveals the transit of feudalism to capitalism. During the 13th to the early 18th centuries, the goal of development was the improvement of social welfare. However, there was no social welfare in feudal society. This lack helped capitalism to flourish, as a free tool for its creation. Likewise, in the age of competitive capitalism (1700–1860), political and economic power moved from the feudal aristocracy to the capitalist bourgeoisie, first in Europe and then in the rest of the world. Capitalism was exported to the rest of the world through the colonial system. Adam Smith's classical political economy and Karl Marx's historical materialism emerged in that period, followed by the age of imperialism (1860–1945). During the imperialism period, small industries collapsed, and big industries emerged in Europe. Neo-classical economic theory and the classical theory of imperialism were the products of that period. Lenin, Marshal, and Keynes were the major thinkers of that time. Keynes's theory of unemployment influenced the new steps to expand imperialism. The creation of the International Monetary Fund and the World Bank can be taken as examples of products of imperialism (Todaro and Smith 2002). These organizations are considered the major stakeholders in diffusing the notion of globalization.

In this regard, various organizational sociologists have analyzed organizations in terms of global change and developed innovative approaches to study complex organizations. There are debates among the authors about the degree of the impact of globalization; however, all accept the notion of a changing social, economic, and political global environment. There are also debates about the impact of globalization on international organization governance. Junne (2001) has noted that globalization might strengthen the role of international organizations through interactions. International organizations gain legitimacy through countries' specific (and global) legal

Introduction 135

procedures, justice, correct procedure, representation, effectiveness, and charisma. Globalization can make an impact on international organizations through (1) worldwide media coverage, (2) the expansion of worldwide trade, (3) the explosion of foreign direct investment, (4) the integration of financial markets, (5) the rise of the internet, (6) international labor migration, (7) global environmental problems, and (8) the globalization of crime (Junne 2001, page 200). Globalization has created demand and an environment for international organizations through international cooperation, coordination, and networks. International organizations may not be able to cope with the demands of the globalized world, because the organization may not be able to change their working modalities fast enough for public demand, because of life cycles, bureaucracy, posturing, and a lack of coordination (Junne 2001). However, to cope with the globalized world order, international organizations have been modifying their working procedures and creating their regimes to atomize and continue their impacts on both the northern and southern worlds. Globalization is an unseen force that has been insisting that international organizations learn to survive and maintain themselves according to a changing global environment (through technological advancement). There is not much research on how traditional organizations are shifting with and incorporating the unique environment. This could be a new area of key research in the future.

As I have noted above, globalization has both positive and negative connotations. Among the latter, it is not creating favorable conditions for the global environment. Rischard (2001) has nicely summarized the environmental challenges posed through globalization in three major headings: (1) "sharing our planet: issues involving and global commons, such as global warming, biodiversity loss, deforestation and desertification, water deficit, fisheries depletion, maritime security, and pollution." He has also identified the major issues to be considered urgently in section (2), "sharing our humanity: issues requiring a global commitment; such as the fight against poverty, peacekeeping and conflict prevention, education for all, global infectious diseases, digital divide, natural disaster prevention and mitigation"; and in section (3) "sharing our rulebook: issues needing a global regulatory approach; reinventing taxation for the 21st century, biotechnology rules, global financial architecture, illegal drugs, trade, investment and competition rules, intellectual property rights, e-commerce rules, and international labor and migration rules" (Rischard 2002, page 6, as cited by Held 2004, page 12). International non-governmental organizations have been highlighting those issues and creating a high-pressure environment through globalized connectedness and the mass media (mostly focused on the global

136 *International Organization and Organizational Sociology*

commons). This notion of connectedness and networking is a positive aspect of globalization that international organizations have been utilizing to create an international regime (Bhandari 2017, 2018, 2019, 2010). This principle of globalization is equally applied in the global, social, economic, and political movements (human rights, women's rights, and environmental conservation) and used in social knowledge construction.

So far, I found that international organizations have been in the mainstream as a subfield of political science from 1900 onwards. Studies of international organizations published before the Second World War ignore or do not incorporate the contribution of classical organizational theorists such as Weber, Taylor, and Fayol. In sociology, organization theory was in practice but was not fully developed as a subfield of study (it became a major field of study only from the 1970s) as it was in political science. Organizational theory is a wide discipline with deep roots in sociology. On the other hand, the theory of international organizations is rooted in political science and has been examined by political actors. In addition to the sociologists and political scientists, scholars from anthropology, public administration, social psychology, and economics have also been contributing to organizational theory building. The organizational study is recent as a discipline in sociology. Political scientists have propounded numerous ideas back to ancient Rome and philosophers go even farther back in time, while religious scholars trace their studies of organized religious organizations beyond that time. It is difficult to pinpoint the exact time sociologists became interested in theories of organization, and this seems a fruitful subject for further investigations.

One of the major international organizational theorists and authors of international organizations, Professor Clive Archer (2008) (in my email correspondence), supports my investigation that the first complete book on the international organization was by Leonard Woolf (1880–1969) (husband of Virginia Woolf, 1882–1941) which published in 1916, entitled "International Government." Woolf was a political leader who worked on the behalf of League of Nations. However, the first academic textbook of international organizations was published by Pitman Potter in 1922. On the other hand, Professor Richard Scott (2008 in my email correspondence) assures that until 1970, organizational study in sociology was only in its beginning phase. He mentions that "it is a bit difficult to select the first organization sociology textbook. It is a toss-up among the following: J. March and H. Simon, Organizations 1958 (by two political scientists, but an important founding approach), A. Etzioni, A Comparative Analysis of Organizations 1961 and P. Blau and W.R. Scott, Formal Organizations: A Comparative Approach published in 1962." However, with confirmation with Scott, I would consider

J. March and H. Simon's book entitled "Organizations," published in 1958, as the first academic textbook in organizational sociology. This account assures that organizational studies in sociology are young but have been capturing great attention since the 1980s. However, these publications also indicate that study of organizations is not a new phenomenon in sociology, which gives an option to search for the link and gap between these two major fields of study.

Potter indicates that the study of the international organization was in practice even before 1900, in the discipline of law, which covers international intercourse, cosmopolitanism, international politics, laws, treatises, negotiations, conferences, international bureaucracy administration, international control and international relations with the concrete example from the "League of Nations" – its role and its formation. The study of international relations, which is very associated with the study of international organizations, was begun in 1919 as a separate field of study in the United Kingdom. These accounts provide grounds to state that there was a long tradition of disciplinary distinction between organizational sociology and the study of international organizations. However, both fields developed from the same historical root of social sciences and have been contributing to the resolution of geopolitical and socioeconomic problems. Institutions, international relations, regime, globalization, and organizational network theories are most commonly used in both international organizations and organizational sociology literature. The scholars of political sciences examine these agendas through positivist, constructivist, realist, neo-realist, liberal, neo-liberal, and pluralist perspectives, and sociologists examine organizations through rational, natural, and open perspectives. However, in terms of the application of theories, both incorporate general social sciences theories (needless to state: functionalism to post-modern, feminism, or radical). Robert Cox's (1981) principle of theory building applies in both cases because the basic aim of the foundation of organizations is to attain certain goals. The commonalities between organizational sociology and international organizations theory are mostly found in the literature published after the Second World War and most importantly after the 1970s when multidisciplinary approaches began to flourish in the social sciences.

Scholars of contemporary international organizations have been advocating interdisciplinary approaches (Friedrich Kratochwil, Michael Barnett, Martha Finnemore, Margaret Keck, and Kathryn Sikkink). They argue that the role of international organizations has been expanding from the state-centric framework to the people-centric perspective. In the current context, the study of international organizations not only covers nation-states, international regimes, and security alliances but also the international

138 *International Organization and Organizational Sociology*

form of organizations that focus on non-state actors. In this context, the role of international organizations is not solely centered on the implementation of political agendas but also focuses on the social, cultural, and economic power dynamism. Therefore, the study of international organizations not only belongs to the political scientist but also to the sociologist and includes a range of social science discourses.

Insofar, in this section, I tried to explain what we know about the study of international organizations and how international organization theories are associated (broadly) with sociological theories and especially with organizational sociology. In the following section, I will very briefly outline organizational sociology's major approaches and try to connect with how these approaches can be applied to study international organizations.

Organizational Sociology

"The study of organizations provides a theoretical framework for knowledge about human behavior in organizations and reviews the empirical evidence for the propositions that make up the theory. The theory emphasizes the motivations for organizational participation and the processes of decision making within organizations" (Simon 1979).

Organizational sociology can be described as the study of formal groups organized to achieve or attain specific goals efficiently. Organizations have been leading the socio-political scenarios of the world for at least the last two centuries. In other words, organizations have been changing the world's socioeconomic landscape (Perrow 1991). As Perrow notes, "organizations are the key to society because large organizations have absorbed society. They have vacuumed up a good part of what we have always thought of as society and made organizations once a part of society into a surrogate of society" (1991, page 726, as cited by Scott and Davis 2007, page 340). This influence, which has increased gradually over time, mostly in the developed regions of the world during the 20th century, can be found in our everyday lives. Now, we are in organizational firms from birth to joining the workforce, as well as in our prayers, and we even die in organizations; along the way, we derive our identities from our associations with them. Organizations are related to every aspect of our daily life. Organizations are not only the building blocks of our societies, and a basic vehicle for collective action, but they are also our life forms. They bring into being the social structure of our societies and form our futures. Organizations are a fundamental part of contemporary societies; we enthusiastically turn to them or create them when a need or crisis exceeds our person or resources. Moreover, organizations are at the core spirit of every society and nation. Through organizations, we make difference in our society and achieve collective goals. Theoretically, organizations are dedicated to extending the idea of creating a new base to create new opportunities. These broader contexts of organization theories apply not only to the domestic organizational environment but also, equally, apply in the case of international organizations.

Sociologists have developed various perspectives and paradigms to analyze organizations based on the major classical writers of sociology. Organizational theory before 1900 emphasized the division of labor and the importance of machinery to facilitate labor. In the 1910s, the concept of scientific management arose, which describes management as a science with employers having specific but different responsibilities and encouraged the scientific selection, training, and development of workers and the equal division of work between workers and management. In the same era, the classical school listed the duties of a manager as planning, organizing, commanding employees, coordinating activities, and controlling performance; basic principles called for the specialization of work, unity of command, a scalar chain of command, and coordination of activities. In the 1920s, the concept of human relations was introduced, which focuses on the importance of the attitudes and feelings of workers and recognizes that informal roles and norms influence performance. The classical school in the 1930s re-emphasized the classical principles, followed by group dynamics, in the 1940s, which encouraged individual participation in decision-making and noted the impact of workgroups on performance.

International organizations' literature is silent about this sociological history of organizational development. Historical knowledge of the organization can be informed to see the similarities and differences between organizational sociological theory and theory building relevant to international organizations. I am interested in investigating the historical background of theories because I think history yields ideas that will enable me to categorize contemporary thoughts. This helps me to make judgments about how knowledge was developed and processed. Further, historical accounts document the experiences faced by the authors, explain their relationships to contemporary society, explore their research and analysis methods, and provide information about the debates and explanations within their context as well as their connections to previous authors (predecessors, allies, and rivals) (Chapoulie 2004).

Classical sociological theories have been criticized by contemporary organizational theorists since the late 1950s. As alternatives, contemporary

140 *International Organization and Organizational Sociology*

sociologists have developed more theories and methods grounded in the same roots but with new models (Kuhn 1962; Gibson Burrell and Gareth Morgan 1979; Morgan 1980; Ness and Brechin 1988; Taylor 2002; Scott 2003). Argyris (1957) states that the classical organizational theorists did not consider the workers' perspectives and that workers have minimal control over their working lives. Likewise, Salaman (1979) states that "a genuine sociology of organizations is not assisted by the efforts of some organization analysts to develop hypotheses about organizations in general, lumping together such diverse examples as voluntary organizations, charities, and political organizations ... It also obstructs the analysis of those structural elements which are dramatically revealed in employing organizations, but not necessarily in all forms of organization" (Salaman 1979, page 33, as cited by Thompson and McHugh 2002, page 6). Zey-Ferrell (1981) has summarized the major criticisms of organizational theories, mostly concerning the comparative structural and structural contingency approaches.

Organizations are formed by the contexts or environments in which they are established. Modern organizations replicate the impact of their historical origins in societies characterized by growing privileged circumstances and conflicts over the control and distribution of products and services. Organizations come in many puzzling forms because they have been designed to deal with a wide range of social, cultural, economic, and political problems (Bhandari 2010, 2011, 2012, 2014). Because they have emerged under widely varying environmental conditions, they have to deal with complexity within and emerging externalities. However, this complexity is not a new phenomenon for organizational theorists.

To address the complexity and the criticisms of organizational theories, various systems perspectives have been developed, particularly from the late 1950s. These system perspectives examine organizations as rational (embedded through the work of classical organizational theorists, Taylor, Fayol, Weber, Simon, March, and others), natural (including conflict approach and functionalist analysis of the organization, by theorists such as Durkheim, Malinowski, Radcliffe-Brown, and Parson), Barnard's cooperative system; Selznick, Perrow, and Mayer: the institutional approach, in which new institutional theorists are generally working under the open systems perspective; this focuses on the broader importance of the environment although institutional theory does discuss the issue of organizational survival [not efficiency] which is a natural system perspective; Mayo: Hawthorne effect, and open system (based on social movements; Bertalanffy, Boulding: Systems, Simon, and March 1958, etc.) (Scott 2003). According to Kuhn (1983), all three – the natural, rational, and open systems – perspectives

Organizational Sociology 141

co-exist and are important, but each has different methodologies. Each of them has different values, and each is based on different rhetoric. Kuhn's summary captures the notion of the systems perspective because they are interlinked in one way or another. Similar notions can be found in the works of Granovetter (1985), Weick (1976), and Pfeffer (1982) who have extensively analyzed organizational theory with combined perspectives. These authors' arguments are based on Weber's bureaucratic principles, as well as sociological approaches dealing with social systems, socially negotiated orders, social structures of power and domination, symbolic constructions, and social power structures. In other words, most of the social sciences' epistemologies have been applied to study different aspects of organizations such as economics (Williamson 1975: transaction cost approach), market and labor (Pfeffer and Cohen 1984), ecology (Carroll 1984; Graham 1985), environment (Tushman and Anderson 1986), and the organization as networks (Fligstein 1985; Chandler 1962; Harrison 1994; Uzzi 1996; Powell 1990). In terms of organizational theories, there is a wide range of applications. Specifically, organizational theorists concentrate mostly on contemporary theories such as contingency theory (Lawrence and Lorsch 1967; Galbraith 1974), bureaucracy (Weber 1946), cultural theory (Weick 1985), critical (Marxist) theory (Burawoy 1979; Burrell and Morgan 1979), feminist organizational theories (Putman 1992; Mohanty 1984; Brewis 2005; Calas and Smircich 1996), conflict theory (Burawoy 1979), and economic theory (Friedman 1953; Granovetter1985; Polanyi 1944; Williamson 1975).

Likewise, institutional theory has been applied to analyze organizations (Stinchcombe1959; Selznick1984; Rowan 1982; Meyer and Rowan 1977; Hirsch 1972; DiMaggio and Powell 1983), network theory (Powell 1990, and others), and organizational learning (Baum and Jintendra 1994; Cohen and Levinthal 1990). Similarly, population ecology theory has been used to study organizations (Astley 1985; Carrol and Hannan 1989). Organizations have also been analyzed with the application of post-modern approaches (Gergen 1992; Martin 1990), and with the application of Foucaultdian, Gramscian, and radical feminist approaches. Authors like Pfeffer and Salancik (1978) and Pfeffer (1982, 1992) have repeatedly applied resource dependency theory, Weick (1976) has applied sense-making theory to analyze organizations, and most commonly many authors have applied networks theory.

These sociological approaches could contribute to the theoretical basis for the study of international organizations. How, in what context, and when depend on the nature and role of the international organizations. However, several such approaches can be applied to study a given international

142 *International Organization and Organizational Sociology*

organization. The choice of approaches depends on the nature and purpose of the study as well as the complexity of the organization.

Organizations as Complex Phenomena

Organizational sociologists have extensively highlighted the complexity of organizations, which can be one of the major organizational sociological knowledge that can be transferred or inform the study of international organizations. Jeffrey Pfeffer and Gerald R. Salancik in their various articles and particularly in their recent book "The External Control of Organizations" note that a resource dependence perspective argues that the world of organizations has changed in several important ways, including the increasing externalization of employment and the growing use of contingent workers; the changing size distribution of organizations, with a larger proportion of smaller organizations; the increasing influence of external capital markets on organizational decision-making and a concomitant decrease in managerial autonomy; and increasing salary inequality within organizations in the US compared both to the past and other industrialized nations. These changes and their public policy implications make it especially important to understand organizations as social entities. Likewise, Fligstein and Neil (1987) state that one of the causes of organizational complexity is organizations' internal and external power struggles which leads to claims from various actors about the goals and resources of the organization. Those who control are those who can use the resources available to force their view of appropriate organizational behavior. In the largest firms, there are two bases of control: formal ownership and authority. This preceding theory draws on theories of sub-unit power (Perow 1970, 1972), political economy (Zald 1969, 1970), strategic contingencies (Hickson, Hinings, Lee Schneck, and Pennings 1971), and resource dependence (Pfeffer and Salancik 1978). Pfeffers (1981) attempts to synthesize these theories of power. Actors' claims to power must rest on two sources: their positions within organizational structures and their claims to define and resolve important problems in an organization.

Karl Marx's notions also explain the cause of organizational complexity as due to power struggle. Marx considers market despotism to be the only factory regime compatible with the exigencies of capitalist development. Four conditions for the existence of market despotism are (1) competition among firms, (2) the real subordination of workers to capital, the separation of conception from execution, (3) the workers' dependence on the employer, on the sale of labor for a wage, where dependence on a particular capitalist

Organizations as Complex Phenomena 143

is consolidated by a reservoir of surplus labor, (4) that the state would preserve only the external conditions of productions, and that it would not directly regulate either relation among capitalists or the process of production and its apparatuses (from Burawoy 1987). Burrell, Gibson, and Gareth Morgan (1979) state that the sociology of regulation is concerned with the organization is complex because according to them, in the society, (a) radical change, (b) structural conflict, (c) modes of domination, (d) contradiction, (e) emancipation, (f) deprivation, and (g) potentiality are always playing a key role. Patrick Kenis (2002) states that organizational complexities and problems are related to the societal/unspoken, legal, and bureaucratic procedures and control mechanisms of the internal and external environment. They bring the empirical evidence of organizational control mechanisms from "Personal Centralized Control" (Child 1984), "Coordination by Feedback" (March and Simon 1958), "Control Through Supervision" (Blau and Scott 1963), "Behavioral Control (direct)" (Ouchi 1977, 1979, 1980), "Bureaucratic Control" (Child 1984), "Programs (Activity Coordination)" (March and Simon 1958), "Rules and Regulations" (Blau and Scott 1963), "Behavioral Control (Rules and Procedures)" (Ouchi 1977, 1979, 1980), "Output Control" (Child 1984), "Programs (Output Coordination)" (March and Simon 1958), "Performance Records" (Blau and Scott 1963), "Output Control" (Ouchi 1977, 1979, 1980), "Cultural Control" (Child 1984), "Recruitment and Training" (Blau and Scott 1963), and "Clan Control" (Ouchi 1977, 1979, 1980).

Likewise, Joel A. C. Baum and Tim J. Rowley (2005) show organizational complexity with the illustration of several authors in three levels: (1) intra-organizational level where they claim organizations are complex because of complex adaptive systems, differentiation in agents, variations on decision making and problem-solving techniques and networks, and information technology and algorithmic complexity; (2) organizational level: complex adaptive systems, loose coupling and models, edge of chaos, simple rules and complex behavior, emergence, and recombination and evolution; and (3) interdependence, cellular automata, micro-behavior and macro-structure complex inter-organizational dynamics, sensitivity to initial conditions, and path dependence.

Furthermore, organizations, which provide security in the society, provide the environment to share and cope with problems and produce goods, deliver services, maintain order, and give a way to survive from the individual level to the societal stage. They help to minimize the challenges and establish order in society. Concerning linkage with day-to-day individual and societal settings, organizations are the fundamental building blocks of

144   *International Organization and Organizational Sociology*

modern societies, and the basic vehicles through which collective action is undertaken. The eminence of organizations in modern society is obvious when we consider some consequences of their actions.

I think, in the present time, organizations are becoming more complex and difficult to understand because of the rapid development of computer applications in an organization, communication, and information technologies, growing international competition for products and production, an increasing trend toward industrial deregulation and its expansion, and narrowing life cycles of product and process because of modern technology and increasing diversity in the workforce. In terms of social complexities, globalization, multiculturalism, and externalism are other parameters which are leading to greater complexities.

In my general literature survey, I did not find the utilization of these thick sociological theories of organizational complexities applied in the study of international organizations. The theoretical perspectives discussed could usefully contribute to the study of international organizations. However, sociologists and political scientists commonly use networks and institutional theories. In the following paragraphs, I will briefly illustrate how political scientists and sociologists deal with the institutional theory and its usefulness, and conclude this essay.

Application Network Theory in the Study of International Organizations

Networks are often viewed as the locus of innovation of knowledge and technology (Powell et al. 1996; Stuart et al. 1999; Ahuja 2000; Owen-Smith et al. 2002); they can create trust and increase tolerance in the situation of unwanted consequences (Piore and Sabel1984; Uzzi 1997) and often inspire conformity in thought and action (Galaskiewicz and Burt 1991; Mizruchi1992) and they may also shape the diffusion of certain technologies (Rodgers 1962; Coleman et al. 1966) and organizational practices (Davis 1989; Strang and Macy 2001). Further, network theory can be utilized to understand the formal contractual relationships among member organizations (Owen-Smith and Powell 2004); their affiliations, shared memberships that suggest connections (Beckfield 2003, 2008; Boehmer et al. 2004; Boli et al. 1999), and informal inter-organizational relationships flow through people such as director interlocks, employee mobility that crosses organizational boundaries (Fleming et al. 2007).

Analysis of networks is a common phenomenon in both physical and social sciences. There is a long tradition of network analysis in sociology,

Organizations as Complex Phenomena 145

and anthropology literature and various models have been developed. In sociology, networks are embedded in all micro, macro, and meso social environments in which large-scale social forces influence the social structure in a casual process (Ahuja and Carley 1998; Freeman 2004; Hill and Dunbar 2002; Krebs 2006; Bassuk, Glass, and Berkman 1999). Network theory in the social sciences was originated by the German psychologist Jacob Moreno in 1937. In his publication on the network model, he showed how human social groups are interconnected. Moreno introduced a sociogram to represent the relationship between individual and social group (Tesson 2006). In 1956, D. Cartwright and F. Harary used network theory to explain the graph theory to interpret structural balance with the mathematical application. They argued that Moreno's sociogram can be analyzed using mathematics. Cartwright and Harary also applied the sociogram qualitatively (Scott 2003). In 1967, Stanly Milgram developed the concept of "the small world problem" where he argued that within a social group, any person could contact any other person through a surprisingly small number of links. Milgram conducted research that is commonly known as degrees of separation (Tesson 2006). The full emphasis on network theory came after the publication of Granovetter's article, then *American Journal of Sociology* in 1973, entitled "The Strength of Weak Ties." Granovetter's research proves the small world hypothesis proposed and partly proved by Milgram. Granovetter conducted extensive interviews of job applicants and tried to find out the ties among job applicants. He used the question "whether the person whose information that led to a job was a friend" and the answer was "NO, just an acquaintance" (Tesson 2006). Based on research results, Granovetter develops the idea that the significant links in a network are not strong connections but weak ties.

Granovetter states that "Analysis of social networks is suggested as a tool for linking micro and macro levels of sociological theory. The procedure is illustrated by elaboration of the macro implications of one aspect of small-scale interaction: the strength of dyadic ties. It is argued that the degree of overlap of two individuals' friendship networks varies directly with the strength of their ties to one another. The impact of this principle on the diffusion of influence and information, mobility opportunity, and community organization are explored. Stress is laid on the cohesive power of weak ties. Most network models deal, implicitly, with strong ties, thus confining their applicability to small, well-defined groups. Emphasis on weak ties lends itself to the discussion of relations between groups and to the analysis of segments of social structure not easily defined in terms of primary groups" (Granovetter 1973, page 1360). Granovetter paved the path for the analysis of networks which became a most focused field of study in the 1980s. There

146 *International Organization and Organizational Sociology*

was not a meaningful change in network theory and its application until the 1990s. In 1998, D. J. Watts and S. H. Strogatz published a paper on NATURE entitled "Collective Dynamics of 'Small World' Networks" where they applied the mathematical approach to analyze the small world phenomena focusing on the organization of the graphs of small world, where they found that small world network was neither random nor regularly organized. Their conclusion supports what Granovetter had proposed in 1973.

In the field of international organizations, analysis of networks has been in practice since 1909 when the Union of International Associations began to collect information about the international organizations. However, they did not mention that they are using any theory to categorize and explore the links with various international organizations of that time. I found several authors who have focused on the networks of international organizations before 1973. The following are the examples of such publications. George Beal et al. published a book on "System Linkages Among Women's Organizations" in 1967, Clyde Mitchell published a book on "Social Networks in Urban Situations" in 1969, Anthony Judge published an article on "The Visualization of the Organizational Network" in 1970, and Scott Boorman published an article on "Outline and Bibliography of Approaches to the Formal Study of Social Networks" in 1973. There was an extensive list of such publications before 1977. In 1977, Groom and Paul Taylor edited the book entitled "International Organizations: A Conceptual Approach" which was published by Frances Pinter, London, where several authors analyze networks perspectives of international organizations.

In the introduction chapter, A. J. R. Groom and Paul Taylor (1977) cite William Evan (****) who states that "One basic assumption, however, has unified researchers from diverse disciplines and vantage points, viz. that a significant amount of the variance of organizational phenomena can be accounted for by concentrating on intra-organizational variables... In recent years, one can detect a rising tide of discontent with the intra-*organizational* focus of organizational research. One expression of this discontent is as follows: 'Too much sociological theory arid research has been based on the model of a single organization, and attention has been focused on its internal processes. Surely this dominant model is not sufficient to analyze newer arid more complex organizational forms such as the interlocking networks of organization in the civil service, the multi-campus state university, regional consortia of educational institutions, and multi-outlet distributive organizations in business, and multi-plant industrial concerns. Having become rooted in its social and technological environment arid more complex ways, organizations find themselves both constraining and being constrained by these environments in new ways. Yet investigators of formal organizations have barely begun to attack these new relationships." (Groom and Paul Taylor 1977, in the introduction: International Organization Networks: A Complementary Perspective).

This account of William Evan clearly shows the importance of inter-organizational networks to examine the complex form of international organizations. The documentary evidence shows that the international organizational networks analysis has been fostered since United Nations was established (Groom and Paul Taylor 1977). In the contemporary world, network analysis is one of the major perspectives to investigate how and what level organizations are contributing to meet the demand of a globalized world (Bernstein and Cashore 2000). In the context of social networks, both sociologists and political scientists are equally applying the networks theory to analyze the connectedness and disconnectedness of organizations both national and international.

Social Networks

In a current neo-liberal global world, we cannot imagine surviving or managing ourselves without interpersonal, growing, up and social relationships and links or relationships are built based on multiple networks. Networks are the sets of actors and sets of links between actors (individuals, groups, societies, nations, and the globe). Such links can have multiple chain relationships with multiple values. Normally, links and relationships can be examined with nodes of connections.

Social network theory examines the social relationships in terms of mutual benefits and attachments between and among the social actors. Network theory explains how such relationships are embedded and connected (nodes) in social settings and examines the connection of individual actors within the networks and searches for the relationship between various actors. In another word, social network theory examines the map of interconnectedness between individuals to individuals, groups to groups, societies to societies, and at the national and the global levels. This interconnectedness can be a simply one-disciplinary approach to multidisciplinary dimensions. In this context, network theory can be seen in multiple situations of multiple niches. Environmental networks niche can be one of them.

Social networks are important because it examines the socially embedded interrelationships of the social actor (individual to the nation and the global phenomenon). To understand social activities, it is essential to

148 *International Organization and Organizational Sociology*

understand the social actor's social relationships. The network provides the linkages of actors to each other as well as to the groups where social actors play important roles to find the opportunities to survive and grow. The social environment is dynamic and networks study is the study of social dynamism. Social networks are necessary for understanding social dynamics and interactive social action, their connectedness, and social as well as politico-cultural processes. Network analyses are also important to understand the local social processes which combine with the cumulative to the broader sociologically interactive phenomena (Bhandari 2018, 2019, 2020).

Social networks exist because it examines the strong and weak ties between social actors. It helps to analyze the social structure or structural dynamism of relationships among actors in local to international contexts. The social system (almost in every society) involves diverse types of identities, i.e., individual persons, groups, culture, organizations, beliefs, and geographical and locational variations. In the current context, this contextual analysis is more important because of the growing interdependence between various social, political, and geographical phenomena. Social structures bear various regularities and govern by multiple links and relationships within and in an external context. There are three major complex views of network analysis. In the first stage, it remains at personal level connectedness, in the second stage associations among actors and other social entities, and finally connections of groups to groups, and societies to societies. In the current context, these phenomenological links and interconnectedness go beyond the national boundary. Such a network context has a long history; however, there is not much research on this contextual frame. We can examine this network in terms of density (webs of networks), reciprocity, clustering, and connectivity, and it links with the central feature (object and casual connections). There are several studies of these types (both formal and informal).

Social networks analysis involves from the individual level to the global social system (Kadushin 2004), and such network analysis is more powerful in the recent global socioeconomic-political system. Network analysis is primarily based on network theory, which deals with the various sets of interrelationships. In other words, a network contains several sets of objects, social, economic, and political mapping in terms of their interconnectedness. Such interconnectedness analysis is popular in sociology (in environmental and organization sociology), anthropology, sociolinguistics, geography, social psychology, information science and organizational studies, and other academic disciples. Various research works in the above field operate at various levels (individuals, groups, nations, and international levels) to determine the cause of social problems and to resolve such problems. In the current context, network analysis is commonly in use to analyze organizations (how they run, operate, structure, and function) and how individual actors act to achieve their goals in the management field (Scott 2004).

Borgatti and Foster (2003) have examined the growing literature trend in the management field. They have done a conventional review of the recent literature, organizing the work around accepted research areas and pointing out current issues in various categories such as social capital, embeddedness, network organizations, board interlocks, joint ventures, inter-firm alliances, knowledge management, social cognition, and a catch-all category we have labeled "group processes" (cf., Borgatti and Foster 2003, pages 992–993). According to them, a broader network analysis has been done to analyze the social capital and power relationships in a globalized socio-political context.

Likewise, Arvind Parkhe, Stanley Wasserman, and David A. Ralston (2006) have done a meta-analysis on the recent trend of network theory development, where they have provided the exponential growth of literature in this field.

Network analysis is equally important in the environmental conservation field. Several studies suggest that the increase in environmental concern is both a local and global phenomenon (Brechin and Kempton 1994, 1997; Dunlap

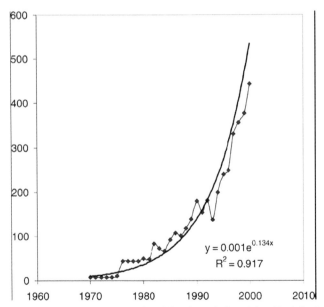

Figure 3.1 The exponential growth of publications indexed by Sociological Abstracts containing "social network" in the abstract or title. Source: S.P. Borgatti, P.C. Foster / Journal of Management 2003 29(6) 991–1013.

150 *International Organization and Organizational Sociology*

and Mertig 1995, 1997; Inglehart 1995; Escobar 2001). Global environmental concern is also growing as political agenda and has global connection and networking. Conservation movements were begun through group awareness and personal and group networking. The global environment conservation movements are the best examples of networking. These movements can be related to both political and social networks.

At the beginning of the section, I noted that there is no theoretical gap between sociology and political sciences in the application of network theory in organizational studies. One of the major roles of both formal organizations and international organizations is to establish relationships among stakeholders. An organization is best depicted as a network (Groom and Paul Taylor 1977). Therefore, analysis of network form is a common phenomenon. However, there is a distinction in application procedures. Political scholars examine the state-centric power dynamism of networks and sociologists focus on social networks embedded in society. As Groom and Paul Taylor (1977) note, "political theory rarely manages networks with several distinct types of relationships, each with its configuration of links. It is precisely such networks that are of most interest in sociology. "It also tends to exclude networks in which some of the points have links back to themselves, and it is often just such networks that are important in representing social structures.

There is not much research on how social networks have been influential in the political ground of international relations and regimes.

Application of Sociological Institution Theory in the Study of International Organizations

The study of institutional theory is a common phenomenon in social science. Scott (2004) states that the roots of institutional theory run richly through the formative years of the social sciences, enlisting, and incorporating the creative insights of scholars ranging from Marx and Weber, Cooley, and Mead, to Veblen and commons. The institutional theory examines the deep and flexible aspects of social structure. This theory analyzes how institution processes affect social behavior including in social structures, schemas, rules, norms, and routines, and how authoritative guidelines develop in society. It goes into investigation of structure norms, etc., and explores how they are created, diffused, adopted, and adapted over space and time; and how they fall into decline and disuse (Scott 1987; DiMaggio and Powell 1983; Oliver 1991). The broader subject of institutional theory is to examine the social structure and order, conflict, consensus, and conformity. The founding authors such as Philip Selznick (old institution), Paul Dimaggio, and Walter Powell (new institution) are equally cited by the sociologists as well as by the political scientists (Cook 1992; Lash 1971; Norton 1998; Otto 1996; Archer 1983, 1992; Hall and Taylor 1996; Barnett and Finnemore 2004). Most importantly, new institutional theory has drawn more attention from the political scientists (Hall and Taylor 1996); however, the scholars of international organization and international relations also do not ignore historical institutionalism and sociological institutionalism. Political scientist Nielsen, Klaus (2001, page 505) notes that DiMaggio distinguishes three new institutionalisms: rational-action neo-institutionalism (RAN), social-constructivist neo-institutionalism (SCN), and mediated-conflict neo-institutionalism (MCN). The typology transcends the disciplinary boundaries although the three institutionalisms are originating from economics, sociology, and political science, respectively. Likewise, the founder of the new institutional theory DiMaggio (1991) states that social constructivist neo-institutionalism "originated in sociology, although it too gained adherence among political scientists" (Nielsen 2001). The major institutional theorists of political science, Marsh and Olsen (1989), note that institutionalism, as that term is used here, connotes a general approach to the study of political institutions, a set of theoretical ideas and hypotheses concerning the relations between institutional characteristics and political agency, performance, and change. Institutionalism emphasizes the endogenous nature and social construction of political institutions. Institutions are not simply equilibrium contracts among self-seeking, calculating individual actors or arenas for contending social forces. They are collections of structures, rules, and standard operating procedures that have a partly autonomous role in political life (cf., by Marsh and Olsen 2005, page 3). The only differences in the application of institutional theory between political perspectives and sociological perspectives are first looking at the political ground of society and second examining social order, structure, norms, rules, and regulations authorized through institutions. Marsh and Olsen (2005) make clear the notion that institutional approaches are not limited to political science. They state that there is wide diversity within and across disciplines in what kinds of rules and relations are construed as "institutions." Moreover, approaches to political institutions differ when it comes to how they understand (1) the nature of institutions, as the organized setting within which modern political actors most typically act, (2) the processes that translate structures and rules into political impacts, and (3) the processes that translate human behavior into structures and rules and establish, sustain,

152   *International Organization and Organizational Sociology*

transform, or eliminate institutions (Marsh and Olsen 2005[1], page 4). This shows that political vision differs from the sociological approach but uses the same perspectives such as institutional, rational actors, cultural community, etc. Marsh and Olsen accept that perspectives can be differed according to the socio-political environment. They state that the key distinctions are the extent to which a perspective views the rules and identities defined within political institutions as epiphenomena that mirror environmental circumstances or predetermined individual preferences and initial resources; and the extent to which a perspective pictures rules and identities as reproduced with some reliability that is, at least in part, independent of environmental stability or change (Marsh and Olsen 2005, page 5). "Institutions are not static, and institutionalization is not an inevitable process; nor is it unidirectional, monotonic, or irreversible" (Weaver and Rockman 1993, cf., Marsh and Olsen 2005). This notion indicates that it is obvious to have various paradigms of institutional analysis because the institutional theory is still in the maturation phase. Even the founders are actively working and reframing their ideas (see the shift of thoughts in DiMaggio and Powell, Marsh, and Olsen, Keohane and Scott's writings of the 1980s and 2000 onwards).

Similarly, international relations scholars use realism, neo-realism, pluralism, and other approaches to study the institutional role in transnational situations. In this connection, Robert Keohane (1988) compares the rationalistic and reflective approaches to studying how international institutions work and change. He states that "Institution may refer to a *general pattern or categorization* of the activity or a *particular* human-constructed arrangement, formally or informally organized." Both types of institutions "involve persistent and connected sets of rules (formal and informal) that prescribe behavioral roles, constrain activity, and shape expectations (Keohane 1988, page 383). Keohane (1988) focuses on institutions that can be identified as related complexes of rules and norms, identifiable in space and time (page 383). This account of Keohane does not differ from what

---

[1] Institutionalism, as that term is used here, connotes a general approach to the study of political institutions, a set of theoretical ideas and hypotheses concerning the relations between institutional characteristics and political agency, performance, and change. Institutionalism emphasizes the endogenous nature and social construction of political institutions. Institutions are not simply equilibrium contracts among self-seeking, calculating individual actors or arenas for contending social forces. They are collections of structures, rules, and standard operating procedures that have a partly autonomous role in political life. The paper ends with raising some research questions at the frontier of institutional studies. James G. March & Johan P. Olsen (2005), Elaborating the "New Institutionalism." http://www.inomics.com/cgi/repec?handle=RePEc:erp:arenax:P0011

sociologists such as Scott, DiMaggio, and Powell are explaining about the institutional theory. It is a general notion that the rationalistic approach to international institutions argues that institutions emerge to reduce the costs of cooperation to facilitate mutually beneficial agreements and reduce transaction costs (the costs of specifying and enforcing contracts) and certain types of ambiguity.

Keohane argues that through the rationalistic approach, we should expect international institutions to appear whenever the costs of communication, monitoring, and enforcement are low compared to the benefits to be derived from the political exchange (Keohane 1988, page 387). Likewise, the reflexive approach according to Keohane (is a sociological approach) stresses the role of impersonal social forces and the impact of cultural practices, norms, and values that are not based on utility maximization. This account of Keohane which is supported by many contemporary political science institutional theorists (Duffield 2007; Hall and Taylor 1996; Thelen 1999) gives ground to state that there is equal focus on institutional theory from both an organizational sociologist and political scientists, especially from international relation and international organization field. However, as Marsh and Olson (2005) note, scholars who deal with political institutions are less concerned with *whether* institutions matter, than to what extent, in what respects, through what processes, under what conditions, and why institutions have influence (page 9). On the other hand, sociologists go into in detail and examine the embedded ground of institutions. DiMaggio and Powell (1983) three contrasting mechanisms for diffusion of institutions such as coercive, normative, and mimetic can be taken as examples of vivid analysis of institutions. Furthermore, Strang and Meyer's (1993) notion of relational versus the cultural concept of institutions, Oliver's (1992) analysis of pressures on the institution toward deinstitutionalization functional, political, and social, Barley's (1986) micro-level institutional change, Greenwood and Hinings' (1993) organizational-level institutional change, and macro of Scott (2000, 2004) are other best examples of the vividness of institutional analysis from the sociological perspectives. Similarly, Nielsen's analysis of institutionalist approaches in social sciences which explores the contemporary debates and typology or institution, Hall and Taylor's (1996) examination of the institution through political perspectives (historical, rational choice, sociological, and comparing institutionalism), and Duffield's (2007) reflection, evaluation, and integration of international institutions are some of the examples of political analysis of institutions. Likewise, John J. Mearsheimer (1995) in his article "The False Promise of International Institutions" examines three institutionalist IR theories as

154   *International Organization and Organizational Sociology*

liberal institutionalism, collective security, and critical theory, where she argues that institutions push states away from war and promote peace. Mearscheimer[2] (1995) criticizes liberal institutionalism for ignoring security issues, ignoring the other major obstacles to cooperation, and failing to prove it from an empirical perspective. Mearscheimer (1995) also criticizes the critical theory stating that critical and incomplete theory does not provide a satisfactory explanation for how states overcome their fears and learn to trust one another, too easily the satisfaction of an extraordinarily complex network of requirements and little support from the historical record.

These authors extensively use both sociological and political explanations of the institutional theory. Therefore, there is not much knowledge gap between these two disciplines in the application of institutional theory (both old and new institutional theories). I am not arguing that there are no variations in paradigms of institutional theory but arguing that both political scientists and sociologists are focusing on the same subject matter.

In the following paragraphs, I will briefly discuss what major sociologists (institutional theorists Scott, DiMaggio, Powell, Jepperson, and Haveman) state about the new institutional theory followed by a comparative chart developed by Danish political scientist Theret (2000), adopted by Klaus Nielsen (2001), which gives an overall account of how institutional theories are interlinked with social sciences.

Scott (1991), on unpacking institutional arguments, evaluates how various institutional theorists treated institutions and elaborates on the major concepts. He brings the notion of rational myths and explains institutional and technical environments' influence. Further, he explains organizational legitimacy where he examines the degree of cultural support for an organization. He describes how the changes that have occurred over time in how organizational theorists have conceived of the environments within which organizations operate with the empirical evidence. He states that the new institutionalism is a social theory that focuses on developing a sociological view of institutions, the way they interact, and the effects of institutions on society: "Compliance occurs in many circumstances because other types of behavior are inconceivable; routines are followed because they are taken for granted as 'the way we do these things." He explains how environmental

---

[2] According to John J. Mearscheimer (1995), "The optimistic assessment of the promise of international institutions, underpinned by the three institutionalist theories, is not warranted. There are serious problems with the causal logic of each theory, and little empirical evidence for any of them. Misplaced reliance on institutional solutions is likely to lead to more failures in the future." http://www.people.fas.harvard.edu/~olau/ir/archive/mea3.pdf.

elements are singled out for attention and what the important influential or causal mechanism institutions are and affect the organizational structure. He says there are no fixed rules and regulations to describe the organization. He states that organizations confront multiple sources and types of symbolic or cultural systems, and they exercise some choice in selecting the systems in which they connect. R. L. Jepperson (1991) supports Scott's notion of institutional unpacking. Jepperson elaborates that institution is a social order or pattern that has attained a certain state or property, which, according to him, is a process of such attainment that depends on standardized interaction sequences.

Jepperson brings main points such as (1) institutionalization is not equivalent to stability or survival, (2) practice in an institution is relative to particular contexts, (3) within any system having multiple levels or orders of organization, (4) primary levels of the organization can operate as institutions relative to secondary levels of the organization, (5) an institution is relative to a particular dimension of a relationship, and, finally, (6) an institution is relative to centrality. Whereas, J. W. Meyer and B. Rowan (1991) argue that institutionalization is a process by which social processes, obligations, or actualities come to take a rule-like status in society for action. They state that the formal structure of an organization is a blueprint for activities which includes a listing of offices, departments, positions, and programs. These elements are linked by explicit goals and policies that make up a rational theory of how, and to what end, activities are to be fitted together. They further state that the formal structures of many organizations in post-industrial society dramatically reflect the myths of their institutional environments instead of the demands of their work activities. W. P. Powell (1991) evaluates institutions as dependent on technical environments. He states that organizations can be evaluated by their outputs and appropriateness of their form and institutional and competitive processes. He states that institutionalized organizations are not passive, inefficient manipulators of symbols rather than substance. He evaluates organizations through both sources such as heterogeneity in institutional environments and the processes that generate institutional change, where he also brings the concept of institutional isomorphism. According to him, new institutionalism recognizes that institutions operate in an environment consisting of other institutions, called the institutional environment. Every institution is influenced by the broader environment through institutional isomorphism. In this environment, the main goal of organizations is to survive. To do so, they need to do more than succeed economically; they need to establish legitimacy within the world of institutions. He suggests four opportunities for institutional reproduction: the exercise

156 *International Organization and Organizational Sociology*

of power; complex interdependencies; taken-for-granted assumptions; and path-dependent development processes. D. Strang and J. W. Meyer (1994) argue that the development of the organization and its specification depend on abstract categories and the formulation of patterned relationships such as chains of cause and effect. He elaborates more on the theory's diffusion. He states that diffusion processes often look more like complex exercises in the social construction of identity than like the mechanical spread of information.

Based on these, scholars state that new institutionalism deals with the common influence of institutions on human behavior through rules, norms, and other frameworks. Jeannette Colyvas and Walter W. Powell (2006) with the illustration of various authors (Meyer and Rowan 1977; Zucker 1977; DiMaggio and Powell 1983; Scott and Meyer 1983) argue that the basic point of institutionalization and new institution is legitimacy, and according to them, it is also crucial to various lines of research in organizational theory more generally (Hannan and Freeman 1989; Hannan and Carroll 1992; Aldrich and Fiol 1994; Dacin, Goodstein, and Scott 2002). To elaborate more on intuitional legitimacy, Haveman (2000) goes on this notion and notes that without precision in measurement, the adoption of organizational structures and even the global spread of managerial and institutional theory can lack the agreement of core concepts. Institutional actors according to Powell and others are those who (1) define who can participate in the particular political arena, (2) shape the various actors in political strategies, and (3) influence what these actors believe to be both possible and desirable. In new institution, Powell and others discuss the basics points of convergence and disagreement with institutionally oriented research in economics and political science and locate the "institutional" approach to major developments in contemporary sociological theory. I find it much more relevant to illustrate Walter Powell and Paul J. DiMaggio's (1983) article which is supportive of their new theme on the institution in 1983; they describe institutional change as institutions or organizations becoming increasingly similar. Powell and DiMaggio argue that the grounds of bureaucratization and rationalization have changed. The challenge is that organizational change occurs as a result of processes that make organizations more similar without necessarily making them more efficient. Their goal was not to explain the efficiency but legitimacy of the organizations. They explain that isomorphism comprises the institutional definition of an organizational field because of the activities of a diverse set of organizations. The homogenization of institutions on the periphery of the field, vis-à-vis the field, makes up the second stage (Powell and DiMaggio 1983). In this case, I see strong links between the concepts of new institutions and hierarchy, and network forms of organization of Powell were bringing four basic points to support his argument: (1) firms blurring the boundary between hierarchy and market; (2) exchanges in networks are indefinite and sequential, normative, and reciprocal; (3) networks involve strategic alliances and partnerships; and (4) three critical components for networks are know-how, demand for speed, and trust. Even further back in 1974, J. R. Galbraith, P. Lawrence, and J. Lorsch (1967) had explained the institutional challenges as (1) more uncertainty, more info process, dependent on handling non-routine acts and slack, self-contained, vertical, and lateral; (2) problems on balancing and differentiation and integration to simpler tasks; (3) function of exposure to the environment and organizational performance determines by ability but how to cope with the environment and each subsystem and differentiates their exposure to the environment. My concern here is how new institution mitigates these challenges. How to separate connecting mechanisms in institutional theory because it relies on historical tracing of an event, how institutional logic competes with each other and how to address them, what would be the conditions, and how do contemporary competing institutions retain power during periods of instability? These points are subject matters of further study both from the political and sociological perspectives.

So far, this essay gives how sociologists and political scientists examine the institution with the same theoretical approach but apply different perspectives. This account also shows that there is no knowledge gap between the two disciplines at least at the epistemological level. Institutional theory is still young and various perspectives have been developed. Still, the founders of the institutional theory are active and refining their thoughts; therefore, scholarly argumentation is not over about the disciplinary boundary. More than that I think, there should not be disciplinary demarcation but need to develop a multidisciplinary approach to the local to global institutions. Figure 3.2 developed by Danish political scientist Theret (2000), adopted by Klaus Nielsen (2001), gives a visual of the complexity of institutionalism.

In addition to Figure 3.2, Theret (2000) adds more points to show the complex phenomena of institutionalism. In this connection, Neilsen (2001) also adds some points such as American neo-institutionalism, institutional-evolutionary economics, new economic sociology, new institutionalism in political science, historical institutionalism, and the cognitive-institutional approach as an additional typology of neo-institutionalism (page 512). He further argues that there should be a clarification on methodological approaches in connection to political and sociological institutional perspectives such as the distinction between the open system and closed system methodology. There is a clear distinction between positivist and post-positivist approaches, and within post-positivist approaches, the distinction between realist and

158 International Organization and Organizational Sociology

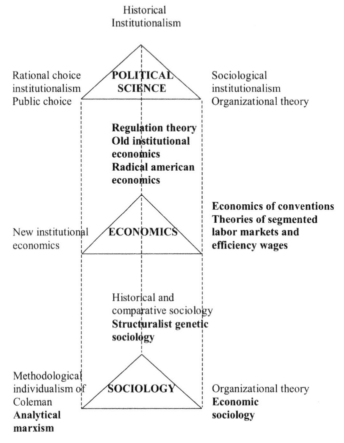

Figure 3.2 The visual of the complexity of institutionalism.
Source: Theret (2000), adopted by Klaus Nielsen (2001).

idealist ontologies. I conclude this section with two major points that Nelsen has raised. First, he criticizes DiMaggio and Powell for their less concern about the practical explanation of new institution theory in the transnational situation, which I agree with; second, he is accepting and bridges the gap between political and sociological perspectives of intuitional theory. With the examples from DiMaggio and Powell (1998) of rational action, social constructivism, and mediated conflicts institutionalism, he presents the change mechanism of the institution through strategic action and selection, diffusion, and political conflict of the intuitionalism. Nielsen (2001) concludes that there is always a tradeoff between internal development within coherent frameworks on one side and cooperation among different approaches – currently there seems to be much to say in favor of cross-fertilization, joint work, and even merging of the approaches (Nielsen 2001, page 514). I agree with Nelsen's conclusion. The current world is interconnected economically, culturally, socially, and politically due to technological development and the globalization process. The diffusion of knowledge is also spreading at an accelerating rate to the entire world. The demand for international laws was never as high as it is because of transnational problems HIV/AIDS, terrorism, as well as the globalizing, social, economic, and biophysical environmental problems. Institutions create "sets of rules, typically formalized in international agreements, and embodied in organizations that stipulate how states should cooperate and compete with each other. They prescribe acceptable forms of state behavior and proscribe unacceptable kinds of behavior" (Mearscheimer 1995); therefore, multidisciplinary approaches are needed to study the international institutions or to explore the role, and demands, and create the new institution as needed.

The Green Economic Initiatives (As Theory) and International Organization

Broadly, since 2008, the global conservation movements have taken a different path, with a special focus on the green economic initiatives. The major stakeholder of global environmental governance the United Nations has been advocating in the international forums to integrate the conservation and development themes and establish a collaborative platform, where all concerned stakeholders could contribute to the health of the planet (Bhandari 2018, 2019, 2020).

In fostering this concept, the UNEP called for a Global Green New Deal, in the wake of unprecedented economic stimulus packages. A recent UNEP report released in December 2008 called for a Global Green New Deal and a subsequent Policy Brief to G20 heads of states urging them to turn the crisis into an opportunity by enabling a global green economy driven by massive job creation from more efficient use of resources, energy-efficient building and construction, widespread use of modern clean public transport, the scaling up of renewable energy, sustainable waste management as highly lucrative sectors, and sustainable agriculture that reflects the latest thinking in ecosystem management and biodiversity and water conservation (UNEP-GRID 2009, page 4). The concept of a GE, and its policy implications, will apply differently across countries, reflecting national circumstances and priorities. However, for developing countries, in particular, widespread opportunities exist to strengthen economic development, including poverty reduction as well as food and water security in developing countries, through

160　*International Organization and Organizational Sociology*

improved environmental and natural resource management (UNEP 2010; Bhandari 2017, 2018, 2019, 2020).

The green economy theory especially captures the notion of the vulnerability of human welfare, which can be understood as the result of the widespread application of an unsustainable model of economic development. With the linkages of recent year's economic and environmental crises, the United Nation Environment Program (UNEP) urges the cooperative efforts to address bringing the economy and environment together, on the root thesis of the "environment" is where we live; and development is what we all do in attempting to improve our lot within that abode. The two are inseparable" (from the Our Common Future as in UNEP 2007, page 1). Along the same line, the IUCN also notes the urgency of cooperative work. In its program plan for 2008–2012, it notes that there is an urgent need to re-align our economies with the basic principles of sustainability and to bring our political representatives and society at large to understand that true prosperity is only possible if economies effectively support – and do not undermine – environmental systems. As is increasingly apparent from the effects of climate change, the resilience of the global economy is fundamentally determined by environmental factors and the capacity of societies to understand, manage, and adapt to natural processes. Unfortunately, the full values of wild nature and the benefits of sound environmental management are still poorly recognized and excluded from economic thinking. A crucial step in the transition to a more sustainable global economy is the fuller integration of ecosystem values in economic policy, finance, and markets (IUCN 2009, page 1). The green economy theory itself was coined and theorized by the United Nations to deal with the current global environmental crisis; however, it is not being highlighted as it should be. The green economy theory is still an infant and the potential that international organizations and scholars will add more value to this discourse.

The Stakeholder Theory and International Organization

With regard to stakeholder theory, I have drawn from Friedman and Miles (2002) and focus on the importance of understanding the conflicts and controversies that arise from different stakeholder groups. The stakeholder theory was pioneered by R. E. Freeman in 1984. Freeman states "A stakeholder in an organization is (by definition) any group or individual who can affect or is affected by the achievement of the organization's objectives" (Freeman 1984, page 48). Donaldson and Preston (1995, page 68) state that stakeholders are all those persons or groups with legitimate interests

Social Networks 161

participating in an enterprise/organization to obtain benefits, and there is no prima facie priority of one set of interests and benefits over another. Donaldson and Preston (1995, page 70) define a stakeholder as an "entity through which numerous and diverse participants accomplish multiple, and not always congruent, purposes." Similarly, Brenner and Cochran (1991, page 452) claim that stakeholder theory helps to understand "how organizations operate and to help predict organizational behavior" (Bhandari 2019, 2020).

The Governance Theory and International Organization

Discussions of global governance theory can be found throughout the social sciences. Global governance is a concept that has been used in almost any example where actors from the international level engage nation-states in nation-building efforts or related shared governance issues (Kahn and Zald 1990). The term has been used to illustrate so many diverse types of engagements that it has lost any precise meeting; it has become an uncritical term (e.g., Hewson and Sinclair 1999; Douglas 1999; Murphy 2000). Governance engenders several perspectives and definitions. For example, James Rosenau states that governance occurs on a global scale through both the coordination of states and the activities of a vast array of rule systems that exercise authority in the pursuit of goals that function outside normal national jurisdictions (Rosenau 2000, page 172). Further, Rosenau describes governance as a process as "a pervasive tendency ... in which major shifts in the location of authority and the site of control mechanisms are underway on every continent, shifts that are as pronounced in economic and social systems as they are in political systems" (1995, page 18) and characterizes global governance as systems of rule at all levels of human activity – from the family to the international organization in which the pursuit of goals through the exercise of control has transnational repercussions (1995, page 13).

Similarly, Finkelstein notes that global governance is governing, without sovereign authority, relationships that transcend national frontiers. Global governance is doing internationally what the government is doing nationally (Finkelstein 1995, page 369). FAO (2009) states that "the term "governance" covers both: (i) the activity or process of governing; (ii) those people charged with the duty of governing: and (iii) the manner, method, and system by which a particular society is governed." Likewise, Gerry Stoker (1998) goes on to summarize governance in five propositions: (1) governance refers to a set of institutions and actors that are drawn from but also beyond government; (2) governance identifies the blurring of boundaries and responsibilities for tackling social and economic issues; (3) governance identifies the power

162 *International Organization and Organizational Sociology*

dependence involved in the relationships between institutions involved in collective action; (4) governance is about autonomous self-governing networks of actors; and (5) governance recognizes the capacity to get things done which does not rest on the power of government to command or use its authority (Stoker 1998, page 18).

These definitional claims of Rosenau, Finkelstein, FAO, and Stoker are useful to examine the relationships between IUCN and its members including INGOs, NGOs, national governments, and private enterprises. From the definitions above, there appears to be a consensus on global environmental governance among scholars that global governance includes both nation-state and the non-state actors (INGOs, NGOs, civil society organizations, and private sectors) (McKormick 1999; Kauffman 1997; Schreurs 1997; Litfin 1993). In the social sciences, governance is also sometimes explained in Foucaultian terms (Baldwin 2003; Agrawal 2005), where government means less of the political or administrative structures of the modern state but the people's internalization of the rules that leads to types of self-governance, which is governance without active external enforcement (Foucault 1991). Foucault's work is notable; it (philosophically) illustrates extensive social and political structures, including the state, bureaucracy, and professions which will be helpful to explore how knowledge and power utilize by the hybrid international organization (such as IUCN) at the state and transnational levels (Bhandari 2018, 2019, 2020).

Conclusion

Social science epistemologies have historically been developed to tackle social problems, and formal and informal organizations were formed to address social issues as they appeared. When socioeconomic and political problems cross borders, international organizations form to tackle those issues on an international scale.

The term "international organizations" was first used by a Professor of Law, James Lorimer, in 1867 and became a major field of study in political science by 1900. In the contemporary world, the role of international organizations is universal. International organizations represent a form of institution that refers to a formal system of rules and objectives, a rationalized administrative instrument (Selznick 1957). There are varieties of international organizations according to their objectives and their functions. There are three categories of organizations: intergovernmental organizations, international non-governmental organizations (INGOs), and multinational enterprises. To consider any organization as international, there should be a formal instrument of agreement between the governments of nation-states including three or more nation-states as parties to the agreement and possessing a permanent secretariat performing ongoing tasks. A formal technical and material organization should have a constitution, local chapters, physical equipment, mechanics, emblems, letterhead stationery, a staff, an administrative hierarchy, and so forth (Duverger 1972 as cited by Archer 1992, page 2).

According to political science literature, international organizations form to attain certain goals of the governments and have specified rules and regulations formulated by the governments. In this regard, IOs are strongly associated with international relations theory, regime theory, and globalization theory. There are various perspectives for the analysis of the political environment which include positivism, constructivism, realism, neo-realism, liberalism, neo-liberal, globalism, and so on.

Sociologists "who study organizations have been and are rendering more valuable services to organizational theory and practice by maintaining the sociology of organization as a more or less distinct specialty than by simply joining hands with others in an interdisciplinary approach to the field" (Lammers 1981). Differing from the political scientists, sociologists examine organizations through three major perspectives such as rational, natural, and open and developed various approaches from functionalism, neo-functionalism, structuralism, and neo-structuralism to post-modernism along with the other theories such as contingency, network, institution, resource dependency, transaction cost, ecology, demographic, and so on.

The distinction between formal organizational studies and studies of international organizations is minimal because both help to widen the idea of creating an original position for better combinations of favorable circumstances or situations in human affairs. Organizations can inspire and bring people in concert to achieve combined goals. They are accountable for determining the intelligence needed to meet their goals. Both can be found acting in every aspect of social life at the local, national, and international levels accommodating diversity in society and achieving communal goals. However, there is not much interdisciplinary research between organizational sociology and international organizations and also a huge gap in the literature. This is still an important field of future research. In other words, there is not much literature that explores paradigms and explores the interconnectedness of the sociology of organizations and international organization theories. Organizational sociologists Ness and Brechin (1988) made an early attempt

164　*International Organization and Organizational Sociology*

to explore this connectedness. They broadly rejected the functionalist notion of organizational study and instead follow contingency theory (according to Galbraith (1973) in contingency theory, there is no one best way to organize, and any way of organizing is not equally effective) to show the matching approaches (international relations, institutionalization, regime formation, realism, neo-realism, liberalism, globalism, etc., of political sciences and rational, natural and open system perspectives and networks, transactional cost, institution, etc., of organizational sociology) between organizational sociology and international organizations. In addition to that, there have been few efforts made in search of matching the common ground of organizations and international organizations from a sociological point of view. On the other hand, political scientists (Nye 2004; Friedman 2006; Agnew 2005; Slaughter 2005; Ba and Hoffmann 2005; Howard 2002; Finnemore and Sikkink 1998; Barnett and Finnemore 1999; and many others) have investigated the sociological ground of international organizations and elaborated on their political views to link with sociological organizational theory. Political scientists have been engaged on these topics; however, relatively little has been written by organizational sociologists who have not focused on this important field of research. This essay is the first step of my journey along this path.

The study of international organizations can be a lifelong research topic for individual scholars. There is a large literature and potential for investigations with the application of many differing perspectives. Investigating the theories and perspectives of organizations is challenging. This essay provides very a brief outline of what we know about international organizations. During my literature search, I found that organizational sociologists have extensively used social theories that exist in the scholarship of social sciences to investigate the past, present, and future roles, and the complexity of formal organizations. Similarly, international organization scholars have followed the same epistemology of the social sciences to investigate the roles of international organizations. Therefore, it was difficult to make recommendations regarding which organizational sociological theories and perspectives can be informed for the study of international organizations because most aspects are relevant. However, I think organizational sociological perspectives such as rational, natural, and open systems theory (which are not extensively utilized in the IO and IR) can be utilized to study international organizations. Similarly, from organizational sociological knowledge, approaches such as contingency, resource dependency, transaction cost, ecology, demographic, and so on are among sociological approaches that can be transferred to the study of organizations.

I have provided only a glimmer of international organizations theory, origin, historical account, definitions, and utilization of the contemporary academic world intertwined with the international relations, regime, and globalization as well as the organizational sociological theories and perspectives that can be utilized to study international organizations. I have given a general scenario of the available literature and theory, as I have found it. Several epistemologies in social sciences mutually can be applied to study both formal organizations and international organizations; however, there is a gap in theories (not in all, because institutional and networks theories are mutually applied in the study of the organizations as well as international organizations) as well as methods and their applications. To bridge this gap, it is essential to conduct parallel research both from political and sociological perspectives as several multidisciplinary team projects.

As I feel it:

There are ample things to know, this first step is small and slow,
There are countless theories to grow, words to weave, and miles to go.

"The woods are lovely, dark, and deep, But I have promises to keep, And miles to go before I sleep, and miles to go before I sleep." (Robert Frost)

References

Adib, A. and V. Guerrier (2003) "The Interlocking of Gender with Nationality, Race, Ethnicity, and Class: The Narratives of Women in the Hotel Work." Gender, Work and Organizations Vol.10, No. 4 (August)

Adler, P. S. (1993). "Time and Motion Regained." Harvard Business Review,(January-February): 97-108.

Agard Walter R. (1960) What Democracy Meant to the Greeks (Madison, University of Wisconsin Press, 1960).

Agnew John, Hegemony: The New Shape of Global Power (Philadelphia: Temple University Press, 2005).

Ahuja, M., & Carley, K. (1998). Network structures in virtual organizations. Journal of Computer-Mediated Communication, 3(4).

Alice Ba and Mathew Hoffmann. (2005) Contending Perspectives on Global Governance: Coherence, Contestation and World Order. Routledge.

166 *International Organization and Organizational Sociology*

Allen, N., and J. Meyer (1990). "Organizational Socialization Tactics: A Longitudinal Analysis of Links to Newcomer's Commitment and Role Orientation." Academy of Management Journal, 33(48): 847-858.

Allen, T. J. (1977). Managing the flow of technology, Cambridge, MA, MIT Press.

Alter C. (2007) Bureaucracy and democracy in organizations: Revisiting Feminist Organizations, The Sociology of Organizations, Wharton A.S. editor, Roxbury Publication Company

Ansell, C.K.; Weber, S. (1999) Organizing international politics: sovereignty and open systems. International Political Science Review, 20.

Anthony Judge (1970) The visualization of the organizational network. *International Associations*, 22, May 1970, pp. 265-268

Aquinas Saint Thomas (1953) Political Ideas of St. Thomas Aquinas (New York, Hafner Library of World Classics # 15, 1953).

Archer, Angus (1983) Methods of Multilateral Management: The Interrelationship of International Organizations and NGOs, in the US, the UN, and the Management of Global Change 303, 309 (Toby Trister Gati ed., 1983), United Nations.

Archer, Clive (1992) International Organizations (2nd Edition), Routledge, USA.

Arensberg, C. 1951. Behavior and organization: Industrial studies. In Social Psychology at the Crossroads, eds. J. H. Rohrer and M. Sherif, pp. 324-352. New York: Harper.

Argyris, C. (1957) Personality and organization: The conflict between system and the individual, Harper.

Argyris, Chris, (1972) Applicability of organizational sociology, Cambridge University Press.

Aristotle, Aristotle's Politics and Poetics (New York, Viking Press, Compass Books, 1957).

Aristotle, Ethics (tr. by J. A. K. Thomson, Baltimore, Penguin). Ernest Barker, Greek Political Theory: Plato and His Predecessors (New York, Barnes & Noble, 1951).

Armstrong, J. D. (James David), (1982) Rise of the international organization: a brief history, London: Macmillan & Co

References 167

Arvind Parkhe, Stanley Wasserman, David A. Ralston (2006) Introduction to Special Topic Forum, New Frontiers in Network Theory Development, _ Academy of Management Review 2006, Vol. 31, No. 3, 560–568.

Astley, W. G. (1985). "The two ecologies: population and community perspectives on organizational evolution." Administrative Science Quarterly, 30: 224-241.

Baran, B. (1987). "The technological transformation of white-collar work: a case study of the insurance industry" in H. I. Hartman. Computer Chips and Paper Clips. Washington DC, National Academy Press.

Barker, J., R. (1993). "Tightening the iron cage: concretive control in self-managing teams." Administrative Science Quarterly, 38: 408-437.

Barkin, J. Samuel, (2006) International organization: theories and institutions, Palgrave, Macmillan.

Barley, S. (1986). "Technology as an occasion for structuring: Evidence from observations of CT scanners and the social order of radiology departments." Administrative Science Quarterly, 31: 78-108.

Barley, S. R. (1992). "Design and Devotion: Surges of Rational and Normative Ideologies of Control in Managerial Discourse." Administrative Science Quarterly, 37: 363-399.

Barnard C. I. (1940) The Functions of the Executive, Cambridge: Harvard University Press, 1940, p. 115.

Barnes, Harry E. (1920) Durkheim's Contribution to the Reconstruction of Political Theory, Political Science Quarterly, Vol. 35, No. 2. (Jun. 1920), pp. 236-254.

Barnett Michael & Martha Finnemore. 1999. The Politics, Power, and Pathologies of International Organizations. (In Martin & Simmons)

Bassuk, S.; Glass, T.; and Berkman, L. (1999). "Social Disengagement and Incident Cognitive Decline in Community-Dwelling Elderly Persons." *Annals of Internal Medicine* 131:165–173.

Baum, J. A. C., and V. S. Jintendra (1994). "Organization-Environment Coevolution" in J. Baum and V. S. Jitendra. The Evolutionary Dynamics of Organizations. New York, Oxford University Press: 379-402

Beal George et al (1967) System Linkages among Women's Organizations, Iowa State University, Department of Sociology and Anthropology. 1967.

168 *International Organization and Organizational Sociology*

Becker Howard and Harry Elmer Barnes, Social Thought from Lore to Science, 3 vols. (New York, Dover Publications).

Beniger, J. R. (1986). The Control Revolution: Technological and Economic Origins of the Information Society, Cambridge, MA, Harvard University Press.

Bennett, A LeRoy (1984) International Organizations, (3rd Edition), Prentice-Hall, Inc.

Benny Hjern, Chris Hull (1984) Going Interorganizational: Weber Meets Durkheim Scandinavian Political Studies 7 (3), 197–212. doi:10.1111/j.1467-9477.1984.tb00301.x

Berkman, L. F. (1995) "The Role of Social Relations in Health Promotion." *Psychosomatic Medicine* 57: 245–254.

Berkman, L., and Syme, S. (1979). "Social Networks, Host Resistance, and Mortality: A Nine-Year Follow-up of Alameda County Residents." *American Journal of Epidemiology* 109:186–204.

Bernstein, S., & Cashore, B. 2000. "Globalization, four paths of internationalization and domestic policy change: The case of eco-forestry in British," Canadian Journal of Political Science, 33: 67-99.

Berton H. Kaplan (1968) Notes on a Non-Weberian Model of Bureaucracy: The Case of Development Bureaucracy, Administrative Science Quarterly, Vol. 13, No. 3, Special Issue on Organizations and Social Development. (Dec. 1968), pp. 471-483.

Bhandari, Medani P. (2004) An Assessment of Environmental Education Programs in Nepal, Environmental Awareness, *International Journal of Society of Naturalist, Vol.27, No.1. (ISSN 0254-8798)*

Bhandari, Medani P. (2012) Environmental Performance and Vulnerability to Climate Change: A Case Study of India, Nepal, Bangladesh, and Pakistan, "Climate Change and Disaster Risk Management" Series: Climate Change Management, Springer, New York / Heidelberg, ISBN 978-3-642-31109-3

Bhandari, Medani P. (2014) "Civil Society and Non-Governmental Organizations (NGOs) Movements in Nepal and terms of Social Transformation". Pacific Journal of Science and Technology. 15(1):177-189.

References 169

Bhandari, Medani P. (2014). "Is Tourism Always Beneficial? A Case Study from Masai Mara National Reserve, Narok, Kenya." Pacific Journal of Science and Technology. 15(1):458-483.

Bhandari, Medani P. (2019), The Development of the International Organization and Organizational Sociology Theories and Perspectives. **Part 1**-The Origin, Scientific Journal of Bielsko-Biala School of Finance and Law, ASEJ 2019; 23 (3): 5-9 DOI: 10.5604/01.3001.0013.6523 ISSN: 2543-9103 | E-ISSN: 2543-411X | ICV: 100 | MNiSW: 7 - https://asej.eu/resources/html/article/details?id=196026

Bhandari, Medani P. (2019), The Development of the International Organization (IO) and Organizational Sociology Theories and Perspectives. Part 2- Definitions and Types of IO, Scientific Journal of Bielsko-Biala School of Finance and Law, ASEJ 2019; 23 (3): 10-14; DOI: 10.5604/01.3001.0013.6524 ISSN: 2543-9103 | E-ISSN: 2543-411X | ICV: 100 | MNiSW: 7, https://asej.eu/resources/html/article/details?id=196028

Bhandari, Medani P. (2019), The Development of the International Organization (IO) and Organizational Sociology Theories and Perspectives. Part 3 - Definitions and Types of IO, Scientific Journal of Bielsko-Biala School of Finance and Law, ASEJ 2019; 23 (3): 15-18; DOI: 10.5604/01.3001.0013.6525 ISSN: 2543-9103 | E-ISSN: 2543-411X | ICV: 100 | MNiSW: 7- https://asej.eu/resources/html/article/details?id=196029

Bhandari, Medani P. (2019), The Development of the International Organization (IO) and Organizational Sociology Theories and Perspectives. Part 4 - Definitions and Types of IO, Scientific Journal of Bielsko-Biala School of Finance and Law, ASEJ 2019; 23 (3): 19-35- DOI: 10.5604/01.3001.0013.6527 GICID: 01.3001.0013.6527 ISSN: 2543-9103 | E-ISSN: 2543-411X | ICV: 100 | MNiSW: 7- https://asej.eu/resources/html/article/details?id=196031

Bhandari, Medani P, (2019). Live and let others live- the harmony with nature /living beings-in reference to sustainable development (SD)- is the contemporary world's economic and social phenomena favorable for the sustainability of the planet abounding, Nepal, Bangladesh, and Pakistan? Adv Agr Environ Sci. (2019);2(1): 37–57. DOI: 10.30881/aaeoa.00020 http://ologyjournals.com/aaeoa/aaeoa_00020.pdf

Bhandari Medani P. (2019). "Bashudaiva Kutumbakkam"- The entire world is our home, and all living beings are our relatives. Why do we need to worry about climate change, concerning pollution problems in the major

170 *International Organization and Organizational Sociology*

cities of India, Nepal, Bangladesh, and Pakistan? Adv Agr Environ Sci. (2019);2(1): 8–35. DOI: 10.30881/aaeoa.00019 (second part) http://ologyjournals.com/aaeoa/aaeoa_00019.pdf

Bhandari, Medani P. (2018). The Problems and Consequences of the Biodiversity Conservation: A Case Study from Bangladesh, India, Nepal, and Pakistan. *Socioeconomic Challenges, 2*(1), 6-20. http://armgpublishing.sumdu.edu.ua/wp-content/uploads/2016/12/files/sec/volume-2-issue-1/Medani%20P.%20Bhandari_SEC_1_2018.pdf

Bhandari, Medani P. (2020) Second Edition- Green Web-II: Standards and Perspectives from the IUCN, Policy Development in Environment Conservation Domain concerning India, Pakistan, Nepal, and Bangladesh, River Publishers, Denmark / the Netherlands. ISBN: 9788770221924 e-ISBN: 9788770221917

Bhandari, Medani P. (2020), Getting the Climate Science Facts Right: The Role of the IPCC, River Publishers, Denmark / the Netherlands- ISBN: 9788770221863 e-ISBN: 9788770221856

Bhandari, Medani P. (2018) Green Web-II: Standards and Perspectives from the IUCN, Published, sold, and distributed by: River Publishers, Denmark / the Netherlands ISBN: 978-87-70220-12-5 (Hardback) 978-87-70220-11-8 (eBook).

Bhandari, Medani P (2018). The Role of International Organization in Addressing the Climate Change Issues and Creation of Intergovernmental Panel on Climate Change (IPCC). Adv Agr Environ Sci. 1(1) 1-17: 00005. http://ologyjournals.com/aaeoa/aaeoa_00005.pdf

---- (2011) "Viewpoints: What do you think should be the two or three highest priority political outcomes of the United Nations Conference on Sustainable Development (Rio+20), scheduled for Rio de Janeiro in June 2012? Natural Resources Forum 36, 251-252 (Wiley-Blackwell)

---- (2011) The conceptual problems of Green Economy and Sustainable Development and the Theoretical Route of Green Economy Initiatives, Applicability, and the Future, Compilation Document - Rio+20 - United Nations Conference on Sustainable Development, United Nations, New York, (Major groups), 141-153 http://www.uncsd2012.org/rio20/content/documents/compilationdocument/MajorGroups.pdf

---- (2012) Centre for Integrated Mountain Development (ICIMOD) [for conservation and management of the Hindu Kush-Himalayas

References 171

– Afghanistan, Bangladesh, Bhutan, China, India, Myanmar, Nepal, and Pakistan Environment], in Ritzer, George (Ed.) Blackwell Encyclopedia of Globalization, Wiley-Blackwell Publication Volume 3, 1076-1078.

---- (2012) International Union for Conservation of Nature (IUCN) [Implication of the global conservation policies and its contribution to the biodiversity conservation in the developing world], in Ritzer, George (Ed.) Blackwell Encyclopedia of Globalization, Wiley-Blackwell Publication Volume 3, 1086-1088.

---- (2012) South Asian Association for Regional Cooperation (SAARC) [Problems and opportunities in improving the livelihood of its member countries: Sri Lanka, India, Pakistan, Afghanistan, Bhutan, Maldives, Bangladesh, and Nepal], in Ritzer, George (Ed.) Blackwell Encyclopedia of Globalization, Wiley-Blackwell Publication, Volume 4, 1891-1898.

---- (2012) The Intergovernmental Panel on Climate Change (IPCC) [The fourth assessment reports on climate change: a factual truth of contemporary world], in Ritzer, George (Ed.) Blackwell Encyclopedia of Globalization, Wiley-Blackwell Publication Volume 3, 1063-1067. 15, 1995, p. 177.

Bimber, B. (1994). "Three Faces of Technological Determinism" in M. R. Smith and L. Marx. Does Technology Drive History. Cambridge, MA, MIT Press.

Blau, P. M. (1955) The Dynamics of Bureaucracy. Chicago: University of Chicago Press.

Blau, P. M. (1964) Exchange and Power in Social Life. New York: Wiley.

Blau, P. M. (1970) A formal theory of differentiation in organizations. Am. Social. Rev. 35:201-218.

Blau, P. M. (1973) The Organization of Academic Work. New York: Wiley.

Blau, P. M. (1974) Parameters of social structure. Am. Social. Rev. 39:615-635.

Blau, P. M. (1977) Inequality and Heterogeneity: A Primitive Theory of Social Structure. New York: Free Press.

Blau, P. M. (1994) Structural Contexts of Opportunities. Chicago: University of Chicago Press.

Blau, P. M. (1995) A circuitous path to macrostructural theory. Annu. Rev. Social. 21:1-19.

172 *International Organization and Organizational Sociology*

Blazer, D. (1982) "Social Support and Mortality in an Elderly Community Population." *American Journal of Epidemiology* 115:684–694.

Boorman, Scott (1973) Outline and Bibliography of Approaches to the Formal Study of Social Networks, Harvard University, Department of Sociology, 1973 (Fels Discussion Paper, no. 87). H.C. While, Do Networks Matter? Harvard University, Department of Sociology, 1972, p. 35.

Borgatti, S. P. and P. C. Foster (2003) The Network Paradigm in Organizational Research: A Review and Typology, Journal of Management, December 1, 2003; 29(6): 991 - 1013.

Bowen, D. E., G. E. J. Ledford, et al. (1991). "Hiring for the Organization, Not the Job." Academy of Management Executive, 5(4): 35-51.

Braverman, H. (1974). Labor and Monopoly Capital: The Degradation of Work in the Twentieth Century, New York, Monthly Review Press.t

Brechin S.R. and W. Kempton (1994) Global environmentalism: a challenge to the post-materialism thesis, *Social Science Quarterly* 75 (2) (1994), pp. 245–269.

Brechin S.R., W Kempton (1997) Beyond Postmaterialist Values: National versus Individual Explanations of Global Environmentalism, Social Science Quarterly, 1997, 78:11, 1-43.

Brechin Steven R. (1997), Planting Tree in the Developing World, A sociology of International Organization, The Johns Hopkins University Press, Baltimore.

Brechin Steven R. (2003) Comparative Public Opinion and Knowledge on Global Climatic Change and the Kyoto Protocol: The U.S. versus the World? International Journal of Sociology and Social Policy, 23(10), pp. 106-134, October 2003.

Brechin Steven R. and D. Freeman (2004) Public Support for both the Environment and an Anti-Environmental President: Possible Explanations for the George W. Bush Anomaly, the Forum: A Journal of Applied Research in Contemporary Politics, 2(1), Article 6, January 2004.

Brechin Steven R., Peter Wilshusen, Crystal Fortwangler and Patrick West (2002) Beyond the Square Wheel: Toward a More Comprehensive Understanding of Biodiversity Conservation as Social and Political Process, Society and Natural Resources, 15, pp.41-64, January 2002.

References 173

Brechin, Steven R., and Bhandari, Medani P. (2011) Perceptions of climate change worldwide, *WIREs Climate Change* 2011, Volume 2:871–885.

Brewis Joanna (2005) Othering Organization Theory: Marta Calas and Linda Smircich, The Editorial Board of the Sociological Review, 2005, Blackwell Publishing, Ltd.

Brown, Reva (2004) Consideration of the origin of Herbert Simon's theory of "satisficing? (1933-1947)Management Decision, Volume 42 Number 10 2004 pp. 1240-1256

Burawoy, M. (1979). Manufactured Consent, Chicago, University of Chicago Press.

Burrell, G., and G. Morgan (1979). Sociological Paradigms and Organizational Analysis, Heinemann.

Calas, M.B. and L. Smircich. 1996. "From 'The Woman's Point of View: Feminist Approaches to Organizational Studies" Handbook of Organizational Studies, Sage Publications.

Carrol, G. R., and M. T. Hannan (1989). "Density dependence in the evolution of populations of newspaper organizations." American Sociological Review, 54: 524-548.

Cartwright, D. and Harary, F. (1956), Structural balance: a generalization of Heider's Theory. Psychological Review, 63:277-293.

Chandler, A. (1984). "The Emergence of Market Capitalism." Business History Review, 58(winter): 473-503.

Chapnis, A. (1983). "Engineering Psychology" in M. D. Dunnette. The Handbook of Industrial and Organizational Psychology. New York, Wiley: 697-744.

Charnitski Christina Towel (2002), Gauging the Readiness of an Institution of Higher Education to Implement Change in Its Distance Education Program in Ways that are Consistent with the Paradigm of Organizational Agility, Doctoral thesis, Drexel University

Cicero, "On Old Age," Selected Works, Edited by Michael Grant (London: Penguin, 1971), p. 218.

Clark, Ian (1999) Globalization and international relations theory, Oxford University Press.

Cohen, S.; Underwood, S.; and Gottlieb, B. (2000) *Social Support Measures and Intervention.* New York: Oxford University Press.

174 *International Organization and Organizational Sociology*

Cohen, W. M., and D. A. Levinthal (1990). "Absorptive Capacity: A New Perspective on Learning and Innovation." Administrative Science Quarterly, 35: 128-152.

Conicoid Jean-Marc and Veijo Heiskanen (edited 2001) Legitimacy of international organizations, United Nations University Press.

Collins, R. (1979). The Credential Society: An Historical Sociology of Education and Stratification, Orlando, FL, Academic Press.

Cook, Blanche Wiesen (1992) Eleanor Roosevelt: Volume One, 1884-1933. New York: Viking Press, 1992, 259-260.

Cooperrider David L., Jane E. Dutton, (editors 1999) Organizational dimensions of global change: no limits to cooperation, Sage Publication.

Cusimano, M.K. (1999) The challenge to institutions. In Beyond sovereignty: issues for a global agenda. Bedford/St Martin's, Boston, MA, USA.

Cusumano, M. (1989) Japanese Automobile Industry, Boston, Harvard University Press.

Dalton, M. (1959). "Men Who Manage" in M. Granovetter and R. Swedberg. The Sociology of Economic Life. Boulder, CO, Westview Press.

DeVault Marjorie (2002) Institutional Ethnography: Using Interviews to Investigate Ruling Relations (With Liza McCoy). Pp. 751-76 in Handbook of Interview DeVault Marjorie Research, eds. Jaber Gubrium and James Holstein. Thousand Oaks, CA: Sage Publications, 2002.

DeVault Marjorie (2004) What is Description? (One Ethnographer's View). Perspectives (ASA Theory Section Newsletter), 27 (#1): 4, January 2004.

DiMaggio, Paul, J., and Walter W. Powell (1983) "The iron cage revisited: Institutional isomorphism and collective rationality in organizational fields," American Sociological Review 48: 147-160.

Disney, Jennifer Leigh, Joyce Gelb (2000) Feminist Organizational "Success": The State of U.S. Women's, Movement Organizations in the 1990s, Women & Politics, Vol. 21(4) 2000.

Dore, R. (1983). "Goodwill and the Spirit of Market Capitalism." British Journal of Sociology, 34: 459-482.

Drori Gili S., John W. Meyer, and Hokyu Hwang (editors 2006) Globalization and organization: world society and organizational change, Oxford University Press

Dunlap Riley E. and Angela G. Mertig (edited 1992) American environmentalism: the U.S. environmental movement, 1970-1990, Taylor and Francis.

Dunlap, Riley E., and Angela G. Mertig (1995) "Global Concern for the Environment: Is Affluence a Prerequisite?" Journal of Social Issues 51:121–37.

Dunlap, Riley E., and Angela G. Mertig (1997) "Global Environmentalism: An Anomaly for Postmaterialism." Social Science

Durkheim, Emile [1893] 1964. The Division of Labor in Society. Tr. George Simpson. New York: Free Press.

Durkheim, Emile. [1897] 1951. Suicide: A Study in Sociology: Tr. John A. Spaulding and George Simpson. Glencoe, IL: Free Press.

Durkheim, Emile. 1915. The Elementary Forms of the Religious Life: A Study in Religious Sociology. Translated by Joseph Ward Swain. New York: Macmillan.

Eccles, R., and N. Nohria (1992). Beyond the Hype, Cambridge, Harvard Business School Press.

Eller Shafritz, J. M., J. Steven Ott, and Yong Suk Jang (2005) Classics of Organization Theory, 6th Edition, Thompson/Wadsworth, 2005.

Elliott, Lorraine (1994) International Conference on Diplomacy and the Changing Role of NGOs, in Australian and New Zealand Society of International Law: Proceedings of the Second Annual Meeting 223, 225 (1994).

Emirbayer, Mustafa (1996) Useful Durkheim, Sociological Theory, Vol. 14, No. 2. (Jul. 1996), pp. 109-130.

Engels, F. (1958 [1894]) "The Peasant Question in France and Germany." In: Karl Marx and Frederick Engels: Selected Works, II, pp. 420–440. Moscow: Foreign Languages Publishing House.

Escobar, Arturo (2001) Culture sits in places: reflections on globalism and subaltern strategies of localization, Political Geography, Volume 20, Issue 2, February 2001, Pages 139-174

Falk Richard (1987) The Global Promise of Social Movements: Explorations at the Edge of Time, 12 Alternatives 173 (1987).

Faunce, W. A. (1965). "Automation and the Division of Labor." Social Problems, 13: 147-160.

176 *International Organization and Organizational Sociology*

Faure Michael, Joyeeta Gupta, Andries Nentjes (edited 2003) Climate change and the Kyoto protocol: the role of institutions and instruments to control global change, Edward Elgar Publisher

Fincham R and Rhodes, P (1999) 'Principles of Organizational Behavior', Oxford University Press.

Finnemore Martha (1996) National Interest in International Society, Cornell University Press, Ithaca, 1996.

Finnemore Martha (2004) The Purpose of Intervention: Changing Beliefs about the Use of Force (Ithaca: Cornell University Press, 2004)

Finnemore Martha and Kathryn Sikkink,(1998) "International Norm Dynamics and Political Change," International Organization, 52, no. 4 (Autumn 1998): 887-917.

Fisher, C. D. (1986). "Organizational Socialization: An Integrative View." Research in Personnel and Human Resources Management, 4: 101-145.

Fleming, L., C. King III, and A. I. Juda (2007) Small Worlds and Regional Innovation Organization Science, November 1, 2007; 18(6): 938 – 954

Frank, R. (1985). Choosing the Right Pond: Human Behavior and the Quest for Status, New York, Oxford University Press.

Freeman, L.C. (2004) The Development of Social Network Analysis: A Study in the Sociology of Science. Vancouver: Empirical Press.

Friedman Thomas, The World is Flat (New York: Farrar Straus Giroux, 2006).

Friedman, M. (1953). "The Methodology of Positive Economics" in M. Friedman. Essays in Positive Economics. Chicago, University of Chicago Press.

Frost, P. J., L. F. Moore, et al., Ed. Eds. (1985). Organizational Culture. Beverly Hills, Sage.

Galbraith, J. R. (1974). "Organization Design: An Information Processing View." Interfaces, 4: 28-36.

Gallarotti, G.M. (1991) The limits of international organization: systematic failure in the management of international relations. International Organization, 45.

Garvin, D.A. (1993) Building a learning organization. Harvard Business Review, Jul-Aug.

Gay Paul du (edited 2005) Values of bureaucracy, Oxford.

References 177

Geertz, C. (1978). "The Bazaar Economy: Information and Searching Peasant Marketing." American Economic Review, 68(May): 28-32.

Gergen, K. J. (1992). "Organizational Theory in the Post-Modern Era" in M. Reed and M. Hughes. Rethinking Organizations: new directions in organization theory and analysis, Sage Publications: 207-226.

Gerschenkron, A. (1952). "Economic Backwardness in Historical Perspective" in M. Granovetter and R. Swedberg. The Sociology of Economic Life. Boulder, CO, Westview Press.

Giddens, A. (1979). "Agency, Structure" in A. Giddens. Central Problems in Social Theory. Berkeley, University of California Press.

Glass, T.; Dym, B.; Greenberg, S.; Rintel, D.; Roesch, C.; and Berkman, L. (2000). "Psychosocial Intervention in Stroke: The Families in Recovery from Stroke Trial (FIRST)." *American Journal of Orthopsychiatry* 70(2):169–181.

Goldenweiser A. (1917) Religion and Society: A Critique of Émile Durkheim's Theory of the Origin and Nature of Religion, The Journal of Philosophy, Psychology, and Scientific Methods, Vol. 14, No. 5. (Mar. 1, 1917), pp. 113-124.

Goodspeed, Stephen S. (1967) Nature and function of an international organization, Oxford University Press.

Granovetter, M. (1973), The Strength of Weak Ties. *American Journal of Sociology*, 78:1360-1380.

Granovetter, M. (1985). "Economic Action and Social Structure: The Problem of embeddedness." American Journal of Sociology, 91: 481-510.

Granovetter, M. (1995). Getting a Job: A Study of Contacts and Careers, Chicago, University of Chicago Press.

Grant Charles (2001) "A European View of ESDP," Centre for European Policy Studies working paper (April 2001).

Grazia Alfred De (1962) Political Behavior, the Elements of Political Science (Volume One), New, Revised Edition, Chicago university.

Gregory, Allan W., and Gregor W. Smith (1990) "Calibration as Estimation." Econometric Reviews 9:1 (1990): 57-89.

Gregory, K. L. (1983). "Native-View Paradigms: Multiple Cultures and Culture Conflicts in Organizations." Administrative Science Quarterly, 28: 359-376.

178 *International Organization and Organizational Sociology*

Griffin James M. (edited 2003) Global climate change: the science, economics and politics, Edward Elgar Publisher

Haas, E.B. (1990) When knowledge is power: three models of change in international organizations. University of California Press, Berkeley, CA, USA.

Haas, P.M.; Haas, E.B. (1995) Learning to learn: improving international governance. Global Governance, 1995.

Hackman, J. R. (1975). "On the Coming Demise of Job Enrichment" in E. L. Cass and F. G. Zimmer. Men and Work in Society. New York, Van Nostrand Reinhold Company: 97-115.

Hackman, J. R. (1985?). "Designing work for individuals and groups" in J. R. Hackman, E. E. Lawler, and L. W. Porter. Perspectives on behavior in organizations. New York, McGraw-Hill Book Company: 242-258.

Hackman, J. R., and R. Wagemen (1995). "Total Quality Management: Empirical, Conceptual and Practical Issues." Administrative Science Quarterly, 40: 309-342.

Hamilton, G. (1994). "Civilizations and the Organization of Economics" in N. Smelser and R. Swedberg. Handbook of Economic Sociology: 183-205.

Hamilton, G. G., and N. W. Biggart (1988). "Market, Culture, and Authority: A Comparative Analysis of Management and Organization in the Far East." American Journal of Sociology, 94 (Supplement): S52-S94.

Hannan, M. T. and J. Freeman (1989). Organizational Ecology, Cambridge, Harvard University Press.

Hannigan, John A (1995) Environmental sociology: a social constructionist perspective, Routledge, UK

Hardin, G. (1968). "The Tragedy of the Commons." Science, 162(December): 1243-1248.

Harper John Lamberton (1996) American Visions of Europe: Franklin D. Roosevelt, George F. Kennan, and Dean G. Acheson (Cambridge University Press, 1996)

Hatala, J.P. (2006) Social Network Analysis in Human Resource Development: A New Methodology, Human Resource Development Review, March 1, 2006; 5(1): 45 - 71.

Heckscher, C.; Donnellon, A., (ed. 1994) The post-bureaucratic organization: new perspectives on organizational change. Sage, Thousand Oaks, CA, USA.

Held, David (2004) Global covenant: the social democratic alternative to the Washington Consensus, Polity Press.

Higgins, T.E. (1996) "Anti-Essentialism, Relativism, and Human Rights" Harvard Women's Law Journal.

Hill, L. A. (1992). Becoming a Manager, Boston, Harvard Business School Press.

Hill, R. and Dunbar, R. (2002) "Social Network Size in Humans." Human Nature, Vol. 14, No. 1, pp. 53-72.

Hirsch, P. M. (1972). "Processing Fads and Fashions." American Journal of Sociology, 77: 639-659.

Hirschman, A. (1982). "Rival Interpretations of Market Society: Civilizing, Destructive, or Feeble?" Journal of Economic Literature, 20(Dec.): 1463-1484.

Hoffmann, Matthew J. Ozone depletion and climate change: constructing a global response / Matthew J. Hoffmann. 2005

Hopp, W. and M. L. Spearman (1996). "1: Manufacturing in America" in. Factory Physics. Chicago, Irwin.

Hounshell, D. A. (1984). From the American System to Mass Production -- 1800-1932, Baltimore, Johns Hopkins University Press.

House, J.; Robbins, C.; and Metzner, H. (1982). "The Association of Social Relationships and Activities with Mortality: Prospective Evidence from the Tecumseh Community Health Study." *American Journal of Epidemiology* 116:123–140.

Howard Michael (2002) The Invention of Peace and the Persistence of War, 2d revised ed. (London: Profile Books, 2002).

http://www.uncsd2012.org/rio20/index.php?page=view&type=510&nr=138&menu=20   http://www.uncsd2012.org/rio20/content/documents/138apec. pdf

Huntington Samuel P. (1999) "The Lonely Superpower," Foreign Affairs (March-April 1999).

180 *International Organization and Organizational Sociology*

Hutchins, E. (19XX). "The Technology of Team Navigation" in J. Gallagher, R. E. Kraut, and C. Egido. Intellectual Teamwork: Social and Technological Foundations of Cooperative Work. Hillsdale, NJ, Lawrence Erlbaum Associates: 191-221

Ireland Ekko C. van, Joyeeta Gupta, Marcel T.J. Kok. (Edited 2003), Issues in international climate policy: theory and policy, Edward Elgar Publisher

Ingelhart, Ronald (1995) "Public Support for the Environmental Protection: Objective Problems and Subjective Values in 43 Societies." PS: Political Science & Politics 28:57–72.

Jayaram N.; forward by Satish Saberwal (editor 2005) All India Sociological Conference (26th: 2000: University of Kerala) On civil society: issues and perspectives, Sage Publications.

Kaplan, G.; Salonen, J.; Cohen, R.; Brand, R.; Syme, S.; and Puska, P. (1988) "Social Connections and Mortality from All Causes and Cardiovascular Disease: Prospective Evidence from Eastern Finland." *American Journal of Epidemiology* 128:370–380.

Karns Margaret P. and Karen A. Mingst (2004) International organizations: the politics and processes of global governance, Lunne Rienner Publisher.

Kaufman, Herbert (1964) Organization Theory and Political Theory, the American Political Science Review, Vol. 58, No. 1. (Mar. 1964), pp. 5-14

Kawachi, I.; Colditz, G. A.; Ascherio, A.; Rimm, E. B.; Giovannucci, E.; Stampfer, M. J. et al. (1996) "A Prospective Study of Social Networks about Total Mortality and Cardiovascular Disease in Men in the U.S.A." *Journal of Epidemiological Community Health* 50:245–251.

Kerr, S. (1975). "On the Folly of Rewarding A, While Hoping for B." Academy of Management Journal, 18(4): 769-783.

Kiesler, S., and T. Finholt (1988). "The Mystery of RSI." American Psychologist, 43(12): 1004-1015.

Knapp, Peter (1986) Hegel's Universal in Marx, Durkheim, and Weber: The Role of Hegelian Ideas in the Origin of Sociology, Sociological Forum, Vol. 1, No. 4. (Autumn, 1986), pp. 586-609.

Knowles, M. (1984) The Adult Learner: A Neglected Species (3rd Ed.). Houston, TX: Gulf Publishing.

Kolb, D. A. (1984). Experiential learning: Experience as the source of learning and development, Englewood Cliffs, New Jersey, Prentice-Hall, Inc.

Kothari Rajni (1993) The Yawning Vacuum: A World Without Alternatives, 18 Alternatives 119 (1993).

Krasner, S. (1983). International regimes. Ithaca: Cornell University Press.

Krebs, Valdis (2006) Social Network Analysis, A Brief Introduction. (Includes a list of recent SNA applications)

Kuhn, Thomas (1983b) "Rationality and Theory Choice", Journal of Philosophy 80: 563-70.

Kuiper Edith and Drucilla K. Barker (Editors 2006) Feminist economics and the World Bank: history, theory, and policy,

Langer William L. and S. Everett Gleason (1952) The Challenge to Isolation, 1937–1940 (Harper Bros., 1952), 14.

Lash, Joseph (1971) Eleanor and Franklin. New York: W.W. Norton & Company, 1971, 346-348.

Lawler, E. E. I., and S. A. Morhman (1985). "Quality Circles After the Fad." Harvard Business Review,(January-February): 65-71.

Lawrence, P., and J. Lorsch (1967). "Differentiation and Integration in Complex Organizations." Administrative Science Quarterly, 12: 1-30.

Levinthal, D. A. and J. G. March (1981). "A Model of Adaptive Organizational Search." Journal of Economic Behavior and Organization, 2: 307-333.

Levinthal, D. A. and J. G. March (1993). "The Myopia of Learning." Strategic Management Journal, 14: 95-112.

Levitt, B.; March, J.G. (1988) Organizational learning. American Review of Sociology, 14.

Lewis Douglas (edited 2006) International and regional organizations, Oxford.

Locke John, Of Civil Government, (Chicago, Regnery).

Louis, M. R. (1980). "Surprise and Sensemaking: What Newcomers Experience Entering Unfamiliar Organizational Settings." Administrative Science Quarterly, 25: 226-251.

Louis, M. R. (1985). "An Investigator's Guide to Workplace Culture" in P. J. Frost, L. F. Moore, M. R. Louis, C. C. Lundberg, and J. Martin. Organizational CLouis - Investigators Guide to Workplace Culture. Beverly Hills, Sage: 73-93.

182 *International Organization and Organizational Sociology*

Louis, M. R. (1985). "Perspectives on Organizational Culture" in P. J. Frost, L. F. Moore, M. R. Louis, C. C. Lundberg, and J. Martin. Organizational Culture. Beverly Hills, Sage: 27-29.

Lucas, Robert E. "Econometric Policy Evaluation: A Critique." The Phillips Curve and Labor Markets. Eds. Karl Brunner and Allan Meltzer. Amsterdam: North-Holland, 1976: 19-46.

Luterbacher Urs and Detlef F. Spring (edited 2001) International relations and global climate change, MIT

Maanen, J. V. and S. R. Barley (1985). "Cultural Organization: Fragments of a Theory" in P. J. Frost, L. F. Moore, M. R. Louis, C. C. Lundberg, and J. Martin. OrVan Maanen & Barley - Cultural Orgs Fragments of a Theory Organizational Culture. Beverly Hills, Sage: 31-53.

Macaulay, S. (1963). "Non-Contractual Relations in Business: A Preliminary Study." American Sociological Review, 28: 55-67.

Machiavelli Niccolo, The Prince, and the Discourses (New York, Random House, Modern Library College Editions).

Manning, P. K. (1977). "Talking and Becoming: A View of Organizational Socialization" in R. L. Blankenship. Colleagues in Organization: The Social Construction of Professional Work. London, Wiley & Sons: 181-205.

March, J. G. (1991). "Exploration and Exploitation." Organization Science, 21(February): 71-87.

March, J. G. (1991). "Organizational Consultants and Organizational Research, J of Applied Communication Research." Journal of Applied Communication Research, 19: 20-31.

March, J. G. (1994). A Primer on Decision Making, New York, The Free Press.

March, J. G. (1994). Three Lectures on Efficiency and Adaptiveness in Organizations. Helsingfors, Sweden, Swedish School of Economics and Business Administration

March, J. G. (1995). "The future, disposable organizations and the rigidities of imagination." Organization, 2: 427-440.

March, J. G. (1996). "Learning to Be Risk Averse." Psychological Review,

March, J. G., and J. P. Olsen (1975). "The Uncertainty of the Past: Organizational Learning Under Ambiguity." European Journal of Political Research, 3: 147-171.

March, J. G., and J. P. Olsen (1995). Democratic Governance. New York, The Free Press.

March, J. G., and Z. Shapira (1971). "Managerial Perspectives on Risk and Risk Taking." Management Science, 33(11): 1404-1418.

March, J. G., and Z. Shapira (1992). "Variable Risk Preferences and the Focus of Attention." Psychological Review, 99(1): 172-183.

March, J. G., L. S. Sproull, et al. (1991). "Learning from Samples of One or Fewer." Organization Science, 2: 1-13.

Marcson, S. (1960). The Scientist in American Industry: Some Organizational Determinants in Manpower Utilization, Princeton, NJ, Industrial Relations Section, Princeton University.

Martin Lisa L. and Beth A. Simmons (edited 2001), International institutions: an international organization reader, MIT Press.

Martin, J. (1990). "Deconstructing organizational behavior taboos: The suppressions of gender conflict in organizations." Organization Science, 1: 339-359.

Marx, Karl, and Friedrich Engels, 1930. The German Ideology. New York: International Publishers.

Marx, Karl, and Friedrich Engels, 1962. Selected Works, 2 vols. Moscow: Foreign Language Publishing House.

Marx, Karl, 1973, Grundrisse. New York: Vintage.

Marx, Karl. 1848/1954. The Communist Manifesto. Henry Regnery Company: Chicago.

Marx, Karl. 1964. Selected Writings in Sociology and Social Philosophy. (Translated by T.B. Bottomore). London: McGraw-Hill.

Marx, Karl. 1964b. Early Writings. Translated and edited by T. B. Bottomore. New York: McGraw-Hill.

Marx, Karl. 1845. Eleven Theses on Feuerbach.

Marx, Karl. 1959. Toward the Critique of Hegel's Philosophy of Right, in Marx and Engels, Basic Writings, Lewis S. Feuer (ed). New York: Doubleday & Co., Anchor Books.

184 *International Organization and Organizational Sociology*

Mathiason, John, and Bhandari, Medani P. (2010) Getting the Facts Right: The Intergovernmental Panel on Climate Change and the New Climate Regime, Journal of International Organization Studies, Volume 1, Number 1, (September 2010) 58-71 http://www.journal-iostudies.org/sites/journal-iostudies.org/files/JIOS1014.pdf

Mathiason, John, and Bhandari, Medani P. (2010) Governance of Climate Change Science: The Intergovernmental Panel on Climate Change and the New Climate Change Management Regime, the UNITAR-Yale, Geneva, USA, 2nd Issue (2010).

Mearsheimer John (2002) Tragedy of Great Power Politics, W.W. Norton, New York 2002

Merton, Robert K (1968) Social Theory and Social Structure. New York: Free Press.

Meyer Birgit and Peter Geschiere (edited 1999) Globalization and identity: dialectics of flow and closure, Blackwell Publisher.

Meyer, J. W., and B. Rowan (1977). "Institutional organizations: formal structure as myth and ceremony." American Journal of Sociology, 83: 340-363.

Milgram, S. (1967), The small world problem. *Psychology Today*, 2:60-67.

Miller, V. D., and F. M. Jablin (1991). Information seeking during organizational entry: Influences, tactics, and a model of the process." Academy of Management Review, 16(1): 92-120.

Mills, A.J. (2002) "Studying the Gendering of Organizational Culture Over Time: Concerns, Issues, and Strategies." Gender, Work, and Organizations. Vol. 9, No. 3 (June).

Mills, Albert J, Corman, Steven R Poole, Marshall Scott (2002) Perspectives on Organizational Communication. Finding Common Ground, Canadian Journal of Sociology. Fall 2002.Vol. 27, Iss. 4.

Mintz, B., and M. Schwartz (1985). The Power Structure of American Business, Chicago, University of Chicago Press.

Mitchell, J. Clyde (1969) Social Networks in Urban Situations, Manchester University Press,

Mohanty, C.T. (1984) "Under Western Eyes: Feminist Scholarship and Colonial Discourses" boundary 2, Vol. 12, No. 3 On Humanism and the University I: The Discourse of Humanism. (Spring-Autumn): 333-358.

Moran, Robert T. Philip R. Harris, William G. Stripp. 1993Moran, Robert T., 1938- Developing the global organization: strategies for human resource professionals /

Mumby, D.K. and L.L. Putman (1992) "The Politics of Emotion: A Feminist Reading of Bounded Rationality." The Academy of Management Review, Vol. 17, No.3: 465-486.

Nature, 393:440-442.

Nelson Richard R. (1994) "Economic Growth Via the Coevolution of Technology and Institutions," pp. 21-32 in Loet Leydesdorff and Peter Van den Besselaar, eds., Evolutionary Economics and Chaos Theory: New Directions in Technology Studies, New York: St. Martin's Press, 1994.

Nerfin Marc (1986) Neither Prince nor Merchant: Citizen--An Introduction to the Third System, in World Economy in Transition 47 (Krishna Ahooja-Patel et al. eds., 1986).

Ness Gayl D. and Brechin Steven R (1988), Bridging the gap: international organizations as organizations, International Organization 42, 2, spring 1988.

Noble, D. F. (1979). "Social choice in machine design: The case of automatically controlled machine tools" in A. Zimbalist. Case Studies in the Labor Process. New York, Monthly Review Press.

Norton, Mary Beth, (et al eds 1998) A People and a Nation. Boston and New York: Houghton Mifflin Company, 1998, 657-660.

Nye Joseph (2004) Soft Power (New York: Public Affairs, 2004).

Orlikowski, W. J. (1991). "Integrated Information Environment or Matrix of Control? The Contradictory Implications of Information Technology." Accounting Management and Information, 1: 9-42.

Orlikowski, W. J. (1995). "Improvising Organizational Transformation over Time: A Situated Change Perspective." Information Systems Research WP #3865-95 November 1995, http://dspace.mit.edu/bitstream/1721.1/2598/1/SWP-3865-34131434.pdf

Orr, J. (Forthcoming). "About Copier Technicians" in. Talking About Machines: An Ethnography of a Modern Job. Ithaca, NY, ILR Press.

Orth-Gomer, K., and Unden, A. (1987) "The Measurement of Social Support in Population Surveys." *Social Science Medicine* 24:83–94.

186 *International Organization and Organizational Sociology*

Otto, Dianne (1996) Nongovernmental Organizations in the United Nations System: The Emerging Role of International Civil Society, Human Rights Quarterly 18.1 (1996) 107-141

Padgett, J. F. (1995). "The emergence of simple ecologies of skill: a hypercycle approach to the economic organization" in B. Arthur, S. Durlauf and D. Lane. The Economy as a Complex Evolving System.

Palacios Juan J. (edited 2008) Multinational corporations and the emerging network economy in Asia and the Pacific, Gulf Pushing Company.

Pangle Thomas L. and Peter J. Ahrensdorf, (1999) Justice among Nations: On the Moral Basis of Power and Peace (University Press of Kansas, 1999), 200–201.

Papaconstantinou George (1995) "Globalization, Technology, and Employment: Characteristics and rends," STI Review, No.

Parente, D. H. (1998) Across the manufacturing-marketing interface: Classification of significant research. International Journal of Operations & Production Management, 18 (12), 1205.

Parker, M. (2002) "Queering Management and Organization" Gender, Work and Organization. Vol. 9. No.2 p. 146-166.

Parkinson C. Northcote (1958) Evolution of Political Thought (New York, Viking Press, Compass Books, 1958).

Parsons, Talcott (1951) The Social System. Glencoe, IL: Free Press.

Parsons, Talcott (1971) The System of Modern Societies. Englewood Cliffs, NJ: Prentice-Hall.

Pennix, B. W.; van Tilburg, T.; Kriegsman, D. M.; Deeg, D. J.; Boeke, A. J.; and van Eijk, J. T. (1997). "Effects of Social Support and Personal Coping Resources on Mortality in Older Age: The Longitudinal Aging Study, Amsterdam." *American Journal of Epidemiology* 146:510–519.

Perin, C. (1991). "The moral fabric of the office: Panopticon Discourse and Schedule Flexibilities" in P. S. Tolbert and S. Barley. Organizations and Professions, Volume 8, Research in the Sociology of Organizations. Greenwich, CT, JAI Press.

Perrow, C. (1983). "The Organizational Context of Human Factors Engineering." Administrative Science Quarterly, 28: 521-541.

Peter R. Baehr & Leon Gordenker (1992) The United Nations in the 1990s 116 (1992); United Nations.

Pfeffer, J. (1982). Organizations and Organization Theory, Pittman.

Pfeffer, J. (1992). Managing with Power: Politics and Influence in Organizations, Boston, Harvard Business School Press.

Pfeffer, J. and G. Salancik (1978). The External Control of Organizations, Harper & Row.

Pickering, J. M., and J. King (1995). "Hardwiring Weak Ties: Inter-organizational Computer-Mediated Communication, Occupational Communities, and Organizational Change." Organization Science, 6(4): 479-486.

Polanyi (1944). The Great Transformation, Boston, Beacon Press.

Polanyi, K. (1957). "The Economy as Instituted Process" in m. Granovetter and R. Swedberg. The Sociology of Economic Life. Boulder, CO, Westview Press.

Posner, Michael H. (1994) The Establishment of the Right of Nongovernmental Human Rights Groups to Operate, in Human Rights: An Agenda for the Next Century 405 (Louis Henkin & John L. Hargrove eds., 1994).

Potter Pitman B. (1935) The Classification of International Organizations, I, The American Political Science Review, Vol. 29, No. 2. (Apr. 1935), pp. 212-224.

Potter, Pitman B. (Pitman Benjamin) (1928) Introduction to the study of an international organization, Century Company, USA.

Pugh Derek S., David J. Hickson (2007) Writers on organizations, Sage Publications.

Quarterly 78:24–29.

Ragnar Frisch, (1933) "Editorial." Econometrica 1 (1933a): 1-4.

Rajagopal Balakrishnan (2003) International Law from Below (New York: Cambridge University Press, 2003).

Robbins, L. (1932). An Essay on the Nature and Significance of Economic Science, New York, New York University Press.

Roethlisberger F. J. and Dickson W. J. (1941) Management and the Worker, Cambridge: Harvard University Press, 1941, p. 524.

Rohlen, T. (1973). "The Education of a Japanese Banker" in Unknown. The Future of Organization Design: 526-534.

188 *International Organization and Organizational Sociology*

Roloff, M. E. (1981). Interpersonal Communication: The Social Exchange Approach, Beverly Hills, CA, Sage.

Ross, David P. (1993). Family Security in Insecure Times. National Forum on Family Security, Canadian Council on Social Development. http://workinfonet.bc.ca/lmisi/Making/CHAPTER2/TANDG1.HTM

Rousseau Jean-Jacques (1954) Social Contract (New York, Hafner Library of World Classics # 1, 1954).

Rowan, B. (1982). "Organizational Structure and the institutional environment: the case of public schools." Administrative Science Quarterly, 27: 259-279.

Rowlands, Ian H (1995) Politics of global atmospheric change, Manchester University Press.

Roy, D. F. (1959). "Banana Time: Job Satisfaction and Informal Interaction." Human Organization, 18: 158-168.

Sakamoto Yoshikazu (edited 1994) Global transformation: challenges to the state system, United Nations University Press.

Scarselletta, M. (Forthcoming). "The infamous lab error: education, skill, and quality in medical technician's work" in S. Barley and J. Orr. Between craft and science: technical work in US settings. Ithaca, NY, ILR Press.

Schein, E. (1996). "Culture: The Missing Concept in Organization Studies." Administrative Science Quarterly, 41(2): 229-240.

Schoenbach, V.; Kaplan, B.; Freedman, L.; and Kleinbaum, D. (1986). "Social Ties and Mortality in Evans County, Georgia." *American Journal of Epidemiology* 123:577–591.

Scott W. Richard, John W. Meyer, and associates (1994) Institutional environments and organizations: Structural complexity and individualism, Sage Publications.

Scott, J. (2000). Social Network Analysis: A Handbook 2nd Ed. Newberry Park, CA: Sage.

Scott, W. Richard (2003) Organizations: Rational, Natural & Open Systems 5th Edition

Seeman, T. (1996) "Social Ties and Health: The Benefits of Social Integration." *Annuals of Epidemiology* 6:442–451.

Seeman, T., and Berkman, L. (1988). "Structural Characteristics of Social Networks and Their Relationship with Social Support in the Elderly: Who Provides Support." *Social Science Medicine* 26(7):737–749.

Seeman, T.; Berkman, L.; Kohout, F.; LaCroix, A.; Glynn, R.; and Blazer, D. (1993) "Intercommunity Variation in the Association between Social Ties and Mortality in the Elderly: A Comparative Analysis of Three Communities." *Annals of Epidemiology* 3:325–335.

Seidman, S. (1994) "Queer-Ing Sociology, Sociologizing Queer Theory: An Introduction." Sociological Theory, Vol. 12, No.2: 166-177.

Selznick, P. (1984). "Guiding Principles and Interpretation: A Summary" in. TVA and the Grass Roots. Berkeley, UC Berkeley Press: 249-266.

Selznick, Philip (1943) An Approach to a Theory of Bureaucracy, American Sociological Review, Vol. 8, No. 1. (Feb. 1943), pp. 47-54.

Selznick, Philip (1948) Foundations of the Theory of Organization, American Sociological Review, Vol. 13, No. 1. (Feb. 1948), pp. 25-35

Selznick, Philip, (1949) TVA and the grassroots; a study in the sociology of formal organization, University of California Press.

Shafritz, J.M., Ott, J.S. (Eds.2001): "Classics of Organization Theory", 5th Ed., Harcourt, 2001

Shah AH, Bhandari Medani P. Al-Harbi NO, Al-Ashban RM (2014) Kaff-E-Maryam (Anastatica Hierochuntica L.): Evaluation of Gastro-Protective Activity and Toxicity in Different Experimental Models. Biol Med 6: 197. DOI: 10.4172/0974-8369.1000197

Shea, G. F. (1994). Mentoring: Helping Employees Reach their Full Potential, American Management Association.

Simon, Herbert A.: "Applying Information Technology to Organizational Design", in Public Administration Review, Vol. 33, No. 3, May/June 1973, pp. 268-278.

Simon, Herbert A.: Administrative Behavior. A Study of Decision-Making Processes in Administrative Organization, Third Edition, The Free Press, Collier Macmillan Publishers, London, UK, 1976.

Simon, Herbert A.: The Sciences of the Artificial, the Massachusetts Institute of Technology, the Murray Printing Company, USA, 1969.

Simpson Gerry (1991) False Harmonies and Tragic Ironies: Human Rights in the New World Order, Int'l Legal Sec. J. 5, 6 (1991).

190 *International Organization and Organizational Sociology*

Simpson Gerry (1992) Some Recent Theoretical Orientations in International Law, in Proceedings, supra notes 73, at142, 146.

Slaughter Ann-Marie (2005) A New World Order (Princeton: Princeton University Press, 2005).

Smircich, L. (1983). "Concepts of Culture and Organizational Analysis." Administrative Science Quarterly, 28(3): 339-358.

Smith, A. (1776). A wealth of Nations, Chicago, University of Chicago Press.

Smith, M. R. (1994). "Technological Determinism in American Culture" in M. R. Smith and L. Marx. Does Technology Drive History? Cambridge, MA, MIT Press: 1-35.

Steven Everts (2001) "Unilateral America, Lightweight Europe? Managing Divergence in Transatlantic Foreign Policy," Centre for European Reform working paper (February 2001).

Stinchcombe, A. L. (1959). "Bureaucrats and Craft Administration of Production: A Comparative Study." Administrative Science Quarterly, 4(2): 168:187.

Strauss, G. (1955). "Group Dynamics and Intergroup Relations" in W. Whyte, F. Money, and Mot. New York, Harper & Row.

Sugisawa, H.; Liang, J.; and Liu, X. (1994). "Social Networks, Social Support and Mortality among Older People in Japan." *Journal of Gerontology* 49:S3–S13.

Taylor, Paul Graham (1993) International organization in the modern world: the regional and the global process, Pinter Publisher.

Terry Maley (2004) Max Weber and the Iron Cage of Technology, Bulletin of Science Technology Society 2004; 24; 69

Tescal Fernando R. (1992) The Kantian Theory of International Law, 92 Colum. L. Rev. 53 (1992).

Tesson, K.J. (2006), Dynamic Network: An interdisciplinary study of network organization I biological and human social system, Doctoral theses, University of Bath, UK.

Thiele Leslie P. (1993) Making Democracy Safe for the World: Social Movements and Global Politics, 18 Alternatives 273 (1993).

Thomas, M. Franck (1992) The Emerging Right to Democratic Governance, 86 Am. J. Int'l L. 46 (1992).

References 191

Thompson, P. and McHugh, D. (2002) Work Organizations, 3rd edition, Palgrave.

Tilly, Charles (1978) From Mobilization to Revolution. Reading, MA: Addison-Wesley.

Tilly, Charles (1981) "Useless Durkheim." Pp. 95-108 in As Sociology Meets History New York: Academic Press.

Tiryakian, E.A. (1981) The sociological import of a metaphor: tracking the source of Max Weber's 'iron cage' Sociological inquiry 51,1: 27-33

Tolbert, P. S., and L. G. Zucker (1983). "Institutional sources of change in the formal structure of organizations: the diffusion of civil service reform, 1880-1935." Administrative Science Quarterly, 28: 22-39.

Trist, E. L. (1978). "On socio-technical systems" in W. A. Pasmore and J. J. Sherwood. Socio-technical Systems. La Jolla, CA, University Associates.

Trist, E. L., and K. W. Bamforth (1951). "Some social and psychological consequences of the longwall method of coal getting."

Turkle, S. (1985). The Second Self: Computers and the Human Spirit, New York, Simon & Schuster.

Turner J. H. (1990) Emile Durkheim's Theory of Social Organization, Social Forces, Vol. 68, No. 4. (Jun. 1990), pp. 1089-1103.

Tushman, M. L., and P. Anderson (1986). "Technological discontinuities and organizational environments." Administrative Science Quarterly, 31: 439-465.

Van Maanen, J. (1977). "Experiencing Organization: Notes on the Meaning of Careers and Socialization" in J. Van Maanen. Organizational Careers: Some New Perspectives.

Van Maanen, J., and E. H. Schein (1979). "Toward of Theory of Organizational Socialization." Research in Organizational Behavior, 1: 209-264.

Van Maanen, J., and S. Barley (1984). "Occupational Communities: Culture and control in organizations." Research in Organizational Behavior, 6: 287-365.

Vaubel Roland (1986) A public choice approach to an international organization, Public Choice 51:39-57 (1986.

Viotti Paul R., Mark V. Kauppi (1999) International relations theory: realism, pluralism, globalism, and beyond, Allyn and Bacon 3rd edition.

192 *International Organization and Organizational Sociology*

Voegelin Eric, Plato, and Aristotle, in Order and History (Baton Rouge: Louisiana State University Press, 1957), pp. 3-268.

Vogt, T. M.; Mullooly, J. P.; Ernst, D.; Pope, C. R.; and Hollis, J. F. (1992) "Social Networks as Predictors of Ischemic Heart Disease, Cancer, Stroke, and Hypertension: Incidence, Survival, and Mortality." *Journal of Clinical Epidemiology* 45:659–666.

Wasserman, S., & Faust, K. (1994) Social Networks Analysis: Methods and Applications. Cambridge: Cambridge University Press.

Watts, D.J. and Strogatz, S.H. (1998) Collective dynamics of 'small world' networks.

Weber Max (1904-05/1992) The Protestant Ethic and the Spirit of Capitalism. trans. T. Parsons/intro. A. Giddens. London: Routledge.

Weber Max (1949) "Objectivity in social science and social policy" in the methodology of the social sciences, translated by Edward A Shils and Henry A Finch, New York: Free Press 1949.

Weber Max (1961) Basic Concepts in Sociology, (New York, Citadel Press.

Weber, Max (1946) "Science as a Vocation" in H.H. Gerth and C. Wright Mills (Translated and edited), From Max Weber: Essays in Sociology, pp. 129-156, New York: Oxford University Press, 1946.

Weick, K. (1985). "The Significance of Corporate Culture" in P. J. Frost, L. F. Moore, M. R. Louis, C. C. Lundberg, and J. Martin. Organizational Culture. Beverly Hills, Sage: 381-389.

Weiss, R. S. (1974) "The Provisions of Social Relationships." In *Doing unto Others,* ed. Z. Rubin. Englewood Cliffs, NJ: Prentice-Hall.

Welin, L.; Tibblin, G.; Svardsudd, K.; Tibblin, B.; Ander-Peciva, S.; Larsson, B. et al. (1985) "Prospective Study of Social Influences on Mortality: The Study of Men Born in 1913 and 1923." *Lancet* 1:915–918.

Wellman, B. and Berkowitz, S.D. (1988) Social Structures: A Network Approach. Cambridge: Cambridge University Press.

Westley Frances R. and Philip S. Miller (edited 2003) Experiments in consilience: integrating social and scientific responses to save endangered species, Island Press.

Wieland, George F. (1974) The Contributions of Organizational Sociology to the Practice of Management: A Book Review Essay, The Academy of Management Journal, Vol. 17, No. 2. (Jun. 1974), pp. 318-333.

Wiggenhorn, W. (1990). "Motorola U: When Training Becomes an Education." Harvard Business Review, 5(4): 35-51.

Williamson, O. (1975). Markets and Hierarchies, The Free Press.

Williamson, O. (1985). "Contractual Man" in. The Economic Institutions of Capitalism, the Free Press: 43-63.

Williamson, O. E. (1981). "The Economics of Organization: The Transaction Cost Approach." American Journal of Sociology, 87(3): 548-577.

Yadong Luo, (2007), Global dimensions of corporate governance, Blackwell Publishing.

Young, Oran R. (1989) International cooperation: building regimes for natural resources and the environment, Cornell University Press.

Young, Oran R. (2002) Institutional dimensions of environmental change: fit, interplay, and scale, MIT Press.

Zacher, M.W. (1999) The United Nations and global commerce. Department of Public Information, United Nations, New York, NY, USA.

Zelizer, V. A. (1978). "Human Values and the Market: The Case of Life Insurance and Death in 19th-Century America." American Journal of Sociology, 84: 591-610.

Zey-Ferrell, Mary (1981), Criticisms of the Dominant Perspective on Organizations, the Sociological Quarterly 22 (Spring 1981):181-205

Zuboff, S. (1984) In the Age of the Smart Machine, New York, Basic Books.

4

Sustainability Theory

Sustainable Development – Is This Paradigm the Remedy of All Challenges? – Does Its Goals Capture the Essence of Real Development and Sustainability? Concerning Discourses, Creativeness, Boundaries, and Institutional Architecture[1].

©medani.bhandari

"The Sustainable Development Goals (SDGs) are the blueprint to achieve a better and more sustainable future for all. They address the global challenges we face, including those related to poverty, inequality, climate, environmental degradation, prosperity, and peace and justice. The Goals interconnect and to leave no one behind, we must achieve each Goal and target by 2030" (UN 2015). *"The Sustainable Development Goals (SDGs), otherwise known as the Global Goals, are a universal call to action to end poverty, protect the planet and ensure that all people enjoy peace and prosperity"* (UNDP 2019).

Outline

Prof. Bhandari is a globally known environmentalist, conservationist, and expert on climate change impact, sustainability, social empowerment, and educationalist, who has devoted his entire life to the conservation of nature and social services. Prof. Bhandari is a theoretically and practically equipped social scientist who has a deep understanding of current global challenges – environmental, geographic, and socioeconomic – poverty, hunger, health, and inequality. Our objective is to bring this wealth of knowledge for the benefit of all concerned stakeholders of the world who thrive for a peaceful sustainable world. In the previous interview (in the *International Journal*

---

[1] Partly, this chapter was published at the *Scientific Peer-Reviewed Journal – Socioeconomic Challenges (SEC)*, Vol. 3(4), 97–128. https://doi.org/10.21272/ sec.3(4).97-128.2019.

196   *Sustainability Theory*

on Advances in Agriculture and Environmental Science), Prof. Bhandari explained why "Bashudaiva Kutumbakkam" the entire planet is our home, and all living beings are our relatives, which explained why climate change is a severe problem in human history, how pollution problems severely harming to major cities of India, Nepal, Pakistan, and Bangladesh. He also explains the social dimensions of environmental challenges and how geographical, and socio-cultural environments on personal motivation building. He also explained why and how he became interested in the conservation of nature and natural resources, what the problems were, and how he overcame and continuously worked on the same track with the same focus in his entire life. In another interview (in the *International Journal on Advances in Agriculture and Environmental Science*), he discussed "Live and let other live- the harmony with nature /living beings-in reference to sustainable development (SD)- and to how India, Nepal, Pakistan, and Bangladesh are coping with the agendas of sustainable development. The previous two interviews discussed how personal background makes people's perceptions of nature and society, the role of spiritualism/tradition, and how Indigenous knowledge can motivate himself or herself to devote to the conservation of nature and social empowerment. Prof. Bhandari shared the essence of education – how as a poor subsistence farmer's child who suffered to find educational options (six hours walk for school, swim across three rivers for schooling – only four hours sleep, experiencing death). How heavenly was sleeping in buffalos' back and how enjoyable was walking six hours for school, or even hunger and thirst were not an abnormal circumstance for poor students of the developing world. Prof. Bhandari also elaborates on the essence of sustainable development; agreed, particularly sustainable development goals have a crux to minimize the global challenges but not a readymade solution to the current global crisis. However, it has emerged as the maturing domain of development with future hope. In previous interviews, he briefly covered a historical account of SD, its goals, theory, and practices. These challenges are heavily explored and explained by many scholars, international organizations, governments, civil societies, and media houses. More importantly, United Nations has been vigorously working to overcome these challenges through various initiatives. In this regard, United Nations has been pioneering to minimize global challenges throughout its history. United Nations declared four decades (1960–1990) as a development decade with the objective of total development primarily in the developing world. In 1990, the UN presented Human Development Report 1990, and in 2000, UN declared millennium development goals (2000–2015). However, goals were only partially achieved. With this experience, the UN declared

"Transforming our World: The 2030 Agenda for Sustainable Development," which declared 17 sustainable development goals and 169 targets. Having this background, we posed theoretical questions to Prof. Bhandari. In response to the questions, Prof. Bhandari explains what the epistemological stand of sustainable development is, how discourses are developed, what the limitation is, boundaries, how creativeness is incorporated into the sustainability domain, whether SDGs are achievable, and whether governments are ready to cope with the domestic and international challenges. Hopefully, all concerned stakeholders will enjoy reading and utilizing the acquired knowledge for the sake of future generations (the essence of sustainable development).

Prof. Bhandari has been witnessing the development scenario of sustainable development since "Our Common Future 1987." He has published many scientific papers within the sustainability domain and published poems, plays, and songs. In his recent books "Green Web-II: Standards and Perspectives from the IUCN" and "Reducing Intra- and International Inequalities and Disproportions Towards SDGs" (edits jointly with Hanna Shvindina), he explains how collectively we can resolve the global environmental crisis and how SDGs can be achieved. A brief biography and contact details of Prof. Bhandari are included at the end of this interview. Prof. Bhandari states that "My intention, of life, is to pay back; give or contribute to the society in fullest whatever I have, earned, or experienced." Hopefully, readers will enjoy reading and will be benefited from this true and intrinsic motivational story with the evidence of scientifically grounded facts.

Introduction – Questions – Coverage

Q: Prof. Bhandari, thank you for taking the time to speak with us. In the last two interviews (in the *International Journal on Advances in Agriculture and Environmental Science*), you discussed your career in environmental protection as well as problems and consequential impacts of climate change, especially pollution impact on major Asian cities. In the interview titled "Bashudaiva Kutumbakkam – the entire world or earth is our/your family," you internalize the learned, listened, and practiced rituals to make the guiding principle of your dedication to nature conservation. Your academic work and publications also show that your primary expertise is in sustainability and your environment conservation journey was embodied within the principle of Live and Let Them Live, which was depicted in the interview titled "Live and let other live- the harmony with nature /living beings-in reference to sustainable development (SD)- and to how India, Nepal, Pakistan, and Bangladesh." In previous interviews, it was agreed that until or unless we understand the

198   *Sustainability Theory*

root cause of the problem, it is hard to develop actual tools – mechanisms to resolve them. Interviews also reveal that the thirst for acquire-get- gain and poses more and more- without compromising others' needs is the root of the current global challenges- environmental crisis, climate change, biodiversity loss, inequality (haves and have nots, sex, race, gender, invisible walls created by various traditions or so on), poverty, hunger, epidemics, drought, flood, land slight .... In "live and let other live," we also discussed that the notion of sustainable development emerged as a remedy for all solutions (that is not a correct assumption), and slightly we discussed how "World Conservation Strategy: Living Resource Conservation for Sustainable Development 1980" and "Our Common Future 1987" paved the pathways for sustainable development concept. In this discussion, we want to know how theoretically the sustainability discourse developed. What are the boundaries and what is the linkage with creativeness? Does the sustainability notion help to foster creativeness and innovation? What are the boundaries of the sustainable development paradigm?

As illustrated in many academic papers, books, monographs, and, most importantly, in the United Nations' declarations of 2015 (Transforming Our World: The 2030 Agenda for Sustainable Development), sustainable development goals are considered powerful tools to overcome the global challenges. Are SDGs achievable? What institutional architecture is required?

A: Thank you very much for inviting me to discuss this complex issue. Let me begin with the question "are SDGs achievable?" In the simplest term, yes; however, to achieve SDG goals and meet the targets, there is a need for real commitments; so far, commitments are limited on the paper or in the political slogans. United Nations and its member nations are taking SDGs as a remedy to all problems. For example, the UN declaration 2015 states that *"The Sustainable Development Goals are the blueprint to achieve a better and more sustainable future for all. They address the global challenges we face, including those related to poverty, inequality, climate, environmental degradation, prosperity, and peace and justice. The Goals interconnect and to leave no one behind, we must achieve each Goal and target by 2030"* (UN 2015). This statement is enough to show hope; however, the entire declaration openly and equally treats haves and haves not countries as the UN stands for. However, none of the documents disclose why inequality gaps (in every span of socioeconomic environment) are widening throughout history – rapidly increasing in recent decades? Who are responsible, and why is it increasing despite numerous efforts from related stakeholders? Are individual countries capable enough to implement the SDGs? What is the cost of *poverty, inequality, climate,* and *environmental degradation*? And where are the resources? Are global international development agencies willing to support developing nations without (agency's income return) any stirring? Will development agencies support developing nations without interventions in their national strategies? So far, we have not seen any agency support agency conditions. These conditional supports primarily create super strata as supporters and recipients automatically remain in lower strata. There is no freewheel as well as free will to developing countries who have to rely on others' mercy to tackle the accelerating environmental problem for which they were and are not responsible. I would say that SDGs have created a temporary emotion of hope; however, most countries of the global south may or may not be able to bring the desired outcome. The current trend so far in the developed world (G20) shows questionable results. As Bertelsmann Stiftung and Sustainable Development Solutions Network 2018 indicate, the lack of economic resources, appropriate institutional arrangements, suitable monitoring evaluation tools, and shortage of appropriate professional workforce are the major challenges toward achieving SDGs. Bertelsmann Stiftung and Sustainable Development Solutions Network 2018 report summarize the following:

- Most G20 countries have started SDGs implementation, but important gaps remain.
- No country is on track toward achieving all SDGs.
- Conflicts are leading to reversals in SDG progress.
- Progress toward sustainable consumption and production patterns is too slow.
- High-income countries generate negative SDG spillover effects.
- Inequalities in economic and social outcomes require better data (page IX).

If so, what is the condition of developing countries? Unknown. It will remain unknown because they are still in the planning phase, or for the report purpose, they might have some framework; however, implementation is a matter of big question mark (?). "To achieve the SDGs, countries must undertake major transformations of education, health, energy systems, land-use, urban development, and many other dimensions. Each transformation requires long-term changes involving large numbers of stakeholders from government, business, and civil society. Since such complex transformations cannot be implemented by markets alone, governments must take the lead in mobilizing stakeholders, planning for the transformations, designing supporting policy processes, and mobilizing the public funding" (Bertelsmann Stiftung and Sustainable Development Solutions Network 2018, page 1).

200 *Sustainability Theory*

Similarly, Egron-Polak (2019) rightly shows the future directions to achieve the SDGs: "SDGs address all nations – North, South, East, and West; The 17 SDGs are all inter-connected and show that solutions are interdependent; need holistic (multi-disciplinary) approaches; No SDG can be achieved without involvement – through research, education, and outreach – of higher education institutions; None can be achieved without international collaboration and commitment; Current trajectories of development (including in HE) are unsustainable – economically, socially, and politically; International education and research can serve to raise awareness, be at forefront of the search for alternatives, demonstrate the centrality of both knowledge and collaboration, gain new impetus by building on other broad agendas." SDGs are global agendas and unified international efforts are needed to achieve them practically. Institutionalization is processed (Scott 2001) and has to cross several prerequisites; similarly, internationalization also needs combined efforts at the multinational level. Therefore, it is hard to judge and also too early to predict. Based on past experiences (United Nations development decades 1960–1990; agenda 21; millennium development goals), there is a rational ground state that SDGs may be partially achieved by 2030. Even to achieve partial, indeed, there is a need for strong commitments of governments, regional and global collaborations, and strong institutional architecture for monitoring and evaluation.

The following questions are complicated and complex as the notion of sustainability:

1. *How theoretically and practically is sustainability discourse developed?*
2. *What are the boundaries and what is the linkage with creativeness?*
3. *Does the sustainability notion help to foster creativeness and innovation?*
4. *What is the institutional architecture to attain the SDGs?*

I will try to respond to each question separately as much as possible; however, there are overlaps among all five domains.

1. How Theoretically and Practically Sustainability Discourse is Developed?

A "theory" is not a collection of assertions about the behavior of the actual economy but an explicit set of instructions for building a parallel or analogue system--a mechanical, imitation economy. A "good" model, from this point of view, will not be exactly more "real" than a poor one, but will provide better imitations. Of course, what one means by a "better imitation" will depend on the particular questions to which one wishes to answer (Lucas 1980, page 697).

Discourse is what we understand and share the meaning of ideas, concepts, and opinions (written or unwritten). "The routine day-to-day usage of the term discourse simply refers to a stretch of text or spoken utterances that cohere into a meaningful exposition" (Chris Barker 2004, page 54).

Sustainability as such is a complex term: "sustain" – survive, maintain, bearing or holding capacity, and ability to be able of. However, in a definitional statement, mostly scholarly world cites from Our Common Future report (1987) which states "development that meets the needs of the present without compromising the ability of future generations to meet their own need" (Our Common Future 1987). In definitional terms, sustainability and sustainable development are used interchangeably, which builds on three major areas: environmental sustainability, economic sustainability, and social sustainability.

"The current state of scientific knowledge (particularly insights obtained in the last few decades) about natural and social phenomena and their

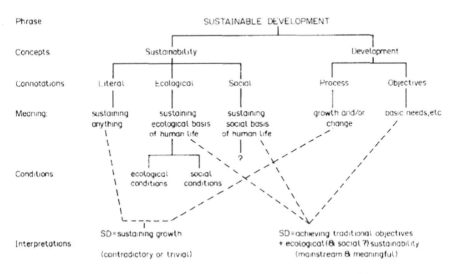

Source: Lele (1991, page 608) ("the existence of the ecological conditions necessary to support human life at a specified level of well-being through future generations, what I call ecological sustainability" (Lele 1991, page 609).

Figure 4.1 The semantics of sustainable development (as in Lele 1991, page 608).

202 *Sustainability Theory*

interactions leads inexorably to the conclusion that anyone driven by either long-term self-interest, or concern for poverty, or concern for intergenerational equity should be willing to support the operational objectives of SD" (Lele 1991, page 612).

Lele (1991) nicely presents the complexity of sustainable development (SD) from concepts to the implementing phase, which reveals the fact that SD depends on many aspects and can be implemented with the application of multidimensional approaches. The following table gives the general scenario of SD coverage (self-explanatory).

Sustainability is a complex issue which is interchangeably in use with sustainable development. Various authors have used the term in various ways and defined various categories to illustrate the issue they are addressing (health, development, policy, environment, climate change, weather variation, etc.) (Corral-Verdugo et al. 2009; Betsy 2010; SDSN 2014; Boucher 2015; UN 2015; WHO 2015; Mitchell and Walinga 2017; Tahvilzadeh, StigMontin, and Cullberg 2017; Bhandari 2018). The term sustainability discourse stands to maintain the equilibrium between nature and society and fulfill the societal demands (which could be environmental, economic, and social). Sustainability scholarship is to search the know-how of how development can be maintained without hampering the natural ecosystem and how the global major problems, i.e., environmental problems and socioeconomic problems – poverty, hunger, and health, can be solved or at least minimized.

Sustainability discourse is the overall scenario of how the concept began and how all concerned stakeholders use, develop, and adjust to it. Discourse can be seen as "social interaction, discourse as power and domination, discourse as communication, discourse as contextually situated, discourse as social semiosis, discourse as natural language use, discourse as complex, layered construct, sequences and hierarchies in discourse, abstract structures versus dynamic strategies in discourse, and types or genres of discourse" (VanDijk 2011). As Barker (2004, page 54) notes, "discourse is said to 'unite' language and practice and refers to regulated ways of speaking about a subject through which objects and practices acquire meaning." Sustainability discourse captures the notion of how the theories and practices have been developed and how the concerned stakeholders utilized them in the established scenario. Sustainability discourses can be seen as the creation of the sustainability regime creation, by which various rules, regulations, norms, values, and policy have been created. Sustainability discourses are accepted notions in the contemporary political, social, economic, and environmental policy domains.

As such, sustainability discourse can be seen in IUCN, UNEP, and WWF document "World Conservation Strategy: Living Resource Conservation for Sustainable Development" in 1980.

 **The Symbol** The circle symbolizes the biosphere—the thin covering of the planet that contains and sustains life. The three interlocking, overlapping arrows symbolize the three objectives of conservation: – maintenance of essential ecological processes and life-support systems; – preservation of genetic diversity; – sustainable utilization of species and ecosystems.	The World Conservation Strategy is intended to stimulate a more focused approach to the management of living resources and to provide policy guidance on how this can be carried out by three main groups: - government policymakers and their advisers; - conservationists and others directly concerned with living resources; - development practitioners, including development agencies, industry and commerce, and trade unions. 1. The World Conservation Strategy aims to achieve the three main objectives of living resource conservation: a. to maintain essential ecological processes and life-support systems; b. to preserve genetic diversity; c. to ensure the sustainable utilization of species and ecosystems. 6. The World Conservation Strategy ends by summarizing the main requirements for sustainable development, indicating conservation priorities for the Third Development Decade (section 20).
IUCN-UNEP-WWF (1980-vi-vii). https://portals.iucn.org/library/sites/library/files/documents/WCS-004.pdf	

The world conservation strategy, the symbol, and the text clearly emphasize the importance of sustainability, which also paved the foundation of

204 *Sustainability Theory*

sustainability discourses. However, one can trace the originality of discourses when people began to think about the limitation of natural resources and interrelated harmony relationships between humans and nature. In this respect, we can see the modern environment conservation history and the efforts to conserve them, particularly in terms of environmental problems – climate change. Sustainability discourse developed as a problem-solving tool. The meaning of sustainability has been modified as its application became popular. The following table adapted from Klarin (2018, page 77) provides a chronological overview of the meaning of sustainable development.

Table 4.1 The chronological overview of the meaning of sustainable development in the period 1980–2018.

Authors/ publication and year	Meaning and understanding of sustainable development
IUCN 1980	World Conservation Strategy
WCED, 1987	Sustainable development is a development that meets the needs of the present without compromising the ability of future generations to meet their own needs
Pearce et al. (1989)	Sustainable development implies a conceptual socioeconomic system that ensures the sustainability of goals in the form of real income achievement and improvement of educational standards, health care, and the overall quality of life
Harwood (1990)	Sustainable development is an unlimited developing system, where development is focused on achieving greater benefits for humans and more efficient resource use in balance with the environment required for all humans and all other species
IUCN, UNDP, and WWF (1991)	Sustainable development is a process of improving the quality of human life within the framework of the carrying capacity in the sustainable ecosystems
Lele (1991)	Sustainable development is a process of targeted changes that can be repeated forever
Meadows (1998)	Sustainable development is a social construction derived from the long-term evolution of an overly complex system – human population and economic development integrated into ecosystems and biochemical processes of the Earth
PAP/RAC (1999)	Sustainable development is development given by the carrying capacity of an ecosystem

Introduction – Questions – Coverage 205

Table 4.1 Continued

Authors/ publication and year	Meaning and understanding of sustainable development
Vander-Merwe and Van-der-Merwe (1999)	Sustainable development is a program that changes the economic development process to ensure the basic quality of life, protecting valuable ecosystems and other communities at the same time
Beck and Wilms (2004)	Sustainable development is a powerful global contradiction to the contemporary western culture and lifestyle
Vare and Scott (2007)	Sustainable development is a process of changes, where resources are raised, the direction of investments is determined, the development of technology is focused, and the work of different institutions is harmonized; thus the potential for achieving human needs and desires is increased as well
Sterling (2010)	Sustainable development is a reconciliation of the economy and the environment on a new path of development that will enable the long-term sustainable development of humankind
Marin et al. (2012)	Sustainable development gives a possibility of time-unlimited interaction between society, ecosystems, and other living systems without impoverishing the key resources
Duran et al. (2015)	Sustainable development is a development that protects the environment because a sustainable environment enables sustainable development
Bhandari (2018)	Sustainable development is a fundamental basis of development practice and way of thinking ahead

Source: Klarin (2018, page 77).

This change of sustainability meaning is based on its complexity – in coverage – economic – social and environment and its subsidiaries. According to Daly, "*Standard economics defines sustainability as a non-declining utility over generations. Ecological economics considers this unworkable because the utility is not measurable, and more importantly cannot be bequeathed. Also, it is throughput, not utility, that impinges on the environment. Ecological economics, therefore, defines sustainability as the bequest to future generations of an intact resource base, a non-declining stock of natural capital (strong sustainability). Some economists define sustainability as a non-declining total capital stock (the sum of natural*

206 *Sustainability Theory*

and man-made capital) on the neoclassical assumption of easy substitution between the two. The usual ecological economists' view of complementarity, with natural capital being the limiting factor, argues for the nonreclining natural capital definition" (Daly 2007, pages 254–255).

Primarily, sustainability discourse was developed to overcome the worrisome triggered by environmental change and to search the technological tools to monitor the environmental challenges and impacts.

Table 4.2 The development trend – the worrisome of environmental damage and mainstreaming of sustainability.

Year	Activity	Description
1969	UN published the report Man and His Environment or U Thant Report.	Activities focused to avoid global environmental degradation. More than 2000 scientists were involved in the creation of this report.
1972	First UN and UNEP World Conference on the Human Environment, Stockholm, Sweden.	Under the slogan, Only One Earth, a declaration and action plan for environmental conservation was published.
1975	UNESCO Conference on Education about the Environment, Belgrade, Yugoslavia.	Setting up a global environment educational framework, a statement known as the Belgrade Charter.
1975	International Congress of the Human Environment (HESC), Kyoto, Japan.	Emphasized the same problems as in Stockholm in 1972.
1979	The First World Climate Conference, Geneva, Switzerland.	Focused on the creation of the climate change research and program monitoring.
1981	The First UN Conference on Least Developed Countries, Paris, France.	A report with guidelines and measures for helping underdeveloped countries.
1984	Establishment of the United Nations World Commission on Environment and Development (WCED).	The task of the Commission is the cooperation between developed and developing countries and the adoption of global development plans on environmental conservation.

Introduction – Questions – Coverage 207

Table 4.2 Continued

Year	Activity	Description
1987	WCED report Our Common Future or Brundtland report was published.	A report with the fundamental principles of the concept of sustainable development.
1987	Montreal Protocol was published.	Contains results of the research on harmful effects on the ozone layer.
1990	The Second World Climate Conference, Geneva, Switzerland.	Further development of the climate change research and monitoring program and the creation of a global Climate Change Monitoring System.
1992	United Nations Conference on Environment and Development (Earth Summit or Rio Conference), Rio de Janeiro, Brazil.	In the Rio Declaration and Agenda 21 Action Plan, principles of sustainable development were established and the framework for the future tasks as well.
1997	Kyoto Climate Change Conference, Kyoto, Japan.	The Kyoto Protocol was signed between countries to reduce CO_2 and other greenhouse gas emissions, with commencement in 2005.
2000	UN published the Millennium declaration.	Declaration containing eight millennium development goals (MDGs) set by 2015.
2002	The World Summit on Sustainable Development, Johannesburg, South Africa.	Report with the results achieved during the time of the Rio Conference, which reaffirmed the previous obligations and set the guidelines for implementation of the concept in the future.
2009	The Third World Climate Conference, Geneva, Switzerland.	Further development of the global Climate Change Monitoring System with the aim of timely anticipation of possible disasters.
2009	World Congress Summit G20, Pittsburgh, USA.	G20 member states agreed on a moderate and sustainable economy.
2012	UN conference Rio +20, Rio de Janeiro, Brazil.	Twenty years from the Rio conference, report the future we want to renew the commitment to the goals of sustainable development and encouraged issues of the global green economy.

208 *Sustainability Theory*

Table 4.2 Continued

Year	Activity	Description
2015	UN Sustainable Development Summit 2015, New York, SAD.	The UN 2030 Agenda for Sustainable Development was published, setting up 17 millennium development goals which should be achieved by 2030.
2015	UN Conference on Climate Change COP21Paris Climate Change Conference, Paris, France.	Agreement on the reduction of greenhouse gases to reduce and limit global warming.

Source: UN 2015; UNFCCC, 2016 (recited from Klarin 2018, page 72).

Environmental change detection was only possible through technological enhancement and the use of enhanced tools to detect the change. If we go even back, we can find how the Greeks began to explore the position of the Earth and atmospheric variation through geology and geography (geology: meaning Earth and its speed in Greek; geography (Tuan 1991): "ge" for the earth and "graph" for "to write"), from where the exploration of climate variation and change came into the research agenda. The concern about environmental change can be seen in the Greek era; however, it was only within a certain group of people. The geological and geographical study of the Earth's system paved the ground for research on scenarios of climate variation; these are the oldest disciplines of the academic world. Longwell (1954) examines the root of geological exploration – the first step in the detection of environmental change (Bhandari 2017). However, the concerned people were only elites/ scholars and scientists. Historically, we can find many concerned scientists about the impact of environmental damage on humans; however, it was also the subject of discussion in the political arena. "The history of life on earth has been a history of interaction between living things and their surroundings ... Considering the whole span of earthly time, the opposite effect, in which life continually modifies its surroundings, has been relatively slight. Only within the moment represented by the present century has one species— man—acquired significant power to alter the nature of his world" (Rachel Carson, Silent Spring 1962).

In the modern era, 1972 was the milestone year for the institutionalization of environmental concern and sustainability discourse formalization, through the first World Conference on Global Environment, which recommended establishing the United National Environment Program. Similarly, the Club of Rome also published its most authentic report "The Limits to Growth"

Introduction – Questions – Coverage 209

(1972), which draws global attention to the global environment. There is no direct challenge to the research outcome of the Rome Club. The "Limits to Growth" report states that if the present growth trends in world population, industrialization, pollution, food production, and resource depletion continue unchanged, the limits to growth on this planet will be reached sometime within the next one hundred years (Bhandari 2012). The most probable result will be a rather sudden and uncontrollable decline in both population and industrial capacity. This was a second shock after Rachel Carson's book *Silent Spring* (1962), which largely drew the attention of the general public regarding the seriousness of global climate change (Brechin and Bhandari 2011). Having growing concerns and evidence of the global impact on the environment, UNEP continued its consultation with the scientific and government agencies to reach a mutual understanding.

"Human history has traditionally been cast in terms of the rise and fall of great civilizations, wars, and specific human achievements. This history leaves out the important ecological and climate contexts that shaped and mediated these events. Human history and earth system history have traditionally been developed independently...and there have been few attempts to integrate these histories ... across these fields of study" (Robin and Steffen 2007, page 9).

The environmental history helps to pave the future direction through its failure or success stories.

It is an established notion that the sustainability discourses emerged very recently; however, it has a long route to be accepted in the mainstream political, social, economic, and environmental agendas. The growth of international concern of governments, scientific agencies, the non-profit sector, and the general public dealing with the environment began to accelerate from the beginning of the 20th century and continues. The sustainability discourse is uniformly accepted, used, and being utilized.

The sustainability discourse became so paramount that it has its niche in the development arena of the current time. It can be stated that discourse became an established and accepted principle; in other words, it can be seen as a sustainability regime. "Regime is sets of implicit or explicit principles, norms, rules and decision-making procedures around which actors' expectations converge in a given area of international relations" (Krasner 1983). Maintaining sustainability is a national, transnational, multinational, and global concern. Socioeconomic and environmental problems have been increasing on a global scale (HIV/AIDS, inequality, transnational migration, terrorism, environmental problems – climate change, etc.), and these problems

210 *Sustainability Theory*

themselves create certain types of the regime and format their networks and relationships.

In the current scenario, sustainability discourses are seen in the form of agreement on the facts, norms, rules, and procedures. The United Nations has been playing a critical role in sustainability regime formation with factual scientific results and is influential in international policy formation to obtain sustainable development goals.

In this regard, it is necessary to understand that *"discourse is not a neutral medium for the formation and transfer of values, meanings, and knowledge that exist beyond its boundaries, rather, it is constitutive of them. That is, discourse is not best understood as an innocent reflection of non-linguistic meaning, nor simply in terms of the intentions of language users. Rather, discourse constructs meaning. Though material objects and social practices have a material existence outside of language, they are given meaning or 'brought into view' by language and are thus discursively formed. Discourse constructs define and produce the objects of knowledge in an intelligible way while excluding other forms of reasoning as unintelligible. It structures which meanings can or cannot be deployed under determinate circumstances by speaking subjects"* (Barker 2004, page 54). In sustainability discourse, sustainability is no more a word with complex meaning; however, it is the framework of maintaining the *"development that meets the needs of the present without compromising the ability of future generations to meet their own need"* (Our Common Future 1987). And how, the sustainable development goals (SDGs) are the pathways and various policies are the directives, and countries' plans are the future directives. The goals are set with the experience of millennium development goals (MDGs) implementation's output. As such, MDGs were only a partial success; SDGs have incorporated the shortfalls of the past and created the future directives through 17 goals and hundreds of policy directives.

Sustainability is a complex issue that is built on the necessity created by the overutilization of natural resources, due to accelerated development intervention in nature. As Costanza et al. (2007) note, *"the most remarkable phenomenon on Earth in the 20th century was the "Great Acceleration" the sharp increase in human population, economic activity, resource use, transport, communication, and knowledge–science–technology that was triggered in many parts of the world…following World War II and which has continued into this century… Other parts of the world, especially the monsoon Asia region, are now also amid the Great Acceleration. The tension between the modern nation-state and the emergence of multinational corporations and international political institutions is a strong feature of the changing human-environmental relationship. The "engine" of the Great Acceleration is an interlinked system consisting of population increase, rising consumption, abundant cheap energy, and liberalizing political economies"* (Costanza et al. 2007, page 4 as cited in Robin and Steffen 2007, page 7). The anthropogenic disturbance in nature has been its acceleration and impact on the planet's environment drawing the attention of concerned stakeholders. This urgency was documented (one can state them as sustainability discourses at large) in various forms, i.e., research papers, books, monographs, thesis, dissertations, etc. (IUCN 1980; Paehlke 1989; Eckersley 1992; Litfin 1994; Hajer 1995; Dryzek 1997; van Dijk 1998; Sawyer 2002; Palmer 2003; Barker 2004; Diamond 2005; Costanza et al. 2007; Lorek and Fuchs 2011; Veen, et al. 2013; James 2015; Tahvilzadeh et al. 2017; and so on). The Silent Spring (1962); The Limits to Growth (1972); World Conservation Strategy (1980); Our Common Future (1987); and many UN and other agencies world summit on earth (1972–2012) are examples of sustainability discourse.

In addition, other major treaty events that boasted the sustainability discourses are the Ramsar Convention, Stockholm Declaration of the United Nations Conference on the Human Environment, The Rio Declaration on Environment and Development, Convention on Biological Diversity, Convention on Long-Range Trans-boundary Pollution, Convention on the Prevention of Marine Pollution by Dumping of Wastes and Other Matter, Convention on International Trade in Endangered Species(CITES), Basel Convention on the Control of Trans-boundary Movements of Hazardous Wastes and Their Disposal, Convention Concerning the Protection of the World Cultural & Natural Heritage, United Nations Convention to Combat Desertification, United Nations Convention on Law of the Sea (UNCLOS), United Nations Framework Convention on Climate Change and the Kyoto Protocol on Global Warming and many others. These treaty events captured the notion of international multicultural and socioeconomic politics. Many researchers have examined the successes and failures of international treaties and agreements. These researchers accept the role and responsibilities of the nation, international organizations, civil societies, NGOs, and advocacy groups. The hegemonic power relationship is still in force within the current neo-liberal world (Bhandari 2018).

However, the major step in fostering sustainability begins with the first UN Conference on the Human Environment, Stockholm (1972), followed by the second Earth Summit in Rio de Janeiro in 1992, where 172,108 people participated including heads of the states, business personnel, and other experts. For the first time, about 2400 representatives of non-governmental organizations (NGOs) participated in the Rio summit. Summit produced

212   *Sustainability Theory*

agenda 21 declaration on environment and development, the statement of forest principles, the United Nations framework convention on climate change, and the United Nations convention on biological diversity. Since Rio summit, global concern on environment management and policy reform became common agenda for the entire world. Most of the states in the world started to focus on and monitor patterns of production (i.e., toxic components, gasoline, and poisonous waste) and investigate an alternative to the fossil fuels (which is a major cause of global climate change) and alternatives for the public transportation (to reduce air pollution and smog) and water resource management. Blueprint provides a comprehensive structure for the modernization of national/transnational environment protection and environment reform which includes the framework for sustainability and offers the links between economic growth using science and technology to solve the environmental problems with the application of multi-driven approaches. The world conferences based on sustainability and environmental reforms have been broadly focusing on natural resource management, searching for options to reduce the environment impact due to economic activities with the application of new technology. As a result, sustainability discourse became a prime field of consideration in the development agendas of global concern.

In sum, the agenda of sustainability is institutionalizing, blueprints are becoming common, nations are more receptive to addressing the socioeconomic and environmental problems, and the diffusion of such concern is accelerating.

2. What Are the Boundaries of Sustainability?

In general terms, the word meaning of boundaries can be understood as a limitation, edge, or limit. According to the Cambridge English Dictionary, an edge or limit of something or a limit of a subject or principle can be understood as an administrative boundary, natural boundary, or certain range within or beyond the limit. As seen in the synonyms, the term boundary is that which has a limitation. However, connecting with sustainable development is defined as "Sustainable development is a development that meets the needs of the present without compromising the ability of future generations to meet their own needs" (Brundtland 1987).

As noted in the above question (discourse of sustainability), the global focus on sustainability began in earnest with the 1980 publication of the World Conservation Strategy by the International Union for Nature and Natural Resources (IUCN). The World Conservation Strategy is the first warning of resource limitation in another world – there, a limitation or boundary and societal, social, economic, and environmental development should not cross the borders. This bold statement highlighted the scope and limitations (boundaries) of our planet's natural resources and ecological systems. Though it presented a great scope of future development with the wise use of available resources, it also presented a scenario of how humankind's current and future uses of resources would diminish the carrying capacities of our ecosystems. Though neo-liberalists might disagree with the arguments of limiting carrying capacity given the new innovative measures, the Brundtland Commission on Sustainable Development (CSD) in 1987 realized the possibility of deteriorating ecosystem services if the present trend of resource consumption continues without alternatives. Brundtland Commission on Sustainable Development coined the term sustainable development (SD) for the wise of resources so as to store their availability for future generations. The Brundtland report gained importance at the UN Conference on Environment and Development (UNCED) in Rio de Janeiro in 1992. Agenda 21 of this UNCED emphasized much on the sustainable aspect of ecosystem services. Since then, SD got more importance both in concept and practice. Today, the UN and its agencies are embedding the term SD in each of their activities as envisioned by the CSD (Bhandari 2017, 2018).

As listed in Table 4.2, in 1969, UN published the report Man and His Environment or U Thant Report, which first outlined the environmental damage and its impact and proposed the activities focused to avoid global environmental degradation. This indicated that overuse of natural resources is crossing the **boundary or limitation**. And all efforts through United Nations, international development agencies, international intergovernmental, non-governmental organizations, and warning calls from scholars (through publications, seminars, presentations, dissertations, etc.) have been trying to aware society, showing evidence that anthropogenic activities negatively impact the environment. In 1987, the WCED report Our Common Future or Brundtland report was published, which paved the fundamental principles of the concept of sustainable development and provided a clear indication that if we continue what we are doing in the name of economic development (this is beyond the limit of nature), future generation may not have natural privilege as we have now. As depicted in Table 4.2, the declaration and action plan for environmental conservation in 1972, the 1975 Conference on Education about the Environment, the 1975 Summit on Human Environment, the 1992 Conference on Environment and Development, the 2000 Millennium declaration, the 2002 World Summit on Sustainable Development, the 2012 UN conference Rio +20, the 2015 Sustainable Development Summit, which set up 17 millennium development goals, and the 2015 COP21 Paris Climate

214 *Sustainability Theory*

Change Conference (holding the increase in global average temperature below 2 or 1.5 °C above pre-industrial levels), all focused on environmental damage hampering earth sustaining mechanisms and earliest action has to be taken and implemented. Agenda 21, millennium development goals, and the most recent one Sustainable Development 17 Goals and 169 Targets to achieve them are the framework problems illustrations and plans for not to cross the boundaries and maintain the health of the planet as well as resolve the challenges of "poverty and hunger everywhere; to combat inequalities within and among countries; to build peaceful, just and inclusive societies; to protect human rights and promote gender equality and the empowerment of women and girls, and to ensure the lasting protection of the planet and its natural resources....resolve also to create conditions for sustainable, inclusive and sustained economic growth, shared prosperity and decent work for all, taking into account different levels of national development and capacities (UN 2015-https://sustainabledevelopment.un.org/post2015/transformingourworld). This warning and the call of action to resolve the problems, the sustainable development is a proposed method, plan of action, and procedures of implantation. The underlying assumption is the current development which is mostly based on the exploitation of nature and natural resources needed to shift toward harmony with nature. Therefore, the boundaries of sustainable development are seen through environmental constraints ("carrying capacity," "sustainable consumption and production," "guardrails," "tipping points," "footprints," "safe operating space," or "planetary boundaries") (Rockström et al. 2009, 2013, page 3).

Table 4.3   Planetary boundaries and quantification.

Planetary boundary	Boundaries quantified
1. Climate change	CO_2 concentration in the atmosphere should be limited to 350 ppm and/or a maximum change of $+1$ W m^{-2} in radiative forcing
2. Biological diversity loss	An annual rate of a maximum of 10 extinctions per million species
3. Biogeochemical cycles	Nitrogen (N) cycle – limit industrial and agricultural fixation of N_2 to 35 Mt N yr^{-1}) and phosphorus (P) cycle (annual P inflow to oceans not to exceed 10 times the natural background weathering of P
4. Global freshwater use	Limited to 4000 km^3 yr^{-1} of consumptive use of runoff resources

Introduction – Questions – Coverage 215

Table 4.3 Continued

Planetary boundary	Boundaries quantified
5. Land system change	Not more than 15% of the ice-free land surface used as cropland
6. Ocean acidification	Mean surface seawater saturation state concerning aragonite at not less than 80% of pre-industrial levels
7. Stratospheric ozone	Maximum 5% reduction in O_3 concentration from a pre-industrial level of 290 Dobson Units
8. Chemical pollution	No boundary defined
9. Atmospheric aerosol loading	No boundary defined

Source: Rockström et al. (2013, pages 26–27) – "The planetary boundary framework below is based on a decade's research suggesting a safe operating space for humanity."

This was brought forward as a priority in the report from the UN Secretary Generals High-Level Panel "Resilient People Resilient Planet" (UNs Secretary General's High-Level Panel on Global Sustainability 2012). It stated that we should "defend the science that shows we are destabilizing our climate and stretching planetary boundaries to a perilous degree" (page 25). Rockström et al. (2013, page 21) summarize as follows: (1) the science of planetary boundaries makes clear that we are on an unsustainable trajectory; (2) achieving the sustainable development trajectory will require an unprecedented global effort by all countries – rich and poor – that will only be possible under a shared global framework for sustainable development. The planetary boundary image by Rockström et al. (2009) gives a clearer picture of the same circumstances.

The boundaries of sustainable development can also be seen in terms of its three-pillar infusion – social, economic, and environmental. The environmental boundary is depicted in Table 4.2. Many scientists/scholars have shown the interrelationship of sustainability planetary boundary (Barnosky 2012; Steffen et al. 2011; Carpenter and Bennett 2011; Cornell 2012; Erb et al. 2012; Foley et al. 2011; Folke et al. 2011; Folke and Rockström 2011; Ingram 2011; Rockström and Karlberg 2010; Running 2012; and others). There is a gap in research on sustainability boundary setting with the social, economic, cultural, and political lenses.

Social boundaries of sustainability can be seen in individual, family, and cultural differences, and their relationships, and how they perceive sustainability in their pursuits. Understanding of sustainability awareness

216   *Sustainability Theory*

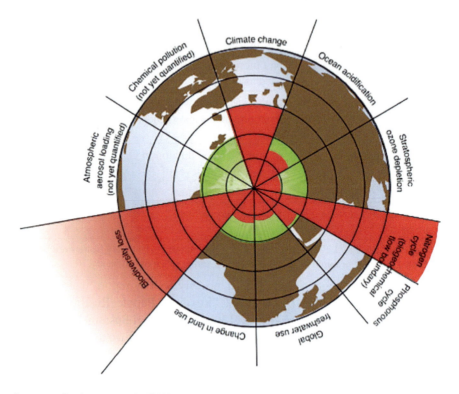

Source: Rockström et al. (2009) and also in Steffen et al. (2015, page 736) as cited also in Stockholm Resilience Centre website: www.stockholmresilience.org. (Estimates of how the different control variables for seven planetary boundaries have changed from 1950 to the present. The green shaded polygon represents the safe operating space.) The red areas in image 1 show the position of each boundary. The safe operating space for the boundaries is within the green area. Out of these nine boundaries, at least three have already been passed: climate change, biodiversity loss, and the nitrogen cycle.

can be seen at the individuals to the societal level – the awareness about own ecological footprint; carrying capacity of local niche; valuing the nature on social interactions – regular behavior pattern – waste disposal system or water use pattern, etc., shows the regular pattern of understanding of sustainability through behavior. The conflict among societies in resource use and utilization, the social strata, and cultural variations are also among the other boundaries of social phenomena. Economic boundaries of sustainability can be seen in the eyes of the victims of poverty and hunger, in the inequalities within and among countries. Political boundaries of sustainability are a whole different scenario of discussion. The major cause of the conflict, division, wars, segregation, and separation are major boundaries. Table 4.1, development scenarios of sustainable development can be considered as minimizing the boundaries impacts and acting collectively to resolve the environmental, social, and economic challenges the world is facing. UN 2015, in "Transforming our World: The 2030 Agenda for Sustainable Development" states that it "determined to mobilize the means required to implement this Agenda through a revitalized Global Partnership for Sustainable Development, based on a spirit of strengthened global solidarity, focused on particular on the needs of the poorest and most vulnerable and with the participation of all countries, all stakeholders and all people" (Transforming our World: The 2030 Agenda for Sustainable Development – UN 2015). As noted in Scoones (2016), "there has been a growing consensus on the endpoints of sustainability, combining environmental, social, and economic goals—now parsed in terms of circular, low-carbon, or green economies -there has been less discussion of how to get there and of the social, cultural, institutional, and political challenges that arise" beyond the national and political borders. The Sustainable Development 17 Goals and 169 Targets (UN 2015) present the current scenario of the problems (which shows where the current trend of development crossed the boundary) and provide the pathway to move forward.

The boundaries of sustainable development can be seen, analyzed, and interpreted within the coverage of sustainable development goals (1: No Poverty; 2: Zero Hunger; 3: Good Health and Well-being; 4: Quality Education; 5: Gender Equality; 6: Clean Water and Sanitation; 7: Affordable and Clean Energy; 8: Decent Work and Economic Growth; 9: Industry, Innovation, and Infrastructure; 10: Reduced Inequality; 11: Sustainable Cities and Communities; 12: Responsible Consumption and Production; 13: Climate Action; 14: Life Below Water; 15: Life on Land; 16: Peace and Justice Strong Institutions; 17: Partnerships to Achieve the Goal) (UN 2015) and beyond. These goals are interconnected, multidimensional, and have underlined constraints (each holds different boundary discourse of sustainable development) (Rockström et al. 2013).

The boundaries of sustainable development can also be seen and evaluated in terms of institutionalization process and organizational process. So far, sustainability is formalized, organized, and institutionalized frame of development paradigm (Anaedu and Lars-Goran 2002; Bertelsmann Stiftung and Sustainable Development Solutions Network 2018; Robert et al. 2005; Maser 1997); therefore, the boundaries of sustainable development can also be evaluated in terms of formal organization. "Formal organizations are typically understood to be systems of coordinated and controlled activities that arise when work is embedded in complex networks of technical

218 *Sustainability Theory*

relations and boundary-spanning exchanges. But in modern societies, formal organizational structures arise in highly institutional contexts. Organizations are driven to incorporate the practices and procedures defined by prevailing rationalized concepts of organizational work and institutionalized in society. Organizations that do so increase their legitimacy and their survival prospects, independent of the immediate efficacy of the acquired practices and procedures. There can develop a tension between, on the one hand, the institutionalized products, services, techniques, policies, and programs that function as myths (and ceremonially adopted), and efficiency criteria on the other hand. To maintain ceremonial conformity, organizations that reflect institutional rules tend to buffer their formal structures from the uncertainties of the technical activities by developing a loose coupling between their formal structures and actual work activities" (Meyer and Rowan 1977). In terms of sustainability, the structured rules, directives, and articulative principles can be seen as the boundaries of sustainable development. The notion of complexity of organization applies in the context of sustainable development. As sustainability is an integral part of resolving the constraints of developmental discourses and has various challenges in maintaining interrelation boundaries of social, economic, and environmental connections, "The most effective organizations achieve a degree of *differentiation* and *integration* in organizational boundary-spanning functions which is compatible with environmental demands" (Lawrence and Lorsch 1967). The sustainable development boundary is thin if worked with the multinational, multidimensional, and at the scholarly level multidisciplinary approaches. However, addressing boundaries? ... essential to explore more to pave the future direction.

To outline the boundary of sustainable development is tremendously difficult because of its complexity, coverage, and multicriterial nature in development paradigms. The boundaries of sustainable development shift as the SDG are achieved. As UN 2015 in Transforming Our World: The 2030 Agenda for Sustainable Development notes, "a call for action by all countries – poor, rich, and middle-income – to promote prosperity while protecting the planet. They recognize that ending poverty must go hand-in-hand with strategies that build economic growth and address a range of social needs including education, health, social protection, and job opportunities while tackling climate change and environmental protection." As measurable outcomes are visible, the boundary will change (Bhandari 2018). The boundary and definition of sustainable development change with the advancement of the epistemology of sustainability. As Hannan and Freeman (1989) state, "the boundary definition of organizations is itself a variable that

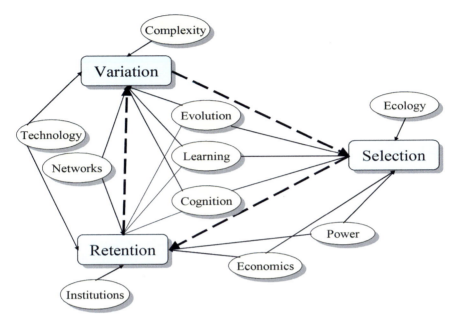

Source: Baum and Rowley (2005).

Flowchart 1: Organizational complexity.

changes as technology and other environmental forces affect it. Determining how to exactly classify a particular organization is becoming increasingly more difficult." This notion completely applies to the complex notion of sustainability and is also useful for boundary setting.

Sustainable development complexity can be analyzed through the organizational theoretical lenses on three levels – first organizations are complex because of complex adaptive systems, differentiation in agents, variations in decision making and problem-solving techniques and networks, information technology, and algorithmic complexity, second, organization hold complex adaptive systems, loose coupling and models, edge of chaos, simple rules and complex behavior, emergence, and recombination and evolution and thirdly, organizational interdependence, cellular automata, micro-behavior and macro-structure complex inter-organizational dynamics, sensitivity to initial conditions and path dependence (Baum and Rowley 2005). Adaptation of sustainable development and multisectoral development has past experienced through complex adaptive systems because each country has different social, cultural, geographical, and political limitations or boundaries. The complexity also exists in the decision-making system

220 *Sustainability Theory*

because each country's definition of public participation may differ due to its governance system.

Baum and Rowley's (2005) depiction of the meta-frame (flowchart 1) of an organization can be helpful to see the complex structures of sustainable development. However, there is a need for modification based on sustainability parameters. The implementation and evaluation of sustainable development perspectives depend on how sustainability principles (in the current scenario, SDG goals and targets) are interrelated with each other and how this complexity can be minimized. There is a research gap on sustainability complexity and its boundaries. The sustainability boundaries also are evaluated through the lenses of institutional perspectives, which is another field of further research. As nicely illustrated in Pesch's (2014) descriptions of institutional domains, on the one hand and of second-order problems that are related to these domains, and on the other hand, we may conclude that we are faced with a dilemma in the case of promoting sustainable development. In its very essence, sustainable development pertains to problems that transcend the boundaries of institutional domains. To resolve environmental degradation and the depletion of resources, we have to fulfill the following necessities: appropriate knowledge has to be produced; the external effects of our economic system have to be integrated into private transactions, having major effects on the distribution of economic wealth and economic burdens; effective collective decisions have to be made that transcend national boundaries and that are subject to broad societal consent, and the creation and implementation of sustainable technologies have to be facilitated. In all, the tendencies of institutional domains to displace goals have to be overcome (Pesch 2014, page 48).

Sustainable development boundaries can be obstacles to achieving progress and there is a need for new policy formation which can create instruments to promote boundary-crossing collaborations, to achieve the sustainable development goals. Understanding how best to move along the road toward sustainability, as contrasted with understanding the levels and types of unsustainability, is an issue that has not yet been addressed in detail. "Sustainability is a systems problem, one that defies typical piecemeal approaches such as follows: Will there be enough ore in the ground for technological needs? Will there be enough water for human needs? How can we preserve biodiversity? Can global agriculture be made sustainable?" (Graedel and Voet 2010, page 3). This concern of Graedel and Voet (2010) provides another gap in sustainability discourse; however, the efforts to

Introduction – Questions – Coverage   221

answer the posed questions provide the pathway to the scholarly world. In advancing sustainable development epistemology, each stakeholder has an unavoidable role and responsibility; however, core responsivities lie with higher educational institutions (Wallendorf 1989; Yao and Bai 2008; Waheed et al. 2011; Yarime and Tanaka 2012; Versteijlen et al. 2017).

"The boundaries of the sustainability system are determined by four dimensions based on the finiteness of the fossil energy system, the development of a post-fossil energy system, the problem of climate change, and the chosen sustainability paradigm. This sustainability approach could enable sustainable development opportunities for the present generation without affecting the welfare of future generations" (Schlor et al. 2015, page 52).

The sustainable development notion provides hope in the world, by reviving security in the society, providing the environment to share and cope with problems and produce goods, delivering services, maintaining order, and giving a way to survive from the individual level to the societal stage. The sustainability notion hopes to minimize the challenges and helps to establish order in the society (Richter 2009; Meuleman 2013). About linkage with day-to-day individual and societal settings, the SDGs are the fundamental building blocks of modern societies, and the basic vehicles through which collective action is being undertaken. The eminence of sustainable development discourses is new paradigms of the modern world and it is obvious to be prepared to face various consequences, particularly in implementation, since limitless boundaries have to be identified and addressed. The sustainability notion has to cross various isomorphism processes which create boundary-spanning demands for economic development (Bhandari 2018). Further, to achieve the sustainable development goals, the concerned stakeholders have to incorporate structural elements isomorphic process (which will create more boundaries) to address the complexity and interdependent boundaries.

3. What Are the Linkages Between Creativeness and Sustainability?

"Truth reveals itself in degrees, and we can progress from an incomplete to a more and ever more complete comprehension of truth. Truth is not a thing, not an object that we either have in entirety or have not at all" Johann Wolfgang von Goethe (1749–1832).

"Creativity is understood as the human capacity, through imagination or invention, to pro use something new and original to solve problems. It is

222 *Sustainability Theory*

a unique and renewable resource. Creativity enables individuals to expand their abilities and develop their full potential. In today's global, knowledge-based societies, creative assets are generating new forms of revenue and employment that are spurring growth, in particular among youth. Releasing diverse sources of inspiration and innovation, creativity contributes to building open, inclusive, and pluralistic societies. As a multi-faceted human resource that involves processes, environments, persons, and products, creativity can inspire positive transformative change for future generations. Creativity, embracing cultural expression and the transformative power of innovation, can contribute to finding imaginative and better development outcomes" (UNESCO 2013, pages 1–2).

The notion of sustainability and creativity has an interchangeable, interrelated, and interdependent relationship. In difficulties, the living being adapts to the surroundings and sustains according to the existing or changing environment. The survival with the fittest notion can work here in the biological environment. When the social dimension is involved, survival with the fittest still exists; however, it goes further on searching for options for survival. We can see these characteristics among the animal species of various ecosystems. If we look back to human development and evolution, at least from primitive society to modern society, we can see how humans developed adaptability to survive and how creativity was applied in the process of survival and development.

The notion of sustainability through creativity has a long history as the history of human survival and development. However, at least in terms of the concept and applicability, we can track as back as the written history began. The development process was, to some extent, on the planet until the industrial revolution began. The notion of development changed to competition with nature and human creativity disturbed the natural process to co-exist and development. Human creativity to sustain began to dominate nature.

Many countries have been working on how to continue economic growth without harming the environment; as a pathway, the concept of sustainable development (SD) has been discussed and utilized for the last two decades or so. Green Economy (GE) and the Creative Economy (CE) initiative initiated by two United Nations (UN) agencies, UN Environment Program (UNEP) and the UN Conference on Trade and Development (UNCTAD), try to capture the notion of the vulnerability of human welfare, caused by the degradation of the global environment, which can be understood as a result of the widespread application of an unsustainable model of economic development; however, attaining global sustainability theory still is a fuzzy assumption – in attaining the global sustainability. The Green Economy

(GE), which can be considered a part of creativity, does not alter with SD; however, it provides further steps practically and theoretically. This training program aims to provide theoretical and practical aspects of GE and equip participants to be able to prepare a strategic plan for green growth and skilled them for professionalism and effectiveness in the performance of their duties in their respected organizations.

Both initiatives capture concerns raised over the past 40 years to address climate change to frame the treaty agreements. The establishment of the IPCC, UNFCC, Kyoto Protocol, and Clean Development Mechanism are among notable outcomes. One can take GE and CE initiates as untested tools that assume too much about greening as an engine for growth, sectoral opportunities, hurdles and enabling conditions, the value of ecosystems and biodiversity, and the vicious cycle of environmental losses and persistent poverty. Both GE and CE emphasize green industry and business, but they lack the means to provide the know-how to perceive global economic growth. GE and CE also fail to address strategic uncertainty such as the likelihood of adverse effects; the consequences of change; the speed of change; discontinuities; and especially uncertainty over the effectiveness of policy instruments.

Both GE and CE initiatives are silent on how social and institutional capital can be enhanced and how creativity can be fostered. I argue that to overcome these problems, there is a need for existing structures to evolve and to create a new institutional framework that can coordinate and manage the activities of all related stakeholders. It requires an effective institutional structure, strong policy, and framework for policy implementation and can work effectively, efficiently, equitably, and transparently. To frame this, one needs to define a new, innovative, and ambitious architecture which can foster social capital.

Many scholars have tried to examine creativity and sustainability/sustainable development (Giddings et al. 2002; Callanan and Ferguson 2015; Mitchell and Walinga 2017; Basadur, Gelade, and Basadur 2014; Cheng, 2018; Corral-Verdugo et al. 2009; Bhandari 2017, 2018). Table 4.4, adopted from Mitchell and Walinga (2017, page 1875), provides a glimpse of how creativity is applied to sustainability.

Table 4.4 Examples of factors facilitating creativity for sustainability.

Factors facilitating creativity	Applied to sustainability
Stimulating and rewarding curiosity and exploration	Creating a comfortable and non-threatening environment

224   *Sustainability Theory*

Table 4.4 Continued

Factors facilitating creativity	Applied to sustainability
Building internal motivation	Designing an environment that supports and rewards sustainability-focused ideas and solutions. Leaders may motivate creative thinking by getting employees to identify with a vision
Building confidence and willingness to take risks: eliminating defensiveness and self-doubt; building favorable self-perception	Fostering recognition and awareness of self-doubt. Using brainstorming techniques
Encouraging divergent thinking: fluency and flexibility in thinking	Utilizing thinking aids that facilitate the application of divergent thinking and elicitation of innovative ideas
Encouraging acquisition of domain-specific knowledge. Relevant knowledge is a prerequisite for creative functioning	Fostering more sustainability-specific knowledge. The more sustainability knowledge and expertise an individual posse, the more he/she is likely to generate sustainable solutions and ideas
Encouraging openness to ideas	Challenging prejudgments and using different domains of knowledge, analogies, metaphors, and exercises in imaginative play
Encouraging building on, or combining ideas from others	Sharing sustainability ideas can stimulate members of a group or network to think of other even more novel or radical ideas

Source: Mitchell and Walinga (2017, page 1875).

Quantifying creativity is not easy; however, through economic parameters, quantifiable or visual outcomes can be drawn. As Giddings et al. (2002) note, "the economy is often given priority in policies and the environment is viewed as apart from humans. They are interconnected, with the economy dependent on society and the environment while human existence and society are dependent on, and within the environment. The separation of environment, society, and economy often leads to a narrow techno-scientific approach, while issues to do with a society that is most likely to challenge the present socioeconomic structure are often marginalized, in particular the sustainability of communities and the maintenance of cultural diversity" (Giddings et al. 2002, page 187). Here, the notion of green economy, creative economy, ecosufficiency, and sustainable development is broadly aimed to foster the global economy without hampering the earth ecosystem and boosting social justice. According to the UNEP (2010), social justice may include: (1) not compromising future generations' capability to meet their needs; (2) the rights of poor countries and poor people to development and the obligations of rich countries and rich people to changing their excessive consumption levels; (3) equal treatment of women in access to resources and opportunities, and (4) ensuring decent labor conditions. Additionally, issues of good governance and democracy are also seen as critical for ensuring social justice and equity (UNEP 2010, page 2).

Another way of looking at creativity can be as Callanan and Ferguson (2015) note "Creativity. We hack it. We map it. We study it. We rate it. We take it places. We build industries around it. We invest in it. We recognize we need it, even when it hurts. We know our future depends on it... Creativity is the spark. When the spark catches, it catalyzes an expression, an experiment, a "creation." If the spark turns into an invention, an entrepreneur can build an enterprise around it." This can be seen in different phases, i.e., generation, conceptualization, optimization, and implementation (Table 4.2; Basadur, Gelade, and Basadur 2014).

Table 4.5 Different phases of creativity.

Quadrant IV	Quadrant I
IMPLEMENTING: Creating options in the form of actions that get results and gaining acceptance for implementing a change or a new idea	GENERATING: Creating options in the form of new possibilities – recent problems that might be solved and new opportunities that might be capitalized upon
Quadrant III	Quadrant II
OPTIMIZING: Creating options in the form of ways to get an idea to work in practice and uncovering all the factors that go into a successful plan for implementation	CONCEPTUALIZING: Creating options in the form of alternative ways to understand and define a problem or opportunity and innovative ideas that help solve it

Source: Basadur, Gelade, and Basadur (2014, page 82).

226 *Sustainability Theory*

Sustainability and creativity have strong interconnections. In other words, maintaining sustainability, creativity, innovation, improvement, and empowerment of all concerned stakeholders are necessary.

"Any group that attempts to manage a common resource (e.g., aquifers, judicial systems, pastures) for optimal sustainable production must solve a set of problems to create institutions for collective action; there is some evidence that following a small set of design principles in creating these institutions can overcome these problems" (Elinor Ostrom 1990).

According to UNESCO (2013), "Creativity is understood as the human capacity, through imagination or invention, to pro use something new and original to solve problems. It is a unique and renewable resource. Creativity enables individuals to expand their abilities and develop their full potential. Similarly, sustainability can be understood as the "development that meets the needs of the present without compromising the ability of future generations to meet their own need" (Our Common Future 1987). How to meet the needs of the present with minimal effort or without harming nature? The millennium development goals were the attempt to minimize the anthropogenic disturbances on nature and natural resources. However, they were not quantifiable, and the evaluation mechanism was not strong enough. The sustainable development goals (which have 17 major goals and hundreds of targets) have established a rigorous way of program planning, and implementation with a clear evaluation process.

Creativity and sustainability are intertwingled. Moreover, sustainability can only be attained properly, when concerned stakeholders incorporate the innovation, and cooperation beyond the political boundaries, with the involvement of governments, enterprises, research institutions, public bodies, civil society associations, financial institutions, and other related bodies (Fusco 2010). To achieve the goals of sustainability, a proper mechanism of the evaluation process as well as institutional arrangements needs to be implemented.

4. What Is the Institutional Architecture to Attain the SDGs?

"Institutions are not static, and institutionalization is not an inevitable process; nor is it unidirectional, monotonic or irreversible" (Weaver and Rockman 1993).

"Institutionalism, as that term is used here, connotes a general approach to the study of political institutions, a set of theoretical ideas and

hypotheses concerning the relations between institutional characteristics and political agency, performance, and change. Institutionalism emphasizes the endogenous nature and social construction of political institutions. Institutions are not simply equilibrium contracts among self-seeking, calculating individual actors or arenas for contending social forces. They are collections of structures, rules and standard operating procedures that have a partly autonomous role in political life" (Marsh and Olsen 2005, page 3).

"Institutions are the rules of the game in a society or, more formally, are the humanly devised constraints that shape human interaction. Three important features of institutions are apparent in this definition: (1) that they are "humanly devised," which contrasts with other potential fundamental causes, like geographic factors, which are outside human control; (2) that they are "the rules of the game" setting "constraints" on human behavior; (3) that their major effect will be through incentives" (North 1981, 1990, page 3 as in Acemoglu and Robinson 2008, page 2). This notion of operation with the incorporation of rules, norms, and values is the fundamental principle for the institutionalization process.

The sustainability concept is already institutionalized, with established discourses, and is a major pillar for socioeconomic and environmental policy, planning, and implementation. Sustainability is a core prerequisite for the United Nations member countries. As noted in the UN (2015) in the preamble of "Transforming Our World: The 2030 Agenda for Sustainable Development."

"This Agenda is a plan of action for people, the planet, and prosperity. It also seeks to strengthen universal peace in larger freedom. We recognize that eradicating poverty in all its forms and dimensions, including extreme poverty, is the greatest global challenge and an indispensable requirement for sustainable development. All countries and all stakeholders, acting in collaborative partnership, will implement this plan. We are resolved to free the human race from the tyranny of poverty and want to heal and secure our planet. We are determined to take the bold and transformative steps which are urgently needed to shift the world onto a sustainable and resilient path. As we embark on this collective journey, we pledge that no one will be left behind. The 17 Sustainable Development Goals (SDGs) and 169 targets that we are announcing today demonstrate the scale and ambition of this new universal Agenda. They seek to build on the Millennium Development Goals and complete what these did not achieve. They seek to realize the human rights of all and to achieve gender equality and the empowerment of all women and girls. They are integrated and indivisible and balance the

228 *Sustainability Theory*

three dimensions of sustainable development: the economic, social, and environmental" (UN 2015, page 3).

It is noteworthy to note that the preamble explains the UN commitment to sustainability and to achieving the 2030 agendas of SDGs in an institutionalized way. Further, partnership documents state **"Partnership"** – *"We are determined to mobilize the means required to implement this Agenda through a revitalized Global Partnership for Sustainable Development, based on a spirit of strengthened global solidarity, focused in particular on the needs of the poorest and most vulnerable and with the participation of all countries, all stakeholders, and all people. The interlinkages and integrated nature of the Sustainable Development Goals are of crucial importance in ensuring that the purpose of the new Agenda is realized. If we realize our ambitions across the full extent of the agenda, the lives of all will be profoundly improved and our world will be transformed for the better"* (UN 2015, page 3). The declaration also openly offers partnerships with civil society organizations, international organizations, higher education institutions, and other stakeholders.

The declaration document states that each country must prepare its plan to achieve 17 SDGs and 169 targets with its institutional setup. There are 91 points in the declaration, and SDGs are under point 59. Before the document declares the goals and target, it states *"59. We recognize that there are different approaches, visions, models, and tools available to each country, by its national circumstances and priorities, to achieve sustainable development; and we reaffirm that planet Earth and its ecosystems are our common home, and that 'Mother Earth' is a common expression in several countries and regions"* (UN 2015, page 14).

These all efforts can be taken as the preparation of the institutional architecture of sustainability. These bold steps to attain sustainability highlight the scope and limitations of our planet's natural resources and ecological systems. Though it presented a great scope of future development with the wise use of available resources, it also presented a scenario of how humankind's current and future uses of resources would diminish the carrying capacities of our ecosystems. The UN Declaration 2015 point 53 accepts this notion *"53. The future of humanity and our planet lies in our hands. It lies also in the hands of today's younger generation who will pass the torch to future generations. We have mapped the road to sustainable development; it will be for all of us to ensure that the journey is successful and its gains irreversible."*

The member governments have accepted this urgency of declaration and have created legal instruments and institutions within their governments since the 1972 Stockholm Conference. Regarding the importance of institutions on sustainability, the Vice-Chairs of WSSD Anaedu and Engfeldt wrote:

"Ensuring an effective institutional framework for sustainable development at all levels is key to the realization of the goals of sustainable development. To achieve these goals and to meet the emerging challenges, the sustainable development governance architecture needs to be strengthened at the international, regional, and national levels as these are inextricably linked and mutually interdependent. There is a clear need to enhance the responsiveness of the current institutional arrangements for the full implementation of Agenda 21, bearing in mind all relevant principles, including, in particular, the principle of common but differentiated responsibilities of States" (2002, page 2).

The above statement embraces the definition that Brundtland outlined in 1987: "development that meets the needs of the present without compromising the ability of future generations to meet their own needs" (page 41). In line with the SD, the WSSD (2002) suggested focusing on six major areas to attain global sustainability. These include poverty eradication; sustainable management and conservation of natural resources; making globalization fit with the sustainable goals; improving governance at all levels; and providing funding for research to find alternative means through scientific and technological innovation to sustain the development (WSSD 2002; Schomberg 2002). Anaedu and Engfeldt (2002) proposed strong institutional development at the international, national, and regional levels to improve functioning in these areas. Before the WSSD meeting, the UN urged that its Rio declaration signatory countries must submit a profile of their institutional strengths and weakness and should show their commitments to SD (Bhandari 2017).

An institutional perspective on organizations suggests that the processes and structure of an organization are a product of pressures exerted by the state, professions, and other members of an organization's field. Under this perspective, organizational structures are not only a product of their objective functionality and market dependency as suggested by contingency, agency, and transaction cost theories, but rather are a combination of social meaning, symbolism, and "action-generating properties" (Tolbert and Zucker 1999, page 171).

230 *Sustainability Theory*

Theoretically, institutions can be seen as social structures that have attained a high degree of resilience. Institutions are composed of cultural-cognitive, normative, and regulative elements that, together with associated activities and resources, provide stability and meaning to social life. Institutions are transmitted by various types of carriers, including symbolic systems, relational systems, routines, and artifacts (Scott 2004, page 48). Institutions operate at different levels of jurisdiction, from the world system to localized interpersonal relationships. Institutions, by definition, connote stability but are subject to change processes, both incremental and discontinuous. Likewise, in relating to the environmental frame, institutions provide the platform for the social practices, assign roles to the participants in these practices, and govern the interactions among the occupants of the various roles (Young, Schroeder, and King 2002, page xiv; Bhandari 2018).

Institution covers a large spectrum in the social context which includes social networks, gender roles, legal system, politico-administrative system, and the state more generally – all of which interact with each other. Institutions are either state or non-state. State institutions cover many aspects, such as the public provision of basic education and health services, public order and safety, and infrastructure. The nature of governance will determine the availability and quality of these public services and, hence, the extent to which the poor have access to them. Non-state institutions are social institutions, values, and norms. A key social institution is a social capital, which consists of informal norms or established relationships that enable people to pursue objectives and act in concert for common benefit. Social capital is particularly important for the poor. Ethnicity and gender roles, which remain pronounced in the global context and lead to discrimination against minorities and females, are other institutions that underlie poverty and inequality (ADB 2002, page 2). As indicated in the ADB report, institutional characteristics are explained in terms of economic institutions fueled by political power and political institutions. Economic institutions matter for economic growth because they shape the incentives of key economic actors in society. In particular, they influence investments in physical and human capital and technology and the organization of production. Economic institutions not only determine the aggregate economic growth potential of the economy but also the distribution of resources in the society. Likewise, political power in society is also endogenous; which includes the political institutions as the form of government, a system of governance like democracy versus dictatorship or autocracy, and the extent of constraints on politicians and political elites (ADB 2002; as in Acemoglu and Robinson 2008, pages 6–7).

Introduction – Questions – Coverage 231

Table 4.6 Definitions.

Institution: A cluster of rights, rules, and decision-making procedures, which gives rise to social practice, assigns roles to participants in the practice, and guides interactions among occupants of these roles. *Multilevel governance* that operates at two or more levels of social organization (e.g., local, regional, and national levels). *New institutionalism* is a school of thought that explores the role of social institutions as sources of governance. *Organization*: A group of people joined together to achieve a specific purpose. Typically, an organization has the personnel, offices, equipment, a budget, and, often, legal personality (Young, Schroeder, and King 2002, 2008).

In environmental management, institutions can be understood as the body of the environmental regimes' creators. Regimes constitute important components of governance systems at levels of social organization ranging from the local to the global. Institutions are distinct from organizations, which are material entities typically possessing personnel, offices, budgets, a legal personality, and so forth. Organizations play important roles in the administration and management of regimes dealing with a wide range of topics (e.g., the U.S. Environmental Protection Agency, the International Maritime Organization, IUCN, etc.) (Young, Schroeder, and King 2002, page xxi). In such cases, international institutions such as international conservation organizations like IUCN; multilateral agencies such as the ADB and the World Bank; and bilateral agencies such as USAID and DFID have been playing an instrumental role in the institutionalization of environment conservation through explicit arrangements, such as treaties and conventions, that regulate behavior (Choo 2005, page 41) as well as by creating the policy for the governments but also to international organizations (IOs). IOs have been largely focusing on the involvement of concerned stakeholders, beneficiaries, and the community in the selection, design, implementation, and monitoring of environment and development projects. Similarly, IOs are also creating partnerships with civil society groups, such as NGOs and CBOs, and helping them further strengthen. IOs also have been playing an important role in fostering decentralized local government agencies instead of working solely with central government agencies including the local stakeholders of related fields (Acemoglu and Robinson 2008, page 56–57).

The UN is the key player that institutionalizes sustainability. UN has been operating and organizing events and forums throughout its history (Rio Earth Summit in 1992; Johannesburg Summit on Sustainable Development

232 *Sustainability Theory*

in 2002, and so on) (Charnovitz 1996, 1997; Gemmill and Bamidele-Izu 2002, page 8) which boosting to institutionalize the sustainability discourses.

Theoretically, the institutionalization of sustainability itself is a trajectory. Institutionalization of sustainability is still young, and new relevant perspectives, which can fully capture the underlying essence, are still to be developed. There is a need for refining principles and practices to achieve the goals of sustainability. The boundaries of sustainability are beyond the limit. Technically, the world is getting smaller; however, the demands are widening and the gap between the haves and not haves is increasing at an unprecedented rate. Therefore, the path ahead is incredibly challenging. However, theoretically, institutionalization is an active process and many scholars have shown the intuitional changes and process of changes (Lawrence and Lorsch 1967; Galbraith 1967; Williamson 1975; Hannanand and Freeman 1977; Zucker 1977; Meyer and Rowan 1977; North 1981; Keohane 1988; March and Olsen 1989, 2005; Powell 1990; Oliver 1991; Opschoor 1991; Thelen and Steinmo 1992; Hannan, and Carroll 1992; Aldrich and Fiol 1994; Strang and Meyer 1994; Mearsheimer 1995; Charnovitz 1996, 1997; Hall and Taylor 1996; Theret 2000; Valentin and Spangenberg 2000; Nielsen 2001; Young et al. 2002; Scott 2004; Choo 2005; Pfahl 2005; Colyvas and Powell 2006; IUCN 2006; Hák, Moldan, and Dahl 2007; Duffield 2007; Acemoglu and Robinson 2008; Jepperson and Platje 2008; Singh et al. 2009). The isomorphism process occurs within the institution. *"Isomorphism is the constraining process that forces one unit in a population to resemble other units that face the same set of environmental conditions" ...... "We identify three mechanisms through which institutional isomorphic change occurs, each with its antecedents: 1) coercive isomorphism that stems from political influence and the problem of legitimacy; 2) mimetic isomorphism resulting from standard responses to uncertainty; and 3) normative isomorphism, associated with professionalization. This typology is an analytic one: the types are not always empirically distinct. For example, external actors may induce an organization to conform to its peers by requiring it to perform a particular task and specifying the profession responsible for its performance. Or mimetic change may reflect environmentally constructed uncertainties.' Yet, while the three types intermingle in an empirical setting, they tend to derive from different conditions and may lead to different"* (DiMaggio and Powell 1983, page 150).

About institutional sustainability, the concern is getting deeper, and more innovative approaches are emerging. The 2015 declaration "Transforming Our World: The 2030 Agenda for Sustainable Development" paves a positive pathway for the future; however, the outcome depends on how actual stakeholders to act, plan, and progress for the institutionalization of sustainability architecture. Higher educational institutions are key stakeholders in transferring or communicating sustainability agendas through the curriculum. As such "sustainability does not simply require an 'add-on' to existing structures and curricula but implies a change of fundamental epistemology in our culture and hence also in our educational thinking and practice" (Sterling 2004, page 50). However, it is necessary to examine on "how far institutions and higher education as a whole are able sufficiently to the wider context of the crisis of unsustainability and the opportunities of sustainability. The common perception is often that little more than a change in teaching or curriculum is necessary – that is, an adaptive adjustment in learning provision. A full response, however, commensurate with the size of the challenge, implies a change of educational paradigm – because sustainability indicates a change of cultural paradigm which is both emergent and imperative" (Sterling 2004, page 50). The educational institution has to deal with the super complex scholarship of sustainability; whereas, sustainability touches all aspects of human life (Martins et al. 2006) as well as Earth's carrying capacity.

Conclusion

The current world is interconnected economically, culturally, socially, and politically due to technological development and the globalization process. The diffusion of knowledge is also spreading at an accelerating rate to the entire world. The demand for international laws was never as high as it is because of transnational problems HIV/AIDS, terrorism, as well as the globalizing, social, economic, and biophysical environmental problems. Institutions create "a set of rules, typically formalized in international agreements and embodied in organizations that stipulate how states should cooperate and compete with each other. They prescribe acceptable forms of state behavior and proscribe unacceptable kinds of behavior" (Mearscheimer 1995); therefore, multidisciplinary approaches are needed to build strong institutions (international institutions), which can help to minimize the global problems as listed in the United Nations 2015 declaration "Transforming Our World: The 2030 Agenda for Sustainable Development." "*14. We are meeting at a time of immense challenges to sustainable development. Billions of our citizens continue to live in poverty and are denied a life of dignity. There are rising inequalities within and among countries. There are enormous disparities in opportunity, wealth, and power. Gender inequality remains a*

234 *Sustainability Theory*

key challenge. Unemployment, particularly youth unemployment, is a major concern. Global health threats, more frequent and intense natural disasters, spiraling conflict, violent extremism, terrorism, related humanitarian crises, and forced displacement of people threaten to reverse much of the development progress made in recent decades. Natural resource depletion and adverse impacts of environmental degradation, including desertification, drought, land degradation, freshwater scarcity, and loss of biodiversity, add to and exacerbate the list of challenges that humanity faces. Climate change is one of the greatest challenges of our time and its adverse impacts undermine the ability of all countries to achieve sustainable development. Increases in global temperature, sea-level rise, ocean acidification, and other climate change impacts are seriously affecting coastal areas and low-lying coastal countries, including many least developed countries and small island developing States. The survival of many societies, and the biological support systems of the planet, is at risk" (UN 2015, page 15). The declaration nicely articulates how the people of the planet and the planet itself are in trouble at present, and it tries to address these issues through SDGs. However, the challenges are deeper; the world has not been peaceful politically, socially, and economically, and the biophysical environment is deteriorating every day. There is still a need for illuminating educational theory and practice which will enable humans to think the world is our house and all living beings are our relatives and neighbors "Bashudaiva Kutumbakkam" (Bhandari 2019). There is a tradeoff between the developing and developed world and there are no coherent frameworks or cooperation among the nations and even the various approaches in use to minimize the gap between North and South. So far, there is no clear indication of how the aims of sustainability "to maintain the wellbeing of humans and nature" will achieve.

And, finally, I would like to conclude my responses with a quote from Margaret Mead and Marshall (1961). *"Never doubt that a small group of thoughtful, committed people can change the world. Indeed, it is the only thing that ever has"* (Mead). Yes, the change-maker/charismatic leader, the thinker can be even a person who can influence the betterment of her/his community through the small program and can be a crucial step to empower society to archive desired goals. We have many such examples – Grameen Bank, Bangladesh, Greening program of Kenya, road belt or self-sufficiency-community forest program of Nepal. Here, I would like to directly quote one of the interesting conceptual programs proposed by Poudel (2008).

Poudel (2008) states that if we keep the climate central and manage it properly, sustainably management of other seven aspects, i.e., *water, land, forest, medicinal and aromatic plants, labor, animal,* and *crop plants,* would be easy. Here, a noticeable aspect is public participation in resources management. There are numerous examples of locally sustainably managed landscapes with Indigenous knowledge and techniques. However, such examples do not get highlighted because of unequal participation in decision-making systems. The United Nations (2015) in the "Transforming Our World: The 2030 Agenda for Sustainable Development" declaration-3 states that "We resolve, between now and 2030, to end poverty and hunger everywhere; to combat *inequalities within and among countries*; to build peaceful, just and inclusive societies; to protect human rights and promote gender equality and the empowerment of women and girls, and to ensure the lasting protection of the planet and its natural resources." (Declaration 3, page 3). However, so far, instead of decreasing, inequality has been increased (Bertelsmann Stiftung and Sustainable Development Solutions Network 2018). UN declaration has been effective; however, there are no symbols of poverty reduction, and opportunities are only accessible to rich or who are in the power. The gender gap is not decreased, and the rate of youth unemployment is on the rise. Similarly, the impact of environmental degradation continues, and frequent and intense natural disasters are common globally in recent decades. There are no symbols minimizing conflicts (local, national, and international), and violence, extremism, and terrorism have been uncontrolled. Environmental degradation is one of the major threats to the contemporary world; however, still there is no institutional architecture to address this challenge. Desertification, drought, land degradation, freshwater scarcity, and loss of biodiversity are still common circumstances. Global temperature is increasing, sea level is rising, and ocean acidification continues. Within four years of declaration implementation, there are no remarkable symptoms of improvements in the listed problems. Even the G-20 Nations' scenario of achieving SDGs is insignificant (Bertelsmann Stiftung and Sustainable Development Solutions Network 2018). As such, UN Declaration "Transforming Our World: The 2030 Agenda for Sustainable Development 2015" absolutely adds new hope discourse of sustainability; however, so far, practicality seems questionable.

In principle, sustainability discourses capture the notion of social, economic, and environmental boundaries, creativeness and innovation, and institutional architectures serve as tools to attain sustainability; however, the global challenges are mounted in every sphere of the globe. To achieve real sustainability, strong commitment and instinctive motivation are needed. A program like Astha-J needs to get promoted and implemented. So far, the invisible walls are everywhere, and "my profit first" is the dominant approach

236 *Sustainability Theory*

of current development paradigms. To overcome the global challenges, the concept of "Bashudaiva Kutumbakkam – The entire world is our home, and all living beings are our relatives" and "Live and let others live – the harmony within, community, nation and global" is needed.

And, finally, it is my pleasure to share knowledge and expertise. As I noted earlier, my family, communities, and various societies (wherever I have been), including the nature and culture, traditions jointly nurtured me, without any expectations. My intention, in life, is to give or contribute to society to the fullest whatever I have. I would be more than happy if readers find this information useful. I am open to engaging in any kind of collaborative research, teaching, or any other tasks which can contribute to overcoming or minimizing the devastating impact of climate change and contribute to achieving the SDGs at any level.

References

Acemoglu, Daron, and Robinson, James (2008), The International Bank for Reconstruction and Development / The World Bank, On behalf of the Commission on Growth and Development, The World Bank, Washington, DC http://www.growthcommission.org/storage/cgdev/documents/gc-wp-010_web.pdf

ADB (2002), Poverty Reduction and the Role of Institutions in Developing Asia, ERD Working Paper Series No.10, Economics and Research Department, Asian Development Bank, Manila

Aldrich, Howard E., and C. Marlene Fiol (1994), Fools Rush in? The Institutional Context of Industry Creation, The Academy of Management Review, Vol. 19, No. 4 (Oct. 1994), pp. 645-670

Anaedu, O and Engfeldt, Lars-Goran (2002), Sustainable Development Governance. Paper prepared for consideration in the Second, Week of the Third Session of the Preparatory Committee for WSSD.

And Reserves to Sustainability Boundaries, River Research, and Applications, River. Published online in Wiley Inter-Science, (www.interscience.wiley. com) DOI: 10.1002/rra.1320

Arima A (2009), A plea for more education for sustainable development. Sustain Sci 4(1):3–5

Barbier, E. B., (1987), 'The concept of sustainable economic development," Environmental Conservation, Vol. 14, No. 2 (1987), pp. 101-110.

Barker, Chris (2004), The SAGE Dictionary of Cultural Studies, SAGE Publications, London / Thousand Oaks / New Delhi https://zodml.org/sites/default/files/%5BDr_Chris_Barker%5D_The_SAGE_Dictionary_of_Cultural__0.pdf

Barnosky AD (2012), Approaching a state shift in Earth's biosphere. Nature 486:52-58

Basadur, M., Gelade, G., Basadur, T., (2014). Creative problem-solving process styles, cognitive work demands, and organizational adaptability. J. Appl. Behav. Sci. 50 (1), 80-115. http://www.business-analytic.co.uk/_media/basadur-gelade-jabs-2014.pdf

Bertelsmann Stiftung and Sustainable Development Solutions Network (2018), SDG Index and Dashboards Report 2018-Global Responsibilities, Implementing the Goals, G20 and Large Countries Edition. www.pica-publishing.com, http://www.sdgindex.org/assets/files/2018/00%20SDGS%202018%20G20%20EDITION%20WEB%20V7%2020180718.pdf

Bhandari, Medani P. (2019), "Bashudaiva Kutumbakkam"- The entire world is our home, and all living beings are our relatives. Why do we need to worry about climate change, concerning pollution problems in the major cities of India, Nepal, Bangladesh, and Pakistan? Adv Agr Environ Sci. (2019);2(1): 8–35. DOI: 0.30881/aaeoa.00019 http://ologyjournals.com/aaeoa/aaeoa_00019.pdf

Bhandari, Medani P. (2019), Live and let others live- the harmony with nature /living beings-in reference to sustainable development (SD)- is contemporary world's economic and social phenomena is favorable for the sustainability of the planet about India, Nepal, Bangladesh, and Pakistan? Adv Agr Environ Sci. (2019);2(1): 37–57. DOI: 10.30881/aaeoa.00020, http://ologyjournals.com/aaeoa/aaeoa_00020.pdf

Bhandari, Medani P. (2018), Green Web-II: Standards and Perspectives from the IUCN, Published, sold, and distributed by: River Publishers, Denmark / the Netherlands ISBN: 978-87-70220-12-5 (Hardback) 978-87-70220-11-8 (eBook),

Bhandari, Medani P (2017). Climate change science: a historical outline. Adv Agr Environ Sci. 1(1) 1-8: 00002. http://ologyjournals.com/aaeoa/aaeoa_00002.pdf

Boucher, Lauren (2015). Sustainable Development Goals vs. Millennium Development Goals: What You Need to Know Population Organization.

238 *Sustainability Theory*

https://populationeducation.org/sustainable-development-goals-vs-millennium-development-goals-what-you-need-know/

Callanan, Laura and Anders Ferguson (2015), A New Pilar of Sustainability, Philanthropic-Creativity, Foundation Center, New York, https://pndblog.typepad.com/pndblog/2015/10/creativity-a-new-pillar-of-sustainability.html

Carpenter S, Bennett E (2011), Reconsideration of the planetary boundary for phosphorus. Environmental Research Letters 6: 014009

Carson, Rachel (1962). Silent Spring. Boston: Houghton Mifflin Co. and in Rachel Carson, "Silent Spring," in Diane Ravitch, ed., The American Reader: Words that Moved a Nation (New York: HarperCollins, 1990), 323-325. http://www.uky.edu/Classes/NRC/381/carson_spring.pdf

Charnovitz, Steve (1996), Participation of Non-Governmental Organizations in the World Trade Organization, University of Pennsylvania Journal of International Economic Law 17: 331-357.

Charnovitz, Steve (1997), Two Centuries of Participation: NGOs and International Governance, Michigan Journal of International Law 18(2): 281-282.

Choo, Jaewoo (2005), Is Institutionalization of the Six-Party Talks Possible? EASTASIA, Winter 2005, Vol. 22, No. 4, pp. 39-58.

Clark, W. C., and R. E. Munn (1996-Eds.), Sustainable Development of the Biosphere (Cambridge: Cambridge University Press, 1986).

Colyvas, Jeannette A. and Walter W. Powell (2006), Roads to Institutionalization: The Remaking of Boundaries between Public and Private Science. Research in Organizational Behavior 27: 315-363.

Cornell, S. (2012), On the system properties of the planetary boundaries. Ecology and Society 17:1

Corral-Verdugo, V., Bonnes, M., Tapia-Fonllem, C., Fraijo-Sing, B., Frias-Armenta, M., & Carrus, G. (2009), Correlates of Pro-Sustainability Orientation: The Affinity towards Diversity. Journal of Environmental Psychology, 29, 34-43. https://doi.org/10.1016/j.jenvp.2008.09.001

Costanza, Robert, Lisa Graumlich, Will Steffen (2007), Sustainability or Collapse: What Can We Learn from Integrating the History of Humans and the Rest of Nature?, Ambio

References 239

Dacin, M. T. Goodstein, J. Scott, W. R. (2002), Institutional Theory and Institutional Change: Introduction to the Special Research Forum, ACADEMY OF MANAGEMENT JOURNAL, 2002, VOL 45; PART 1, pages 45-57.

Daly, H. E (2007), Ecological Economics and Sustainable Development, Selected Essays of Herman Daly, Advances in Ecological Economics, MPG Books Ltd, Bodmin, Cornwall http://library.uniteddiversity.coop/ Measuring_Progress_and_Eco_Footprinting/Ecological_Economics_ and_Sustainable_Development-Selected_Essays_of_Herman_Daly.pdf

Daly, H., (1991) 'Sustainable development: From concept and theory towards operational principles," in tt. E. Daly, Steady-state Economics: 2nd Edition with New Essays, Washington, DC: Island Press

DESA (2013), World Economic and Social Survey 2013, Sustainable Development Challenges, Department of Economic and Social Affairs, The Department of Economic and Social Affairs of the United Nations Secretariat, NY

Diamond, J. 2005: Collapse: How Complex Societies Choose to Fail or Survive. New York: Penguin (http://cpor.org/ce/Diamond%282005%29Collapse-HowSocietiesChooseFailureSuccess.pdf)

DiMaggio, P. & Powell, W. W. (1983), The iron cage revisited: Institutional isomorphism and collective rationality in organizational fields. American Sociological Review, 48:147-160.

DiMaggio, P. (2001), Making sense of the contemporary firm and prefiguring its future. In DiMaggio, P. (Ed.), The Twenty-First-Century Firm: Changing Economic Organization in International Perspective. Princeton: Princeton University Press.

DiMaggio, P. J. & Powell, W. W. (1991a). 'The iron cage revisited: Institutional isomorphism and collective rationality. In Powell, W. W. & DiMaggio, P. J. Chicago: University of Chicago Press.

Donald, Betsy (2010), The Creative Economy, Department of Geography Queen's University Monieson Centre Seminar Series, Canada http:// business.queensu.ca/centres/monieson/events/Betsy_Donald_Creative_ Economy.pdf

Dryzek, John S. (1997), The Politics of the Earth: Environmental Discourses, Oxford University Press.

240 *Sustainability Theory*

Duffield J. (2007), Reflection, evaluation, and integration, what are the international Institutions, International Studies Review (2007) 9, 1-22.

Duran, C.D., Gogan, L.M., Artene, A. & Duran, V. (2015), The components of sustainable development - a possible approach. Procedia Economics and Finance, 26, 806-811. Retrieved November 20, 2015, from https://doi.org/10.1016/S2212-5671(15)00849-7.

Erb K-H et al (2012), Pushing the Planetary Boundaries. Science 14 December 2012: 1419-1420

Fleming, James R. (2004). Climate dynamics, science dynamics, and technological change, 1804-2004, Conference on INTERNATIONAL COMMISSION ON HISTORY OF METEOROLOGY, Barocker Bibliothekssaal, Kloster Polling Weilheimer Straße, D-82398 Polling, Germany, http://www.meteohistory.org/2004polling_preprints/docs/polling_program.pdf http://www.meteohistory.org/2004polling_preprints/docs/abstracts/fleming_abstract.pdf (accessed on 04/03/2016)

Foley JA et al (2011), Solutions for a cultivated planet. Nature 478: 337-342

Folke C et al (2011), Reconnecting to the biosphere. Ambio 40: 719-738

Folke C, Rockström J (2011), 3rd Nobel Laureate Symposium on Global Sustainability: transforming the world in an era of global change. Ambio 40: 717-718

Galbraith, J.K. (1967), The New Industrial State, Houghton-Mifflin, Boston, MA

Gilbert, Christine, "Sustainability's Inconvenient Discourse" (2014). Honors College. 177.

Gilbert, R., Stevenson, D., Girardet, H. and Stren, R. (1996) Making Cities Work: The Role of Local Authorities in the Urban Environment. Earthscan, London.

Girard, Luigi Fusco (2010), Sustainability, creativity, resilience: toward new development strategies of port areas through evaluation processes, Int. J. Sustainable Development, Vol. 13, Nos. 1/2, 2010 161

Graedel, Thomas E. and Ester van der Voet (2010), Linkages of Sustainability, The MIT Press

Hák, T. and Moldan, B. and Dahl, A. (2007), Sustainability Indicators: A Scientific Assessment. SCOPE 67, https://www.researchgate.net/profile/Joachim_Spangenberg/publication/227650480_Institutional_

sustainability_indicators_An_analysis_of_the_institutions_in_Agenda_21_
and_a_draft_set_of_indicators_for_monitoring_their_effectivity/links/
5b6d48bca6fdcc87df7095c7/Institutional-sustainability-indicators-An-
analysis-of-the-institutions-in-Agenda-21-and-a-draft-set-of-indicators-for-
monitoring-their-effectivity.pdf

Hall, Peter A and Rosemary C.R. Taylor (1996), Political sciences and three
new institutions, Political studies (1996) XLIV, 936-957.

Hannan, M T., and Carroll, G.R., (1992), Dynamics of Organizational
Populations Density, Legitimation and Competition Oxford University
Press, New York.

Hannan, M.T. and J. Freeman (1989), *Organizational Ecology.* Cambridge,
Massachusetts: Harvard University Press.

Hannanand, Michael T. and John Freeman (1977), The Population Ecology
of Organizations, as Volume 82 Number 5 (March 1977): 929.

Harwood, R.R. (1990), The history of sustainable agriculture. In C.A.
Edwards et al. (Eds.). Sustainable Farming Systems, (pp. 3-19). In Duran,
C.D., Gogan, L.M., Artene, A. & Duran, V.(2015). The components of
sustainable development - a possible approach. Procedia Economics and
Finance, 26, 806-811. Retrieved November 20, 2015, from https://doi.
org/10.1016/S2212-5671(15)00849-7

Håvard Mokleiv Nygård (2017), Achieving the sustainable development
agenda: The governance – conflict nexus, International Area Studies
Review, Vol. 20(1) 3–18

Haveman, Heather A. (2000), The Future of Organizational Sociology:
Forging Ties among Paradigms, Contemporary Sociology, Vol. 29, No. 3
(May 2000), pp. 476-486

Holvino, E., Ferdman, B. M., & Merrill-Sands, D. (2004), Creating and
sustaining diversity and inclusion in organizations: Strategies and
approaches. In M. S. Stockdale & F. J. Crosby (Eds.), The psychology and
management of workplace diversity (pp. 245-276). Malden, Blackwell
Publishing.

Hornborg, A., J. R. McNeill, and J. Martinez-Alier, (2007), Rethinking
Environmental History: World-System History and Global Environmental
Change, AltaMira Press, Lanham, MD

242 *Sustainability Theory*

http://www.adb.org/Documents/ERD/Working_Papers/wp010.pdf

http://www.regional.org.au/au/apen/2003/refereed/020palmerl.htm

https://digitalcommons.library.umaine.edu/honors/177

https://mitpress-request.mit.edu/sites/default/files/titles/content/9780262
013581_sch_0001.pdf

https://s3.amazonaws.com/academia.edu.documents/1730775/   00Valentin
___JS_-_EnvImpact_AssRev_-_Community_indicatiors.pdf?AWSAcc
essKeyId=AKIAIWOWYYGZ2Y53UL3A&Expires=1551372775&Si
gnature=EUezlugypFRsyCb9ebqEaTxuHwA%3D&response-content-
disposition=inline%3B%20filename%3DIndicators_for_Sustainable_
Communities.pdf

https://www.researchgate.net/profile/Mirilia_Bonnes/publication/
38134636_Affinity_towards_diversity_as_a_psychological_correlate_of_
sustainability/links/55394a080cf226723aba1694.pdf

Ingram J (2011), A food systems approach to researching food security and its
interactions with global environmental change. Food Security 3: 417-431

Ingrid Kajzer Mitchell and Jennifer Walinga (2017), The creative imperative:
The role of creativity, creative problem solving and insight as key drivers
for sustainability, Journal of Cleaner Production 140 1872-1884 https://
tudelft.openresearch.net/image/2016/11/11/mitchel_walinga_jocp_2017.
pdf

Ingrid Kajzer Mitchell and Jennifer Walinga (2017), The creative imperative:
The role of creativity, creative problem solving and insight as key drivers
for sustainability, Journal of Cleaner Production 140 1872-1884 https://
tudelft.openresearch.net/image/2016/11/11/mitchel_walinga_jocp_2017.
pdf

IUCN (1980), World Conservation Strategy: Living Resource Conservation
for Sustainable Development. Retrieved November 7, 2015, from https://
portals.iucn.org/library/efiles/documents/WCS-004.pdf.

IUCN (2006), The Future of Sustainability, Re-thinking Environment and
Development in the Twenty-first Century, IUCN, Gland (contributor W.M.
Adams) http://cmsdata.iucn.org/downloads/iucn_future_of_sustanability.
pdf

IUCN, UNDP & WWF, (1991), Caring for the Earth. A Strategy for
Sustainable Living. International Union for Conservation of Nature and

References 243

Natural Resources, United Nations Environmental Program & World Wildlife Fund Retrieved November 8, 2015, from https://portals.iucn.org/library/efiles/documents/CFE-003.pdf

James, Paul (Paul Warren), (2015), Urban sustainability in theory and practice: circles of sustainability / Paul James; with Liam Magee, Andy Scerri, Manfred Steger, Routledge (Earthscan).https://www.academia.edu/9294719/Urban_Sustainability_in_Theory_and_Practice_Circles_of_Sustainability_2015_

Jefferson, Thomas on Climate Change (15.10.2008) http://xroads.virginia.edu/~HYPER/JEFFERSON/ch07.html; Found it in Dr. Richard Keen's Global Warming Quiz, via Roger Pielke, Sr.'s Climate Science. http://omniclimate.wordpress.com/2008/10/15/thomas-jefferson-on-http://american-conservativevalues.com/blog/2010/03/thomas-jefferson-fully-aware-of-climate-change/climate-change/

Jepperson, R. L. (1991), Institutions, institutional effects, and institutionalism. In P. J. DiMaggio & W. W. Powell (Eds.), The new institutionalism in organizational analysis (pp. 143-162). Chicago: University of Chicago Press.

Joost Platje (2008), "Institutional capital" as a factor of sustainable development the importance of an institutional equilibrium, Technological and Economic Development of Economy, 14:2, 144-150

https://www.tandfonline.com/doi/pdf/10.3846/1392-8619.2008.14.144-150

Kates W. Robert, Thomas M. Parris & Anthony A. Leiserowitz (2005), What is Sustainable Development? Goals, Indicators, Values, and Practice, Environment: Science and Policy for Sustainable Development, 47:3, 8-21, DOI: 10.1080/00139157.2005.10524444 http://www.cepn-paris13.fr/epog/wp-content/uploads/2016/01/CONSOLO_Kates-et-al.pdf

Keohane, Robert O. (1988), International Institutions: Two Approaches, International Studies Quarterly, Vol. 32, No. 4, (Dec. 1988), pp. 379-396

Klarin, Tomislav (2018), The Concept of Sustainable Development: From its Beginning to the Contemporary Issues, Zagreb International Review of Economics & Business, Vol. 21, No. 1, pp. 67-94, DOI: https://doi.org/10.2478/zireb-2018-0005 https://content.sciendo.com/view/journals/zireb/21/1/article-p67.xml

Laudel, Grit; Gläser, Jochen (1998), What are institutional boundaries and how can they be overcome? Germany's collaborative research centers

244 *Sustainability Theory*

as boundary-spanning networks, WZB Discussion Paper, No. P 98-401, Wissenschaftszentrum Berlin für Sozialforschung (WZB), Berlin

Lawrence, P. R., Lorsch, J. W. (1967), Organization and environment. Boston: Graduate School of Business Administration, Harvard University.

Lélé, Sharachchandra M. (1991), Sustainable development: A critical review. World Development, Vol 19, No 6, 607-621 https://edisciplinas.usp.br/pluginfile.php/209043/mod_resource/content/1/Texto_1_lele.pdf

Litfin, Karen. (1994), Ozone Discourses: Science and Politics in Global Environmental

Lorek, Sylvia, and Doris Fuchs (2011), Strong sustainable consumption governance e precondition for a degrowth path? Journal of Cleaner Production, xxx,1-8

Mair, Simon, Aled Jones, Jonathan Ward, Ian Christie, Angela Druckman, and Fergus Lyon (2017), A Critical Review of the Role of Indicators in Implementing the Sustainable Development Goals in the Handbook of Sustainability Science in Leal, Walter (Edit.) https://www.researchgate.net/publication/313444041_A_Critical_Review_of_the_Role_of_Indicators_in_Implementing_the_Sustainable_Development_Goals

March, J.G. and J.P. Olsen (1984), The New Institutionalism: Organizational Factors in Political Life. American Political Science Review 78 (3): 734-749.

March, J.G. and J.P. Olsen (1986), Institutional perspectives on political institutions. Governance 9 (3): 247-264.

March, J.G. and J.P. Olsen (1989) Rediscovering Institutions. New York: Free Press.

March, J.G. and J.P. Olsen (1998), The institutional dynamics of international political orders. International Organization 52: 943-69. Reprinted pp. 303-329 in P.J. Katzenstein, R.O. Keohane and S.D. Krasner eds. 1999, Exploration and Contestation in the Study of World Politics. Cambridge Ma: The MIT Press.

March, James G. & Johan P. Olsen (2005), Elaborating the "New Institutionalism" Working Paper No.11, March 2005, Center for European Studies, Oslo, Norway. http://www.arena.uio.no/publications/working-papers2005/papers/wp05_11.pdf

Marin, C., Doroban u, R., Codreanu, D. & Mihaela, R. (2012), The Fruit of Collaboration between Local Government and Private Partners in the Sustainable Development Community Case Study: County Valcea. Economy Transdisciplinary Cognition, 2, 93–98. In Duran, C.D.,

Martins, Antonio A.; Teresa M. Mata and Carlos A. V. Costa (2006), Education for sustainability: challenges and trends, Clean Techn Environ Policy (2006) 8: 31–37DOI 10.1007/s10098-005-0026-3

Maser C (1997), Sustainable community development: principles and concepts, St. Lucie Press

Meadows, D.H. (1998), Indicators and Information Systems for Sustainable Development. A report to the Balaton Group 1998. The Sustainability Institute.

Meadows, D.H., Meadows, D.L., Randers, J. & Behrens III, W.W. (1972), The Limits of Growth. A report for the Club of Rome's project on the predicament of humankind. Retrieved September 20, 2018, from http://collections.dartmouth.edu/published-derivatives/meadows/pdf/meadows_ltg-001.pdf.

Mearsheimer, John J. (1995), The False Promise of International Institutions, International Security, Vol. 19, No. 3 (Winter, 1994-1995), pp. 5-49

Meuleman, Louis (Ed.) (2013), Trans governance: Advancing sustainability governance, ISBN 978-3-642-28009-2, Springer, Heidelberg, http://dx.doi.org/10.1007/978-3-642-28009-https://www.econstor.eu/bitstream/10419/182344/1/978-3-642-28009-2.pdf

Meyer, J.W. and Rowan, B. (1977), Institutionalized Organizations: Formal Structure as Myth and Ceremony. American Journal of Sociology, 83, 340-363. or Brundtland, G., ed. (1987) Our Common Future: The World Commission on Environment and Development, Oxford: University Press.

Mitchell, Ingrid Kajzer and Jennifer Walinga (2017), The creative imperative: The role of creativity, creative problem solving and insight as key drivers for sustainability, Journal of Cleaner Production 140 (2017) 1872-1884 https://tudelft.openresearch.net/image/2016/11/11/mitchel_walinga_jocp_2017.pdf

Nielsen K. (2001), Institutionalist Approaches in the Social Sciences: Typology, Dialogue, and Future Challenges, Journal of Economic Issues, Vol.32, No 2.

246 *Sustainability Theory*

Nielsen, K. (2001), Review of Institutionalist Approaches in the Social Sciences: Variety, Dialogue, and Future Prospects." Research Papers. Network Institutional Theory. No. 7. Roskilde: Roskilde University, 2001.

Norgaard, R. B., (1988), 'Sustainable development: A coevolutionary view," Futures, Vol. 20, No. 6 (1988), pp. 606-620.

North, Douglass C. (1981), Structure and Change in Economic History. New York: W.W. Norton & Co.

OECD. (1998), Sustainability Indicators beyond the Environment. OECD: Paris.

Oliver, C. (1991), Strategic Responses to Institutional Processes, Academy of Management Review, Vol. 16, 191: pp.145-179.

Opschoor H, Reinders L. (1991), Towards sustainable development indicators. In Search of Indicators of Sustainable Development, Kuik O, Verbruggen H (eds). Kluwer: Dordrecht; 7–27.

Ostrom, Elinor (1990), Governing the Commons: The Evolution of Institutions for Collective Action (Political Economy of Institutions and Decisions), Cambridge University Press; edition (1991-03-14) (1800)

Paehlke, Robert C. (1989), Environmentalism and the Future of Progressive Politics, Yale University Press.

Palmer, Len (2003), Discourses of sustainability: a Foucauldian approach, The Regional Institute

PAP/RAC, (1999), Carrying capacity assessment for tourism development, Priority Actions Program, in the framework of Regional Activity Centre Mediterranean Action Plan Coastal Area Management Program (CAMP) Fuka-Matrouh – Egypt, Split: Regional Activity Centre

Pearce, D. (1989). Tourism Development. London: Harlow.

Pesch, Udo (2014), Sustainable development and institutional boundaries, Journal of Integrative Environmental Sciences, 11:1, 39-54, DOI: 10.1080/1943815X.2014.889718 https://www.tandfonline.com/doi/pdf/10.1080/1943815X.2014.889718?needAccess=true

Pfahl, Stefanie (2005), Institutional sustainability, Int. J. Sustainable Development, Vol. 8, Nos. 1/2, 2005

Poudel, D.D. 2008. Management of Eight "*Ja*" for Economic Development of Nepal, *Journal of Comparative International Management*, Vol. 11, No.1, 15-27.

Powell, W. W. (1990), Neither market nor hierarchy: Network forms of organization. In Staw, B. M. & Cummings, L. L. (Eds.), Research in Organizational Behavior, 12 (pp. 295-336). Greenwich, CT: JAI Press.

Powell, W. W., Koput, K. & Smith-Doerr, L. (1996), Interorganizational collaboration and the locus of innovation: Networks of learning in biotechnology. Administrative Science Quarterly, 41, 116-145.

Powell, Walter W., and DiMaggio, Paul J. (1991), The new institutionalism in organizational analysis Chicago, IL: University of Chicago Press.

Raworth K (2012), A safe and just space for humanity. Oxfam discussion paper. 26 pp

Richter, Brian D. (2009), Short Communication Re-Thinking Environmental Flows: From Allocations

Robin, Libby, and Will Steffen (2007), History for the Anthropocene, History Compass, Vol. 5 July 2007, http://www.blackwellcompass.com/subject/history/section_home?section=hico-world (P. Manning, „Proposal for a World-Historical Database Design Group , January 2007, kindly supplied by the author. (This proposal has been successful, pers. com. May 2006).

Rockström J *et. al.* (2009a), A safe operating space for humanity, Nature 461: 472-475

Rockström J et. al. (2009b) Planetary Boundaries: Exploring the Safe Operating Space for Humanity, Ecology, and Society 14(2): 32

Rockström J, Karlberg L (2010), The Quadruple Squeeze: Defining the safe operating space for freshwater use to achieve a triply green revolution in the Anthropocene. Ambio 39: 257-265

Rockström, Johan and Jeffrey D. Sachs with Marcus C. Öhman and Guido Schmidt-Traub (2013), Sustainable Development and Planetary Boundaries, Background Research Paper, Submitted to the High-Level Panel on the Post-2015 Development Agenda, Sustainable Development Network, https://www.researchgate.net/profile/Marcus_Oehman/publication/257873780_Sustainable_Development_and_Planetary_Boundaries/links/0046352601126370850000000/Sustainable-Development-and-Planetary-Boundaries.pdf

Running SW (2012), A measurable planetary boundary for the biosphere. Science 337: 1458

248 *Sustainability Theory*

Sawyer, R. Keith. (2002), "A Discourse on Discourse: An Archeological History of an Intellectual Concept." Cultural Studies 16(3): 433–56.

Schlör, Holger, Wolfgang Fischer, and Jürgen-Friedrich Hake (2015), The system boundaries of sustainability, Journal of Cleaner Production, Volume 88, 1 February 2015, Pages 52-60

Scoones, Ian (2016), The Politics of Sustainability and Development Annu. Rev. Environ. Resource. 2016. 41:293–319

Scott W.R. (2004), Reflections on A Half-Century of Organizational Sociology, Annual Review of Sociology, 30:1–21.

Scott, W. R. (2004) Institutional Theory: Contributing to a Theoretical Research Program, Great Minds in Management: The Process of Theory Development, Ken G. Smith and Michael A. Hitt, eds. Oxford UK: Oxford University Press.

Singh, Rajesh Kumar, H.R. Murty, S.K. Gupta, A.K. Dikshit (2009), An overview of sustainability assessment methodologies, ecological indicators 9 (2009) 189–212 https://s3.amazonaws.com/academia.edu. documents/45427573/An_overview_of_sustainability_assessment_ methodologies.pdf?AWSAccessKeyId=AKIAIWOWYYGZ2Y53UL3A &Expires=1551372572&Signature=7dfLfFOxOxVFIF46bCCblMugLn g%3D&response-content-disposition=inline%3B%20filename%3DAn_ overview_of_sustainability_assessment.pdf

Spangenberg JH. (2001), Investing in sustainable development. International Journal of Sustainable Development 4(2): 184–201.

Spangenberg, JH. (2002), Institutional Sustainability Indicators: An Analysis of The Institutions in Agenda 21 And A Draft Set of Indicators for Monitoring Their Effectivity, Sustainable Development, Sust. Dev. 10, 103–115 (2002) http://tzyy-ling.ukn.edu.tw/seminar4/%E5%B0%88%E8%A8% 8E%E5%A0%B1%E5%91%8A%E5%8F%83%E8%80%83%E8%B 3%87%E6%96%99/%E7%AC%AC%E4%B8%80%E6%AC%A1/% E8%94%A1%E6%83%A0%E6%97%AC/Towards%20indicators%20 for%20institutional%20sustainability%20lessons%20from%20an%20 analysis%20of%20Agenda%2021.pdf

Spangenberg, Joachim H., Stefanie Pfahl, and Kerstin Deller (2002), Towards indicators for institutional sustainability: lessons from an analysis of Agenda 21, Ecological Indicators 2 (2002) 61–77 https:// www.researchgate.net/profile/Joachim_Spangenberg/publication/

227650480_Institutional_sustainability_indicators_An_analysis_of_ the_institutions_in_Agenda_21_and_a_draft_set_of_indicators_for_ monitoring_their_effectivity/links/5b6d48bca6fdcc87df7095c7/ Institutional-sustainability-indicators-An-analysis-of- the-institutions-in-Agenda-21- and-a-draft-set-of-indicators-for-monitoring-their-effectivity. pdf

Steffen W et al (2011) The Anthropocene: from global change to planetary boundaries. Ambio 40: 739-761

Steffen, Will, Katherine Richardson, Johan Rockström, Sarah E. Cornell, Ingo Fetzer, Elena M. Bennett, Reinette Biggs, Stephen R. Carpenter, Wim de Vries, Cynthia A. de Wit, Carl Folke, Dieter Girtin, Jens Heinke, Georgina M. Mace, Linn M. Persson, Veera Bhadran Ramanathan, Belinda Reyers, Sverker Sörlin (2015), Planetary boundaries: Guiding human development on a changing planet, Science 347, 1259855 (2015). DOI: 10.1126/science.1259855 https://openresearch-repository.anu.edu.au/ bitstream/1885/13126/3/1259855.full.pdf

Sterling S. (2004), Higher Education, Sustainability, and the Role of Systemic Learning. In: Corcoran P.B., Wals A.E.J. (eds) Higher Education and the Challenge of Sustainability. Springer, Dordrecht

Sterling, S. (2010), Learning for resilience, or the resilient learner? Towards a necessary reconciliation in a paradigm of sustainable education. Environmental Education Research, 16, 511-528. DOI: 10.1080/13504622.2010.505427.

Stockholm Resilience Centre (2017), Transformation is feasible-How to achieve the Sustainable Development Goals within Planetary Boundaries- A report to the Club of Rome, for its 50th anniversary 17 October 2018, Stockholm Resilience Centre https://www.stockholmresilience. org/download/18.51d83659166367a9a16353/1539675518425/Report_ Achieving%20the%20Sustainable%20Development%20Goals_WEB.pdf

Strang, D. and J. W. Meyer (1994), Institutional Conditions for Diffusion. Institutional Environments and Organizations. W. R. Scott and J. W. Meyer. Thousand Oaks, SAGE Publications: 100-112.

Sustainable Development Solutions Network -SDSN (2014), Health in The Framework Of Sustainable Development, Technical Report for the Post-2015 Development Agenda, Thematic Group on Health for All of the Sustainable Development Solutions Network, http://unsdsn.org/ wp-content/uploads/2014/02/Health-For-All-Report.pdf

250 *Sustainability Theory*

Lorek, Sylvia, and Doris Fuchs (2011), Strong sustainable consumption governance e precondition for a degrowth path? Journal of Cleaner Production xxx (2011) 1-8

Tahvilzadeh, Nazem, Stig Montin & Mikael Cullberg (2017), Functions of sustainability: exploring what urban sustainability policy discourse "does" in the Gothenburg Metropolitan Area, Local Environment, 22:sup1, 66-85, DOI: 10.1080/13549839.2017.1320538

Tahvilzadeh, Nazem, Stig Montin & Mikael Cullberg (2017), Functions of sustainability: exploring what urban sustainability policy discourse "does" in the Gothenburg Metropolitan Area, Local Environment, 22:sup1, 66-85, DOI: 10.1080/13549839.2017.1320538

The Limits to Growth (1972). Abstract established by Eduard Pestel; A Report to the Club of Rome (1972), by Donella H. Meadows, Dennis l. Meadows, Jorgen Randers, William W. Behrens III; http://www.facebook.com/topic.php?uid=9364228327&topic=4478

the Policy Process. Oxford: Clarendon Press

Thelen, K., and S. Steinmo (1992), "Historical Institutionalism in Comparative Politics." In Structuring Politics: Historical Institutionalism in Comparative Politics, edited by S. Steinmo, K. Thelen, and F. Longstreth. New York: Cambridge University Press, 1992, 1-32.

Theret, B. (2000), "Institutions et institutionalismes. Vers une convergence intra et interdisciplinaires des conceptions de l institution?" Paper for the Colloques Organizations et Institutions: "Regles, coordination, 6volution." Amiens, May 25-26, 2000a

Tuan, Yi-Fu (1991). A View of Geography, Geographical Review, Vol. 81, No. 1 (Jan. 1991), pp. 99-107, on page 99 states "What is the intellectual character and core of geography? An answer, from a broadly humanist viewpoint, which may satisfy the genuinely curious and literate public lies in the definition of the field as the study of the earth as the home of people. Home is the key, unifying word for all the principal subdivisions of geography, because home, in the large sense, is physical, economic, psychological, and moral; it is the whole physical earth and a specific neighborhood; it is constraint and freedom-place, location, and space" http://www.jstor.org/stable/pdfplus/215179.pdf (accessed on 04/02/2016).

References 251

UN, United Nations (1972), Report of the United Nations Conference on the Human Environment. Stockholm. Retrieved September 20, 2015, from http://www.un-documents.net/aconf48-14r1.pdf.

UN, United Nations (1997), Earth Summit: Resolution adopted by the General Assembly at its nineteenth special session. Retrieved November 4, 2015, from http://www.un.org/esa/earthsummit/index.html.

UN, United Nations (2002), Report of the World Summit on Sustainable Development, Johannesburg; Rio +10. Retrieved November 4, 2015, from http://www.unmillenniumproject.org/documents/131302_wssd_report_reissued.pdf.

UN, United Nations (2010), The Millennium Development Goals Report. Retrieved September 20, 2015, from http://www.un.org/millenniumgoals/pdf/MDG%20Report%202010%20En%20

UN, United Nations (2012). Resolution „The future we want ". Retrieved November 5, 2015, from?

UN, United Nations (2015). Retrieved September 21, 2015, from http://www.un.org/en/index.html.

UN, United Nations (2015b), 70 years, 70 documents. Retrieved September 21, 2015, from http://research.un.org/en/UN70/about.

UN, United Nations (2015c), Resolution „Transforming our world: the 2030 Agenda for Sustainable Development. Retrieved November 5, 2015, from http://www.un.org/ga/search/view_doc.asp?symbol=A/RES/70/1&Lang=E.

UN, United Nations (2015d), The Millennium Development Goals Report 2015. Retrieved November 5, 2015, from http://www.un.org/millenniumgoals/2015_MDG_Report/pdf/MDG%20

UNDESA-DSD – United Nations Department of Economic and Social Affairs Division for Sustainable Development, 2002. Plan of Implementation of the World Summit on Sustainable Development: The Johannesburg Conference. New York. UNESCO – United Nations Educational, Scientific and Cultural Organization, 2005. International Implementation Scheme. United Nations Decade of Education for Sustainable Development (2005-2014), Paris.

UNDP (2010), Global Human Development Report 2010, Human Development Report Office, New York

252 *Sustainability Theory*

UN-DSD (United Nations Division for Sustainable Development) (2007), Indicators of Sustainable Development: Guidelines and Methodologies (3rd Edition) United Nations, New York http://www.un.org/esa/sustdev/natlinfo/indicators/guidelines.pdf

UNEP (2010), Background paper for XVII Meeting of the Forum of Ministers of Environment of Latin America and the Caribbean, Panamá City, Panamá, 26 -30 April 2010, UNEP/LAC-IG.XVII/4, UNEP, Nairobi, Kenya http://www.unep.org/greeneconomy/AboutGEI/WhatisGEI/tabid/29784/Default.aspx.

UNEP (2012), Keeping Track of Our Changing Environment: United Nations Environmental Program From Rio to Rio+20 (1992-2012). Retrieved November 4, 2015, from http://www.unep.org/geo/pdfs/Keeping_Track.pdf.

UNEP, (2015), Green Economy. Retrieved November 5, 2015, United Nations Environmental Program from http://www.unep.org/greeneconomy/AboutGEI/WhatisGEI/tabid/29784/Default.aspx.

UNESCO (2013), UNESCO's Medium-The Contribution of Creativity to Sustainable Development Term Strategy for 2014-2021, http://www.unesco.org/new/fileadmin/MULTIMEDIA/HQ/CLT/images/CreativityFinalENG.pdf http://www.unesco.org/new/fileadmin/MULTIMEDIA/HQ/CLT/images/CreativityFinalENG.pdf

UNFCCC, (2016), Report of the Conference of the Parties on its twenty-first session, held in Paris, United Nations Framework Convention on Climate Change, from 30 November to 13 December 2015. Retrieved February 15, 2016, from http://unfccc.int/resource/docs/2015/cop21/

United Nations (1990), Institutions, Institutional Change, and Economic Performance. New York: Cambridge University Press.

United Nations (2002), Implementing Agenda 21 Report of the Secretary-General. Commission on Sustainable Development acting as the preparatory committee for the World Summit on Sustainable Development Second session 28 January-8 February 2002.E/CN.17/2002/PC.2/7

United Nations (2015), Transforming Our World: The 2030 Agenda For Sustainable Development A/RES/70/1, United Nations, New York https://sustainabledevelopment.un.org/content/documents/21252030%20Agenda%20for%20Sustainable%20Development%20web.pdf

United Nations (UN). (1993), Earth Summit: Agenda 21, the United Nations Program of Action from Rio. UN: New York.

United Nations Department of Economic and Social Affairs (UNDESA) (1998), Measuring Changes in Consumption and Production Patterns. A Set of Indicators. UN: New York.

United Nations Department of Economic and Social Affairs (UNDESA) (2011) The Transition to a Green Economy: Benefits, Challenges, and Risks from a Sustainable Development Perspective Report by a Panel of Experts* to Second Preparatory Committee Meeting for United Nations Conference on Sustainable Development Prepared under the direction of Division for Sustainable Development, UN-DESA United Nations Environment Program UN Conference on Trade and Development, New York http://www.uncsd2012.org/rio20/content/documents/Green%20 Economy_full%20report%20final%20for%20posting%20clean.pdf

United Nations Educational, Scientific and Cultural Organization (UNESCO) (2009), Bonn Declaration. UNESCO World Conference on Education for Sustainable Development, Bonn, Germany, 31 March to 2 April 2009. http://www.esd-world-conference-2009.org/fileadmin/download/ ESD2009_BonnDeclaration080409.pdf.

United Nations Environment Program and Development Alternatives-UNEP-DA (2008), South Asia Environment Outlook 2009: United Nations Environment Program (UNEP), South Asian Association for Regional Cooperation (SAARC) and Development Alternatives (DA) UNEP, SAARC and DA. http://www.saarc-sec.org/userfiles/SAEO%202009.pdf

United Nations General Assembly. (1987), Report of the world commission on environment and development: Our common future. Oslo, Norway: United Nations General Assembly, Development, and International Co-operation: Environment.

United Nations General Assembly. (1987), Report of the world commission on environment and development: Our common future. Oslo, Norway: United Nations General Assembly, Development, and International Co-operation: Environment.

Valentin, Anke and Joachim H. Spangenberg (2000), A guide to community sustainability indicators, Environmental Impact Assessment Review, 20 (2000) 381–392

254 *Sustainability Theory*

Van Dijk, T.A., (2011), Discourse studies: A multidisciplinary introduction. Sage.

van Dijk, Teun A. (1998), Ideology: A Multidisciplinary Approach, Sage Publications

van Dijk, Teun A. (2006), "Ideology and Discourse Analysis." Journal of Political Ideologies 11(2): 115–40.

Vander-Merwe, I. & Van-der-Merwe, J. (1999), Sustainable development at the local level: An introduction to local agenda 21. Pretoria: Department of environmental affairs and

Versteijlen, M.; Perez Salgado, F.; Janssen Groesbeek, M.; Counotte, A. (2017), Pros and Cons of Online Education as a Measure to Reduce Carbon Emissions in Higher Education in the Netherlands. Curr. Opin. Environ. Sustain, 28, 80–89.

Vos, Robert O. (2007), Perspective Defining sustainability: a conceptual orientation, Journal of Chemical Technology and Biotechnology, 182:334–339 (2007)

Waheed, B.; Khan, F.I.; Veitch, B. (2011), Developing a Quantitative Tool for Sustainability Assessment of Heis. Int. J. Sustain. High. Educ. 12, 355–368.

Wallendorf, M.; Belk, R.W. (1989), Assessing Trustworthiness in Naturalistic Consumer Research. Interpret. Consum. Res. 69–84.

Wals, A., (2009), United Nations Decade of Education for Sustainable Development (DESD, 2005-2014): Review of Contexts and Structures for Education for Sustainable Development Learning for a sustainable world 2009. Paris.

WB, The World Bank (2015), World Development Indicators. Retrieved September 2, 2015, from http://data.worldbank.org/data-catalog/world-development-indicators.

WCED (1987), Our Common Future World Commission on Environment and Development New York: Oxford University Press

WHO (2015), WHO Sustainable Development and Health, Health and Sustainable Development: Key Health Trends 2015, Rome

Williamson, O. E. (1975), Markets and Hierarchies, Analysis and Antitrust Implications: A Study in the Economics of Internal Organization. New York: Free Press.

References 255

World Commission on Environment and Development (WCED) (1987), Our Common Future, Oxford University Press, Oxford, p61. http://www.worldinbalance.net/pdf/1987-brundtland.pdf

World Conservation Strategy (1980), *World Conservation Strategy: Living Resource Conservation for Sustainable Development*. IUCN/WWF, 1196 Gland, Switzerland, and UNEP, Nairobi, Kenya

Wu, SOS, Jianguo (Jingle) (2012), Sustainability Indicators Sustainability Measures: Local-Level SDIs494/598–http://leml.asu.edu/Wu-SIs2015F/LECTURES+READINGS/Topic_08-Pyramid%20Method/Lecture-The%20Pyramid.pdf

Yao, L.J.; Bai, Y. (2008), The Sustainability of Economic and Cultural Impacts of International Students to Regional Australia. Humanomics, 24, 250–262.

Yarime, M.; Tanaka, Y. (2012), The Issues and Methodologies in Sustainability Assessment Tools for Higher Education Institutions—A Review of Recent Trends and Future Challenges. J. Educ. Sustain. Dev. 6, 63–77.

Young, O. R. (2002), The institutional dimensions of environmental change: Fit, interplay, and scale. Cambridge, MA: MIT Press.

Young, O. R. (2008), Building regimes for socio-ecological systems: Institutional diagnostics. In O.R. Young, L. A. King, & H. Schroeder (Eds.), Institutions and environmental change: Principal findings, applications, and research frontiers (pp. 115–143). Cambridge, MA: MIT Press.

Young, Oran R.; Schroeder, Heike and King, Leslie A. Edits (2002), Institutions and Environmental Change, Principal Findings, The Institutional Dimensions of Environmental Change Applications, and Research Frontiers, (Summary for Policy Makers) MIT Press, MA

Zucker, L. G. (1977), The Role of Institutionalization in Cultural Persistence, American Sociological Review, Vol. 42, No. 5 (Oct. 1977), pp. 726-743.

Zucker, L.G (1991), "The role of institutionalization in cultural persistence", in Powell, W.W, DiMaggio, P.J (Eds), The New Institutionalism in Organizational Analysis, University of Chicago Press, Chicago, IL, pp.83-107.

Index

A

Animal, 222, 235
Arlene Daniels, 2, 21
Astha-J, 235

B

Bangladesh, 39, 40, 96, 97, 125, 168, 169,
171, 196, 197, 234, 237
Berton H. Kaplan, 1, 3, 14, 168
Boundaries, 23, 34, 39, 133, 144, 151,
161, 195, 197, 198, 200, 210, 212,
213-221, 226, 232, 235, 236, 238, 240,
243, 246-249

C

Charles Perrow, 1, 3, 17, 19, 27
Climate Change, 28, 40, 96, 97, 98, 134,
160, 168-171, 173, 178, 179, 182, 184,
195-198, 202, 204, 206-209, 211-213,
216, 218, 221, 223, 234, 236, 237,
243, 252
Conflict, 6, 10, 15, 16, 37, 50, 85, 104,
115, 131, 132, 135, 140, 141, 143,
151, 158, 166, 183, 216, 234, 241
Contemporary Theories, 1, 15, 111, 141
Creativeness, 39, 195, 197, 198, 200, 221,
235
Crisis, 72, 113, 123, 139, 159, 160, 196,
197, 198, 233
Crop Plants, 235

D

Death, 37, 59, 193, 196
Deductive, 62, 66, 83, 85

Deforestation, 135
Discourses, 25, 39, 51, 99, 138, 182, 184,
195, 197, 202, 204, 209-211, 218, 221,
227, 232, 239, 235, 244, 246
Dorothy Smith, 2, 6, 7, 21, 81, 98
Drought, 198, 234, 235

E

Émile Durkheim, 1, 2, 12, 45, 177
environmental problems, 122, 132, 135,
159, 202, 204, 209, 212, 233
Epistemological, 6, 62, 63, 71, 74, 76, 77,
79, 83, 157, 197
Epistemology, 4, 5, 6, 7, 12, 27, 30, 39,
61-64, 73-77, 79, 84, 86, 89, 94, 96,
98, 114, 127, 130, 131, 164, 218, 221,
233
Ethical Considerations, 61

F

Feminism, 21-23, 31, 43, 47, 50, 51, 55,
100, 106, 107, 127, 129, 131, 137
Floods, 198
Forest, 134, 212, 234, 235
Frederick Taylor, 1, 13, 16

G

Gender, 23, 24, 32, 36, 37, 40, 41, 42, 50,
51, 52, 56, 57, 85, 106, 165, 183, 184,
186, 198, 214, 217, 227, 230, 233, 235
Gisela Bock, 2, 21
Globalization, 96, 97, 111, 113-115, 119,
122, 125, 131-137, 144, 159, 163, 165
168, 171, 173, 174, 184, 186, 229, 233

257

258 *Index*

Government, 32, 35, 36, 116, 118, 124, 126, 127, 133, 136, 161, 162, 181, 199, 203, 209, 230, 231, 245
Green Economy, 97, 159, 160, 170, 207, 222, 225, 252, 253

H

Henri Fayol, 1, 2, 12, 27, 114
Herbert A. Simon, 1, 2, 13, 27
Human Development, 96, 103, 196, 222, 249, 251
Hunger, 195, 196, 198, 202, 214, 216, 217, 235

I

India, 39, 40, 96, 97, 125, 168, 170, 171, 180, 196, 197, 237
Inductive, 62, 66, 67, 76, 83, 95
Inequality, 18, 24, 31, 77, 122, 127, 132, 142, 195, 198, 209, 230, 233, 235, 258, 261
Institution, 20, 67, 69, 89, 90, 119, 122, 150-153, 155-159, 162-164, 173, 230-233, 250
Institutional Theory, 16, 43, 54, 90, 111, 116, 140, 141, 144, 150-154, 156, 157, 239, 246, 248
International Organizations, 51, 111-126, 128-132, 134-139, 141, 142, 144, 146, 147, 150, 160, 162-168, 174, 178, 180, 185, 187, 196, 211, 228, 231
International Relation, 111, 126, 153
Interpretive, 61-66, 75, 82, 83, 85, 86, 94, 100, 102-105, 118

J

Jacques Derrida, 1, 22
James David Thompson, 1, 17, 19
Jurgen Habermas, 1, 22

K

Karl Marx, 1-3, 5, 9, 12, 30, 44, 134, 142, 175
Knowledge Gap, 154, 157

L

Land, 29, 198, 199, 215, 217, 234, 235
Linda Smircich, 2, 3, 7, 16, 22, 28, 41, 77, 105, 173
Luther Halsey Gulick, 1, 2, 13

M

Manpower, 50, 183
Marjorie DeVault, 2, 7, 21
Martha Calas, 2, 3, 22, 28
Mass Media, 135
Max Weber, 1, 2, 9, 10, 12, 13, 17, 24, 27, 56, 58, 65, 67, 68, 101, 102, 109, 190-192
Medicinal and Aromatic Plants, 235
Methodological principles, 61
Michel Foucault, 1, 22
Millennium Development Goals, 196, 200, 207, 208, 210, 213, 214, 226
Millennium Development Goals, 227, 237, 251
Mixed Methods, 61

N

Nepal, 39, 40, 96-98, 125, 168-171, 257, 196, 197, 234, 237, 246, 261
Network Theory, 16, 141, 144-150, 167

O

Ontological, 62, 63, 65, 73-78, 83, 112
Organizational Sociology, 3, 6, 9, 11, 12, 16, 18, 19, 21 , 26, 27, 39, 42, 54, 58, 59, 87, 111, 114, 137, 138, 163, 164, 166, 258, 138, 169, 192, 241, 248, 261

Index 259

Organizational Theory, 1, 2, 7, 11-13, 15, 17-19, 22, 25, 27, 28, 42, 45, 93, 105, 112, 113, 115, 129, 132, 136, 139, 141, 156, 163, 164, 177

P

Pakistan, 40, 96, 97, 168-171, 196, 197, 237
Paul J. DiMaggio, 2, 3, 17, 156
Peter Blau, 1, 3, 17, 18, 27
Philip Selznick, 1, 3, 17, 27, 113, 114, 151
Philosophical Commitments, 61
Pollutions, 40, 135, 169, 196, 197, 209, 212, 215, 237
Positivism, 7, 11, 27, 30, 61, 65, 68, 69, 71, 73, 77, 84, 127, 163
Poverty, 135, 159, 195, 198, 202, 214, 216-218, 223, 227, 229, 230, 233, 235, 236

Q

Qualitative, 12, 27, 39, 61-108, 118
Quantitative, 39, 61-63, 75, 76, 83, 85, 96, 98, 103, 107, 254

R

Race, 24, 25, 36, 37, 85, 100, 165, 198, 227
Regime Theory, 130, 163

S

Sea Level, 235
South Asia, 253
Stakeholder Theory, 160, 161
Susan James, 2, 21
Sustainability Domain, 197
Sustainable Development, 39 , 97, 169, 170, 195-199, 201-205, 207, 208, 210, 212-215, 217-223, 225-229, 231-249, 251-254, 258, 261

T

Theoretical Grounds, 62, 83

U

UNESCO, 126, 206, 222, 226, 251, 252, 253
United Nations, 97, 118, 119, 121, 147, 159, 160, 166, 170, 174, 186, 188, 193, 196, 198, 200, 206, 207, 210, 211-213, 222, 227, 233, 235, 239, 243, 251-254
United Nations Environment Program, 253

W

Walter W. Powell, 2, 3, 17, 43, 156, 174, 238
water, 135, 159, 212, 216, 220, 234
Water, 217
WHO, 202, 254

About the Author

Medani P. Bhandari holds an M.A. in Anthropology (Tribhuwan University, Nepal), M.Sc. in Environmental System Monitoring and Analysis (ITC-The University of Twente, the Netherlands), an M.A. in Sustainable International Development (Brandeis University, Massachusetts, USA), and an M.A. and Ph.D. in Sociology (Syracuse University, NY, USA). Prof. Bhandari is a well-known humanitarian, author, editor, co-editor of several books, and author of hundreds of scholarly papers on social and environmental sciences: a poet, essayist, environment, and social activist, etc.

Dr. Medani P. Bhandari has been serving as a Professor of inter-disciplinary Department of Natural Resource & Environment/Sustainability Studies, at the Akamai University, USA and Professor at the Department of Finance, Innovation and Entrepreneurship, Sumy State University (SSU), Ukraine. Dr. Bhandari is also serving as Editor in Chief of the international journal The Strategic Planning for Energy and the Environment (SPEE). He is also serving as managing editor at the Asia Environment Daily (the largest environmental journal of the world).

Dr. Bhandari has published several books, and scholarly papers in international scientific journals. His recent books are Green Web-II: Standards and Perspectives from the IUCN (2018); 2nd Edition 2020; Getting the Climate Science Facts Right: The Role of the IPCC; Reducing Inequalities Towards Sustainable Development Goals: Multilevel Approach; and Educational Transformation, Economic Inequality – Trends, Traps and Trade-offs; Social Inequality as a Global Challenge, Inequality – the Unbeatable Challenges, Perspectives on Sociological Theories, Methodological Debates and Organizational Sociology. Additionally, in creative writing, Prof. Bhandari has published 100s of poems, essays as well as published two volumes of poetry with Prajita Bhandari.